# FOB

---

## The Incredible Story
## of
## Fob James Jr.

## Sandra Baxley Taylor

Dedicated to

# Thaddeus Jackson Gomillion

1892–1969

Who loved politics and the written word
above all other worldly pleasures
and imbued his children and grandchildren
with the knowledge that education opens all doors.

ISBN 0-926291-01-7

Copyright © 1990, Greenberry Publishing Company
Mobile, Alabama
(205) 343-0155

PRINTED IN THE UNITED STATES OF AMERICA

# About the Book...

*FOB* is an All-American story which begins in the mill town of Lanett in east central Alabama and takes the reader through an old-fashioned odyssey of tears and triumph. It tells of financial struggle and monetary success, of personal tragedy and of the political victory which put Forrest Hood James Jr. in the Alabama governor's office for a four-year term beginning in 1979.

Prior to his term in office, James started from scratch a plant to produce barbells and turned it into a national manufacturing company.

It is obvious from the news articles generated by press releases that James in his early years was aware of the necessity to spend time and money on public relations. He believed so strongly in the importance of telling his story that in 1978 his supporters on a single day distributed door-to-door more than a half million brochures telling people why they should vote for Fob James.

Between his election and his inauguration as governor, however, James apparently forgot most of what he knew about good public relations.

Teachers did not learn from James that his budgets included double-digit pay increases for them or that his education plan provided them with free liability insurance, smaller classes and renovated school buildings. They heard instead, and believed, Alabama Education Association lobbyist Dr. Paul Hubbert who told them AEA was responsible for the raises and that James sought to cut their benefits.

State employees did not learn from James that their pay scales would be increased through his reclassification plan, the first reform of the merit system in more than 30 years. Neither did they learn that the plan was devised by career merit workers responding to his orders to remove political favoritism from state hiring. State employees heard from lobbyists and rumor mills instead, and believed that James' intent was to cut their salaries and to fire them and demote them.

No matter what the endeavor, what the outcome, the same thread of silence binds together the chapters of the Fob James story.

It is a story of a man who ran for office to increase literacy in

Alabama and did so; a governor who in a role-reversal took from federal judges control of the state's prison and mental health systems; who when he left the office of governor left in place the only law in the nation allowing children to pray in schools.

*FOB* is the hitherto untold story of the man who so quietly set in motion the reforms which revamped dozens of departments of state government that some of his closest friends remain unaware eight years later.

Fob James fought a solid coalition of bankers and special interest lobbies and won, preserving a $449 million oil-lease sale windfall so creatively that he used the money without spending it to pay for a $657 million Public Works Project which put bridges, roads and schools in every district in the state.

*FOB* is a story of the man described by the late Auburn Coach "Shug" Jordan as "the greatest broken field runner" he ever coached, a man who does not know the meaning of the word quit. When it appears his only option is defeat, James with the same stubborn determination which years ago put points on the scoreboard switches direction and sidesteps the obstacles in his path.

Faced with the impossible task of paying the tremendous medical bills of a terminally-ill son, James came up with the money by developing a better barbell which he began mass producing on a one-man assembly line.

When he met defeat in the Legislature, James sat down with legislators and asked their help between sessions and came back again and again with his proposals, successful more than 70 percent of the time.

*FOB* is many stories. It is the story of a kid who was happiest when thinking up new business enterprises or tramping through the woods. It is the story of a football hero, a successful businessman and a governor who not once in office betrayed the trust of the people who elected him.

It is the story of a winner.

# Table of Contents

Introduction    1

Prologue    11

1 — The Years Before    19

2 — The Decision    47

3 — Campaign and Victory    53

4 — The Transition    75

5 — The Inauguration    83

6 — Governor James    93

7 — A Disastrous Year    137

8 — Labor    147

9 — Public Television:
Handshake Ends Seven Year Court Battle    155

10 — The ABC Department:
Money-making Changes    159

11 — Law Enforcement    173

12 — Prisons    185

13 — The 1980 Legislative Session    203

14 — Halfway    233

15 — The 1981 Session    239

16 — The Isolation of the Budget    253

17 — The Second Special Session    263

18 — Preserving a Windfall:
The Third Special Session    267

19 — Roads and Bridges    285

20 — Three Forgotten Agencies                                    295

21 — The 1982 Legislative Session                                303

22 — The First Special Session of 1982                           327

23 — Prayer, Textbooks, and Stabilizing the Retirement System:
    The Second Special Session of 1982              .   331

24 — A Matter of Law:
    The Prayer Case                                       337

25 — The Third Special Session                                   353

26 — James' Clashes with Siegelman and the Alabama
    Supreme Court                                         355

27 — The War Against Illiteracy                                  381

Assessment                                                       413

Index                                                            427

# Introduction

This book represents two years of my life.

Why would anyone spend two years writing a book about a man who eight years ago was governor of Alabama?

Let's get one thing straight right off. It wasn't supposed to be two years of my life. It was supposed to be six months.

After all, as a reporter for the Birmingham *News* who covered politics during Fob James' term, I knew pretty much what went on when he was governor.

I was there. Therefore I thought it might not even take six months to write such a book.

I was there in 1978, sitting at a table at the Malaga Inn in Mobile a few weeks before the Democratic Primary with my husband, Tom, and fellow *News* reporter Ralph Holmes.

The winner of the gubernatorial race, Ralph predicted, would be Fob James.

"Fob who? Come on," I retorted in what was probably a superior tone of voice. "Fob James knows about as much about politics as I do about football, which is limited to being able to tell the inning by looking at the scoreboard. He's a barbell salesman."

My ever-insistent-on-accuracy editor husband probably insisted I acknowledge that he manufactured the barbells he sold, as well as every other kind of fitness and recreation equipment imaginable.

Ralph's voice when he answered me was definitely in a "superior" tone. (You won't find more "superior" tones than when two political reporters discuss politics, I assure you.)

"I've traveled with all the candidates," he said. "James is the only one who has people excited. Everywhere he goes there are crowds. They're waving flags and carrying balloons and cheering. You wait and see. He's the next governor."

I knew more about James than I let on. I love a good argument and few people argue as well as Ralph, an irascible and indefatigable veteran of Alabama political reporting.

I knew a lot—or thought I knew a lot—that had not been printed, in fact.

Most people believed Diversified Products, James' company, was doing well. I had been told otherwise. Earlier in the campaign an individual who was supporting one of James' opponents offered to provide documentation to prove James was running for governor to save Diversified Products from bankruptcy. The only big client he had was Sears, my source insisted. Sears had notified him the contract would not be renewed, he said. If James got elected governor, however, Sears would have to renew the contract because of the influence James would wield.

After learning the documentation reportedly had been taken from a safe at Diversified Products, I wasn't interested. Some statute came to mind about receiving and concealing stolen property...(I did not learn until much later that James had sold Diversified Products the year before.)

Also earlier in the campaign, I had received a call from a man who possessed all the credentials to be considered a "reputable source." He owned his own business and he wore a suit.

James was nothing but a con man, a pyramid scheme salesman, the man said. It all had to do with Nutri-Bio, an amazing vitamin supplement that claimed to do all sorts of wondrous things for the health of those who swallowed it daily. The pyramid scheme consisted of distributors and stratified echelons of investors and salesmen and you were told if you invested in it you would get a percentage of everything sold by the people who came in after you did. James had been one of the top people in the Mobile area.

I wrote that story and a watered down version of it ran. (Any story you read during a gubernatorial race on a gubernatorial candidate in a decent newspaper written by a young, idealistic reporter will have been watered down by editors. Trust me.)

Not long after, I happened to sit by a man on a plane who said he was from James' home town and was a friend of his.

I asked him, why would James want to run for governor?

Fob James had gone as far as he could go in the manufacturing business, the man confided. Being governor of the state would open a world of new opportunities once he left office.

That did it.

I had just finished a long investigation into the banking activities of Melba Till Allen, the state treasurer who developed a bad habit of borrowing money from banks in which she deposited state funds. By the time the Birmingham *News* began its investigation, her loans totaled in the seven figures and she couldn't pay them back. A jury found her guilty of using her office for personal gain and sent her to jail.

When not busy scrutinizing probate records and bank books, I had been deeply involved in an investigation of legislators and ethics and writing stories about how the twain seldom met—at least not as reflected by the financial disclosure statements filed with the Alabama Ethics Commission.

Professionally, I had no opinion on the governor's race.

I was still a citizen, though. I had my rights. And I was firmly convinced that the one thing Alabama needed least was another hotshot politician running for office to enlarge his economic fiefdom.

I did not vote for Fob James in the Democratic Primary, though to the amazement of many, more people voted for him than any other candidate. He faced Bill Baxley in the runoff.

The day before the runoff, James made a swing through Mobile.

I had my list of questions ready for the news conference. Nutri-Bio was at the top of the list. He had been able to evade commenting on it thus far. Today he would have no choice.

The news conference did not go as I anticipated. After I asked my questions, it more or less turned into a shouting match. With the television cameras rolling, both the candidate and I were forced to shout to be heard above the boisterous demonstration of disapproval launched by his supporters at the back of the room.

After it ended, James assumed the role of the ultimate gentleman, walked to my chair, leaned down and kissed me on the cheek. It was obvious he was putting on a show for the evening news—the cameras followed his every step and zeroed in on his smile and apology.

I smiled too, but it hurt. What the cameras did not reveal, you see, was that all the while he was standing on my foot.

I voted for Bill Baxley in the runoff, which James won.

I did not vote for James in the General Election. I voted for Guy Hunt, the farmer from Holly Pond.

Thus ended chapter one in my relationship with Fob James.

Not long after the election, I learned from "sources" that Mobile District Attorney Charlie Graddick, the attorney general–elect of the state, had worn a body mike and taped the first meeting he had with James, which was in a Montgomery motel.

Now, before you start snickering about "sources," I'll tell you that I almost lived in Charlie's office when he was district attorney.

His sister-in-law (at that time) was to be my eldest son's godmother. His brother had been best man in the wedding of the couple who also served as godmother and godfather for two of my children. His chief assistant, Don Valeska, was and is one of my best friends. Valeska is also, you guessed it, godfather to my youngest son. Charlie's one-time chief assistant, Willis Holloway, became my personal attorney when he went into private practice.

I had other good friends in his office. During the investigation of the state treasurer's loans, I repeatedly was unsuccessful in taping conversations in a bar with Mrs. Allen's business manager. He related wild and outrageous happenings, so outrageous in fact that I felt I had to tape our conversations to convince my editors I was not making them up. He would only talk in bars with loud music in the background, however. My recorder, stashed in my purse, picked up nothing but loud music. To whom did I turn for help? Don Bekurs, Charlie's chief investigator. He had me wired for sound and as the juke box blared the theme from Star Wars, DA investigator Ed Odom in a car outside the bar captured every fascinating detail on tape. (As an aside to journalists, it was a dumb thing to do. The tape was for my own private use. Because it was made by a law enforcement agency, however, the tape was eventually subpoenaed from Bekurs by Montgomery District Attorney Jimmy Evans. Evans played it to the grand jury which indicted Mrs. Allen, I am told, and I haven't seen it since.)

Anyway, you get the picture. If I say I had a "source" who knew Graddick had taped James' meeting, I definitely had the source.

I didn't expect Charlie to be happy with my story. He felt I was a friend and a friend should have ignored it. I was, however, first and foremost a political reporter who could not ignore the fact that the attorney general-elect of the state had done the single dumbest thing on record at that time—secretly taped the governor-elect of the state.

I was fair, however. I called him for comment.

"What do you want?" he asked even before denying the story.

He did deny it, of course. I expected that.

What I did not anticipate was James' reaction.

Did he thank me? Did he ask the Department of Public Safety to find out what really happened?

No. The official comment of the governor-elect of the state was that I was dingy. Or maybe he later called me a dingbat. I forget which. I decided he was still angry about Nutri-Bio, which he said was a bad business venture from which he and a bunch of others including Cong. Jack Edwards had not made any money.

Why, James asked, would Charlie bug a conversation in which the primary topics were the prison system and the operational aspects of improving law enforcement?

It was not an auspicious beginning to our relationship.

After Hurricane Frederic leveled the South Alabama landscape of pine trees and sand dunes, I spent a lot of time in Gulf Shores. The building spree there was unbelievable. There were three stories waiting on me anytime I cared to make the hour's drive.

That was when I first picked up hints that James was involved in some shady beach-front deal. Everywhere I went, it seemed Dick Forster, his Conservation chief, had been there right before.

"Forster sat right in that chair, the first time he ever met me, and said, 'I'm head of the Conservation Department, I think we can make some money,' " a land speculator told me.

There was nothing illegal about the statement and I didn't particularly believe Forster had made it. I was wary, however, of him and of the governor who had appointed him.

When I was handed indisputable proof that James had bought unimproved beach property and resold it for a profit after a sewer right-of-way was approved through Gulf State Park, I wrote it. It was the only exposé written during James' term in office.

Before I wrote it, however, I talked at length with James and his partners in, for gosh sakes, Sunshine Joint Venture! Someone plans to rip off the state and they call their venture "Sunshine"?

I guess it was during that conversation that the set-in-concrete image of James, which had built within my mind from our various encounters, cracked a little.

It was a long conversation. He had just bought the Orange Beach Marina, preparing to run it when he left the governor's office. I had a "scoop" if I wanted it. It would have been the first solid confirmation that he wasn't running for re-election.

The story I was after, however, was the one about the sewer permit.

He wasn't arrogant. He wasn't angry. He made it clear he would produce any documentation, any partners, any staff members, that all parties would be directed to answer any questions I had for as long as I wanted.

I spent enough time investigating the circumstances surrounding the permit that I was comfortable with the subject when Moss Stack called me. Moss was a very good friend. He was also the special agent in charge of the Federal Bureau of Investigation for the Southern District of Alabama.

Moss was direct. Did I think James had used his office for personal gain?

I laughed. There was about as much chance of that in this case as there was that Moss had used his office for the same purpose, I told him.

I told him what I had found. Thousands of rights-of-way routinely were signed by the Conservation Department and the governor's office annually. James' name did not appear on the permit. His signature was signed by legal adviser Mike Waters who was unaware it was remotely connected with James.

I also thought it significant that there had been no peep from Forster.

Forster was no longer with James' cabinet. He had been fired by James after it was disclosed he had taken advantage of his position to buy an island from the Conservation Department. If ever a man existed with a motive to "tell all" if there had been anything to tell on James, it would have been Forster.

Most importantly, however, I wondered why the story had so conveniently fallen into my lap complete with documents before the ink was dry on the permit.

I told Moss what I had come to believe: James had been "set up." I did not name the people who were responsible, except to say they believed James to be running for a second term and they were backing another candidate.

I told him why I thought thus.

Was James thrilled that I had investigated deeply enough to learn what really happened?

Not exactly. He referred to me to his staff from that day hence as "the Sewer Lady."

I don't want to mislead you. The relationship was not completely adversarial.

Frequently, in fact, I found myself in the disconcerting position of defending something James was trying to do.

He was not being overly-idealistic when he pushed a constitutional amendment to force legislators to pass budgets before any other legislation, I argued. It was the right thing to do.

He was not naïve when he insisted legislators should refuse to vote on issues which affected their pocketbooks, I insisted. He was right.

By the time he left office I counted several of his cabinet members as good friends.

He was the best governor the state ever had, they insisted.

I said nothing. Or sometimes I commented lamely, "He tried hard."

Other close friends felt differently. A lot differently.

They snickered when his name was mentioned: "The man was so dumb he forgot to sign his own crime package. He's the worst governor in the history of the state and you know it."

I did not know it. But I would not have argued with it.

In 1986 I left the Mobile *Press Register,* where I had been state editor for three years, to work for U.S. Sen. Jeremiah Denton.

I did not plan to work for someone else forever, just long enough to put a little money aside to start the publishing company I had planned for years.

As Alabamians know, the job was far from "forever." The senator lost the election and I started a publishing company sooner than I intended.

It was not the intent of my publishing company to publish books written by me. However, I needed to start with an author who wouldn't demand a hefty advance, someone who wouldn't sue me when the royalty checks didn't arrive like clockwork. Let's face it. There was only one such person. Me. I planned the first six books Greenberry Publishing would undertake, two of which I would write. I would publish a variety of subject matter—the only common trait among them would be that they would be readable, of good quality and would appeal to Southerners. Most importantly, readers would not be able to find anything like them published by any other publishing company.

I planned a cookbook, a travel book, a book on Southern homes from a different slant and several I will keep for a surprise.

The idea for the first book came in Montgomery when I heard the "latest story" of the friendly rivalry between Gerald Wallace, brother of Gov. George Wallace, and Oscar Harper, the man who is number one on the list when news media refer to "Wallace cronies." Oscar's humorous stories of behind-the-scenes in the Wallace years are legendary in political circles.

Oscar and Gerald had both decided their anecdotes would make good books, I learned. Gerald had written a letter to Lewis Grizzard offering to collaborate.

Through a mutual friend, I got with Oscar. He talked and I wrote. The book is called *Me 'N' George, A Story of George Corley Wallace and His Number One Crony Oscar Harper.* I laughed the whole time I was writing it.

I needed two more books before taking to the road to sell them. Fortunately, Jimmy Faulkner of Bay Minette was looking for a publisher for a real winner. It's called *Massacre* and it's the true story of the Fort Mims massacre, which was the biggest slaughter of settlers by Indians in American history. It was written by a descendant of the whites and Indians, Dr. David Pierce Mason. I've never read another book which reveals what the Indians were thinking when the settlers moved west.

My third book had to be on politics. I've lived, eaten and breathed politics since I was a toddler riding around with my Jim Folsom-loving grandfather in Covington County. I wanted to write something challenging, something of which I would be proud, something which would make a difference in politics.

Alabama politics are covered well on a daily basis by the news media. Reporters know that in-depth reporting, however, is limited by time and budget constraints. What kind of book would I have if I started from scratch with a clean slate and built a picture of politics in the state using that daily media coverage as a starting point, filling it in with facts, figures and documentation available since that time in countless reports and journals? What would happen if I wrote not what politicians said they had done or not done but what the record proved they had done or not done?

I realized the irony—I was sounding like a certain governor had sounded a decade ago as he stood in the lobby of the International Trade Club in Mobile.

"I can't understand why you reporters are content to sit down here in Mobile and let politicians tell you what's going on," Fob James had taunted good-naturedly. It was during one of his statewide efforts to enlist support for a key legislative project. "Why don't you come to Montgomery and search through the records for yourself and come up with the truth?" he almost begged. "Why don't your editors send teams of reporters to find out what is really happening?"

He was serious.

I remembered him at a meeting of editors, how he put them on the spot by asking how many had read the constitution, how many had read the new criminal code, challenging them to hire accountants and attorneys, to move their reporters into the Ethics Commission to discover who was running state government and where they were getting their money.

Such thoughts bounced around in my mind for several months as I thought of possible thrusts for my book and narrowed my goals.

When I first approached James to ask permission to go through his personal files, it was with the intent of doing a book on his administration as the four-year period "between" the Wallace years.

George Wallace was a power in this state for a quarter-of-a-century. By comparing state government in the years before Fob James with the years after Fob James, I thought I could get a handle on the reality of state government.

I called him in September of 1987. Would he consent to an interview?

He was polite but he was noncommittal. Within the month, he would be heading for Canada to hunt ducks. Perhaps when he got back...

I headed for the Alabama Department of Archives. Three months later I had called James several times and he was still polite, still non-committal.

We finally got together for lunch right before Christmas. We talked—I mostly talked, he mostly listened, asking a question every now and then to prod me. He was still non-committal. He would call me, he promised. He would be moving to Magnolia Springs by Jan. 1. Maybe I could drop by after he got settled.

Many weeks later, I got the call. I did the required things a woman does when she is interviewing a former governor. I had my car washed, did my hair and wore the newest dress in my closet. James met me at his Magnolia Springs office. He wore fatigues, hunting boots, an old hat and a camouflage jacket. He drove an old dust-covered, open-windowed hatch-back from which emerged Tad, a huge lovable dog who flopped on the floor and followed his master's every move with contented eyes.

I could have access to his files, he said. He would talk to me. But he had two conditions.

I listened.

First, he had to have my promise that I would do a thorough job, that my book would be well-researched. I had to be completely unwilling to settle for anything less than the complete truth.

Certainly. I couldn't write any other kind of book, I told him.

Second, I had to write an assessment of his administration when I finished my research, he said.

Huh? I do windows. I do lunches. But I don't do assessments. I'm not a bleeping editorial writer. I'm an investigative reporter.

If I wouldn't promise to write an assessment, he said, there was no deal.

Okay, I warned him. You get your assessment. But you may not like it.

Fine. I'll take my chances, he said.

Thus began my six-month project which has stretched into two years.

I can hear the groans of a certain segment of my friends: "How in the devil could you spend two years investigating the administration of a governor who didn't do anything?"

Ignore them. Ignore those other voices too, the friends whose judgment is colored by loyalty.

Do as I did. Wipe the slate clean. Begin at the beginning.

Fob who?

The year is 1979.

Turn the page.

# Prologue

The cold clear January day was described by the weatherman as perfect for the inauguration of Forrest Hood James Jr., or "Fob" as he had been known since before he could speak.

It had been looked forward to for four months by friends and campaign workers who so jubilantly savored the heady thrill of victory.

More than 100,000 revelers crowded the roped-off streets of downtown Montgomery, evidence of the adulation that Southerners and Alabamians in particular lavish on their newly-elected governors.

As the school bus in which he rode pulled slowly up Dexter Avenue on its way to the historic white-domed capitol, James waved to the crowds which to be assured of a glimpse of him had lined up behind police barricades before the stores even opened.

Not to get a glimpse of "him," he knew. To see the governor-elect. The governor. The power. The man who would lead the state the next four years.

James was incredulous that simply by winning more votes than his opponent a mortal would be metamorphosed from mere man in the eyes of the multitudes to object of adulation.

"I hope you get it," a kindly little lady had told him with a hug before the election and he had correctly translated "it" to be the tangible brass ring of governorship.

Being the anointed one was not a wholly comfortable feeling.

He knew better than anyone else that he was no superman. Neither did he regard any who had stood in his place as superman. Not U.S. senators, not even Presidents. They were all mere men, charged with clear-cut responsibilities by their fellow citizens. From time to time someone realizing with a start that James felt awe for no mortal would misread this humility and think him a very arrogant man indeed.

Somewhere in the crowd a daddy surely held his small daughter on his shoulders.

"There he is, honey. Fob James. You can tell your children some day you saw Fob James sworn in as governor."

"Is Governor Wallace going to be here?"

It was a natural question that day.

Where was George Wallace? How did he feel about turning over the reins of power to an upstart political novice from Opelika?

For 16 years George Wallace had been governor of Alabama in his own name or in his wife Lurleen's name, excepting a two-year span after she died in 1968 when Albert Brewer sat expectantly in a chair he would never claim by vote.

For 16 years, the people of Alabama had basked in pride or had blanched in shame, depending on their political views, as the national perception of their sovereign state blurred, its hazy parameters enclosing a fiefdom of demagoguery.

To the nation and the world, Alabama's people marched in unity behind a banner of discord, spouting a rhetoric of hate.

To the nation and the world, that discord was synonymous with George Wallace and George Wallace was Alabama and Alabama was George Wallace.

Alabama. What did the world know about Alabama?

That's where Rosa Parks refused to sit in the back of a bus where blacks were "supposed" to sit, and a man named Dr. Martin Luther King Jr. stood by her side.

That's where Ku Klux Klansmen in blatant disregard of every law known to God and man killed and raped and castrated their victims by night and on Sunday bombed to death black children as they prayed in church.

Alabama, where children of every color and background scored lower on national aptitude tests than in any state of the union except Mississippi, and politicians shrugged and told jokes that ended with, "Thank God for Mississippi."

Where politicians and architects ignored the pleas of educators to settle for five well-placed junior colleges and avariciously scattered 22 poorly-funded schools as though a blind man had thrown darts at a map and decreed a school be erected where each dart landed.

Where the roads were so bad and the people so poor and the

education level so low that the only way Yankee smoke-stack industries could be induced to relocate was to exempt them from paying property taxes that were already the lowest in the nation.

That is how the nation and the world saw Alabama.

Not so, insisted Alabamians whose voices over the years grew in strength and in number and in persistency.

The picture of Alabama held up to the world had been unfairly painted with a brush dipped only in the angry colors of the Wallace aura, they argued.

They talked of a different Alabama, of that which was and of that which could be.

They talked of sun streaming through mountain trees making lacy shadows on streams so pretty it hurt to look at them. Of tall forests which sheltered pioneers and of white-steepled churches where brotherhood was not only preached but was spread on tables after church and eaten as the preacher's admonition to love your neighbor took wings and flitted off in the springtime breeze.

To these Alabamians, heirs to a legacy of sadness that walked hand-in-hand with pride through the generations, hand-me-down memories echoed with purpose of a war which scarred the souls of those who fought and of those who waited and of those who did neither.

Faded picture albums told the story, how after that War between the States, that rebellion, that Lost Cause, that Civil War, poverty in Alabama imprisoned blacks and whites with cold impartiality, kindling within both the thirst for education and the ambition for achievement.

The stage was set in the 1940s and the 1950s by Gov. James Elisha "Big Jim" Folsom to harness that ambition and to quench that thirst.

The stage was set, the script was being written, but the production had to be temporarily postponed when Folsom fell by the wayside, a victim of his own weaknesses and of the rising tide of a racism he would not condone.

The stage sat empty, without a leader to fill the main role.

Alabama suffered economically over the next two decades.

In 1978, Alabama ranked 41st out of 50 states in spending to educate its children and 43rd in salaries paid to teachers.

There were only two other states where the working man earned less and only five states had greater need for doctors than Alabama.

In 1976 Alabama had the highest murder rate of any state.

Alabama's economy reflected a mirror image of the nation's recession, with interest rates and inflation at all-time highs and unemployment the highest since the Great Depression.

Medicaid drained one-third of the state's general fund tax revenues off the top and 84 percent of all money collected by the state was earmarked for one purpose or another before it was collected.

Yet welfare payments to the poor and out-of-work in Alabama only provided 53 percent of the poverty level, leaving a family of four to exist on $3,780.

More than 15 percent of the state's total tax intake went toward retirement funds for education personnel, state employees and judges, the richest retirement system in the nation.

Never had the election of a governor been so important.

In 1978, James' ardent supporters believed he was the man they had long awaited who would fling the gauntlet of change at the feet of politicians who knew of no other way but to perpetuate the mistakes of the past.

James would have scoffed at any who tried to place him in crusader's clothing.

A football hero, an engineer, a millionaire industrialist by the time he was 40, James had a simple basic, historical view of government in which elected officials were job holders. They fulfilled transitory roles in the 200-year-old continuing saga of a government which had been laid out completely and effectively by Thomas Jefferson and his colleagues in the 1770s. James' close scrutiny of history revealed to him certain principles that if followed made government work for the people. If the principles were not followed, the opposite would occur.

Our system of government did not need changing. It just needed to be put back on the track from which foolish and selfish political decisions had derailed it.

With that curious turn of mind which at times variously delighted or frustrated those closest to him, James truly had devoted little thought to the administration which had gone before him or to the man who had claimed the office as his own for nearly two decades.

Wallace belonged to the past, as did the achievements or abuses of the Wallace administration. James' thoughts were firmly turned toward the future and toward the part he should and would play as governor.

When James thought of Wallace, if he thought of Wallace, it was with a vague boyhood memory of Wallace sitting under a shade oak in the James' yard talking politics to his father, a supporter.

On his inauguration day, James sat on the platform in the icy wind, his tanned face betraying a lifetime love affair with the outdoors.

No one, not even the thin, frail-beautied red-headed wife by his side, Bobbie, would have dared try reading his mind.

The governor-elect was gloriously ignorant, in the old-fashioned dictionary sense of the word, of the political winds which swirled round him. He knew not, and would have cared less if he had known, that seasoned politicians who sat within talking distance for the most part laughed behind his back and called his plans grandiose, his beliefs naïve and his efforts doomed. Had he known he would have laughed aloud and challenged, "What has their brand of politics delivered that is worth keeping?"

James waited impatiently, unimpressed as ever by ceremony, anticipating the point at which pomp and pageantry would cease and the real work begin.

The smile on his face, his wave, his nod, the showmanship—they were expected of him in the campaign. He not only understood, he undertook it eagerly, from baby-kissing to stump speeches, enjoying the enthusiasm of the sport for what it was, a political campaign in the oldest American tradition.

The pageantry of the inauguration bothered him, however. It symbolized much that was wrong in American politics. It was something he meant to change and would have changed right off if his entire campaign staff had not argued so adamantly.

He had wanted no inaugural festivities. He wanted simply to be sworn in and sit down behind his desk and get started.

His friends and supporters and even his relatives had argued successfully in favor of staging a full-scale inaugural.

His supporters deserved it, they said, and he went uncomfortably along with their advice, even consenting to the purchase of a new suit.

Wallace sat nearby in his wheelchair on the inaugural platform, waiting for the first time in 16 years for someone other than a Wallace to be sworn in after being elected governor.

Leaving office for what everyone assumed was the last time, Wallace was pale and weak, paralyzed from a would-be assassin's bullet in 1972. A shell of his former self, Wallace had difficulty hearing what was being said, even with a hearing aid.

It was a casual secret, known but not acknowledged, that the pain which racked his body 24 hours a day since the shooting forced him more and more into reliance on pain killers which could not fully ease his agony.

Wallace's eyes did not blur with tears on this crisp cold day as they sometimes did when he talked of the state's old and poor.

There was no time, no place, in the ceremony for the denials and explanations which increasingly punctuated his conversation: "You know, I was never a racist. Folks think I was a racist. I was never against the black folks. I was wrong when I opposed integration, but back then that was the law of the state and I was the governor and I was enforcing the law of the state."

It was the ending of his era, and the eager, over-confident idealists who surrounded James would have been scornful of such pronouncements by Wallace, sentiments they would have perceived as rank hypocrisy, mere lip service to the growing black voter strength in the South.

Wallace, those closest to him believed, had really changed. Also, as an avid reader of history he was ever conscious of his role in it, anxious to soften his almost certain depiction by history as a crafty demagogue who rose to power by capitalizing on the most primordial of human emotions, fear and hatred.

Perhaps the only man on the platform that day who would have empathized with Wallace's fears was James, an equally avid reader of history who realized it would be decades before historians would be able to assess the changes he planned to set in motion.

James could have cited the statistics reflecting Alabama's problems as well as anybody in Montgomery that day. He had campaigned on the well-known fact that Alabama's children were not getting the education they needed to take care of themselves.

James knew the frustration of the businessman who is forced to turn down one high school graduate after another because that graduate cannot read or write well enough to fill out a job application.

He had run for governor to change things. Raising the level of literacy in the state was at the top of the list.

There were few problems that could not be solved, he sincerely believed, if one would admit the shortcomings up front (not something politicians liked to do) and then pursue the right solution, no matter how unpleasant it might be. The confidence instilled in him by parents and grandparents made him comfortable with this approach to problem-solving.

He was the person who could zero in on Alabama's problems and pursue the solutions regardless of political consequence, he also believed. Or he would not have run for office.

He had given himself a certain length of time, four years, in which to do it.

By no coincidence that was exactly the length of time he had been elected to serve as governor.

# — 1 —

# The Years Before

**F**ob James Jr. grew up in the old-fashioned manner which writers attempt to capture when they paint pictures of rowdy big families anchored with stern, but warm and approving, patriarchal discipline and matriarchal care.

"I thought I was living in a dream," he says of his childhood. "I had everything a boy could want. I had loving grandparents, a father who was very understanding, very encouraging, yet demanded reasonable discipline and made me make my own decisions. I could hunt, fish and play sports all I wanted. All I had to do in return was pass in school, go to church on Sunday and behave some of the time."

The first years of that childhood were spent in a white frame house in the cotton mill town of Lanett, an Alabama town which abruptly becomes at a certain street the Georgia town of West Point.

The home in which James was born sits today along a neat line of similar homes built for mill workers of what is today West Point Pepperell.

On a slight hill, the house was typical of the small wood-frame homes common to cotton mill towns and other bustling little Southern communities a half-century ago. It had a small front porch and was painted white. It sat between similar houses which differed in trim, but bespoke their common heritage. Fob James Sr. worked at several jobs. He was a history teacher and coach at Lanett High School, as he had been in Enterprise before moving to Lanett. He was also the manager of Lanett's semi-pro baseball team.

The team was sponsored by the sprawling Lanett Mill, one of five owned by what was then West Point Manufacturing Company, predecessor to West Point Pepperell. As the team manager, Fob Sr. was depended upon by "Mr. Rube" Jennings to lead the team to victory each year over the other teams in Langdale, Shawmut, Riverview and Fairfax.

"Mr. Rube," superintendent of the Lanett facility, occupied a position of power in the small town which does not have its equal today. "Mr. Rube" was the management. "Mr. Rube" called the shots. And "Mr. Rube" not only liked Fob Sr., he treated him as a family member.

While beating all the other mill teams was of great importance to "Mr. Rube," he was particularly anxious that Lanett defeat Riverview, where the rivalry had been hottest for years. Fob Sr. had a lot of talent with which to work. Prior to World War II, baseball in east central Alabama was a serious business in which players were paid salaries and key players in the twilight of their careers were recruited fresh from the majors. Some divided their time between the mill teams and pro teams in Atlanta and Mobile. The era ended when a professional baseball team was organized in the area, the Valley Rebels, and the mill teams became purely recreational.

The James' sturdy wood house resounded with the footsteps and scuffling of two growing boys, Fob Jr. and his younger brother, Calvin.

When James was eight years old the family moved a few blocks away to a larger white wood-frame house which had an oak-shaded yard. The yard provided play space for after-school games of football, basketball or baseball. The year after the move, Robert Edward (Bob) was born, the third and last son in the family.

The yard was filled with youngsters kicking, dribbling or throwing balls of one sort or another. On weekends and holidays they were often joined by a crowd of friends and relatives.

"Fob," the nickname shared by father and son, was short for the official birth certificate designation of Forrest Hood James. The name was in memory of two Confederate generals, Nathan Bedford Forrest and John Bell Hood. Hood had commanded Confederate forces in the nearby Battle of Atlanta.

Fob Sr. was an identical twin to his brother, William Everett "Ebb" James. Their nicknames had been bestowed on them by workers on their parents' farm who refused to call the adventurous toddlers by their full names.

The twins in their youth engaged in the antics of identical twins from time immemorial.

Ebb and Fob Sr. looked so much alike that people were often

confused as to which was which, often because the twins purposely confused them. James' mother repeated to a reporter the family story about how Ebb and Fob Sr. would purposely "switch" their children, Linda Lee and Fob Jr., when they were leaving family get-togethers. The twins would wait until they were almost to their cars (with family members chastising them for playing tricks on their young children) before "discovering" their mistake and exchanging children.

Thus their twinship engendered not only a closeness between them but also between their children.

The twins lettered in baseball, football and basketball at Auburn. Their youngest brother, Louie, lettered in basketball.

While playing basketball for Auburn, the twins sometimes changed jerseys when one fouled out and the other one got tired—the referee could never tell the difference and neither could the crowd.

It is apparent that the chief influence on James was the atmosphere which permeated his household, a sports camaraderie and mutual understanding he shared with his father and a closeness with his mother.

James was a late-bloomer in his love of history, but he grew up in the household of a father who taught history and talked to him often about events of the past and their effect upon today.

James' grandfather, James Edward James, was a native of Waverly, Alabama, and to that small town he brought his bride, Willie Bedell, and began to raise his family. His premature death changed the fate of his family. James' grandmother, known affectionately to all who knew and loved her as "Mama James," knew she could not support her four sons in Waverly. She moved with them in 1922 to Auburn.

In Auburn she rented a big house and took in roomers for $26 a month, serving them hot meals three times a day.

Remembered by her family as a "fine manager," Mama James also took over the management of a 1,000-acre farm.

In 1928, she built a house of her own, where she fed 100 college boys and rented rooms to 15 of them. Among her student boarders was Ralph Jordan, who in later life was known as "Shug," Auburn's legendary football coach.

Mama James saw to it that all four of her sons got an education at Auburn, with two of them going on to earn advanced degrees.

While at Auburn, Fob Sr. had a brief stint as a silent movie star, playing the lead male role opposite film star Helen Munday in the Warner Brothers production *Stark Love*. He listened to his mama's advice when she cautioned against pursuing a career in the movies. Fob Jr. later sought in vain to get a copy of his father's movie, but was told the original film was in too poor condition to attempt to copy or to ship.

The four James brothers scattered, but kept in touch.

Ebb James settled in Tuskegee, where he farmed and raised timber.

Edward James became superintendent of schools in Marion, Alabama. In World War II he became a career Army officer. His last assignment was writing a history of elements of World War II, which involved talking with many of the high German troop command.

The fourth brother, Louis—whom everybody calls Louie—was twice mayor of Auburn.

Fob Sr. married Rebecca Ellington, daughter of Sue Reece Robertson and Calvin Ellington of Opelika and Gold Hill.

"Mr. Cal," an Opelika city commissioner for many years, was a familiar sight to neighbors, a huge man who sold groceries and tobacco for a wholesale house in his younger days and worked the latter part of his life for Equitable Life Insurance Company.

"Fob's Ellington grandparents adored him and he adored them, particularly Mama Sue," Bobbie James remembered of her husband's grandparents.

"Loved but not indulged," is how she sums up her husband's boyhood. "His parents both worked hard and the boys were expected to carry their own weight from early childhood."

Carrying your "own weight" in Alabama in the forties meant earning your own money, an enterprise into which James jumped rather than was pushed from almost his toddler days.

He got his first paper route when he was eight years old, rising before dawn to pick up his papers and deliver them on his bicycle.

One morning while on his paper route, he was hit by a car, or that is what reporters wrote when putting together a biography of him.

He remembers the incident as one in which he pedaled his bicycle at foolish speed down a customer's driveway on a foggy morning and ran into a slow-moving car driven by an elderly man.

The old gentleman was so upset, James said, "that my parents were worried more about him than they were about me."

The leather belt and the hickory stick played a big part in James' early childhood development.

A rambunctious youth, James knew if he got a whipping at school his parents would each give him another whipping when he got home. "My parents believed the teacher was always right—no questions asked—and in my case, my parents were right," he said.

"I got a lot of whippings at school," he would later remark as governor when explaining to teachers why he so firmly believed in strong discipline in schools.

His teachers were aware of the James family policy and, on occasion, James remembers, would send messages to his parents begging them not to whip him again because he had already been punished.

At Christmas, James cut and sold cedar trees off a truck to customers in Lanett and West Point. With the money he earned, he made a bee-line for the nearest roadside stand to buy firecrackers for the holidays.

In their pre-teen years, James and his brother Calvin earned money by parching peanuts and selling them at ball games.

"I had to work, because it was a thing my folks strongly believed in," James says. "But I wanted to work. I never found anything strange about it. It was just something you did."

At age 12, James' picture appeared in the newspaper for the first time. A yellowed clipping still cherished in a family scrapbook is mute testimony to the pride evoked in his family by the story which labeled him a hero for rescuing a younger child from drowning.

The two were fishing from a boat on a pond at Gold Hill, Alabama, owned by near-relatives whom he called "Uncle Dan" and "Aunt Florence." The boat began to take on water. First the tackle went under, then the string of fish, then the two children. James' companion, son of a farm hand, panicked because he couldn't swim. James calmed him down by assuring him he could pull him to shore, then did so. The article recounted that "Uncle Dan" watched helplessly from the bank.

James' new house was within walking distance of the woods. At that point he entered the glorious period he refers to as "the quiet years," the days and weeks-on-end when his parents allowed him to ramble and roam by himself in the environment he came to love the most—the forests and streams and lakes of east central Alabama and west Georgia, and the Chattahoochee River which cuts between the states as a sometimes silent, sometimes swift, watery boundary.

It was a call from deep within which James obeyed when he took to the woods. His father, without talking of it, made it clear that he understood his son's feelings. Only once did that silent understanding erupt into words. Once, when on a stormy, rain-swept day James donned his gear, grabbed his gun, and headed for the woods, his mother stopped him. The weather was too bad for him to leave the house, she said. It was one of the few times in his life that he was aware that his parents differed. "Let him go," Fob Sr. said and his mother, without commenting, did.

On one occasion James and a friend in Tom Sawyer-style literally moved to the woods by the river to live for a month. It was not looked upon as "different" or anything to talk about. It was just something he had to do and something he did, as he would do in later life each year, growing restless when autumn beckoned, watching the sky and thinking of Canadian geese and being called by a nameless desire. Each October, his wife would watch him quietly and understand as had his mother before the call which lured him to a wild, uninhabited place where he could wander days-on-end by himself, hunting a bit but mostly thinking, his soul feeding on the nourishment of solitude.

In 1940, Fob Sr. was awarded the concession rights in the Lanett Mill in an agreement with "Mr. Rube." Fob Sr. left the employ of Lanett City Schools and the Lanett Mill to start a business handling all concessions within the Lanett Mill. A typical small town business-man of his day and a role model for his son's future diversified inter-ests, Fob Sr. at the same time also owned a wood, coal and ice yard, delivering the necessary items in a mule-drawn wagon in the early days of his business.

At that time, none of the huge mills had cafeteria facilities for workers. Fob Sr.'s agreement with "Mr. Rube" was to provide food for the mill workers. He set up at one end of the mill a complete facility for preparing, storing and serving food.

During workers' breaks, Fob Sr. delivered food and snacks to them on a huge wagon which had to be pushed by hand.

Family pictures show James as a sandy-haired high school student who during vacations and after school hours could be found pushing his father's heavy "dope wagon" throughout the three floors of the Lanett mill, stopping at appointed places and pulling up the "window" of the wall-high rolling kitchen, dispensing milk, hot dogs, aspirin, BC medicine powder or crackers and gum and cigarettes to the workers. (The cart was called dope wagon because it carried Coca-Cola, ru-mored in those days to contain cocaine as a secret ingredient.) Fob Sr. was at one time one of the largest retailers of Coca-Cola in the state of Alabama.

The wagon was a heavy, burdensome thing, with cold drinks packed in ice boxes and hot food heated by compartments which held hot water. At the beginning of each day, Fob Jr. was forced to take a running start to push the heavy wagon up the slanted walkway into the mill. Most times he made it. Sometimes it backed him back down and he had to start over. It built muscles and stamina and he swears he lost five pounds from start to finish of a shift.

James may have loved his solitude. But the impression he made on others near his age paints a slightly different picture. One of his boyhood friends, Don Bryan, remembers James as a youngster who did not fit into any mold. Several years younger than James, Bryan said James was "a special type of person, even as a child, a young person growing up. He was different. Ever since I've known Fob, whatever group he has been in, he has been the leader. He didn't get involved in some of the escapades we did. Maybe it was that he had a certain amount of more maturity. I know we looked at him as a leader. He was someone you looked to, to make decisions about what you were going to do."

When James was in 10th grade, his father made the decision to send him to Baylor Military Academy in Chattanooga, Tenn., where the academic standards would be as tough as the competition he would face on the football field.

The decision was based primarily on Baylor's reputation as a tough school on discipline, James said, though his parents were aware of an equal reputation for academic excellence.

"I don't think Fob's parents were particularly impressed with the way he was handling his studies," says James W. "Jimmy" Long of Birmingham. Long roomed with James at Baylor. Their fathers had played football together.

"I was very much in need of the regimentation I got at Baylor," James says.

James fought against going to Baylor, his mother said.

The move paid off, however.

During his junior and senior years at Baylor he lived up to the reputation for athletic excellence set by his father, proving himself a natural athlete as he lettered in track, football, baseball and soccer.

"To say I was a scholar would be to lie," James said of his school years, admitting his literary interests revolved around western novels, war tales and detective stories written by Mickey Spillane.

His grades were decent enough to pass, however.

Long remembers the Baylor years: "Fob wasn't real humble. He was pretty much sure of his abilities. But he was humbled a few times at Baylor."

Long remembers one winter day when the two went to a nearby frozen pond to skate on the ice. Long, a heavier boy, said to get on the ice you had to take a running start and jump. He said he took a running start, jumped on the ice and skated off.

"Fob took a running start, jumped on the ice and it broke and he went 'plop' in the water. I laughed so hard he took his skates and went home and didn't speak to me for three days," Long said.

James, Long says, "was more or less just one of the boys."

Reporter Nancy Harris later wrote of James the Baylor student:

> "His air, his voice, his looks, an honest soul, speak all so movingly in his behalf," rhapsodized the Baylor yearbook in 1952, the year he graduated. He was known as "Poss."
>
> It was short for Possum, said English teacher Dr. James E. Hitt, who gave him the nickname. "He always had what I used to call those cold eyes of his and one day, I told him his eyes looked like a 'possum. No one that I know of could ever strike a note of fear in Fob....He was a really smart kid, not what I'd call an intellectual. Still, he was no dummy. He was a really good football star here and also a baseball star too...he just had such an indomitable will, he'd just go out there and do it," Hitt said.
>
> "He is a person who is absolutely firm. Don't think he can't make a decision. He can and he'll stick to it," said Hitt, an author whose books include *Tennessee Smith*.

Harris wrote that the headmaster remembered James as "serious-minded, even as a kid...very disciplined. He was not a party guy. He was a natural leader and when he was doing something, he was all business."

James was voted All State and All Southern for his sports activities at Baylor.

In December of 1951, the 5-foot-10-inch 170-pounder was awarded a scholarship to attend Auburn University. He also received an appointment to the Naval Academy at Annapolis, where head football coach Homer Hobbs had at one time been an Auburn coach and was aware of James' athletic ability.

James said he toyed with the idea of attending Annapolis but never seriously considered going anywhere but Auburn to play under "Shug" Jordan. Jimmy Long, his roommate from Baylor, also was recruited by Auburn to play football. He and James roomed together, along with several others including future University of Georgia Coach Vince Dooley.

Attending Auburn was returning home.

His coach had been a friend of the family since his own college days when he boarded with James' grandmother.

That friendship did not mean James was able to get away with anything, however.

Jordan told a reporter of one incident.

On Saturday mornings, he discovered, James was slipping away before dawn to shoot ducks or doves, even on the days when big football games were scheduled.

Jordan called James to his office.

In the office sat James' father. Stacked next to him were James' gun, shells, hunting gear, and fishing tackle.

"You are here to study, not to hunt and to fish," his father told him.

The equipment all went home with Fob Sr. and stayed there until James redeemed it at the end of the school year.

In the fall of 1952 there was also in the freshman class a petite redhead of Irish descent named Bobbie Mooney. A Decatur, Alabama, native, she had planned to attend Birmingham Southern on a scholarship, deciding only a month or so before school to go to Auburn instead.

Bobbie's grandparents, Eliza Fleming and Thomas Coy Mooney, had settled in Indiana after emigrating to the United States from Ireland not long after the Civil War. In 1875 they traded their Indiana farm for one in Morgan County, Alabama.

Bobbie's father, R. F. Mooney, got a job clerking in a dry goods store in 1911. The next year he added his $200 savings to money given him by his mother and opened his own store.

By 1916 Mooney owned a fancy buggy pulled by a "high stepping horse" in which he courted Newtia Gladys Tuten, a petite Rogersville girl who wore a size four-and-a-half shoe. They married in August of that year. Her pictures show a turn-of-the-century beauty: coal black hair and black eyes, high cheek bones which were said to be the legacy of a distant Indian ancestry. There is no hint in the face of the healthy-looking young woman that tuberculosis would prevent her from reaching her 40th birthday. An ominous warning was sounded when her mother, Lucendy Wallace Tuten, died of cancer just eight days after her daughter's wedding.

Early married life revolved around the new store Mooney had built. The couple lived in the back of it, where he kept an old wooden box his father had brought from Ireland. In it he placed the "tobacco twists" he made from the tobacco he grew to sell in his store for customers to smoke. He sold sugar and flour in 100-pound barrels and specialized in the livestock feed he carried for farmers in the area.

Bobbie Mooney was born just 18 months before her mother died of the tuberculosis discovered shortly after her daughter's birth. Bobbie was by far the most frail of any of the Mooney children, giving her parents cause to fear that the newborn would develop tuberculosis also. Great care was taken by her parents to prevent her from further exposure, including the hiring of a wet nurse who took the small baby to her breast with her own newborn child.

When she knew she was dying, Bobbie's mother instructed her older girls to "take care of the younger ones."

Bobbie was the seventh child. Though she was too young to remember her mother's death, it haunted her childhood. The depth of her sense of loss is grippingly revealed in a book she later wrote but did not publish:

> ...There was only one thing I feared in all the world...Disease. Especially lung disease. I thought of Mama whom I had never known...Mama, who had wasted away to nothing and finally died and was buried in February in the snow...Mama, whom we never mentioned because it was too painful...who had, it seemed, somehow always been with me just the same...Especially on the special days. I knew that she was watching. And I tried to be good that she wouldn't be disappointed in me, her little golden haired baby girl, wan and thin who grew up sitting on the drummers' knees in the small country store that Papa ran. She had suffered greatly, I had overheard and we didn't talk about it. Papa never mentioned her but once or twice that I could remember.

Mooney moved the toddler and her bed to his store after the death of his wife. There, he had help looking after her from salesmen, or drummers, and from the regular patrons.

"I never lacked for love," she says. "I also had five older sisters looking after me."

Love could not take the place of a mother, however. There would always be moments when she wished desperately and fervently that she had a mother, such as the moment in first grade when the teacher asked her if her mother was coming to PTA.

At Auburn, she quickly became best friends with suitemate Linda Lee James, who informed her two months after school began, "I have a cousin I want you to meet so you can marry him and we can be cousins."

The daughter of Fob Sr.'s twin, Ebb, Linda Lee introduced Bobbie to her cousin, Fob.

"We went bowling on our first date," Bobbie James remembers. "Fob was straight from Baylor and acted such a gentleman that every-time I got up to throw my bowling ball he escorted me. When I got back to the dorm I told Linda Lee, 'Your cousin is the funniest boy I ever met.' But I knew from that first date I wanted to see more of him."

Bobbie Mooney was not particularly interested in sports, definitely not a wide-eyed coed awed by dating a football hero. James thought her "the prettiest girl I had ever seen."

She was thin, five-and-a-half feet tall, a waif with large eyes and a seriousness about her which was obvious even at age 18.

Fob and Bobbie dated for nearly three years, though Bobbie left Auburn after her first year to attend Florence State for one semester. She returned to Auburn the next quarter and then spent several months in Washington, D.C., caring for an ailing sister. She returned to Decatur to work as a secretary to the comptroller at Redstone Arsenal and they continued to date.

Neither had a car. On weekends, when Bobbie came to Auburn, James would borrow his Uncle Ebb's car for double-dates with Linda Lee and her friends. They went bowling and to the movies, fought and broke up and made up as youthful lovers do everywhere.

James, unaware at that moment that fate had settled his future, continued a life which revolved around football, enjoying to the fullest his life as a football hero.

The sports pages of state and regional newspapers were filled with pictures of him. The caption under one picture referred to him as carrying on "in the tradition of his daddy and uncle, once famed as Auburn's halfback twins."

At Auburn, the football season peaked in those days with the annual confrontation with Georgia Tech.

"We had about 8,000 students at Auburn," James said. "Friday before the Tech game it seemed like at least 6,000 of them would hop a train to Atlanta. All the rats (freshmen) were told to bring back Tech rat hats. There were fights all night before the game and the fights lasted until everybody got back to school. Those games were really something to see."

Tech beat Auburn each of James' first three years. It was in James' junior year in the game against Tech that he picked up the nickname which follows him today.

"We were behind seven points and there was less than 10 minutes left in the game," he said. "We were on the Tech two-yard line; I was given the ball on a dive play but dropped it as I crossed the goal line. There was a huge argument and finally the officials ruled the touchdown didn't count."

Long said James had been sick before the game and went into it with a fever. "After the game he really felt terrible. Everyone was mad about the play. Back then there was a student laundry at Auburn which picked up your clothes and washed them and brought them back in a bag. Well, when they brought Fob's laundry back Monday it had a tag on it, 'Fumbling Fob.' "

"Auburn folks have called me that ever since," James says.

Dooley says there is a little bit more to the story: "Fob had a little bit of a problem fumbling because he had a tendency to reach with the ball to make the extra foot or the extra yard. It was a habit he had to overcome. He was a scrapper. But on the day of this game, Fob shouldn't really have played. He had been in the hospital for several days and was obviously weak. I think it was a coaching error that he was there, but his being there lifted the morale of the team and the spirits of the Auburn people."

James' revenge came the next year when in his senior year his team became the first Auburn team in 15 years to beat Tech.

James' younger brother, Calvin, played for Georgia Tech after James graduated from Auburn.

James was one of the 1954 backfield which Jordan labeled the greatest he ever coached, the foursome of Bobby Freeman at quarterback, Joe Childress at fullback, Dave Middleton at right halfback and James at left halfback.

"Fob was a breakaway threat," Jordan said. "He had eyes in the back of his head."

"Fob was always an individual," Dooley said. "In football and in everything else, he dared to try something everybody else said couldn't be done. Most times, when he set his mind to it, he did it."

In 1955, columnist Max Moseley wrote, "That swirling wizard of the gridiron—Auburn's Fob James Jr.—has been almost personally responsible for the Auburn Tigers unbeaten team...(James) has scored four of the six Tiger touchdowns thus far...has bolted into third place in the nation in rushing by his great performance last Saturday against Kentucky..."

Other papers weekly touted James' accomplishments with such headlines as, "Fob pulls Auburn over in scorcher. Says Jordan: Better left half than James?—where is he?"

James in his off-time was as busy with sideline ventures as he had been in his childhood.

An article in the university's newspaper tells of one such endeavor. The head reads: "Haberdashery Big Part of James' Toils: Plainsman Halfback Sells Clothes From Graves Center Men's Store."

The article stated: "The Lanett junior has a small-scale men's wear shop in his cabin at Graves Center.

"Fob says that he spent the summer trying to think of an idea of something he could do this year to make a little spending money," the article stated.

He finally came up with the idea of selling sports clothing. Roy Sewell, a large manufacturer of men's clothing, was an Auburn backer. He allowed James to buy his inventory wholesale. James would borrow a car, drive to Bremen, Ga., buy his inventory and display it in a corner of the Graves Center cottage he shared with roommates Long, Dooley and Frank Reeves.

"His secret of success is that he has no overhead and the fact that he obtains the merchandise straight from the manufacturers," the article stated.

James, however, laughs today and remembers the venture was not a financial success. "I got into trouble by extending credit to all my friends," he says.

While at Auburn, he also sold class rings to seniors and janitorial supplies to fraternities.

James' leadership abilities surfaced in an episode that Don Bryan remembers as a situation which "could have turned into something ugly" without James' intervention.

Retired Auburn Dean James Foy, venerated Dean of Students at Auburn and prior to that much-loved administrator at the University of Alabama, was adviser to the Auburn publications board in 1955. He remembers well the situation of which Bryan speaks.

The editor of the 1955 *Glomerata* had a sense of humor which other students apparently did not share. Instead of the usual dull but flattering descriptions of the various sororities and fraternities on campus, editor John Sellers wrote satirical spoofs poking fun at them.

A feature writer on the staff of the student newspaper, the *Plainsman,* got an advance copy and wrote an editorial denouncing Sellers, Foy said. Students began to gather in groups, feeding upon mass anger.

"I've seen it happen before," said Foy. "What starts out as a group of angry people becomes a mob."

After tossing yearbooks into a bonfire, the students began to march toward a fraternity house where they thought Sellers would be, chanting, "Where's John? Where's John?"

Foy got a call from Sellers asking for help, saying, "They're after me."

As a method of crowd control, Foy said he asked James and several other responsible students who were known by most of the student body to mingle with the crowd and calm things down.

"The students came storming in on campus, headed for the frat house where the editor was," Bryan said. "I remember Fob stopping them in front of the house, standing in front of the door and telling them nobody was going to destroy property or hurt someone, no one was going to come through that door."

Foy said James reminded students everybody had exams the next day and said he knew they had to study like he did and why didn't they go on home and let the publications board take care of the yearbook editor.

James says he really doesn't remember much about the incident.

The crowd dispersed.

Meanwhile, the relationship between James and Bobbie Mooney had blossomed from the traditional love at first sight to talk of marriage.

They talked of future plans, as all couples do, but politics was not in that talk.

At that time, Bobbie recalls with a laugh, the only "dream" James voiced was that someday in the future he would like to own his own restaurant.

"The most I ever wanted was a rose-covered cottage," Bobbie James said. "Fob was different. He was the most different boy I had ever met. I knew he would do something someday. He was unusual."

Fob and Bobbie eloped in August prior to his senior year, a romantic spur-of-the-moment decision.

During her husband's senior year, Bobbie worked for the Auburn Extension Service. Her income was supplemented by his athletic scholarship and the income he made from odd jobs.

In his senior year James was All Southeastern and All American. He was also named most valuable player in the Southeastern Conference by the Atlanta *Journal-Constitution* and was invited to play in the Senior Bowl in Mobile with other top seniors from across the nation.

James' team made it to the Gator Bowl three straight years. In his four years, he gained 1,913 yards on 317 carries, which set a Tiger rushing record not to be broken for two decades. He played safety on defense, ran back punts and kickoffs, held the ball for extra points and did the punting.

"The Southeastern Conference ruled out two-platoon football at the end of my freshman year," James explains. "Everybody had to play both defense and offense. It was much later that the conference changed the rules again to allow free substitution."

After his Auburn football career ended, James took a year off from his studies to play pro football for the Montreal Alouettes. A $2,000 bonus came with the contract he signed.

"We hotfooted it straight down to the Ford dealership and bought a $2,000 Fairlane," Bobbie said.

The year they spent in Montreal was for James the beginning of a love affair with Canada which continues today. The year ended with the birth of their first-born son, Fob III, and a return to Auburn for James' final two quarters. Because he was born in Montreal, Fob III enjoys both U.S. and Canadian citizenship.

After James got his degree in civil engineering in 1957, he drew a six-month tour of active duty at the U.S. Corps of Engineers School at Ft. Belvoir, Va., near Washington, D.C. There, he completed the Engineer Officers Basic Course and played football.

Those were the days after the Korean War, when football competition between various branches of the service was very keen and there was active recruiting by the services of the best college and professional athletes. On the day of a big game, the brass would arrive in chauffeured cars, accentuating the importance placed on the game.

His performance in these games earned James the sports award he has most cherished. The Army Times named him the Outstanding

Soldier Athlete in the U.S. Armed Forces.

James' first engineering job was in Montgomery as an earthmoving engineer for Burford-Toothaker Tractor Co., the Caterpillar dealer in South Alabama and West Florida.

The James family was living there when their second son, Greg, was born in September of 1958. It would be five months before Gregory Fleming James would be diagnosed as having a little known but lethal congenital disease, cystic fibrosis. The disease was understood to be a generalized disorder of the exocrine system.

The unpublished book by Bobbie James, written six weeks after Greg's death in 1967, was about him. The book begins soon after she brings her newborn home. Suffering massive headaches from the spinal tap given her during childbirth, Bobbie describes the frustration of being almost unable to take care of him:

> ...the first time I noticed the grayish color was when he was only a few days old...Something in me registered fear — fear that something wasn't right. But perhaps I was mistaken...The inner voice continued that all wasn't well with this child — our Greggie boy — or better, Mr. Greg which we had already begun to call him. He was such a man even from the beginning that it would have been absolutely impolite to refer to him as simply Greg.
>
> There were coughs in the night, first just little hacking dry coughs that I could hear from my bedroom where I lay...unable to care for this little boy, nor for Fob, my two-year-old son. I made my way holding my head to keep it on to his room...I covered Greg, closed the window fearing a draft might be causing him to take cold...and crept back to my bed in much pain and confusion. Surely this was not the way it should be to bring home a new baby boy, the second son of parents who would love and adore him...Perhaps the pain would go away...I couldn't understand why I had been given a spinal...and now I had those damnable spinal headaches that could last for months...I who had never known a headache in my life and the baby was coughing and Fob was working...

Over the months, the worry turned into fear as Greg's color grayed, his coughing increased and he seemed to spit up more food than he retained. Then a friend, reluctantly, gave them a copy of a magazine article on the newly-discovered disease called cystic fibrosis.

> Cautiously I mentioned the words to Dr. Nolan. He removed the stethoscope from Greg's chest and looked squarely into my eyes. He seemed grave. He didn't laugh...Quietly he answered, 'I

know enough to send this baby to Birmingham' and a stab of cold fear seared my very soul. I wasn't silly after all. Greg could have it. But he wouldn't, I told myself. It would be only a scare. I began to bargain with God. 'Now God, I know you won't let this be. You simply can't let this happen to me, not little Bobbie Mooney. You know I've always tried to be good. You know I've never wanted but one thing in my whole life, to have a Christian home, to be a good mother, have some children, to love and tend them. I haven't been that bad, have I...?'

So I dangled between heaven and hell...for God to change his mind before our appointment in Birmingham...

The diagnosis was cystic fibrosis.

'For the thing I greatly feared has come upon me,' I recalled from Job...

Dr. Hare's office was starkly furnished and I listened intently to the finality with which this fine old gentleman spoke to Fob and me...as he told us that our five-month-old could not possibly reach the age of six...

...In essence we were to take Greg home to die a slow, lethal death by suffocating. The body would literally drown in its own fluids. The lungs would close with thick sticky mucus...

...When I stopped crying I knew I wouldn't cry again for a long time...The floodgates close. You buckle up, draw in a deep breath, say okay, God, you know I can't take this. It's too big for me. You'll have to do it for me. And then suddenly you're okay again. You don't know why. You just have the strength to carry on...Occasionally, wistfully, you ask God 'why?'

The prologue was over. Now to get down to business. We would do all we could. We would hope. We would pray. We would never accept futility nor despair...

We went back to Dr. Nolan. He said, 'well, where there's life, there's hope.'

It was all we needed, a ray, a piece of hope.

And thus began what turned out to be an almost nine-year saga which would change the entire course of the James' lives.

Bobbie's book paints a heartrending picture of the young family of four.

A tent to fit a five-month-old baby is rare but we found one to fit over his head while we administered the aerosol solution that was to keep his breathing passages clear...

...his color improved daily and we began to play a game with ourselves, a pretending game, that it wasn't so, that our baby wasn't sick...that (the) doctor had made some huge mistake or that God had secretly healed Greg and made him well...And the games lasted sometimes for a few days when Greg wasn't coughing...Those were the golden days, days he seemed completely normal...Hope had turned into real faith and the strength to bear each day...

The bills began to pile up...Fob decided to leave Montgomery (for) a job in Mobile...His salary would be small but he would receive a portion of the profits as each project was completed. He would begin his new career as construction superintendent for Laidlaw Contracting Co., completing six miles of interstate highway...

Mobile was wet. It rained the first six weeks...I was beginning to be depressed...It came down in sheets and rainy weather wasn't good for Greg. He seemed to cough more...and I began to complain to Fob...

Meanwhile Fob was working 12 to 14 hours a day to keep our heads above water...There wasn't time to think...There were doses of medicine to be given and each one had to be worked in between inhalation therapy...But we were happy. Except for the weather. I began to wonder if we were supposed to be in Mobile.

Fob was working too hard and gone too much. I complained when he came in. He was my sounding board and he always comforted me. Everything was okay when he came home, but sometimes, sometimes, well, I needed to lean a little bit. I needed him to reassure me that Greg was gonna live.

Oh God, let him live. Let him fool everybody...Please take all the suffering away...

I began to study cystic fibrosis...I knew there must be an answer somewhere...perhaps there was something our doctors didn't know about...

Gee (the name Greg gave Rebecca, Fob's mother) was on a train to Memphis...the woman next to her related that a Dr. Harrison in Houston was working with the disease...

...We boarded the plane (for Houston) a few days afterward, I and my 14-month-old baby boy, by that time glowing with health; bright-eyed, sharp, golden haired...I had packed with great care...I took peanut butter and jelly and bread since Greg was used to a midnight snack since his stomach emptied much too often and he only digested a small portion..."

There was no cure in Houston, nor would there be anywhere else. But there was hope. The doctor was delighted the diagnosis had been made so early. He thought Greg had a chance to make it.

> Make it? What's that in the life of a terminal illness? Who knows? We found that there were teen-agers living with CF, even some adults...

There was also despair in Houston. It was the first time Bobbie had seen a child in latter stages of CF.

> ...Greg's disease would never go this far, I assured myself as I watched the pitiful little bird-like girl take in a deep breath on the positive pressure breathing machine.
> "Oh no God, don't ever let it happen," I silently begged with everything in me. "Oh God, don't ever let Greg suffer," I pleaded. "I would rather You take him than make him a thing of pity, one that people would have to feel sorry for. Oh, God, don't ever let anyone have to feel sorry for Greg. That, dear God, I could not stand."
> Mobile was cold, damp and rainy and the weather began to become my enemy as I watched its effects on Greg. I silently cursed the dampness, and the colds came closer together and finally pneumonia crept in...It was Greg's first hospitalization and complications set in...I knew I must get him out of the damp, muggy climate and the weather began to eat on me like an albatross around my very existence. I was watching my baby go down...I began to nag Fob about getting out of Mobile.

James, meanwhile, was constantly searching for some business opportunity which would bring in the money he needed to pay his son's ever-increasing medical bills.

"Fob didn't used to be serious, the way he is today," says his roommate from Baylor and Auburn, Jimmy Long. "What changed him was Greg. He realized that he had to come up with some way of making money for Greg's care. He centered all his thoughts on that, devoted all his energy to that."

Even though he had never lifted weights, James was aware of negative aspects of the iron barbells on the market. They rusted easily and damaged wood floors when dropped.

In 1961, at age 27, he set out to develop a material and a manufacturing process with which he could produce plastic-coated barbells which would compete favorably with cast iron.

First, he explored the possibility of coating a pre-formed concrete disk with plastic.

"It was totally impractical, from a cost and strength standpoint," he said.

After trial and error, James developed a blow-molded polyethylene disk which could be filled with a high-density material. As it solidified, the disk and material became one substance. He picked the trade name Orbatron, the first two syllables taken from materials used in the process—barite ore—and "tron" because it was the "catchword" of the day.

To decide if his barbell would sell, he put together a crude version and called on a number of sporting goods stores to get the reaction of salesmen and potential customers.

Everywhere he went in the sporting goods world, he was met with enthusiasm. He did not get that enthusiasm from his friends, however.

"He called me to come see what he was doing," Dooley says. "He was so excited. He had this barbell and he told me there was cement in the middle and I thought he was about half crazy. But I thought that on other things, too."

"I only gave Fob advice twice in my life," Long says. "The first time I told him he was crazy if he thought he could make a living making barbells. The second time I told him he could never be elected governor."

James had not been personally involved in the activity he was getting into.

"Heretofore, my coaches had always discouraged weight-lifting," James said. "They felt it would make their players muscle-bound."

Enthusiastic after his reception from the sporting goods salesmen, James knew his next step was to put together the financing for a manufacturing company to produce the barbells.

James headed to home turf, to Opelika where he had spent so much time with his Ellington grandparents. He outlined his plans to Sam Morgan, president of the Opelika National Bank. "Mr. Sam" was gung-ho because he was aware that a local foundry was making weights and could not make them as fast as they could sell them, James said. He became a catalyst in raising the money to begin Diversified Products, calling together other businessmen to listen to James' spiel.

When James was certain he could put together the money to begin his company, he and Bobbie made ready to move from Mobile to Opelika.

Bobbie James wrote of that time:

> It was Thanksgiving and I was pregnant but unafraid and no
> one mentioned that another baby was forthcoming. It was too
> embarrassing. Our genes didn't jibe, we had been told in the begin-
> ning of Greg's illness. Not only were we given a death sentence for
> our precious child, we were mechanically told that we had a one
> out of four chance of having another child with CF...It was no
> wonder that no one said anything...
>
> There was a house for rent; one house in the whole town...Fob
> rented the house and went back to Mobile to move our things...

Thus James began what would be a 17-year saga which was not
without difficulty and close financial calls.

He had financial and moral support. Fob Sr. backed his son to the
hilt; Jacob Walker Jr., a prominent attorney, incorporated the company as Diversified Products.

Opelika businessman Jud Salter describes some of the other men
who participated.

"You had a lot of the wealth and business talent of Opelika in that
group, including Bill Samford, John Lewis Whatley, Holmes Floyd,
Jud Scott Jr., Yetta Samford, Jack Moore and Billy Hitchcock," Salter
said. "You had contemporaries of my father who knew how to build
successful businesses."

Moore was a local sporting goods dealer. Scott was of the Scott
Bridge Co. Hitchcock had been a major league baseball player and
later managed the Atlanta Braves.

Samford was a member of the family which had produced the
Alabama governor of that name in the early part of the century. An
attorney, he was counsel for Auburn University. He helped James in
the formation of capital and remained a close adviser until his death
in 1965.

Whatley started Dairyland Farms, a company which branched out
over the years to deliver milk and ice cream to towns near Opelika,
from Alexander City down into Phenix City. Dairyland was eventually
sold to Meadow Gold.

In 1962 James sold his backers $25,000 in stock to raise capital to
begin Diversified Products Corp., and "borrowed every dime I could
and mortgaged everything but the kitchen stove." He would serve as
president and board chairman until 1978.

The first year was an humble one, to say the least. It was spent in
the back shed of a 2,000-square-foot cotton warehouse. He had two

employees, his secretary Dot Millican and Eldridge Cockrell, a retired lieutenant colonel who was married to Bobbie's sister, Liz. Desks consisted of apple crates turned upside down. Mrs. Millican's apple crate vibrated when she typed.

The process of developing the material later to be trade-named Orbatron to compete with cast iron took longer and cost more than James had anticipated.

Salter, whose grandfather had founded a printing shop in Opelika in 1894, dropped by often during the tedious months of trying to get Diversified off the ground.

"I did the printed forms he needed," Salter said. "He would tell me what he was trying to control with the forms and I would design them. They were very simple."

Salter as an uninvolved observer noted the difficulties James was encountering.

"I thought most of the production work went out the door and wondered how in the hell anyone expected to make a living making barbells," said Salter. "They were mixing certain materials and trying to pour the mixture into a polyethylene shell through a hole the size of a quarter and make it solidify without air pockets. If the mixture was too dry it wouldn't pour and if it was too wet it would leave air pockets. Also, cement generates heat and expands when it cures, so there were all sorts of technical problems."

After many such months of experiment, James hit on the right techniques and developed machinery and procedures which accomplished his goal by using high frequency vibration on the materials and the shell.

James' manufacturing business was begun on about as small a scale as could be possible. He operated the first filling machines himself, one day slicing off the end of a finger while loading an electrical motor in the back of a pickup truck.

The production rate of what started out as a one-man operation accelerated under James' management to the point where he was turning out more than 50,000 pounds of weights per hour.

Diversified Products Corporation financed its early growth by borrowing each week from the Opelika National Bank to buy materials and to make the next week's payroll. Collateral was the "accounts receivable." Or, in layman's language, each week's growth enabled the company to borrow for the next week, admittedly a "nip and tuck" financial arrangement.

Within two years, the plastic barbell was accepted as an improvement for home use over conventional iron weights. The American public was just beginning its romance with the idea of physical fitness.

The leisure time sporting goods market was beginning to boom. Sports and physical fitness had been emphasized nationally from the day physically-fit John Kennedy was elected president. Diets were in fashion. It was stylish to be trim.

Diversified Products was in exactly the right place at the right time.

The company got its first big break when Sears contracted to purchase a large quantity of weights to be marketed under its Ted Williams brand for catalogue and retail sales.

At the same time, efforts to sell customers like J. C. Penney, K-mart and other department and sporting good stores were resulting in increased orders. When Diversified Products reached the point at which it was manufacturing 70 percent of the barbells sold in the country, its products were sold as Hawthorne at Ward's, Foremost at Penney, Golden Pro at discount houses, and Health Disc in department and sporting goods stores.

Calvin James joined his brother as head of sales in 1963. The company by then had 21 employees and had moved to a bigger building on the Columbus Parkway. When Orrox Corporation moved out of its larger building in Opelika, Diversified Products moved into it.

Salter described James' life during those years as a hectic one of long days and evenings at work punctuated by frequent travel to call on customers and suppliers throughout the U.S. James used to joke, Salter said, that if he had a quarter for every time he went through the Atlanta airport he would be rich.

The travel was not of the fly in/fly out the same day nature. James worked extensively with suppliers, tool and die shops and customers in cities and towns for days on end, educating himself at the same time on how grass-roots America thought and lived. What he learned would play a part in a big decision he would make in the future as to whether he would run for public office. James discovered that the majority of Americans with whom he came in contact thought and felt the same way about most things as he did, which was the same as did folks in Lee County, Alabama.

On the weekends, when not working, Fob and Bobbie James spent the time like most couples of the era, barbecueing or going to ballgames with two new neighbors who were to become their closest friends, Cynnie and David James (no relation).

David James also became a business associate when Castone
Corp. was set up under the umbrella of Diversified Products in 1963.
The company manufactured precast concrete panels which are used
in the construction of buildings. The panels are loaded on flat-bed
trucks and taken to construction sites where they are bolted to steel-
frame buildings during construction. The panels can be obtained in a
variety of finishes, from round smooth gravel or crushed gravel to
green tinted rock finish.

Castone Corp. split off from Diversified Products when it soon
became apparent that the construction-oriented precast concrete business and the consumer-oriented fitness products required entirely
different manufacturing and marketing approaches, James said.

James gives complete credit to David James, president of Castone
Corp. since its inception, for making the company into what is today
one of the leading manufacturers of precast panels in the south.

Timothy Ellington James was born three months after Fob and
Bobbie moved to Opelika.

The James household continued to revolve around the needs of a
terminally-ill child.

In the remaining years of Greg's life, his mother wrote, "Money
would come and go. Business would thrive and die. People would
come and go. Feelings, frustrations would rise and melt."

There was only one concrete thing, she said. "There would always
be more praying than anything else."

Greg, meanwhile, grew into a happy, "delightful" child.

> He never thought of himself as sick...We roughhoused, disci-
> plined, spanked, prayed, ate, played games. Greg's favorite was
> "billy goat." He and Fob III made it up.

Fob III went off to school, "and Timothy had come, all pink and
rosy and the healthiest looking baby I had ever seen. He was so tough-
looking with hair that stuck straight up and he ate Dorothy Perkins
Hormone Creme for Dry Aging Skin one Sunday morning for breakfast."

Business thrived. They bought a pony named "Blueboy," guineas,
a hamster who ate the baby turtle's head off. Greg knew everything
there was to know about Bart Starr and kept the family in stitches with
his ability to mimic athletic stars. It took an hour before school in the

morning to rid him of the mucus and he had to take a dozen pills before he left, but he could do 65 push-ups.

Close to both his parents, Greg carefully balanced praise for each. His mother wrote that he told her one day, "You know, Mama, my daddy is just about perfect." Then he added, "Well, except landscaping." Landscaping was one of his mother's talents.

The day had to come which the family had dreaded.

Greg died in 1967 at age eight and a half.

"We kissed our special child, the darling of our life, God's special gift to us, goodbye, several times," his mother wrote.

"Greg was the impetus that drove us, financially, spiritually and in every other way," his mother says. "We were challenged to be all that we could be as we watched a brave little boy battle a horrendous disease daily with a cheery smile, courage unprecedented, never a complaint."

James said his son "is an integral part of our lives. He gave us an example of grace under pain and suffering that has not left us for a single moment of our lives."

Their fourth son, Patrick, was born four days after the anniversary of Greg's birth in 1968.

Diversified Products was doing well. James decided to branch out. Diversified Products moved into related exercise equipment—hand stretch exercisers, exercise bicycles, weight lifting benches, etc.

By 1965, DP had sales of $5 million a year and James had added subsidiary plants in Torrance, California, and Montreal, Canada.

Diversified Products was turning out 4,000 sets of barbells a day. It was also manufacturing under the Health Disc name slant boards, chest pulls, jump ropes, hand grips, isometric exercisers, exercycles and head-strap neck developers as well as distributing horseshoe sets and putting shots.

Within the plant, James and his employees knew each other on an informal, friendly basis. He had physically done every job in the plant, from filling the weights to loading the trucks to sweeping the floors and they knew it. Consequently, in many cases, they did not look upon him as boss but as working companion.

In 1966, with Diversified Products in the process of rapid expansion, James bought Superior Industries Corp. of West Haven, Conn. The purchase put DP into the poker, tennis and pool table business but almost proved disastrous to the company he had built from scratch.

Diversified's fast growth, and the acquisition of Superior, was financed with debt, debentures and borrowings on inventory, plant, equipment and future income.

In the three-year period from 1965 to 1968, sales jumped from $5 million a year to more than $20 million a year, but the bottom line showed a loss of over $1 million.

James said, "It was disastrous. I recall very clearly the day it dawned on me that we were broke because I had got caught up in the acquisition fever so rampant during the mid-60s. It was the time of an overpriced stock market, ridiculous price-earnings ratios for electronic and leisure stocks, the so-called glamour stocks. It was the time of growth for the sake of growth."

James also attributes the downslide to "the irresponsibility and stupidity of debt and leveraging caused by somebody's ego trip—in this case mine. I should have been fired.

"On the other hand, I knew there was only one way out and it was not easy or quick," he said. "I had to reverse my field and get back to fundamentals: cut costs everywhere, but above all, reduce overhead; improve productivity and profit margins; control inventory and increase inventory turn; not ship to those who didn't pay; reduce debt at all costs; and no corporate frills. Period."

Those who were there at the time report that this course was followed "relentlessly without exception."

"Fob is the toughest guy I've ever met. He doesn't know what the word 'quit' is," Cal James once said of his brother.

In the next two years, the books reflect that DP gradually regained the ground James said he lost by trying to grow too big too fast.

Sales dropped in those two years from $22 million to $16 million, but by 1970 the company was once again showing a hefty profit. James attributes the upturn to a board of directors which stuck with him and to "loyal employees and customers and bankers who hung in there."

In 1989, James assessed the experience, "Attempting unwise acquisitions forces you to get honest with yourself in respect to costs. It taught me some very valuable lessons about ego trips."

During the last eight years James was at the helm of Diversified Products, real strengths were developed throughout its structure.

A national sales force called on more than 5,000 retail and catalogue accounts.

His trucking company utilized over 200 tractor/trailer rigs to deliver orders throughout the United States to some 25,000 retail outlets. The trucks did not return empty to Opelika. They carried materials needed for the manufacturing process back to DP. An article written about DP observed that the unique method of distribution gave Diversified customers cheaper freight rates and dependable delivery, which enabled retailers to stage promotions assured of quick delivery if they ran out of merchandise.

In 1977, Diversified Products became part of the Liggett Group of Durham, North Carolina. The corporation consisted of a group of operating companies formed when the Liggett-Myers Tobacco Company decided to expand into non-tobacco markets. It had sales of about $1 billion, excellent financial strength and stability, and a long record of paying high dividends.

As a result of the merger, Diversified Products' stockholders received one share of Liggett Common Stock for 2.1 shares of Diversified Products common stock. The transaction concluded at a $32.50 per share price of Liggett common stock resulting in a value of $15.50 per share for Diversified Products common stock. Many of the early Diversified Products stockholders had bought their stock for less than $1 per share. Newspaper accounts have stated James received Liggett stock valued at slightly more than $3 million. He and his brother Calvin were given contracts to continue as principal officers, with Calvin remaining as president today.

Financial disclosures filed with the Securities and Exchange Commission reflect that the deal James made with Liggett also provided that he would benefit from future profits of the company.

Most importantly, the transaction insured that no matter what happened to James, his family was more comfortably provided for than most families ever dared dream.

He was young. He was healthy. He was wealthy.

Whatever else in the world could he want?

A clause in his contract with Liggett stipulated that he could take a leave of absence from his job, if he so desired, to run for the office of governor of the state of Alabama.

# — 2 —

# The Decision

**W**hy would Fob James Jr. want to run for governor?

The answer lies in what happened to him in the 20-year interval between the day the football hero graduated as a civil engineer in 1957 and the day he sold his manufacturing company for millions in 1977.

Somewhere along the way, the good-time-loving hunter and fisherman whose most serious literature was a Zane Grey western matured into the father of four sons who read history at night and worried that the United States of America was being seduced away from the principles on which it was founded.

Fob and Bobbie James settled into a set routine in the evening hours from the days when they were in their late 20s. Each night after Bobbie got the children to bed, she and Fob would settle in to read.

"I was heavy into the scriptures and he was heavy into history," Bobbie said.

The books James turned to over the years included anything written on the American revolution and books written by or about the founders and leaders of the nation.

He read, and re-read, Tom Brodie's *Thomas Jefferson,* anything about or by Winston Churchill, *The Decline and Fall of the Roman Empire* and other books about ancient and western civilizations.

One book, *15 Decisive Battles of History,* influenced him tremendously. "He must have read it 15 times," Bobbie said. The book describes battles from ancient to modern times which changed the direction of history, making the point that one event or one group of people can make a difference.

As he read through the years, James formed his own view of government and of elected officials and of what government should be doing and not doing for its citizens.

When did he start thinking about running for governor? Not even his best friend can say.

"I haven't the foggiest notion what Fob is thinking. On the deep things, nobody can read that man's mind," said his wife. "He didn't come ask me about whether to run or not. I think he knew full well that I'd support him."

James, looking up from his books, could see what was happening.

The national government was out of control. Inflation and debt were unrestrained. Congress had gone wild spending money. When they ran out they just printed more, plunging the nation deeper and deeper into debt.

The courts had gone crazy, turning loose criminals because of technicalities discovered by expensive attorneys.

Some of the elderly were starving while money which should have gone to feed them fed instead a burgeoning bureaucracy.

However, it was the children for whom James was vitally concerned. A great many were leaving school with diplomas they were unable to read. Teachers were at the bottom of the professional totem pole in salary. Worse, the respect with which teachers had historically been treated had eroded to the point where they worked often in physical fear of students, and emotional fear that parents might sue if their children were disciplined.

In Alabama, state problems paralleled the erosion of national moral and fiscal values.

More and more, James' thoughts revolved around how he could become a force speaking up against the insanity he saw, how he could somehow influence a return to the values he found in the words he read nightly written by the nation's founding fathers.

More and more, he felt that he could make that stand, yell and scream until he were heard, if he were governor of Alabama, one of the sovereign states forming the Union.

Holding office was not an idea foreign to his family. His father had run for mayor of Lanett and lost by six votes. His grandfather had been an Opelika councilman and his uncle had been mayor of Auburn. Bobbie had unsuccessfully run as a Republican for the State Board of Education in the old 3rd congressional district.

James' thoughts can be easily deduced from studying the speeches he gave, speeches which were not written in the customary political manner.

It is an acceptable custom for candidates running for public office to pay others to write their major speeches, retaining influence on the wording in varying degrees. A candidate might meet with his speech writer and outline in broad fashion what he wishes to say. He might jot a few observations down and give it to a speech writer to smooth up a bit. Some candidates probably deliver speeches word for word as written by an ad agency which drew inspiration from polls revealing what people want to hear. Others change a word here and there, leaving out entire paragraphs and sections, adding their own thoughts, thereby molding the speech into a form which reflects their beliefs.

It is a defensible act, relying on a speech writer. Demands are great on a candidate at any level. He simply does not have the time to research and write. Most were trained in a different field and a professional writer can better get their messages across.

James, however, looks on the writing of a major speech not as a chore but as an opportunity to corner a captive audience and tell them in his own words what he wants them to know. It is the one chance to talk heart-to-heart knowing no third party will translate erroneously or read nuances where there were none.

To write a speech, James closes himself off in an office, takes pen in hand and does not look up until he has finished the draft of what he wants to say.

The neatly-typed speeches in his files betray his addiction to last minute changes. All have words or sentences penciled through with hastily scrawled substitutions in the margins, the markings of a perfectionist intently searching for just the right word, just the right quote.

James' speeches thus reveal his pattern of thought:

> ...Government is neither complex nor complicated. It has been made to appear that way. This started in the mid 1960s when pragmatism, form, charisma and cosmetic appeal replaced philosophy and substance as our nation's ideals. Under the disguise of rhetoric such as The New Frontier, The Great Society, The New Federalism, the federal government promoted the false notion that it could cure all social ills.
>
> It completely jumped the tracks during the Vietnam War as we simultaneously pursued a guns and butter course for the first time in our national history. The classical responsibilities of our national government to provide a currency that holds value from generation to generation, to insure a monetary policy that prices money

within reach of the average American, the average business, the average farm, were all but forgotten.

We must understand the nature of our government changed during the last two decades. It became a government totally opposite from the one envisioned by Thomas Jefferson, and I quote, 'A wise and frugal government, which shall restrain men from injuring one another, shall leave them otherwise free to regulate their own pursuits of industry and improvement and shall not take from the mouth of labor the bread it has earned.'

I yearn to hear from the White House the trumpeter's call, loud and clear, a call to change directions, now, abruptly, to act without equivocation, so America can and will defend her vital interests anywhere, anytime and let the whole world know it; and following that to veto any and all federal bills that stand in the way of a balanced budget. To stop the printing presses of the federal government from printing money faster than our real growth in goods and services...

Corporate welfare violates every principle of fair play and the free enterprise system. It is a disgrace to the working people of America, the housewife, the farmer. It is wrong for government to give subsidy to that which the American people have rejected in the marketplace...

...No one in Washington plants a crop or produces a product or provides a service or solves a problem in Lafayette, Alabama. America's problems get solved only when its people throughout 50 states, in hundreds of towns and cities and farm communities, become determined to help themselves and to help their fellow citizens.

I know two things we ought to get serious about. Our state has the fourth lowest per capita income in the nation. Many are having a hard time making ends meet. We need more jobs and better paying jobs. Twenty years of my life have been spent working in shops, factories, market places, construction projects all over Alabama and throughout the nation. We are short of skilled craftsmen, tool and die setters, machinists, lathe operators, mechanics, electricians, and welders. We cannot attract the higher paying industries unless we have the skills and leadership to support it. From these ranks...come the front-line supervision of any production facility. They are to a plant what the 1st sergeant is to the Company B. They make it happen...We must kindle interest by showing high school students they can earn a good living, can get good paying, responsible jobs if they will prepare themselves by mastering a basic trade skill. Then we must provide the training and incentive necessary to convert their interest into reality...

...I've noticed many young people coming by our place looking for work can hardly read, write, add and subtract. Some have a diploma, some don't. Now, I'm not an educator, nor am I a Ph.D., but I know when we turn a youngster loose in today's world to make a living without the basics of reading, writing and arithmetic, he's handicapped for life, and that's a tragedy everytime it happens. I understand there are complexities and difficulties in our schools. But any system needs to be accountable, quality-wise as well as quantity-wise. These deficiencies are a reflection on all of us. It will get better the day we become determined to make it better and are willing across this state to make sacrifices to improve and to measure that improvement.

I've learned the hard way that to make progress I must first get honest with myself, to admit my shortcomings in order to correct them. You can't change anything without first admitting to yourself that it needs changing.

Abraham Lincoln said..."The fiery trials through which we pass will light us down to honor or dishonor to the last generation..."

The dog-eared books on the shelves in James' home reflect more than two decades of reading and re-reading history, biography, and economic commentary. Some bindings are loose. Comments are penciled in the margins and they fall open on their own to pages bearing most-loved quotes.

James scattered quotes from these pages in his speeches, perhaps hoping the language used by history's greatest thinkers would buttress the arguments he made to his listeners.

Quoting Abraham Lincoln:

You cannot bring about prosperity by discouraging thrift.

You cannot help the wage earner by pulling down the wage payer.

You cannot further the brotherhood of man by encouraging class hatred.

You cannot build character and courage by taking away a man's initiative.

You cannot help men permanently by doing for them what they could and should do for themselves.

Quoting Thomas Paine:

Government, even in its best state, is but a necessary evil; in its worst state, an intolerable one.

Quoting Woodrow Wilson:

> Liberty has never come from the government. The history of
> liberty is the history of limitation of governmental power, not the
> increase of it.

It may have been an observation from Lincoln which prompted
James to take to the stump.

Lincoln said, "With public sentiment, nothing can fail; without it,
nothing can succeed. Consequently, he who molds public sentiment
goes deeper than he who enacts statutes or pronounces decisions."

James had made his decision. He would run for governor.

# — 3 —

# Campaign and Victory

In early 1977 Mobile consultant and pollster Jack Friend was in Tuscaloosa on business when he got a telephone call from James.

"He and Starr Smith had tracked me down. They wanted to know if I could stop off in Montgomery on the way home to Mobile," Friend said. Smith was in advertising and public relations and had done some work for Diversified Products. "I said I could. We met at a Howard Johnson restaurant, me on one side of the table, Fob and Starr on the other. After the small talk, Fob folded his hands, sort of bent over, cocked his head and asked me a question."

James said, "Let me pose a hypothetical question. Suppose a fellow who is a businessman who has been a little active politically, but not really, decided to run for governor. Would he have a chance?"

"I knew at that moment he was running," Friend said.

The conversation started a series of events that culminated in a poll which Friend said "was designed to tell whether someone not well known could jump right in and win."

The results of the polls gave a green light to James' plans, revealing that almost half of the 1,000 Alabama voters polled would as soon vote for a newcomer to politics as for a veteran officeholder.

Of equal if not more importance, the polling revealed each of the known contenders commanded no more than 13% hard support (former Gov. Albert Brewer, Attorney Gen. Bill Baxley, Lt. Gov. Jere Beasley and state Sen. Sid McDonald.)

Armed with results of the poll, James hired the Memphis firm of Walker & Associates to do his advertising and began recruiting the people who would form the nucleus of his campaign organization.

Walker & Associates, at that time, had won in 35 of its 39 gubernatorial and senatorial campaigns. The agency's advertising campaigns
had played prominently in Dale Bumpers' toppling of J. W. Fulbright
in Arkansas and in James R. Sasser's successful senatorial challenge
of Republican national committeeman Bill Brock in Tennessee.

Deloss Walker after the 1978 election described to the Press Club
of Mobile the test a candidate must pass in order to be accepted by
him as a client in a political race.

He said the candidate must be a Democrat with integrity, honesty
and an ability to carry out the plans of which he talks.

Walker, the then 47-year-old son of a Baptist minister, was a
college music major who was "always involved in civic work.

"It was just natural to feel the necessity of getting involved in the
political process," he said. "You soon learn that effectiveness has to
come through political leadership."

His Memphis office had a staff of 30, but most of them worked on
general advertising, Walker said. He noted people were usually surprised when they learned political work accounted for very little of his
total business.

Politics is more or less a personal hobby, and he said he would not
increase the number of campaigns he did "for love or money."

"First of all, form a game plan and stick to it," he told the Press
Club. "Don't pick up the newspaper each day and change your strategy after seeing what the press reaction to you is."

"Go from county to county," he said. "Build grass roots support.
And above all, be natural."

What Walker tried to do with James, he said, "was to show him as
he was. If you package someone up with fresh shirts and every hair in
place, they're not going to be believable. I wanted people to see Fob
just as I did in that factory—himself."

He also warned against appearing negative to the voters.

"People look for the positive. They want someone to give them
hope, to lead them down the right pathway," he said. "Above all, don't
get involved in personalities."

Smith had been involved in prior political work and was able to
get James "in" to the National Democratic Convention in 1976. James
went to look and to listen. He confided to a few people that he was
thinking of running for governor.

Mobilian Ruby Noonan, a yellow-dog Democrat, was one of those
in whom he confided.

Most people thought former Gov. Brewer would be a formidable opponent, not to mention Beasley and Baxley.

"I told Fob he had as good a chance as any of the others," Noonan said, "if he ran as a Democrat, that is."

Before there could be a campaign, there had to be an organization.

"I was in the back shop of my printing company when one of my employees told me Fob was out front," Jud Salter remembered. "He asked if I had a minute to talk. That was in the spring of 1977. I'd heard rumors he was going to run for governor and that the house next door to David James was being fixed up to serve as a head-quarters. But he hadn't said anything to me about it."

The house was a huge old one at the corner of North 10th Street and 4th Avenue, dubbed "The Crossroads."

James told Salter he was running for governor and asked for his help. Salter said he was not in the least interested in getting involved, but did not tell James that directly.

"I told him I'd never been involved in politics, even on the local level," Salter said. "He gave me the literature he had on Deloss Walker and it was fantastic. He also had the grey line proofs of the big tabloid he intended to put out which listed everything he wanted to do as governor. Fob asked if I'd take the time to read it and I told him sure I would. Anything to get him out the door."

Salter said he scoffed, as did most others, at James' plans. "He had no city politics in his background, very little civic involvement. He thought he could just walk out of a plant and into the governor's office."

It was not Salter's political experience but his fund-raising abilities that interested James. He had been chairman of every fund-raiser in Opelika, from the United Way to church work. He had always succeeded or gone over his goal in pledges.

A week later, James called to ask if Salter had read his campaign literature. Salter said he wished him well but declined to get involved.

"I told him I had about as much as I could say grace over taking care of my business," Salter said. "It wasn't three days later that Mr. T. K. Davis called me and asked me if I had time to come by and talk."

Davis owned the Davis-Dyer company and had been mayor of Opelika for many years. He was also one of the backers of Diversified Products, and Salter's print shop did the printing for Davis' company.

"Few people turned Mr. T. K. down when he asked them to drop by," Salter said.

He dropped by.

"Have you heard the news?" Davis asked Salter.

"Everybody in Opelika had heard the news," Salter said. But he let Davis tell him the news.

"Fob's going to run for governor."

"I think that's great."

Davis had a little favor to ask of Salter.

"Jud, he needs some help," he said.

Davis reminded Salter that First Methodist Church had been $300,000 in debt until Salter headed a fund drive and got it in the black.

"You're a citizen of Opelika and of Alabama," Davis told him. "We'd like you to help Fob get his finances structured and off the ground."

Salter reluctantly agreed to help a little, just to point James in the right direction.

He said he was barely back to his print shop when he got a call from James.

"I wonder if we could get together," the candidate said.

Salter said he shrugged and agreed to meet him at Diversified. "I figured I could get away easier if I was in his office than if he was in mine," he said.

The upshot of the meeting was that Salter agreed to help James raise some money "if" within one week's time James could successfully elicit contributions from 15 of 20 people Salter listed on a sheet of paper. In addition, they had to agree to solicit money from five to ten other people. James could not call them on the phone. He had to go sit down and talk to them.

Salter, unaware at the time of how much background work James had done, said "I figured I had heard the last of Fob. The men I had named accounted for 75 percent of the wealth of the whole damn county. They were so busy it would be impossible just to find them all in their offices within one week. I knew he wouldn't get more than two or three."

The next Thursday, James called Salter apologetically.

"I haven't done everything you wanted," James said. "I got 16 of the 20."

From that moment, Salter was on board the James campaign bus, though he was eased into it so gently he wouldn't realize it for a few months.

The next Sunday afternoon, Salter was sitting watching a pro football game on television when James appeared at the front door, asking him for "one more favor." James asked him to fly to Mobile with him at 4 a.m. the next morning to meet with the group planning the Mobile area campaign.

At the end of James' short talk in Mobile, however, Salter said he was stunned into momentary silence to hear James introduce him with words that said something like, "I want you to meet the man who is going to head up the finance drive in the state. Come on up here, Jud, and tell them how you're going to do it."

The trip was the first of many. On one occasion, Salter found himself the only man on the plane who did not have a suitcase. No one had told him it would be a three-day trip.

During those early days in the campaign, the philosophy and plan emerged which James used to raise the more than $3 million spent during the primary, runoff and general elections.

Salter summarized: "You get 10 people to give and get them to get 10 more and watch how it spreads. You tell them they have to go see people, not call them on the phone. You can send all the letters you want and make all the phone calls you want and it won't get you the money you need. To raise money you've got to look at a person eyeball to eyeball and sit there until they write you a check. If you let them put you off, you won't get back in to see them the next time you come calling. You want the big contributors, but you also want the $10 contributions. If the man at the filling station donates $10, it probably means more to him than to people who can shell out $5,000 without thinking twice. The man who gives you $10 is going to tell everybody else about his candidate because it was a sacrifice to give it."

It was in those first few months that James and Salter developed the routine Salter calls their "dog and pony show." They spoke to every breakfast, luncheon and dinner meeting in the area. Salter spoke first, reminding those attending of how they had griped in the past about the state's poor education program and of how sick and tired they were of politics as usual in the state.

Then he would say, "If you don't pitch in and help, I don't want to ever hear you complain about state government again."

James would then get up and talk about his goals for education, how he was born and raised in Alabama and how he also was sick and tired of the state always being at or near the bottom in everything when it could do much better.

James' skills in public speaking did not exactly inspire his listeners to throw caution to the wind and follow him, Salter said.

"Fob needed to take remedial public speaking 101," Salter said of his first speeches. "He threw so many statistics in them nobody could keep up with what he was trying to say."

Salter said Opelika-Auburn civic clubs listened to James' poorly delivered speeches because they knew the economic impact Diversified Products had made on the community, how he had begun with two employees and worked his plant up to where it employed 1,200 local folks.

After each speech, Salter would critique it, pointing out to James how he lost people when he quoted so many statistics and how he held their attention when he talked about what he wanted for Alabama.

Very early-on in the campaign, Walker was in the audience when a man in the front row began heckling James with remarks belittling any illusions James might have that a political newcomer could get elected governor.

"That suit you're wearing looks like an undertaker's," the heckler told James, who looked down, paused, smiled and said calmly, "That's because I plan to bury the opposition."

Exclaimed Walker at that point, "We've got ourselves a candidate."

Meanwhile, James flew to Washington to meet the man he had decided sight-unseen should run his campaign, Mobilian John C.H. (Jack) Miller. Miller, who had worked at one time for his cousin, U.S. Rep. Walter Flowers of Tuscaloosa, was in 1977 Deputy to the Chairman of the Federal Deposit Insurance Corporation.

At age 33, Miller qualified as a veteran campaigner.

As a high school senior, he had traveled some 60,000 miles in his Key Club work. He was a youth coordinator in the unsuccessful 1962 gubernatorial campaign of state Sen. Ryan deGraffenried of Tuscaloosa, who was killed in a plane crash during his 1966 campaign for governor.

In 1965, Miller went to work in the campaign of U.S. Sen. John Sparkman, beginning a relationship with the senator which would last until Sparkman died. Sparkman's first youth co-ordinator, in 1966, Miller was state operations chairman of Sparkman's campaign in 1972 when he defeated Republican challenger Winton "Red" Blount of Montgomery, postmaster general of the United States under President Richard Nixon.

Prior to his FDIC post, Miller worked for a period for the U.S. Senate Banking Committee, which was chaired by Sparkman.

At the time James visited Miller in his office across from the White House, the attorney was making final plans to return to Mobile to establish the first law firm in the South specializing in banking law.

The way for James' visit had been paved with a phone call to the attorney from fellow Mobilian and friend John Counts.

Counts' brother, Braxton Counts II, was married to Linda Lee James, the daughter of Fob James Sr.'s identical twin, Ebb.

"John said his brother's close friend was running for governor and that he wanted to stop by to talk with me," Miller recalled.

When Fob walked in Miller's door, he began the conversation by saying, "I understand you know something about Alabama politics."

Miller responded, "I did. I don't know that I do anymore. But I know about banking law."

Miller asked James the question which had been asked before and would be asked again and again.

Why would a 43-year-old man who had made a fortune want to put himself and his family through a tough, uphill race when the odds were against his winning?

"He gave stock answers but I thought then that he was telling the truth and I still do," Miller said. "He said the state was in a hell of a bad condition, that there were too many young people who could not read or write or figure well enough to be trained as skilled workers in the manufacturing sector, that he knew if it was that way in Opelika it was the same all over the state. He said the people of Alabama deserved better and he questioned the honesty and the integrity of existing politics."

That night, Miller dined with Fob and Bobbie James at the Hay Adams Hotel in Washington. They talked politics and philosophy and more politics.

James described the successful campaigns in which Deloss Walker had handled the advertising.

Miller was impressed.

But if James had counted on leaving Washington with Miller on board as campaign manager, his visit was not a success.

Miller demurred.

James flew back to Alabama, undeterred. He stayed in touch by telephone, more than ever convinced after the initial talk that Miller was the man he needed to run his campaign.

Miller continued to give himself reasons why he should not listen to James. His wife, Susan, listed additional reasons why he should not listen to James.

The law firm he was intent upon founding had been a dream for too long to let himself be sidetracked by someone else's dream, they both agreed.

James shot down his arguments one by one. Miller need not put off his plans to open his law firm. He could run the campaign on a part-time basis and work the rest of the time as a banking attorney.

Thus began a dance which continued for several months.

When Miller flew to Orlando, Florida, to attend an FDIC meeting, James asked if he could meet him there to talk campaign one more time. He was bringing with him Walker and his brother, Calvin James.

Susan Miller was alarmed. She knew her husband well and felt he would be vulnerable to such joint persuasive tactics.

She therefore called the couple's best friend, Dr. Robert Lager, and asked him to fly to Orlando to provide moral support to Miller in firmly saying "no" once and for all.

Lager, a Baldwin County, Alabama, native, headed the Russian Department of Georgetown University. He had taught Miller at University Military School in Mobile.

"It didn't work. Fob charmed the socks off Lager, and Lager volunteered on the spot to take a leave from Georgetown and work for Fob's campaign," Miller said.

Miller stopped off on the way back to Washington for a bit of soul-searching in the chapel of his alma mater, Duke University.

"I guess it was a matter of honor," Miller said. "I had preached to anyone who would listen since I was 12 or 14 years old that Alabama didn't have to be the hind teat of the rest of the country. If I didn't run the campaign, it seemed to me there was nobody else who had the time or the inclination who would do so. The (U.S. Sen. Jim) Allen people could have done it, but they were involved completely with the Senate."

Miller's first act as campaign manger was to pay a visit to the Opelika "headquarters" and assess what existed in manpower and equipment.

He found a two-story non-airconditioned house which contained as its only boast to high-tech efficiency a single antiquated copier fit for what he described as "personal use at best."

"No one had heard of WATS lines, telecopiers, or direct feeds to radio stations," Miller said.

Manpower consisted mostly of James' friends and family as volunteers. There were two paid workers, Hal Sumrall, a former Diversified Products executive and college friend of James, and Jon Ham, a journalism graduate who was working on his master's degree.

Reaction was mixed among James' campaign workers when the campaign was taken over by Miller, an extremely competent individual who knew what he wanted done and did not waste or mince words when telling others what parts they were to play in getting it done.

Some were not enthused when Miller moved in and took over. Others were.

Ham and his wife, Kay, were ecstatic that someone had arrived who knew anything about politics.

Ham had little experience except in weekly newspapers.

"When I joined the campaign I knew more about being a press secretary than Jon," Miller said. "That was distinctly not true any more by November of 1978."

It was in July of 1977 that James announced to a Montgomery Civic Club his intention of becoming the first Opelika governor since William Samford in 1901.

"I think people are going to be looking for someone who'll get involved in the real problems of this state and face the facts," he told the audience. He said the facts were that the state's system of elementary and secondary education needed some help from the top. It needed to be made the state's number one priority.

James acknowledged that it was anticipated there would be a crowded field of experienced politicians running for governor. It would be an uphill battle, he admitted.

But he foresaw no obstacles, he said, that could not be overcome with "12 to 14 months of hard work."

The issues he outlined also included the economy in which wages couldn't keep up with double-digit inflation, a state prison system so crowded that prisoners were being refused by the state and sent back to county jails, and unchecked crime on the streets.

In early October, James asked Salter to raise $100,000 in the next two weeks, planning to officially announce his candidacy at a barbecue after the Ole Miss-Auburn game. He planned to get 5,000 people to his kickoff by feeding them free barbecue at Auburn's Duck Samford Stadium. It would get the campaign off to a positive note if Salter could present the check for $100,000 to him at that time.

"I told him he must be crazy. Every freeloader from four counties would show up for the barbecue," Salter said.

"You let me worry about the barbecue and you worry about the $100,000," James told him.

The small group of campaign workers James had recruited worked from can to can't to make the kickoff a success.

When the big day rolled around, Salter said James reaped both the efforts of hard work and of good luck.

"It rained for a while, then cleared. It drizzled through the ballgame. When the last barbecue plate was served, we discovered Fob had contracted for 5,000 plates and had served 4,970."

Salter was not able to present James with a check for $100,000, but he did have pledges for $86,000 which he discovered was far more than James had actually hoped to get.

The candidate was ecstatic.

The *Alabama Journal* reported, "With his old football coach in the rooting section and martial music blaring, former Auburn football player Fob James has launched his longest run, a marathon."

The reporter covering the kickoff reflected political sentiment in the state when he wrote that James' campaign began "under ominous clouds."

"Temporarily he is the leader since he is the first candidate to officially enter," the *Journal* noted.

"The only poll that counts is the one on election day," James commented.

In this first major speech, the media reported that James hammered at his newly chosen theme, "Time for a New Beginning," as he merchandised a business-like approach to government.

James noted rising utility bills and the plight of Alabama's farmers, voiced a desire to abolish taxes on food and drugs, and expressed disgust that Alabama should be near the bottom of the per-capita income totem pole.

He outlined a broad-based platform covering everything from the state's regressive tax system to politicians who "have had their day."

Newspaper estimates varied from 1,700 to 5,000 of the people who braved the threatening weather for James' kickoff. A deputy sheriff sized up the crowd as about 2,500. One reporter observed that there were several hundred people who hungered more for free barbecue than political rhetoric because they drifted away from the "well-advertised kickoff" before the speech making.

One unexpected visitor to the festivities was Montgomery activist attorney Morris Dees who, clad in jeans and T-shirt, rode in on a motorcycle to find out for himself what was happening.

Former Auburn Coach Shug Jordan praised his one-time running back and cautioned the public not to count James out prematurely.

"I've seen him desperate before," Jordan said.

The small inner-circle of campaign advisers put their heads together with James and came up with ideas for most of the advertisements which Walker produced.

"We looked around at what was wrong with the state and that's where our ads came from, not from invective," Miller said. "It was the cleanest gubernatorial campaign I've ever known of."

On their way to find a country restaurant renowned for its quail, Miller and party one night lost their way and wound up on a back road.

"Here we were riding along on a paved road which simply ended in the middle of nowhere," Miller remembers, still incredulous. "It went nowhere. Who in the hell had spent state money paving a highway to nowhere?"

Thus was born the commercial in which James illustrates the innate problems in a state highway department which would pave a "road to nowhere."

Another commercial was born on a visit by young attorney-to-be/campaign worker Bradley Byrne on a trip to Monroeville. In that city, the junior college campus sported a several-years-old auditorium which was essentially unusable because there had never been money provided to buy chairs.

Who would plan an auditorium but lack the foresight to include money for chairs?

Education was the heart and soul of James' reason for running, Miller said. There had to be a way to get across to the public the importance James attached to education.

One day as Miller peered through the venetian blinds of the Birmingham campaign headquarters, he spotted what would become the symbol of the James campaign.

"I yelled for someone to call and see if you could rent a school bus," Miller said.

At that time, you could.

The rented bus was dubbed the "Reading, 'Riting and 'Rithmetic Special." It carried James from one town to another and ended its journey at the inaugural platform in January of 1979.

James' yellow school bus was the last such vehicle which will be ridden into office by an Alabama governor, however. The Alabama Legislature has since approved a law requiring yellow school buses to be repainted a different color when sold for private use.

Friction was inevitable among people of such diverse backgrounds as those making up the inner organizational structure, as it is in all political campaigns.

When Miller would want to spend $20,000 on something, campaign treasurer David James would insist it could be done for $10,000.

Though arguments between the two at times threatened to erupt into free-for-alls, Miller said David James' insistence on staying within a budget, "forced me to marshal a plan before I presented something, to think it out."

Salter, who at times was referee and at times sided with one or the other, said each looked on his role in the campaign with tunnel vision.

"Jack would look at it from the view of what had to be spent to win. David would look at it from the view of what was coming in," Salter said.

Arguments also ensued as to whether to keep the headquarters in Opelika or move to a more central location, like Birmingham.

The lack of space in the crowded campaign headquarters resulted in James spending a lot of time working from his office in Diversified Products.

Miller wanted to move the campaign headquarters to Birmingham. Salter and David James wanted to remain in Opelika. They won.

The organization when Miller joined it had no overall plan as to how to tackle the race from a political standpoint.

"Fob's idea at that time was that you went out and put up a few billboards. He had put up four," Miller said.

To develop a strategy to guide the campaign, Miller took a few days off and sequestered himself high atop Mount Cheaha State Park with only a typewriter and a bottle of Scotch for company.

After four days spent holed-up in the cabin, except for one wild midnight ride down a foggy mountain in search of a new typewriter ribbon, Miller emerged with his "plan," oblivious to the teasing of campaign workers who insisted on referring to it as "the stone tablets brought down from the mountain."

Though changed "a million times," the plan formed the backbone of James' race. It divided the state into nine regions, with a coordinator over each region. Each region was further divided into counties, with each county having two chairmen, one for politics and one for finance. Many counties were further subdivided into cities, which also had finance and political chairmen.

"The first thing anyone does today is to attempt to turn chaos into order, to draw a plan," Miller said. "It was almost unheard of in 1978. My plan was drawn straight from the Sparkman campaign experience."

The biggest task facing Miller, James and David James was in convincing the kind of people they needed to agree to serve as coordinators and chairmen.

"It's not a simple matter to get the type person you want as a chairman in Tuscaloosa when your sole introduction to Tuscaloosa is one billboard on the way into town," Miller said.

Relying on contacts and on small meetings in which contacts were asked to bring friends, the campaign organization gradually took shape.

Each time a county or city appointment was made, a news release and a glossy photograph were sent to nearby newspapers.

Wayne Lord wrote in the Atlanta *Constitution*: "Miller set up and managed the organization and dealt with the toughest parts of political maneuvering while State Coordinator Hal Sumrall solicited the support of small non-political groups. As Sumrall put it, 'I deal with the Christians and Miller deals with the lions.' The general staff of the organization is, according to a long-time Wallace aide, 'the most able and efficient ever assembled in the state.' "

Many relatives of Fob and Bobbie volunteered, as well as their wives and husbands, brothers, sisters, cousins and in-laws.

James' mother, Rebecca, his brother Cal and wife Dora, and his younger brother, Bob, all jumped enthusiastically into the campaign, as did scores of Diversified employees. From James' family also came the volunteer efforts of his Uncle Louie and Aunt Miriam James and their daughter, Dottie, who gave up her voice lessons in New York to return to Alabama for the campaign, and his Uncle Ed and Aunt "Sis" of Decatur.

Fob III took a year off from the University of Virginia and at one point worked North Alabama, spending his days campaigning and his nights scurrying to Nashville to court Beth Cardwell, daughter of John Cardwell, one of James' finance chairmen.

During the campaign, Fob III also teamed up with Braxton Counts III to keep tabs on the "home" counties of Lee, Chambers, and Randolph.

The James campaign also had help from Bobbie James' four North Alabama Mooney sisters—Helen Stewart, Liz Cockrell, Emogene Johnson and "Sis" Lamb—in taking care of Limestone and Morgan counties, along with Marie McLemore of Opelika and brother Roy Mooney Jr. of Decatur, and a whole host of cousins, nephews and nieces.

Don Bryan, James' friend from youth, was named as one of the nine regional coordinators. Another coordinator, Dick Forster, was a newcomer but one who soon proved he "worked like the dickens and was good on details," Bryan said.

In Mobile, Braxton Counts II was an indefatigable worker. James called on two men to serve as local chairmen who had remained close friends since he lived in Mobile, Jimmy Bledsoe and Bob Williams.

David James of Opelika, friend, business associate and hunting buddy of the candidate, played a key role. He held the purse strings and was the one responsible for keeping the campaign fiscally sound and tight. Said Miller, "I can't think of a single major meeting he was not part of. He was essential to the effort, an enormous help."

"We were extremely fortunate in most of our state co-ordinators," Miller said. "Ultimately the team we put in place statewide was one which was unique in the state's political history. Few of them were 'insiders' in any political organization. Many were sick of the Wallace era, though we had a lot of Wallace supporters. Other volunteers were goo-goos (good government supporters). The important thing was that we had volunteers down at the block level who were ready and eager to do whatever had to be done."

Very little money came from off-the-street contributors in the early months.

"I would talk to David James every morning for a report," Miller said. "Many times there had been zero contributions the day before. Some days, we felt good to get $84.32."

Mobilian Arthur Tonsmeire, head of the largest savings and loan association in the state, agreed to serve as state finance chairman. From different parts of the state, people left their jobs and duties to help James get elected. Clint Milstead took early retirement from U.S.

Steel in Birmingham to assist with fund raising in the state's most populous area, Jefferson County. Ebbie Jones, founder of Opelika's First Federal Savings & Loan and former president of Farmers National Bank in the town, also agreed to help raise money. Golf pro Larry Campbell came on board as regional coordinator and Attalla city councilman David Hooks joined the campaign.

James' advertising agency worked closely with top campaign officials.

"Walker did top-notch work on yard signs, on commercials, and on three-color brochures," Miller said. "But the ideas for what went in those commercials and those brochures mostly came from actual circumstances in Alabama."

Before the campaign ended, Alabama had been littered from Florala to Three Forks of the Flint with yard signs, new-sized mini-billboards for yards, bumper stickers and campaign material.

Delivering campaign information to voters on a massive scale was not new to Alabama politics, even though the volume of the material delivered dwarfed other campaigns.

What was unique was that James' campaign material was delivered at precisely the same time in every corner of the state, hitting the courthouse square in Brewton at the same time as the courthouse square in Birmingham, putting into simultaneous action the volunteers on nearly every block of every city in the state.

A lot of background work had to be done before the first mass volunteer delivery of 100,000 pieces of campaign literature took place on a Saturday.

The first step was getting the campaign coordinators together on a regular basis to be filled in on what they were to do between then and the next meeting.

"It was Deloss Walker's idea to stage statewide meetings of the coordinators," Miller said. "I had tried something similar in the Sparkman campaign and I didn't think it would work."

The first meeting was scheduled in Clanton at the Holiday Inn.

"I realized we were onto something when more than 200 coordinators showed up," Miller said. "The format of that first meeting became the format of all future meetings, which we held every two weeks. First we got everyone together in one room. Then we divided into two groups, political workers and finance workers. After each group was given assignments for the next two weeks, we got everyone back together to end with one big pep rally."

At the last meeting before the primary, there were 2,000 strong attending.

"I saw my job as one of seeing that the message got out," Miller said. "I knew if Fob could get enough people to listen, he would win."

Miller was a detail man. He assigned someone to do nothing but call radio stations to offer taped comments from James on the issue of the day.

Yard signs were high on his priority list.

"We made them with wire coat hangers so they didn't flop," Miller said.

Billboards were expensive. There had to be an alternative.

There was.

If you took a piece of 8-by-10-foot plywood and ran off a poster to attach to it, you had a cross somewhere between a yard sign and a billboard. It was big enough to make an impression and small enough to go in people's yards, in front of stores, almost anywhere a campaign worker could get to.

Miller ordered several hundred produced. They were put up by volunteers.

"If you give someone something to do, he has a piece of the campaign," Miller said. "He feels like he has done something. Then, when workers for the other candidates tear it down, he's angry. That prods him to do more."

Volunteers, "more than I could begin to count," got more enthusiastic as the campaign progressed. One youth volunteer claimed as his personal project a major north/south highway and vowed to erect one sign for every mile between Tennessee and the Florida border.

He did it.

In Decatur, an overly enthusiastic coordinator rowed after dark to the middle of the Tennessee River and placed an 8-by-10 foot James sign on a state-owned island.

Another worker, who had access to four small planes, put them all in service. At his expense he designed and had made uniforms for the campaign workers with the campaign insignia sewn on the pockets.

Miller remembers when one of the planes broke down in Atlanta.

He learned of the breakdown when Lager called him after looking out the window and seeing what appeared to be a man in a familiar uniform under the cowl of the plane.

"We've got the Orkin man working on the engine," Lager said. "You send me another plane, Miller."

The planes were in the air 18 hours a day by the end of the campaign. The press office had been expanded to four people to handle the calls and a special department was set up to get outgoing campaign literature ready for UPS pickups. The campaign was supplying the bulk of the UPS business in the area, so voluminous was the amount of material being distributed statewide.

Miller said he literally dreamed one of the ideas which worked so well during the campaign, that of placing volunteers holding James signs every few feet on major thoroughfares during the busiest times of day.

He said he tentatively mentioned the "Miles for Fob" idea to Leonard Hudson, a Morgan County coordinator rated highly by Miller.

"He tried it one Saturday morning on the road to the Tennessee River with only 15 or 20 people, and it worked. People were stopping by the side of the road, waving. We talked about it at the next statewide meeting then did it all over the state."

James' style of campaigning was unique even in a state which engendered Big Jim Folsom's "suds bucket" and George Wallace's oratory.

One aspect of it, however, was similar to Sparkman's campaign style, Miller said.

"Neither one of them would say anything bad about the other candidates. Fob refused to talk about the three Bs (Baxley, Brewer and Beasley). He would only talk about the issues," Miller said.

One of the only references found in news articles that James made to Wallace during the campaign was, "I will have nothing to say against Gov. George Wallace. I am tremendously impressed with the courage this man has shown. Gov. Wallace has made many contributions to Alabama and to the United States. He did much to pave the way for the first Southerner in modern times to be in the White House."

In stressing issues, James hammered away at the need to streamline state government.

It was time, he said, to take politics out of the highway department.

Bill Sloat wrote in *The South Magazine* in January of 1978, "Most of the state's political watchers think James faces a strenuous, uphill fight if he's to capture any attention in the September Democratic primary. They give him little chance of winning. But James seems confident, saying, 'Viewpoint determines whether you are the underdog or not.' "

James ran as a Democrat, but that did not mean establishment Democrats welcomed him with open arms.

In July, 1978, Birmingham attorney Ed Still disputed James' right to run as a Democrat, filing a formal challenge with party chairman George Lewis Bailes Jr. and with the State Democratic Executive Committee.

James was a Republican, Still charged, citing as evidence the fact that James had been a member of the State Republican Executive Committee in 1974.

James had not renounced his affiliation with the GOP and did not mention the Democratic Party in his campaign literature, Still said. As basis for his challenge, Still cited a 1974 Democratic Party resolution which he said required a member of another party to notify the state Democratic Executive Committee a year prior to the qualifying date that he is switching parties and will run as a Democrat. James had not notified the Democratic Party of his intention to run for governor as a Democrat until the fall of 1977, after the qualifying deadline had passed, Still said.

Still said he was filing the challenge because, "I'm firmly committed to the idea that we should have Republicans running in the Republican primary and Democrats running in the Democratic Primary."

James answered, "Someone is tampering with the right of the people to choose their next governor. I suspect that someone is the professional politicians and the special interest groups."

A week later, Miller appeared on his behalf before a committee appointed by Bailes to hear the challenge, disagreeing with Still's interpretation of the 1974 resolution. Miller argued that the resolution dealt not with candidates switching parties to run as a Democrat, but with Democratic office holders who had openly supported candidates of another party. Those who did so, Miller argued, were required by that resolution to file a letter of intent to run as a Democrat with Democratic officials a year prior to qualifying deadline.

Secondly, even if the resolution had applied to James, Miller pointed out, the point was moot because James had in May 1977 notified the Lee County Democratic Executive Committee chairman by letter that he would run for governor. That letter was well before the deadline set by the resolution.

James, asked by the committee to explain his brief involvement in Republican politics, likened it to the prodigal son who "strayed from the Democratic Party but has come home again."

Why did he stray?

"I can sum it up in one name, George McGovern," James said.

It took the five-member committee a matter of minutes to rule that James could run as a Democrat.

Miller was euphoric. "We could not have afforded to buy the publicity we got. The challenge was the springboard of the campaign, the turning point. From then on, we could see daily advances in the polls."

The momentum increased daily. So did the contributions.

"The people who had thought he had no chance all at once were saying, 'I better put a little insurance money on James,' " Miller said.

The James team settled in for a frantic, busy summer.

"Grand strategy never works. Nuts and bolts strategy happens," Miller says. "There is an incredible distance between grand strategy in the mind of the campaign chairman and carrying it out on the streets of Ardmore."

When you decide to distribute 40,000 bumper stickers on the last Saturday of the campaign, as Miller did, you must be aware that such an ambitious effort cannot be undertaken overnight. It had to be planned many months in advance.

On each Saturday leading up to the 40,000–distribution day, the James organization made trial runs, so to speak, handing out a few more thousand each week. The Saturday before the big day, 10,000 bumper stickers were distributed.

On D-Day, Miller said, calls were pouring in from all over the state by the end of the day from youths telling how many bumper stickers they had put out.

"We went 2,000 over our goal," Miller said.

The organization did not attempt to work secretly, but it may as well have. Most people were unaware of the monumental behind-the-scenes effort. Therefore, most people were surprised when James led the slate by 46,000 votes in the Sept. 5 Democratic Primary election.

Baxley, who finished second, had been so certain of whom he would face in the runoff that he had already planned a runoff strategy against Brewer.

The runoff was a fierce one. Tempers flared.

A story in the Birmingham *Post-Herald* angered James so that he filmed on the spur of the moment a retaliatory commercial.

"James may face ethics trouble over liquor stock," the headline on the story by Ted Bryant stated.

> Gubernatorial candidate Fob James, who owns a large block of stock in a firm that sells liquor to the Alabama Beverage Control Board, may face a problem with the state ethics law if he is elected.
>
> Two sections of the ethics law prohibit companies that are owned or partially owned by public officials from doing business with the state.
>
> As a result of a stock exchange, James received more than 85,000 shares of the Liggett Group Inc. when his company, Diversified Products Corporation of Opelika, merged with Liggett early in 1977.
>
> Two subsidiaries of Liggett...are distributors for an expensive brand of bourbon, Wild Turkey, and a well-known Scotch, J&B...
>
> Liggett's sales to the state last year totaled about $2.8 million, a relatively small figure for liquor companies...
>
> ...James said he would place his interests in a blind trust or take whatever other action is necessary to assure there is no conflict if he is elected governor.

Other last minute allegations flew back and forth.

Baxley charged there were "discrepancies" in the financial report James had filed with the party and the Secretary of State, citing minor technicalities. Bailes said Baxley's charges "warrant some investigation."

James said he welcomed the investigation.

James accused Baxley of "serious misrepresentation" in a proposal made by Baxley. Baxley said the state would reap $100 million more tax revenue annually by forcing big industries to pay the same 4 percent utility tax which individuals paid. James said such a move would only create some $3 million in new revenue.

James and Baxley each picked up their share of endorsements.

Baxley got the support of outgoing Gov. Wallace and the volunteer efforts of George Wallace Jr. and his first cousin, Jack Wallace. James got the support of Wallace's mother, his ex-wife, Cornelia Wallace, and his son-in-law, Mark Kennedy.

Baxley, a University of Alabama graduate and a football nut, was endorsed by the legendary Coach Paul "Bear" Bryant.

Monday, Sept. 25, the last day of the Democratic Primary campaign, found James standing on the porch of his mother's freshly-painted 1890 home in Opelika.

Some 500 friends and neighbors gathered in the front yard to hear him end his saga to win the Democratic nomination, tantamount to election in 1978.

"I'm not good with words. In fact, the one bit of campaign wisdom I've picked up in the last 18 months is that the less I say the more support I get," James said.

The first inkling that James would win was when it was learned that he had carried Beat 14 in Elmore County. Hitherto, any candidate who won Beat 14 had always won the governor's race.

From the first vote returns which trickled in after the polls closed, it was apparent to politicos what the pattern would be. The counties whose votes had gone to Brewer on Sept. 5 were going by massive margins to James. It didn't take a political genius to realize that Baxley's fierce attacks on Brewer and Lt. Gov. Jere Beasley in the primary had sent Brewer/Beasley supporters into the James camp by the droves. By the end of the evening, it was apparent James had won by a 55-45 percent margin, 50 of 67 counties.

Miller said the most rewarding results of the election were in the returns from the counties in which James lived and worked (Lee County) and had grown up (Chambers County).

"He won by staggering percentages in those counties," Miller said. "I had never before seen any candidate get that kind of endorsement from the people who knew him best."

From the moment Fob and Bobbie James pulled into the parking lot at the Governor's House Motel in Montgomery for the traditional victory party, the reality of winning engulfed them.

"I remember all those people lining up at the Governor's House," Bobbie James said. "Nothing was ever that exciting."

The campaign had taken its toll. Lager had collapsed at one point with what was thought at the time to be a heart attack and later proved to be exhaustion. Ham collapsed from exhaustion the day of the election and had to be taken to the hospital.

Regardless of personal fatigue, the word euphoria is used repeatedly by James' supporters to describe their mood that night.

Michael D. "Mike" Waters is an attorney who worked in the campaign. He had also worked in the campaign of U.S. Sen. John Sparkman in 1972. Waters remembers "an enormity of difference" in the atmospheres of the two victory parties. "It was astonishing. The electricity in the air was greater, it was something you could feel—and Sparkman was one of the most powerful senators of the day."

James had won the Democratic Primary. He faced Republican Guy Hunt in the general election, but at that time in Alabama's history the Republican Party offered only token opposition to the Democratic nominee for governor. Hunt was a farmer from Holly Pond in Cullman County. James was governor-elect in all but official designation.

"A shirt-sleeved James, a political unknown who came forward in a surprising triumph, delayed claiming victory until almost two hours after Atty. Gen. Bill Baxley conceded defeat in a ballroom only 30 feet away," a reporter wrote.

"James had to be twice escorted by state troopers (to speak to the crowd)...Big Jim Folsom paid a visit."

"Baxley, who had run far behind James in the first primary Sept. 5 but wouldn't give up, told his saddened supporters in Montgomery "this is not our year." He promised to support James against Hunt and said he would "do anything in my power to serve Mr. James as a loyal constituent in helping him in the real tough job he's got coming up."

Despite the tension that marked the closing days of the runoff, Baxley said, "...there was nothing personal...as far as I was concerned...I just believe in giving it all you've got in any effort."

A triumphant James told jubilant followers it was "one of the most interesting campaigns ever [undertaken] and the backbone of it was your hard work...You had a candidate who didn't know what to do and you told him what to do."

The euphoria was short lived, said Bobbie James.

"Then the responsibility hit. We both are serious about the things we're serious about. There were promises to keep, looking after people, taking care of the public interest. Our thought was to get ahead with the task of getting kids educated. The commitments Fob made he would have died before breaking," she said.

# — 4 —

# The Transition

James, as was expected, creamed Republican Guy Hunt when they met head-to-head in the November general election. The Associated Press carried the vote total: James, 539,539; Hunt, 192,586. A candidate who ran on the Prohibition ticket got almost half as many votes as Hunt.

Knowing the big task facing him was getting a hand on how the state spent its money, the governor-elect physically moved into the state finance office for the rest of November and all of December.

Interspersed with the facts and figures to which he devoted his attention were thousands of resumes from job applicants who took James at his word that he was not interested in politics but was seeking the most qualified people to fill appointive positions.

Because Alabama was one of 13 states which provided no transition money to aid turnovers in administrations, seven of James' transition staff members were placed in empty slots on the payrolls of various state departments. They included Bob Geddie, who was to work with the Finance Department, and Don Bryan, who was to serve as legislative liaison with the House of Representatives. Bryan had been associate general director of the Montgomery YMCA prior to going to work for James. The team included two secretaries, Debra Jayne Dahlen and Kay Ham. Waters, a graduate of Duke University and Oxford and a Rhodes scholar, was assigned to coordinate the rewriting of a new state constitution. He was added to the staff of the Supreme Court by Chief Justice C. C. "Bo" Torbert.

News clippings reflect how the James family lifestyle was changing. Constantly in the limelight, James was pictured at a news briefing in

Montgomery, taking dogs Dolly and Stonewall for a romp on his Opelika front lawn, laughing at the donkey given him as a birthday gift by
campaign workers.

Bobbie James was swamped with more than a thousand well-
wisher letters.

James' aides must have quickly become aware that he viewed
events, people and incidents from a different perspective than they
did. But even his closest aides were probably unaware of how wide
was the gap between their viewpoints.

This can be illustrated through the difference in memories James
and his close aides have of their first glimpses of the actual physical
offices which made up the governor's complex in the capitol.

As one aide remembers: One night after the election, the group
which was becoming known as the "James gang" had dinner with Dr.
David Bronner, head of the state retirement funds for teachers and
state employees.

Bronner was an Iowa native who had grown up in Minnesota.

"Because David was 'neutral,' which meant he hadn't been for
anyone on the governor's race, Gov. Wallace agreed that he should
be the one to show us around the governor's office," the aide recalls.
"It was 9:30 or 10 p.m. one night when we decided to go look the
office over."

Wallace had moved out. His staff had moved out. What was left
in the main floor governor's office of the old capitol, and in the basement offices below, was a sight viewed with incredulity by the small
party.

"When we saw the maze of corridors that had no relation to each
other, how the paint was peeling, the inadequacy of the rest rooms,
we wondered how state government could be run efficiently, how
anyone could function efficiently," the former aide says.

More importantly, there was "not a desk, not a chair," he remembers. "I had expected files and studies, but there was not a pencil, a
map, furniture, nothing."

As James remembers the same situation: "The office had everything a governor's office needed. We had all the room we needed. It
had an upstairs and a downstairs. We had cooperation from the Wallace folks. I didn't see what else anyone could have asked for."

Members of James' staff say that he set up an office at the mansion
because there was a lack of privacy and lack of space in the capitol
office. The governor's office opened directly to the public waiting

room. He had to cross the waiting room to get to his legal adviser's office.

"Fob set up an office at the mansion to get more work space," Lager said. "The problem was, you've got show horses and work horses and he was a work horse. He needed room to work, an atmosphere conducive to work, not to politics."

James says there was a simple reason why he needed an office in the mansion. Much of the time, he could work effectively from the capitol office. This was not possible in meetings which lasted for hours, however, because there were constant interruptions at the capitol office. When he realized he needed a two or three-hour uninterrupted stretch of time to accomplish a specific task, he retreated to the office at the mansion.

It was difficult to convince James to do something by telling him that was the way it had always been done, Lager said.

James at first refused to travel with a bodyguard, considering it silly and a waste of money, Lager said.

After discovering that staffers and friends would travel with him if he did not have a bodyguard, and after discovering that staffers and friends talked so much he couldn't get any work done while traveling, James gave in.

He was assigned a security detail of three men, headed by former Opelika Police Chief Ron Dunson. It also included an old friend of James, "Sarge" Banks.

Lager remembers driving up behind Sarge and the governor one day. Because they were moving more slowly than Lager wanted to drive, he passed them, waving as he did so.

"There sat Sarge in the passenger's seat, reading the newspaper with Fob behind the wheel tooling on down the highway," Lager says with a laugh.

Department of Public Safety Sgt. Gene Mitchell, who later became James' chief security officer, says James refused at first to allow state troopers to provide him with security because he believed it was a misuse of talent. Trained law enforcement officers had more important work than to follow a governor around. Mitchell said James maintained his obstinacy until in a series of meetings with top Public Safety officials he was made aware that they considered him to be interfering with their legal directive to protect him and his family.

Though James acquiesced, Mitchell said he insisted throughout his term that a minimum of security personnel be assigned to him.

One by one, James made his cabinet appointments.

A special blend of businessman and super sleuth was needed to head the Alcoholic Beverage Control Agency. In Alabama, the public could buy liquor only in state-licensed bars and restaurants or in state-run stores. James in his campaign had made his views known that the state had no business engaging in what amounted to a monopoly. Also, the ever-changing appointed ABC Board which ran the agency had for decades been so blatantly political in choosing which brands the state stores should stock that exposés had frequently put Alabama in a bad light nationally.

James chose Joe Broadwater for his ABC chief. Broadwater was an Athens, Alabama, native whose career included such widely diverse jobs as 25 years in the CIA and other years on an Alabama farm. Broadwater had an agriculture degree from Auburn University and had been a school teacher.

"I had known Joe for years and got to know him better in the campaign," James said. "We knew we had to straighten out some things at the ABC Board and I felt Joe was just a great guy to have over there. He's bright, bull headed, a bulldog. and he knows how to conduct an investigation. We put Joe there to clean it up. I knew he would be fair and he was. Everybody got treated the same. He was there until he became finance director the last six months of the administration."

Ham, the 31-year-old University of Georgia graduate who had worked as campaign press secretary, was named to that position for the governor.

James named as Insurance Commissioner Hal Sumrall, who had worked prior to that as an aide in charge of screening board and commission appointments. Sumrall prior to joining James' campaign was an executive in a manufacturing firm in Anniston.

Dean James E. Foy was named executive secretary.

It was no surprise when James asked Don Bryan to join the staff as legislative liaison to the House and close personal aide.

Bob Geddie had proven himself indispensable. A graduate of Marion Institute and Auburn University, Geddie worked as a legislative aide to Sen. John Sparkman for three years in the early 70s. He returned to Sparkman's staff to serve as in-state liaison after a stint as associate director of the Alabama Petroleum Council. Geddie had endorsed James and joined his campaign team after losing a low budget race for Congress. He worked out of Opelika during the campaign and moved to Birmingham to coordinate the Democratic ticket after the primary. He was recruited by the new governor to help in the finance office and moved quickly to the job most suited for his considerable talents, liaison to the Senate. Before long, Geddie's title became simply legislative liaison.

W. H. (Hoke) Kerns was picked to be director of the Commission on Aging. Kerns had been top administrator at Baptist Medical Center.

Jerry Shoemaker was a career law enforcement officer in the Department of Public Safety. He did not apply for the job of Public Safety Director. James, asking around, heard so many recommendations for Shoemaker that he named him to the top post.

Jerry C. Ray was a Linden employee of American Can Company. He had also served as president of Local 952 of United Paperworkers International. James named Ray to head the Labor Department.

Rex Rainer, head of Civil Engineering at Auburn University, was named director of the Highway Department. Rainer had worked with James several years before when James headed a citizens' task force to develop a long range highway plan for the state.

He named as Conservation Director Dick Forster, who had worked as a systems analyst doing research on land and waterway use.

David Hooks, former Attalla city councilman and budget director, was named as an executive assistant to the governor.

Ralph P. Eagerton Jr., who had served the state since 1948 as income tax examiner, was named Revenue Commissioner.

Mobilian Gary Cooper, a state legislator who was a highly-decorated Marine Corps veteran and a Notre Dame graduate, was named Commissioner of Pensions and Security.

James named as Adjutant General to run the Alabama National Guard a Princeton University graduate and a businessman, Maj. Gen. Henry H. Cobb Jr.

Ben C. Collier, a colorful self-made millionaire from Montgomery, was named director of the Alabama Development Office.

Jack Miller stayed in Montgomery for a few months to help James get the office organized and appointments made, then he returned to Mobile to begin the long but eagerly anticipated task of building a law firm specializing in banking in the south.

Bobby Davis, former mayor of Fort Deposit, Alabama, and a stalwart James supporter, was known by mayors throughout the state as an expert in working with state grants. James put him in charge of the

State Planning Office and soon moved him to the governor's office. He would retain the planning job for the duration of the term, also becoming executive secretary a year later when Foy returned to Auburn.

Reuben Finney, a 44-year-old Lafayette native and Auburn graduate, was named administrative assistant to the finance department. The Birmingham businessman was also asked to coordinate a committee of private citizens with business and industry experience in a study to determine ways in which to economize in state government.

There were Wallace holdovers in some departments, and in others top merit-system people who had been with the state for decades were promoted to head their departments.

One of these was Kenneth McCartha, who had worked in a Greenville bank until 1963 when he began his career with the State Banking Department. James named him superintendent of banking.

Maida Persons, who had been daughter-in-law of the late Gov. Gordon Persons, was named an executive assistant to the governor. Mrs. Persons had extensive experience in governmental relations.

And so it went. James put together a cabinet in which many held state jobs for the first time.

Education, top on the list of priorities, needed James' 100 percent attention. He named Bob Lager as his education liaison, the first person to hold a position reporting directly to the governor which is geared 100 percent toward carrying out the governor's education program.

A multi-lingual (he speaks nine languages) urbane professor, Lager's political activity prior to the James campaign had been limited to heated philosophical discussions.

It was not politics which brought the two together, however, but a shared conviction that efforts should be concentrated on improving the basics in education. Lager echoed James' fervent belief that education reform had to begin in kindergarten and work its way up grade by grade.

James A. Littleton, personnel manager for Koppers Co. in Bessemer, was named executive assistant for human resources.

Why did James not insist on people who had more political experience?

"We zeroed in on two things," Miller said. "We tried to find people who were expert in their fields who were not the captive of any special interest group."

Birmingham businessman Ed Dixon spearheaded the recruitment.

The most important appointive job, finance director, was not filled for the first 69 days of the administration, James said, for two reasons: there was no one readily available with the qualifications he sought for the job; and he wanted to first get a hands-on understanding of the state's financial condition, long and short term.

Until he got that understanding, James kept Wallace Finance Director Tom Ventress as his assistant. Ventress had served as Wallace's industrial relations director in 1971 and had taken a leave of absence to direct Wallace's reelection campaign in 1974. Wallace had named him finance director after the Alabama Senate refused to confirm Ventress to head the Board of Pardons and Paroles.

James told reporters he and Ventress were "getting into budgets and setting priorities and meeting with department heads."

The only way he could have named someone right off, he said, was if he had found someone who shared his goals, his methods and his way of thinking—and could convince that person to move to Montgomery. There was no such person.

"I can guarantee you that if you're going to turn anything around, unless you've got a finance director that's a blood brother, you've got to do it yourself," James says today. "There is no way of getting familiar with the numbers—as related to costs—unless you dig in yourself."

Geddie said James "sat down with career merit state employees, people who actually did the work, like Becky Beasley (later named State Budget Officer). They went through every department and sub-department and questioned every expense. They looked at the books and said, 'why?' and 'how come?' "

James acquired one cabinet member when he spoke to participants in a 13-states consortium on the future of education.

Sitting near the front was a woman who had worked as a consultant during the Wallace administration for the federally-funded CETA (Comprehensive Employment Training Act) program. It appeared to Lynda Hart that James was looking directly at her when he told the audience, "I need your help."

"I had coordinated an interagency project which studied the agencies charged with delivering federal dollars," Hart said. "It weighed how money and services could best be coordinated."

Prior to James' speech, Hart had dismissed any notion she'd had that the new administration might be interested in the conclusions drawn by her study when James' aide Dick Forster had been uninterested.

"I tried to give him the package," she said.

Forster told her, "If you want a job, why don't you apply for one?"

"That ticked me off and I wrote them off," she said.

When James appealed for help, however, asking those in the audience to stop by to see him if they had ideas on how to help, Hart decided to give it one more chance.

"I said to myself, we'll see how true that is, and I called Dean Foy the next day and told him what the governor had said."

Foy, whom she described as "so polite and a gentleman," laughed and said, "He meant that, too. The only problem is, he just doesn't realize there are only 24 hours in the day. Would you mind telling me what you want to talk with him about?"

Hart, remembering the adamant look in James' eyes, stood her ground.

She said, "I want to talk to him because I want federal programs done right. There's been pork barrel forever."

Foy told her, "You know Fob doesn't like the CETA program."

"I don't blame him, the way it has been run," Hart said.

She left the office with Foy asking if she would consider being "a CETA person." He said he would talk with Sumrall.

That night when she was cooking, the phone rang. It was Foy. He said the governor would like to see her at 10 a.m. the next day.

After talking with Hart for a half-hour, she said James told her, "This is not a 30-minute discussion, is it?"

He asked her to return the next day, which was a state holiday.

"I approached him with the contention that CETA should be viewed as an economic program, not a social program," Hart said. "That made sense to him."

Hart was hired on the spot to "work with" CETA. Mid-way through James' term she was made a cabinet member.

As such, she directed the expenditure of millions of dollars in federal grants fought over by every political subdivision of the state.

"I was so non-political I didn't realize I was being given a political job," Hart said. "He hired me on philosophy and expertise. The loyalty had to be worked out later. It came."

James' two months transition period passed quickly.

The Inauguration Day was January 15, 1979.

# — 5 —

# The Inauguration

**J**ames borrowed a quote from Charles Dickens to set the tone for his inaugural address: "It was the best of times, the worst of times..."

It would be prophetic.

Inauguration Day began for Montgomery police at 6 a.m. as they started blocking off main streets for the 10:30 a.m. parade and the 2 p.m. swearing-in ceremonies.

They had no idea how many people would turn out.

Several factors would influence the turnout.

The day fell on a state holiday, the birthday of Robert E. Lee. It was also the birthday of Martin Luther King. There might be huge crowds. Or there might not.

The weather was bitingly cold with icy blasts of wind, though the fact that the thermometer hovered deceptively in the mid-forties led forecasters to predict the best weather of any inaugural day in 20 years.

Most importantly, in assessing potential crowd size, Gov. George Wallace had not held a big celebration when he was sworn in four years before. The state was ready for one.

All factors considered, the inaugural committee anticipated a crowd of 100,000 to 250,000 people.

As police set up barricades, some 230 parade units, 20,000 bandsmen, beauty queens and politicians began lining up for the 4.8-mile parade.

The cost, revealed a James' spokesman, would be some $175,000. It was being raised by the inaugural committee through sale of ad space in the program and through tickets to the ball.

All Alabama newspapers that day played the inauguration as the top story. Other front page headlines noted, "Shah Leaves Iran Tuesday for Egypt" and "Dr. King Ceremonies Held at Dexter Church..."

The best-selling items on the street that day, hawkers told newsmen, were "Alabama No. 1" banners and Styrofoam hands signifying that fact.

The night before the inauguration there had been an "Alabama Stars Show" at Montgomery's Garrett Coliseum, a black tie event for 9,000 at which newspapers noted that surprise guest Tammy Wynette sang a take-off on her hit, "Stand By Your Man." She sang "Stand by Your Friends."

Inauguration Day began for the James family with a family-dominated, invitation-only service at St. John's Episcopal Church.

Sons Patrick and Timothy took part in the service. Pat was acolyte with his cousin, Cal James Jr. Timothy as crucifer led the procession down the aisle. Ebb Counts, grandson of Fob James Sr.'s twin, Ebb James, carried the flag. Friend David James was the lector who read the scripture and his three sons also took part: Sandy was server in the communion service, Cooper and Michael were torch bearers.

It was a solemn but an uplifting service which lent purpose to the day, one attendee remembered.

The absence of the son who had been lost to cystic fibrosis, Greg, was referred to only in a simple note on the program which read, "At the request of the James family the offering at this service will be sent to the Alabama chapter of the Cystic Fibrosis Foundation."

As James' family and close friends worshipped at St. John's, a 9 a.m. ceremony was being held in front of the Dexter Avenue King Memorial Church commemorating King's Jan. 15th birthday. King had been minister of the church in 1954.

There had been an initial conflict in the planning of King's birthday memorial and James' inauguration. The Dexter Avenue Church sits on the parade route, only blocks away from the capitol.

The conflict was easily resolved when the inaugural committee volunteered a spot in the parade for a float to commemorate King.

James arrived at the reviewing stand shortly after 11 a.m., riding for the last time the school bus the state knew as the Reading, 'Riting and 'Rithmetic Special. Wallace rode with James and his family on the yellow school bus. At least one reporter noted that "George Wallace said nothing, took no part in the ceremonies..."

There was no Forrest Hood James Jr. at the inauguration. He was sworn in as Fob. Nearly every bus, float and store window sported a sign proclaiming "Welcome Fob." Drummers hawked Fob clocks, Fob T-shirts, Fob corsages and Fob programs.

On Morgan County's float the sign read, "We love you, Bobbie." On the back was the afterthought, "You too, Fob."

Space heaters were placed on the reviewing stand. "But Bobbie James realized that wouldn't keep the children on the stand happy, so she served a selection of sandwiches and goodies from a paper plate," Mark Childress wrote in the Birmingham News.

James' kinsman, Charles Robertson Allen, "provided another light moment when he rolled his wheelchair onto the reviewing stand," Childress wrote. "Neatly displayed on his chair were two bumper stickers: 'Tijuana Taxi' and 'Keep on Truckin.'"

The parade kept coming. After three hours, one reporter noted, many of the notables had sneaked away to warm their hands, such as Auburn coach Shug Jordan. James never left the reviewing stand.

Also featured on the inaugural platform were other constitutional officers being sworn in that day.

In addition to the inaugural platform and reviewing stands for state officials, there was a special reviewing stand for the handicapped and the elderly. Tens of thousands of others stood.

The swearing-in ceremony was as family dominated as the church service had been, from the moment Fob III read from the Bible to the point in which Braxton Comer Counts III held the Bible for his mother's first cousin to take the oath of office. The Bible he held was the traditional one which has been used in the ceremony by every Alabama governor since Jefferson Davis in 1861 was sworn in as president of the Confederacy.

James differed sharply from those who had stood on that spot before to take the same oath. He differed also from most judges and district attorneys, legislators and other office holders who watched the ceremony.

Their education in government was bolstered with experience as they worked their way up Alabama's political ladder, learning to maneuver, to compromise when necessary, to retrench when they must, and to work behind the scenes to outwit their opponents. Their classroom was the system itself, in which they had became proficient by watching closely the people who won to see how they did it and by not making the same mistake twice.

James' education in government had come from the books he cherished. His mentors had been men well loved and widely known but long since dead. He had no knowledge of the thousand and one nuances of politics upon which those accomplished in the art seemingly draw without effort.

James was proud to be labeled "outsider" when he observed what mastery of those nuances and that art called politics had done to the state of Alabama. He believed a responsible man could follow but one course. He had no choice but to turn his back on the you-scratch-my-back-and-I'll-scratch-yours form of government, to reinstate that historic concept of a government of checks and balances which since the nation's founding has been a role model for the world.

Where, he asked himself, had Alabama's self-propagating, incestuous politics gotten the state? The answer was evident in the statistics he had quoted while campaigning: At the bottom of most ladders.

It was as a soldier going to war that James took to the campaign trail.

It was as a general determined to rebuild a devastated country that James took office as governor.

James wanted his goals to be clear to the public. He did not want the public to lose sight of what he was trying to do. He needed their support. He wanted them enthusiastically at his side. After he put the essence of his administration into words, he would share them with all Alabama.

This formal notification of intent, this distillation of years of work and study, he decided, would be his inaugural address.

James took pen and paper into his office at his house and long past the midnight hour wrote the final draft of his speech. He was influenced by a word from his wife, a suggestion from a friend, but the bulk surged from deep within as he compacted the tenets in which he deeply believed.

In composing his speech, James wrestled in his mind with the major problems facing the state.

Illiteracy was the biggest problem. On education rested all other aspects of government. A good economy depended on being able to provide jobs for people. Business and industry would not locate in a state which could not supply them with skilled workers or educate the children of their employees. Jobs meant revenue to the state to pay for roads and prisons and help to the poor and elderly. No matter which way you went at it, you always got back to the need for a good education system as critical for all other endeavors.

James worried about the trend which he discerned in state and national governments to plunge deeper and deeper into debt. Staying out of debt was so important in the minds of the founding fathers, he knew from reading their thoughts and words, that they felt no public debt should be entered into for more than the length of a single generation. You don't make debt for your children to pay. His books on history were cluttered with hard times caused by governments which ignored the principle. Alabama had gone crazy with debt. It took $40 million a year of the Highway Department budget just to pay the debt on construction projects of earlier years. The federal government was encouraging debt by policy, and the fortunes of the state, of all 50 states, were irrevocably intertwined with the fortunes of the nation.

James, as he thought of what he would say in his inaugural speech, pondered the responsibility a government has to its people in spending tax dollars. Tax dollars should be treated as carefully and with the same reverence as money taken up in a church offering, he believed. In old-line trust companies they used the word fiduciary. James believed government should display a fiduciary responsibility where tax dollars were concerned. Instead, he saw tax money being spent as carelessly as though it had fallen from the sky.

The effects of squandering tax money were felt most by those who could afford it least, the poor and the elderly. James thought of the vicious circle of poverty from which uneducated people would never emerge if they weren't given more by the state than a check which wouldn't feed and house their families. He believed many of them could be trained in skills which would allow them to earn their own money with dignity and pride.

James noted, as he wrote, a special debt owed to the elderly, those who so few years ago carried the burden of responsibility now shouldered by James' generation.

Lastly, he thought of the incredible effort it took tens of millions of Americans to forge their way across a nation of primeval forests and inhospitable plains. He thought of the legacy of pride and determination left by those pioneers and of the children who sat in Alabama classrooms ready to assume that mantle and pass it to their children and grandchildren if given half a chance.

When James rose from his seat on the inaugural platform to take the oath of office as governor of Alabama, he carried with him the 24 paragraphs he had written.

After he swore to carry out the duties of the office of governor, James moved to the podium and began to read:

> In the words of Charles Dickens, "It was the best of times, it was the worst of times, it was the age of wisdom, it was the age of foolishness, it was the epoch of belief, it was the epoch of incredulity, it was the season of light, it was the season of darkness, it was the spring of hope, it was the winter of despair, we had everything before us, we had nothing before us, we were all going direct to heaven, we were all going direct the other way" — in short the period was so far like the present period, that some of its noisiest authorities insisted on its being received, for good or for evil, in the superlative degree of comparison only.
>
> So it is today as —
>
> I stand before you filled with humility and gratitude for the trust you have placed in me.
>
> I am not one bit in awe of government at any level — nor the trappings of any public office.
>
> I am awe-stricken and thankful for the goodness, the will, the compassion, the genius, the industry, the hope, the strength, the spirit, the integrity, of my fellow citizens — THE PEOPLE OF ALABAMA.
>
> I say to you the character of our government will never equal the greatness of our people — but IT'S TIME to bring the two closer together.
>
> Thomas Jefferson envisioned in his first inaugural address, "A wise and frugal government, which shall restrain men from injuring one another, shall leave them otherwise free to regulate their own pursuits of industry and improvement and shall not take from the mouth of labor the bread it has earned."
>
> Send forth the word this day, that the vision given by God and Founding Fathers is still alive! Let no one mistake my resolve to make that vision a reality for every man, woman, and child in this State.
>
> Here lie the tasks ahead.
>
> Our children cannot seek their own destinies without literacy. Our children cannot be free without literacy. We must have literacy and by the Grace of God, we shall have literacy.
>
> Any government that places the yoke of debt upon its young adulthood borders on tyranny.

Any government that tolerates erosion of the hard-earned, well-deserved retirement income of its elderly is immoral.

Any government that does not hold sacred the tax dollars taken from the labor of its citizenship is dishonest.

I shall launch a frontal attack upon these injustices within the borders of Alabama, and I shall battle those forces beyond that insist upon the economic strangulation of our people.

On this, the birthday of Martin Luther King Jr., I claim for all Alabamians a New Beginning free from racism and discrimination. Let us bury forever the negative prejudices of the past. The same standards of justice, responsibility, and reward are for one and all. I stand on this commitment without equivocation. So be it.

It matters not what I say today; it matters only what we do tomorrow. We must march ahead with dreams grounded in the toil of sweat, as well as hope for the future.

We are confident in the richness of our heritage. Our heroes are many—if only we are not too arrogant to remember—too proud to see.

From Concord to Gettysburg, from World War I through World War II, Korea and Vietnam—American fighting men, the flower of our youth, by the millions made the supreme sacrifice to secure for us government of the people, by the people, for the people. How dare we not now sacrifice to make work for the common good that government purchased with the blood of our sons.

I believe if Robert E. Lee and Martin Luther King Jr. were here today, their cry to us—their prayer to God—would call for "The Politics of Unselfishness"—a people together—determined to climb the highest plateau of greatness.

It is then—We have a New Beginning.

It is time.

I pledge to you my best to this end.

I ask for your prayers.

Thank you—God bless you.

The cheering began. The cameras rolled. The flashbulbs popped.

James walked away thinking he had put his administration firmly on record. He would now put the inaugural address on his desk and adhere to it steadfastly and the public would know where he was coming from and where he was going on every issue.

He was wrong.

The importance James attached to the message was for the most part undetected by the multitudes.

Listeners were conditioned to expect a forest of rhetoric and therefore overlooked the towering trees of commitment and planning which anchored the landscape in this administration blueprint.

There was no indication that either James' closest friends or his cabinet members picked up on the importance of every carefully-chosen word in the lean speech.

Officials who sat on the platform in the bitterly cold wind probably expected James to talk far longer than they were willing to listen. They were veteran speech-listeners who know to clap when the speaker raises his voice to emphasize a point, how to pay just enough attention to later be able to comment intelligently.

"James' speech was interrupted, courteously, with light, polite applause four times. The same politely restrained but totally enthusiastic reception took up exactly 25 seconds at its ending," Charles Black wrote in the *Valley Times-News*.

The closest anyone came to correctly interpreting the thrust of James' short speech may have been the author of an editorial placed by a family member in a scrapbook, but lacking identification as to its origin. It stated: "...It's certainly not often enough that we have a man with sufficient perspective to place all governmental functions in their proper place: Service."

Television reporters faced the ever-present challenge of capturing the tone and mood of James' speech in 10 or 15 seconds to be sandwiched into the newscast between film clips of myriad other happenings of the day.

Print media, also battling a space problem in which it was impossible to relate everything that happened, also had to single out sections of the speech to emphasize.

One respected reporter read political motive into James' warnings against the "yoke of debt" and wrote that it was a swipe at Wallace's $220 million bond issue of the year before.

From one end of the state to the other, the remarks most quoted by media from the speech were those dealing with race. It was felt to be significant, and of course it was, that on what was thought to be the last day of the Wallace era his successor called for a New Beginning free from racism and discrimination.

At the very bottom of the engraved inaugural invitation were two quotes in tiny italics which were unseen by the masses and overlooked by the intimates.

The first was from the Gettysburg address: "...that this nation under God shall have a new birth of freedom, that government of the people, by the people, and for the people, shall not perish from the earth."

The second was from the ninth chapter of Isaiah, verse six, "...and the government shall be upon his shoulder..."

Gov. Fob James Jr.

Fob Jr. and grandfather Calvin S. Ellington

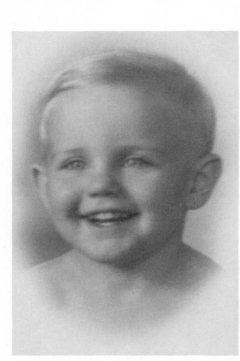

A young Fob James Jr.

Fob Jr. on grandmother's back steps.

Fob Jr., brother Calvin and "Dan."

Fob Jr., Cal holding brother Robert.

"Bubber" (Fob Jr.) on his horse.

*Top:* Barry Heywood, Bill Duncan, Fob
James Jr., Floyd Tees at Baylor Military
Academy.
*Left:* Fob James Jr., 1955.
*Center:* Bobbie Mooney James, 1955, in
wedding announcement picture.
*Right:* Bobbie Mooney, Fob James Jr.,
1953.

All-America halfback Fob James Jr. carries the ball for Auburn.

Four generations: Fob James Jr. holding Fob III; Fob James Sr.; Calvin S. Ellington.

Another look at three Fobs: senior, III, junior.

Gregory Fleming James at 14 months; Bobbie James, Fob III.

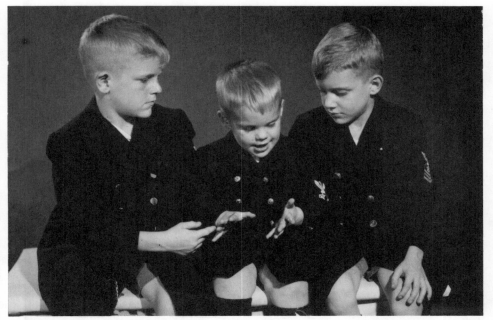

Fob III, Tim and Greg, 1963.

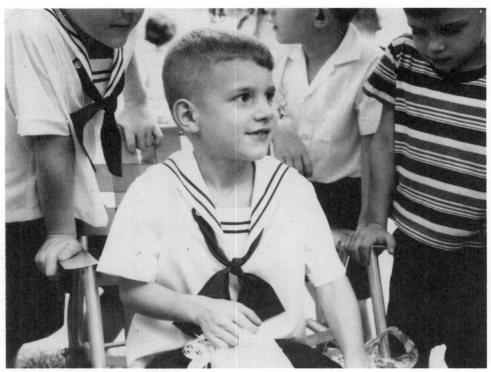

Greg's sixth birthday party.

Fob James Sr., Fob James Jr., 1973.

Rebecca James, mother of Fob James Jr., with her husband's brothers, Ed and Louie , 1978.

The Reading, 'Riting and 'Rithmetic Special, 1978 campaign.

Diversified Products says "Goodbye," 1978.

The "real" Fob James Jr. with Stonewall and Dolly, 1979

In the field...

...On the farm.

The campaign manager 1978: John C.H. (Jack) Miller (left).

The James family, December, 1978; standing, Patrick (in front, Fob III, Tim.

# — 6 —

# Governor James

Though publicly the Legislature appeared to consume the majority of the new governor's time, this was not the case.

During the first months of his administration, James set the pattern he would conform to for the rest of his term in office—he divided his time by priority. A large block of that was devoted to his education program.

The bulk of the rest of his time was spent setting the direction for state government in his administration, making its policy, delving into the nitty gritty of state finances and the operations of the dozens of departments now under his control. His appointment books were filled with meetings with department heads and state employees who knew the inner workings of government. He was undertaking what he considered one of the most important functions of a governor, setting priorities within a budget as to how state tax dollars would be spent the next year.

A lot of clout rests in the hands of those drawing up the language of the budget, James' aides point out, and James' budgets when he signed them into law retained his specific language and unmistakable imprint.

Budgets in the Wallace administrations also reflected the strong imprint of the governor. Speaker of the House and veteran legislator Joe McCorquodale became one of James' closest friends during his four years in office. James' aides and department heads would view McCorquodale differently, but James looked on the twinkly-eyed, pipe-smoking, turkey-hunter as a friend who delivered when he promised and never broke his word. McCorquodale told James that the

difference between the James budgets and the Wallace budgets was
"pork": James' budgets contained none of the politically-motivated
appropriations which benefit specific legislators' districts without regard to the overall population. Wallace's budgets used "pork" to garner support and reward friends.

Historically, governors continued to have major input into the
state's budgets until the administration of Republican Gov. Guy Hunt.
Hunt's budgets were declared "dead" by the Democratic-majority
legislature even before they arrived in the Ways and Means Committee.

The budgets signed into law by Hunt originated in the Legislative
fiscal office under direction of Ways and Means chairman Taylor Harper.

James in working with legislators used what Bobby Davis called a
"straightforward" approach.

James told them, "We don't have the money to do any more than
we've done in this budget. If you pass a budget appropriating more
money, we'll be in proration. If you want to add something to the
budget, make it conditional upon the extra revenue coming in to take
care of it."

Davis said McCorquodale worked closely enough with James and
his staff prior to the first legislative session to observe the efforts being
made to draw up "honest" budgets.

"He knew the governor's figures were more on the mark than
those of the fiscal office and he paid attention to them," Davis said.

Dean Foy, who as executive secretary often was a buffer between
James and those who wanted to talk with the governor, said people
who were familiar with past administrations had to be immediately
aware that things would be different in James' administration.

"The first call I got was from a school superintendent who was
building a new school," Foy said. "He wanted to know who the governor's architect was. I told him the governor didn't have an architect,
for him to hire the firm which would do the best job."

On another day, an inquiry came from troopers wanting a list of
wrecker services which had supported James, Foy said.

They were given the same answer.

Foy said James was aware that politics permeated every layer of
government, but was astounded at how openly political favoritism operated.

Equally astounded, apparently, were many of the people who had contributed to James and been promised "good government" in return.

"They were astounded to learn he was serious," Foy said. "I hadn't been there long when I got a call from a big supporter who asked me, 'What the hell's going on? The man down the street is getting the same state business I am and he didn't support Fob.' "

On another day a civic delegation left James' office miffed because they had asked for state funds for a project and James had laughed. Foy said he told them, smiling but serious, "Get out of here, you do the best job in the state. You don't need state money."

Was James aware of the political bridges he was burning?

"Fob wasn't the ordinary politician," Foy said. "The first thing they think of when making a decision is how it will affect their reelection. Fob had asked for four years. His campaign promises clearly stated he would not seek reelection. He thought he could do in four years what he had committed to do. 'We won World War II in four years,' he used to say. 'Surely we can clean up state government in four years.' You have to think of Fob in the backdrop of being a man who was successful in business, who didn't need a dollar from the state of Alabama. Anytime anyone tried to point out the political ramifications of something, he would say, 'Remember that I'm not running for governor. I *am* governor.'"

Politics and the administration of government should be two separate entities, James believed, two different processes, each equally important as a link in the philosophical and practical chain which binds the American system together.

"Politics is emotion. And emotion. And emotion, particularly during a campaign," James says. "You've got to realize the day you get elected that the campaign is over. During the campaign, emotion is a necessary ingredient to keep you moving and get your message across," James says. "But once you take that office there is no place for emotion. It is the time for substance to be introduced and reality to take over. Facts and figures have got to come into play."

Out went the preconceptions. The slate was rubbed clean. He wrote on a new blackboard as he pondered the approach he would take to the daily routine of governing the state.

"What precisely am I supposed to do as governor?" he asked himself. "Am I supposed to come down here to this office and see people all day and zip around the state and eat all the good cooking the ladies know how to fix in Alabama, and go down to Mobile and tell folks in Mobile how wonderful things are, go to Birmingham and tell folks in Birmingham how wonderful things are? There was a very clear record of that, for years and years that's what governors did."

James decided the primary function of a governor was to run the government in the public interest, period. He therefore in effect put blinders on concerning activities he considered had nothing to do with running government in the public interest.

The ability to do this was, to paraphrase one of his aides, at once his greatest asset and his biggest weakness.

It was this blindness which made him ignore controversy about issues which he felt affected only his personal life—such as the decision to live in a private residence and use the governor's mansion for state functions and meetings and for an office away from the capitol.

When James took office, Fob III was in college. Son Tim was being sent to his father's high school alma mater, Baylor, in Tennessee.

Bobbie James had supported her husband's decision to run for governor as she had always supported him in whatever he wanted to do. She had extracted only one promise from him when he told her he wanted to run for governor—that his duties as governor would not interfere with the homelife of the one remaining son at home, Pat.

James promised her it would not.

On the November night in which James was declared the winner of the general election, and therefore the governor-elect, Bobbie James spotted an architect she knew at the victory party.

She mentioned to him a house she had loved when she and Fob had lived in Montgomery on Perry Street, a house she had thought the most wonderful house she had ever seen as she drove past it daily on her way to work. A home like that would never be for sale. It would stay in a family forever, she told the architect. But did he perhaps know who owned the Thigpen-Hill house?

The house was not only vacant. It was for sale. It was also on the same street as the governor's mansion and close to it. The next morning she asked her husband to go for a ride. She drove into the driveway of the Thigpen-Hill house. James did not even leave the car to look inside the house. He knew what it meant to her. He agreed to buy the house for her.

The Thigpen-Hill house was indeed a "dream house." It had been named by the American Institute of Architects as "most notable" of 55 area residences. Designed by Frank Lockwood, a well-known 19th century architect, it had been built in 1898 for Dr. Charles A. Thigpen, an ophthalmologist. It was owned in 1978 by his grandson, Wiley Hill III and his daughter, Isabel Thigpen Hill. The white clapboard house had undergone only one structural change since it had been built on the two-acre lot.

When news media reflected negative reaction to James' announcement that his family would live in the Thigpen-Hill house, neither he nor his wife attempted to explain to the public why the decision had been made. James saw the issue as a simple one—his purchase of the Thigpen-Hill house had nothing to do with running state government efficiently. The state would not spend any extra money because of the purchase, not even for security.

It therefore fell to close friends of the James, upset when they read flippant references to James because of the incident, to hint to news media that there were "reasons" why Fob James would "give in" to his wife's desire for "privacy." But there they would stop, whether from respect or from ignorance.

Perhaps the worst blows dealt to James, public relations-wise, were by well-meaning administration officials and friends who with well-intentioned motives simply invented what they considered plausible explanations: The governor's mansion suffered from almost 30 years of financial neglect, they said. It had obsolete wiring. The kitchen was unusable. The furniture was falling apart and had not been covered in more years than anyone could remember. There was not enough money in the mansion fund to make it habitable. The towels with embossed State of Alabama seals had been stolen. The china was cracked or broken. The sheets were torn and shabby. The James had the money to buy a better house, so why shouldn't they?

Nothing could have been farther from the truth. But the editorial and political chastisement which resulted from these erroneous "explanations" planted an unfortunate picture of Bobbie James in the public eyes of those who did not know her—the picture of a rich woman for whom the state mansion was not "good enough."

The truth could be found occasionally in sporadic newspaper quotes in the middle of long stories in country newspapers if one spent enough time searching, but those quotes were not widely-enough circulated to have an impact on public opinion. Those quotes are from close friends of Bobbie who had been there with her when a two-room apartment was regarded as a mansion, who knew of the gusto with which she rolled up her sleeves and tackled whatever job needed doing, who were aware of her determination to maintain an everyday, home-cooking-on-the-kitchen-table atmosphere for her husband and son.

James, meanwhile, acted oblivious to the ruckus in sun-up to midnight days in which he got a handle on the state books.

The day-to-day administration of the government is not a glamorous task. A story on such drudgery would not be rated by a television news assignment editor as "sexy."

News coverage of politics tends to focus instead on the "spot story," an event, whether that be an exchange of barbs between legislators or the riveting excitement of a final night of a legislative session.

James draws an analogy to football.

> If you read what sports writers write about football, and I love the game and played it for a long time, football is portrayed as a romantic, legendary thing. That is far from reality. In reality, football is hard practice, discipline, and fundamentals, practice, practice, practice, practice, day in and day out. All the practice is for three hours of glory on a Saturday afternoon. But people would not be interested in reading long stories on how the University of Alabama or Auburn scrimmaged for four hours on Wednesday, and had a drill for two hours on blocking the linebacker on a certain play, and how they practiced it over and over and over and over again until they learned how to do it and that's the reason they won the game against Tennessee. People want excitement and all that's fine, and goes with it, but it's more important to put those points on the board. For a governor, that comes from delivering on campaign commitments.

The necessity of putting the points on the board was as ever-present in the thoughts of James the governor as it had been in the thoughts of James the All-America halfback.

His first year, James remembers, was one in which "we put out a lot of fires and got things under control, got the cabinet people in place and spent our time running the government, that was the main thrust. There wasn't that much time that first session to draft and think out legislation. I thought there were more pressing, immediate problems within the executive department's range, such as the highway department's cash flow problem, the prison systems, finding out how much money we had and setting priorities."

State finances were in a mess when James took over. No one would dispute that.

Ira W. Harvey, a former employee of the State Department of Education, wrote a book detailing education finances through Wallace's last term—*A History of Educational Finance in Alabama.*

He explains in his book the financial situation James found when he took office: the education budget for the 1979 fiscal year had been based by the Legislature on an overly optimistic projection of a 13.52 percent growth in revenue which falsely created a $72.5 million surplus. The Legislature had spent the projected surplus. In the first three months of the fiscal year, October through December, 1978, the increase in revenue was only 12.56 percent. Education was short some $7.6 million.

"When Gov. Fob James took the oath of office...," the Birmingham *News* wrote, "he found that the Alabama Legislature, in its first-ever election-year session, had just spent all of the money earmarked for education, all of the $70 million left over from the previous year—and then 5 percent more."

James had inherited a serious money problem. One of his first duties was to declare a state of proration in Alabama's $1 billion-plus Special Education Trust Fund—the first such declaration in 20 years.

The state cannot spend more than its income. When the income falls short of projections, the spending has to be cut—proration.

Part of the blame was put on the Legislature, but most went to an economy on a downward spiral that hadn't stopped.

The $290 million General Fund wasn't in proration—it is supported by more stable taxes—but the demands on it were strong.

Proration is a misnomer, James says. "We're talking about a balanced budget. Prorate is what you have to do by law to ensure a balanced budget. You can't spend more than you take in."

James and Superintendent of Education Dr. Wayne Teague both emphasized in meetings of the State Board of Education that local school boards should not plan on cutting teacher salaries to "balance their now deficit budgets," Harvey wrote.

The 6 percent proration declared by James should have come as no surprise. Teague had warned school officials at the beginning of the fiscal year that proration was around the corner. He had urged them to trim spending by 5 percent.

Determined to draw up his own budget, James asked his staffers to bring him a solid projection of how much revenue would be available to spend the next year.

There was no "system" for projecting the state's revenue for the next year. There were, however, several projections made available to lawmakers and the governor—all of which normally differed in predictions. They were made by the departments of finance and revenue, the legislative fiscal office and the University of Alabama. In addition, the governor had his own budget officer.

Bobby Davis was involved in every aspect of James' administration. He worked with the Alabama Development Office until a permanent director was chosen. He then moved to the executive office and for the last two years of the administration was executive secretary.

The most accurate and the most conservative revenue projections came from the revenue department, Davis said.

"Fob told his people to get together and come up with one estimate," Davis said.

This narrowed to two the number of conflicting revenue estimates given to James, those of the governor's office and those of the Legislative fiscal office.

"We're going to have to revert to old-fashioned line-item (zero-based) budgeting," James told news media as he literally rolled up his shirt sleeves and retreated to his desk to study revenue projections.

"We've never had a governor before who set the stack of budget requests down on his desk, went and got a box of No. 4 pencils and closed the door to sit down and draw up the budget," Davis said.

Line-item budgeting in simple language meant that each of the departments under James was ordered to justify requests item by item.

"We learned that in the past each department had submitted a budget asking for more than it needed, knowing the request would get cut. James instructed budget officers of various departments not to prepare the kind of budgets he had learned were customarily submitted to the governor's office, Davis said.

"Fob told them he wanted an honest budget. Don't hide money. Don't tell me you need $40 million knowing you can make it on $30 million," Davis said.

Gene Mitchell said he was present when one department head presented his first budget to James.

"The governor studied it, then handed it back to him and said, 'You've squirreled away $2 million in there. Go back and bring me an honest budget,' " Mitchell said.

James developed his first budget department by department, in what aides describe as a methodical, "hands-on" approach, a detail-oriented scrutiny in which no sum was too small to be questioned.

In the past, the actual writing of the budget had been done by the governor's finance and budget officers. That task was too important to be delegated, James believed.

He performed the duties of finance director for the first 69 days of his administration, relinquishing the title to Dr. David Bronner, chief of the state retirement systems.

But, said Davis, who sat in on the budget meetings, James gave up only the title, never the control.

"After that first year, which was an educational experience, Fob would bring in the finance director and the budget officer to advise him on the budget, but it was soon obvious he knew as much if not more about it than they did. He had his own ideas on what he wanted to do and how much he wanted to spend."

In tackling the skyrocketing costs of government and getting them in hand, James was in his element, said Bob Geddie.

In paring down expenses, James regarded the departments under him not as independent, unrelated agencies but as inter-dependent divisions making up the whole of state government.

"The administration of the executive departments, cutting costs to the bone, monitoring—that was Fob James at his finest," Geddie said. "He had his ledger on his desk and got weekly reports of expenses, the epitome of a typical president of a company. When he found an expense had gone up, he'd call the department head in to his office to demand why there were two more employees this week than last week, or why there had been an increase in money spent on supplies.

"Fob knew more about the budgets of those state departments than many of the directors did and more than any finance director has ever made it his business to know. He probably carried it to an extreme," Geddie said.

Ever mindful that his administration functioned amid the backdrop of the worst recession since the Great Depression, James found no expense too insignificant to worry about. To keep his thumb on the soaring amounts spent for in-state and out-of-state travel, James divided the departments among his staff members to monitor.

"Requests for travel from executive departments were sent to us to be approved or rejected," Geddie said. "We knew what the departmental budget for travel was and we had to hold them to it."

In an effort to more easily monitor the travel of agencies assigned to him, Davis said he combined the travel money for some 18 programs into one budget item.

"When Fob got the budget request in front of him he stormed out wanting to know why there was $76,000 in the budget for travel and I explained it was less than in past years, that it looked like a big amount because it was for so many programs," Davis said. "He didn't comment right then, but he didn't forget. Later that year he suddenly walked into my office and said 'Have you spent that $76,000 yet?' "

The monitoring paid off.

For example, in one of the smallest departments in state government, the Aeronautics Department, the director reported the elimination of out-of-state travel during the administration saved $1,500. Reducing instate travel saved some $2,200 in 1981 and 1982.

Jud Salter, appointed chief of staff by James in mid-July, remembers James canceling a three-day convention that employees of one department had planned to hold in Biloxi, Miss.

"They held it in Montgomery instead, and in one day," Salter said.

James took office knowing that legislation was necessary to do some of the things he wanted; other legislative proposals, such as rewriting the state's 1901 constitution, developed as he learned more about the problems of state government and the needs of the departments under him.

The legislative program he put together over a four-month period was an ambitious package, one which he knew he would not pass in its entirety. He kept that knowledge to himself, however, never exuding anything but confidence to everyone else including those whose job it was to work daily with the Legislature to get his programs passed.

James' War on Illiteracy was at the top of his list, though his legislative package included a miscellany of targets ranging from campaign promises to issues discovered after he became governor.

He became aware of the need for a new constitution after taking office and learning that the unwieldy existing one formed an obstacle in the path of many reforms.

A newspaper clipping dated Jan. 15 reflects how strongly a governor can feel about wanting to rewrite a bulky, out-moded constitution.

"The provisions of our present antiquated fundamental-plan constitution [form] inseparable barriers to most of the important reforms necessary to meet modern conditions and to secure greater economy and efficiency in the administration of every department in state government," the governor told legislators.

The newspaper containing that clipping hit the street some 64 years prior to James' inauguration. It quoted Gov. Emmett O'Neal.

Alabama's 1901 constitution, still in effect today, was the state's sixth one. It was written primarily with the intent of limiting black voting. Therefore, said O'Neal, "...little consideration was given to other matters..."

James D. Thomas and William H. Stewart in their book *Alabama Government and Politics* point out that the Civil Rights movement "reversed the bulk of the convention's handiwork." The parts of the 1901 constitution left intact, which are essentially a re-adopted 1875 constitution, address problems of a post–Civil War Alabama which have little similarity to today's problems.

O'Neal was unsuccessful in getting a new constitution as were others who followed him, as described by Thomas and Stewart.

The Brookings Institution, commissioned by Gov. Benjamin M. Miller during the Great Depression, recommended revising the constitution as one means of lowering the cost of operating state government.

During the 1930s and 1940s, the Alabama Policy Commission, a citizens' group, pushed for constitutional revision.

Big Jim Folsom repeatedly called for a constitutional convention to revamp the document.

Gov. Albert Brewer also favored constitutional revision.

Alabama voters, used to seeing constitutional amendments on state ballots, reflected disinterest by ignoring the proposals. More and more frequently, fewer than 10 percent of those voting in an election voted on the proposed amendments. It was therefore relatively easy for a special interest group to muster enough votes to amend the constitution in its favor.

One important part of the constitution pushed by James was a section establishing education as an essential function of the Legislature, Harvey wrote.

No one argued with James' contention that Alabama's 1,210,000-word constitution needed streamlining. The U.S. Constitution said what needed to be said in fewer than 10,000 words. The Alabama constitution had been amended 380 times. Sixty of those amendments had been tacked on in the prior 15 years. Only a third of the 380 amendments applied to the entire state, but all had to be approved by statewide vote.

However, a wholesale rewriting of the constitution brought out every special interest group in the state seeking to protect whatever advantages they had been able to wangle in the form of amendments to the existing constitution.

Selma State Sen. Earl Goodwin predicted that once the Legislature opened the can of worms that is the 1901 constitution, "the crows and hawks may be ready to grab in there."

James did not favor a constitutional convention, believing a new constitution should go before the people for a referendum vote. He felt the Legislature should have the job of rewriting it, preparing enabling legislation to present it for a vote. He wanted input as governor, however. In early December he named 15 private citizens to a Constitutional Revision Committee to develop guidelines. The committee worked under the direction of Yetta Samford, a former prison board member.

Prior to the inauguration, James' staff member Mike Waters devoted his full attention to the constitution. "I spent the first month-and-a-half in the basement of the Alabama Supreme Court building researching Alabama's constitution and those of states in which there had been major reform, such as Virginia and Louisiana," Waters said.

"There were six or seven key items that either the governor or the commission wanted included in the new constitution," Waters said. These included referendum and recall, home rule for counties and the unearmarking of tax revenues.

"Fob wanted to allow the public to recall elected officials and to be able to actually enact legislation," Waters said. "Cities had home rule, but the Legislature had never enacted county codes, so local officials had to go to legislators for power to do what cities did without asking. There was opposition to this from county legislators, who weren't pleased because they would lose a lot of power if county governments were given the same privileges as cities."

In January 1979, Waters was named legal adviser, but he continued coordinating efforts toward writing the new constitution.

Waters said the committee, composed of experts in constitutional law, met regularly. "Lt. Gov. McMillan and Chief Justice Torbert sat in on meetings. Speaker McCorquodale was invited but never attended."

James talked of the new constitution everywhere he went. He told legislators to "cautiously" consider the proposed constitution, urging them at the same time not to wait 20 years to okay it. In January he told members of the Alabama State Bar it might take a year or two before the constitution could be implemented. On another day, he voiced a desire that the new document be "fundamental rather than trying to usurp power as the 1901 constitution does."

In January, a legislative committee was appointed which held public hearings on the proposed constitution drafted by James' committee. The Legislative committee was comprised of 17 senators named by Lt. Gov. McMillan and 15 House members named by McCorquodale.

When he went into office, James was hoping to be able to submit the constitution to voters for their approval in June.

The stack of requests from people who wanted to be heard at the public meetings on the constitution was more than one foot high.

As time drew near for the full Legislature to consider James' new constitution, bookmakers would have given odds that it had little chance of passing.

McCorquodale told James it could not be done, but assured him that it would get a fair hearing in the House.

McMillan committed himself to passing it in the Senate.

"McCorquodale said it would get a fair hearing, but we kept getting a lot of feedback otherwise, undercurrents of opposition from the speaker," Waters said. "McMillan was all for it."

Public attention was focused on the re-writing of the constitution. But many other issues took James' attention. One of these was a proposal to provide money for low-income families through a vehicle called the Alabama Housing Authority.

Repeated attempts to accomplish this had been unsuccessful for nearly a decade. News articles in April of 1973 reported that such a bill was being introduced and that special interests would fight it for the third year in a row.

The bill was aimed at helping families of moderate to low income buy homes they could not otherwise finance through banks and mortgage companies. The housing authority would obtain the mortgage money by issuing tax-free bonds. Proceeds from the bond sale would finance mortgages, the repayment of which would pay off the bond issue.

Similar bills had passed in 22 other states.

Six years before James took office, a news article states that the bill had at that time been killed twice by bankers and mortgage company officials fearful of the competition it would provide.

"It is not a subsidy program. It would not cost the taxpayers a dime," Montgomery attorney Charles Miller in 1973 argued in support of the bill to members of the South Alabama Regional Planning Commission.

"Several members questioned the bill's interest rate provisions in competition with banking interest rates," a reporter covering the meeting wrote.

Six years passed on the calendar, but the need for such housing did not change.

In February, 1977, a Quaker antipoverty group held a press conference in Washington, D.C. and released the results of a study done on housing in Alabama.

Poverty showed no racial preference. Some 147,591 homes in Alabama, half black, half white, were substandard, the study showed. The group called for a "massive housing program" in Alabama and the stepping-up of federal assistance funds.

Soon after James took office, Geddie was visited by several people who asked him to talk with the governor about supporting the bill.

James did not warm up to the idea until he had investigated all monetary ramifications to the state, Geddie said.

"Then he got enthusiastic," Geddie said.

The Alabama Housing Authority bill was added to the growing list of bills James would push.

In nearly every department, career merit workers worked with James' new administrators to suggest legislation needed to carry out James' new efficiency and self-sufficiency directives.

In each session of the Legislature during James' term there were seemingly unimportant bills affecting the departments under him which were routinely passed as "housekeeping" bills.

Spread among some three dozen departments, and channeled to a dozen different legislative committees, the bills did not blatantly appear to be part of any "package," therefore the tremendous overall effects they would engender escaped notice. No administration spokesman heralded their passage as part of what it was—a vast reorganization of state government. No attention was called to the common theme of overhaul and update which bound them together. They moved through the legislative process quietly but steadily, sharing only a lack of fanfare and the common fate at the end of that process of being enrolled by the Secretary of State in the book in which new laws are logged.

The new laws enabled top officials of the various departments, most of whom were merit system employees of long years standing, to put in effect new fee structures which shifted some of the burden of paying for specific government services from taxpayers in general to the shoulders of the people who directly benefitted from those services.

During James' term, banks would be called upon to pay the cost of audits by the state, fish pond owners would be asked to pay for the fish placed in their ponds by the state, applicants for drivers' licenses would be assessed a $5 charge for the test, etc.

The purpose of the measures was to bring more money into the departments, but frequently there were unexpected benefits. Requiring pond owners to pay for the stocking of fish not only brought money into the department, it cut down on the number of requests by pond owners to stock ponds, thus freeing Game and Fish employees for other duties, Commissioner Claude D. Kelley wrote in his four-year-end report. Charging for the driver's tests not only brought money into the Department of Public Safety, it discouraged people from taking tests before they were ready for them, thus cutting down on the number of tests officers had to give, Department of Public Safety Director Jerry Shoemaker stated.

In each department, James coupled the income-producing measures with cost-savings ones, not all of which required legislation. Examples can be found examining the annual reports of every department under his control. Bank accounts were consolidated, as was office space. Weekly magazines published at state expense were changed to bi-weekly and recipients were asked to subscribe for a small fee. Forms for reports were shrunk, the purchase of supplies was centralized and bulk purchasing instituted as well as a hundred other common sense, cost-effective steps taken which had not been taken in the past because no strong advocate of such measures sat in the governor's chair.

Other savings were brought about through research, such as the fifty percent reduction in costs which resulted from the research-inspired switch to using liquid fertilizer for state lakes, Kelley stated. He stated that James' legislation increased the budget of the Game and Fish Division by some 50 percent during his term as governor.

In readying for his first legislation session, it came to James' attention that the two men from his staff who were charged with lobbying his bills in the Legislature would have a lot of company—dozens of state-paid lobbyists from mental health, corrections, education, the court system, etc.

Such lobbyists have been an accepted part of government, routinely coaxing departmental bills through the legislature.

James saw no need for them, however.

"The idea of paying lobbyists for units of state government and institutions to lobby the government itself made no sense," he said.

James was also aware that it was quite possible the lobbyists might seek to undermine his legislation. He banned all such lobbyists who fell under his jurisdiction and intimidated a few others out of the picture temporarily, such as the Auburn lobbyists from his alma mater.

"I called Auburn and told them to send 'em home. We needed priorities and facts, not politics," James said. The move did not make friends among the dozens of other lobbyists paid by higher education.

"We didn't want departmental lobbyists undercutting our programs, trying to increase their appropriations at the expense of our overall program," Geddie said. "Restricting them was a way of getting their attention. Once we got their attention we didn't have to worry about undercutting."

They would be allowed back on the hill in 1980, limited to providing information about specifics when legislators had questions.

Additionally, Geddie said, "We sent a directive that all departmental bills had to be cleared in advance of the session. We didn't want any surprises. We had a first readings committee which met weekly with representatives of major departments. We would review pending legislation and determine the administration's position on each bill introduced. If we found that a departmental bill was interfering with something we were attempting to do, we asked the department head to withdraw support."

The majority of departmental bills in the four years were introduced as administration bills, part of the overall effort to pare down bureaucracy and cut expenditures, Geddie said.

In 1979, examples of the myriad departmental legislation include a bill allowing the Game and Fish Division to increase the cost of resident hunting and fishing licenses. The additional revenue would also allow for the hiring of much-needed enforcement officers.

Additionally, James sponsored a "pet" bill to create a state duck stamp which would bring in about $60,000 a year.

Legislation originated in the Department of Aging to create a network of ombudsmen to hear the complaints of patients in state nursing homes and work out solutions.

The Banking Department, with career merit system worker Ken McCartha at the helm, contributed legislation which would allow it to increase the fees it charged financial institutions it regulated. Passage of the bill allowed the department to become self-supporting during James' term, McCartha said. He said it also allowed the department to save some $33,000 during the 1979–80 fiscal year.

From the Highway Department came legislation which allowed the department to carry over maintenance funds at the end of a fiscal year. Prior to the legislation, unspent funds were theoretically returned to the General Fund. What actually happened, however, was that department heads as the end of the fiscal year drew near found some way to spend the money. If not, they feared, legislators would think they did not need as much the next year and cut their budget. Whether true or not, it was a common joke among news media that the National Guard put all its vehicles into service at the year's end to use up that fiscal year's gasoline allotment. It is certainly true that the "spend it or lose it" theory existed after James left office. In the 1990 budget hearings, Gov. Guy Hunt's ABC administrator, Tandy Little, explained that his department bought 32 enforcement vehicles because the department had the money at the time. The cars, for enforcement officers the department hoped to hire in the future, were bought during a period in which ABC stores were being closed for "lack of money."

Legislation in three of four years was drafted by Insurance Department personnel which strengthened requirements for insurance salesmen. The new laws upgraded the qualifications for new agents, required them to complete a 40-hour educational course and to pass a more comprehensive state examination.

James approached the legislative session with confidence. He worked closely with Lt. Gov. McMillan and House Speaker McCorquodale and had confidence in their vows that his legislative program would be put before legislators for a vote.

Past governors had hand-picked the speaker of the House, key leaders in both Senate and House and key committee chairmen in both houses. This was the way they had managed to pass their legislation.

James announced he had no intention of interfering with the way McCorquodale or McMillan ran their respective bodies. The House elected McCorquodale speaker and that was fine with him. They could pick their chairmen. He saw no need to even have floor leaders as other governors had done. He had been assured that his legislation would come up for a vote and he was sure that he could convince legislators it was the right thing for Alabama. If they did not feel it was right, they should not vote for it.

That was as fair a deal as James figured a governor had a right to expect.

Newspaper columnists were dubious about James "naïveté."

Was he really giving legislators a free hand in organizing their respective houses, asking nothing of them except to vote their conscience on the bills he introduced?

That's exactly what he was doing. Mike Waters says he remembers overhearing James end many sessions with legislators by telling them, "If you think my legislation is good for the state, I ask you to vote for it. If you don't think it's good for the state, don't vote for it."

James in a speech soon after being inaugurated defended his stance and chastised newspapers for criticizing the close manner in which he was working with McMillan and McCorquodale.

He said he was following the constitution, not the columnists, when he supported the leaders of the legislative branch without extracting promises or deals in return.

James had quickly become a personal as well as a political friend of McCorquodale. Not long after he was elected, James invited McCorquodale, McMillan and new Attorney General Charles Graddick to the governor's mansion at Gulf Shores to go over his plans with them.

It was a meeting which lasted several hours and in closing James got up and started to say, "Gentlemen, I'm not going to run for governor again. I just want you to know that."

When he started talking, however, McCorquodale guessed what he was about to say, jumped up and interrupted him and changed the subject.

Afterward, McCorquodale explained to James that he had changed the subject to keep James from making a severe political mistake. Both McMillan and Graddick wanted to be governor, McCorquodale told him. If they knew he did not intend to run for reelection they would be running themselves the entire time he was in office. As candidates, they would be more interested in promoting their programs than in supporting him.

James' first speech to the Legislature was in January prior to his inauguration when legislators met in an organizational session. He called on them for a united front against special interests.

Acknowledging that lobbyists might present legitimate appeals to public officials, James told them his administration would "listen carefully, appreciate the information and input," but would make the decisions based on what was best for the public.

Legislators did not comment on the obvious, which was that they had no intention of spurning the attentions of people whose reason for existence was to pick up their tabs, provide them with campaign donations and hover in constant attendance to ensure their comfort.

There was no need for legislative comment, however. A column written by *Post-Herald* writer Ted Bryant after the session began said it all.

"The first week was a good one for legislators so far as freebies are concerned," Bryant wrote. "On Tuesday a potted azalea plant was on each legislator's desk, courtesy of the Alabama Nurserymen's Association.

"By coincidence, we're sure, a bill that would place nursery supplies in the same category as farm supplies, exempting them from the state sales tax, was introduced.

"All the association executives—which means lobbyists—got together and threw a party for the legislators Tuesday night. The following night, the Associated Builders and Contractors were the hosts at Montgomery's Civic Center.

"Then there were...let's see...framed pictures of the Capitol, peanuts, notepads from the Alabama Education Association bearing the legislators' name and a ballpoint pen that writes in red and black from the Alabama Association of School Boards...," Bryant wrote.

James' first success in getting what he wanted from the Legislature stemmed from a pay increase legislators had voted themselves at the organizational session which occurred before Wallace left office. Legislators passed a resolution approving for themselves a $75 per day salary for each day in session and a $500-per-month, 12-month-a-year expense account.

Wallace signed the resolution.

Bill Sellers, Mobile *Press Register* political columnist, reacted with a weathered view of the proceedings when he wrote: "It will be the same old story in Alabama politics for the next couple of years at least. The script was written by the Alabama Legislature in its organizational session this last week when in rapid fire order a rubber stamp was applied to the policies which spelled disaster to the prior crop of lawmakers."

He wrote that the Senate had put unlimited power in the hands of a small clique headed by McMillan and had then voted themselves a hefty pay raise.

Sellers thought an even more significant indication that McMillan would wield considerable clout was the fact he named with "heavy use" of the gavel his choice for president pro tem, Sen. Finis St. John of Cullman.

James bristled when the pay raise resolution was approved. He told McMillan and McCorquodale, privately, to inform legislators that he would raise a ruckus like they wouldn't believe if they didn't drastically reduce the raise.

In making the threat, James used one of the two strategies he would rely on in dealing with legislators. He labels the strategies defensive and offensive.

Defensively: "I had long thought a governor can defeat anything he knows will be bad for the people simply by threatening in private to scream and raise a ruckus publicly if need be," James says.

Any governor could use a defensive strategy effectively to be "batting 1,000," he says.

Offensively: A governor can propose legislation he believes is needed and use logic and public support to convince legislators to go along with it.

Offensively, a governor can never hope to get 100 percent of what he wants, James says.

Faced with the newly-elected governor's threat, legislators approved a resolution cutting their expense account from $500 a month to $300 per month and reduced the $75 per day figure to $65 per day.

It was his first victory in two areas, in holding down the cost of government and in dealing with the Legislature.

**Setting precedent for a long list of similar actions**, the victory was not a political one, however. Few people except McCorquodale and McMillan were aware that James was the impetus behind the turn-about. Thus there were no headlines or editorials written and placed in newspaper files to serve as source material for reporters attempting in the future to list James' successes and failures.

There were perhaps throwaway lines in political columns or stories which at most piqued the curiosity, such as the one which observed, "Early the next morning James arrived early, ate in the cafeteria, met with his staff while the telephone installers worked and met with Mc-

Corquodale and McMillan. There was some speculation they were discussing the legislative pay raise passed last week and signed by Gov. Wallace."

When reporters later wrote of the pay raise episode, they would background it as did the *Birmingham News* in an April 25, 1979 article: "During the organizational session, the lawmakers passed a resolution increasing its pay from $50 to $75 a day. After a loud outcry from the public, the lawmakers came back and reduced its pay increase to $65 a day and at the same time called for a commission to study legislative pay needs and come up with a report."

James called the legislature into a short special session on Feb. 15 in which the regular session was delayed until April 17.

For House liaison Don Bryan, James's decision not to name floor leaders for his first legislative session meant that, "We had no one there we could get to help with the programs the governor had. And he had some very ambitious programs at the onset."

The constitution was in trouble before the session began, Bryan said. "Joe McCorquodale told us that."

On Feb. 28, the Joint Interim Legislative Study Committee opened hearings on James' constitutional proposals, including a key one giving local governments home rule. It was controversial, as were other provisions.

The first public sign of trouble was when James decided not to present the proposed constitution to a short special session which had been called for "housekeeping measures" and to give the new attorney general supplementary funding for his office.

James said he would wait and present the constitution to the regular session of the Legislature when it met in a few weeks.

The *Birmingham News* reported the popular story going around, that James made the decision because McCorquodale had warned him if he did not that the House would vote to adjourn immediately and go back home. James, so the story went, reluctantly backed down.

McCorquodale told the *News* that was not the way it happened. He said that he and McMillan and others realized the 381 amendments to the existing constitution had not been researched.

"We explained to Gov. James that there just wasn't time. We weren't ready. He understood. He is a reasonable man," McCorquodale said.

Waters said that was not what happened.

"We were to have a big strategy session on the constitution in

McCorquodale's office. The speaker made an impassioned plea with Fob not to present the new constitution. He said there were all these court cases based on the old constitution and a new one would throw the state into court for years every time we turned around. He begged Fob to forget the new constitution and go back to the old one and make changes section by section."

Waters said McCorquodale was wrong in his basic argument. "We had grandfathered in all existing law," he said.

Why didn't Waters speak up? He was a young staff attorney who worked for the governor. The meeting was in McCorquodale's office and the speaker was clearly in charge. Waters protested that too much work had been done to scrap the document and start over three weeks before the regular session. But he did not feel he should confront the veteran lawmaker in front of the governor.

"Also, the governor liked Joe McCorquodale. He trusted him. The only thing I could do was hand the governor a note, 'Go slow. Don't agree now,'" Waters said.

James glanced at the note, but agreed before the session ended that McCorquodale's approach was more logical.

"We tried," Waters said. "We gave it our best shot. We started with the old constitution, got to the verge of the regular session and saw it could not be done. It had taken four to five months to write the first draft. We couldn't do a new one in three weeks."

Waters, Yetta Samford and Jack Miller converged on James one night and explained the problem. Having the advantage over Waters of being able to talk to James on his level, not as a wet-behind-the-ears young staff member, they explained that all sections of the constitution which had been upheld in court had been grandfathered in. James agreed that the original draft was the version which should be presented to the Legislature, Waters said. His only concern was that McCorquodale and the other legislators who had been in the speaker's office for the meeting might think he was breaking his word.

"Fob called Joe and they rode around in his car for an hour-and-a-half and Fob came back and said Joe understood completely and had no problems with us going back to the original draft," Waters said.

"It is important to understand that McCorquodale is the only legislator Fob explained this to," Waters said. "We all assumed he would go back and tell the others in the meeting of the change in plans and the reason for the change."

The first inkling Waters had that McCorquodale had not repeated his agreement with James to anyone came when the constitution was introduced in committee, Waters said.

"House members came up to me and said things like, 'You lying son of a bitch. You said you would start with the old constitution, but you introduced Fob's draft. You double-crossed us,' Waters said. "Once the House *perceived* that Fob had gone back on a commitment, House members started ripping it to shreds with a particular vigor which we didn't expect. House members who had worked with us before did not after that."

Did he repeat the remarks to James?

"It may be difficult to understand, looking back on it, but I didn't," Waters said. "I told Bob Geddie and Don Bryan. I told Jack. But if you are new on the governor's staff, you don't want him to think that every time you walk in the door you're going to bitch about something. The Legislature was not my responsibility. There were enough times I had to go in to Fob with a list of complaints about things I was responsible for not to take on any more. Besides, I didn't know if he would believe me. I was afraid he would think I was paranoid."

The heart of legislative opposition seemed to revolve around two provisions James was insistent upon including. Referred to as "initiative and referendum" and "recall," their inclusion would have enabled voters to bypass the Legislature in initiating legislation and repealing laws and would have allowed voters to call an election to oust politicians from office by getting enough names on a petition.

Newspapers supported James wholeheartedly. As the *Journal* noted, recall would "keep politicians on their toes."

McMillan explained that some legislators were concerned about the two provisions but added that they could be approved with "sufficient safeguards."

James tried to calm legislators' fears, assuring them (as one reporter wrote) that "...the threshold at which recall or initiative and referendum can be invoked must be high enough so that a sensational issue in the media can't incite...when there is not real grass roots support..." He also stipulated that a fixed percentage of voters would have to sign a petition.

Resistance strengthened. James, learning much of the opposition was coming from judges, agreed to exclude judges from the recall provisions.

This gave legislators the artillery for which they had been looking. A story which appeared March 8, 1979 stated, "the governor's proposal to exclude judges from a provision allowing ouster of elected officials drew fire from legislators. Sen. Donald Holmes of Anniston said the public wants judges included. Sen. Douglas Cook of Bessemer said he didn't understand the logic. One legislator said judges "are just as much a political animal as anyone else."

Reform of the constitution was being fired on from all sides.

In a March 8 column, *Post Herald* writer Ted Bryant wrote, "Meanwhile, Mrs. James' husband continues to have problems at the Capitol, particularly with his proposed constitution. We suggested in a previous column that James 'may be giving in too much to legislative pressure on the specific, progressive points he wants in the constitution' such as unearmarking of tax revenue...earmarking remains one of those provisions that can turn a large group of voters against the entire constitution."

## James' First Session

James did not read a prepared speech Jan. 16 when he delivered his first State of the State Address.

Talking from notes, the new governor asked legislators for $20 million for his War on Illiteracy, cautioning, "...dollars won't win the war without mass commitment from parents who will support their children, teachers and principals."

Roads and bridges which needed repair and rebuilding were also on his mind. James set the stage for requesting an increase in the gas tax to pay for the highway needs. The price of gasoline was rising daily, which James felt would swallow any increase in state tax as prices at the tank equaled out in Southern states in the future. He also asked for a few special things such as the elimination of sales tax on food and drugs.

Literacy, however, was clearly number one on his list.

He announced to legislators he intended to actively serve as president of the state school board. By custom, the board member elected as vice president by other members served as the working chairman. The governor's role as president had been looked on as more or less a ceremonial one, though he possessed the same vote as other members.

James told legislators that he wanted to ensure quality in the state's junior colleges and universities.

"But it all starts in grammar school, and all too often, for too many children, in reality it ends there," he said.

James said the great majority of teachers were "competent and dedicated. Those that are not we need to get away from our children."

He urged parents to support teachers when those teachers disciplined their children.

To provide teachers with the support and encouragement necessary to discipline students as firmly as the teachers of his youth had disciplined him, James proposed that the state provide free liability insurance to teachers.

Unknown to James at that time—or for years afterward in fact—two of his proposals were to Dr. Paul Hubbert challenges to battle. The first was his desire to provide teachers with liability insurance. The second was his announcement that he would serve as an active president of the State Board of Education. Hubbert headed the powerful Alabama Education Association (AEA) teacher lobby, which offered liability insurance as its biggest lure to prospective members. AEA claimed 93 percent of all teachers in the state as members. Regarding the State Board, Hubbert prior to James' administration had more clout with the board than any other single individual.

There had been disdain for James in Hubbert's voice prior to this (he had fiercely campaigned first for Brewer then Baxley). After this there would be blatant animosity and hostility. James was obviously, Hubbert believed, out to break AEA. James, on the other hand, remained totally oblivious to Hubbert's distress.

"The governor proposed the allocation of $19,986,000 for elementary schools and kindergartens which he said was to fight illiteracy," Ted Bryant wrote. "Of that amount, $3 million would go to 12 basic skills teams of eight specialists each to assist schools, and $10 million to support the teams' work.

"Another $5.85 million would go to establish 320 more kindergarten teacher units and $1 million would be used for emergency construction where necessary. The remaining $135,000 would cover the cost of liability insurance."

In his message to legislators, James pointed out that nearly 77,000 Alabamians were unable to write, the sixth highest illiteracy rate in the nation. Only 47 percent of white adults and 21.4 percent of black adults had high school diplomas.

James' first General Fund budget, delineating how $278.7 million would be spent, was approved by Ways and Means one day after it was introduced in the Legislature. It was approved by the House the first day it appeared on the calendar.

Bryant wrote that it gained approval of the Ways and Means Committee "with few, if any, changes."

Accompanying the general fund budget was a separate bill granting $14.9 million in supplemental appropriations to help state agencies finish out the current fiscal year.

Bryant predicted the $1.3 billion education budget would "produce fireworks because James is asking institutions of higher learning to hold the line at the current year's appropriations.

"James is asking that all the increase in revenue earmarked for education go to elementary schools to launch his War On Illiteracy," he said.

The reaction of veteran legislators to James' legislative package was that he was biting off more than he could chew in attempting to pass the constitution at the same time as numerous other ambitious programs.

Hubbert, after the speech, told reporters AEA did not oppose eliminating the food and drug tax, "if that money is made up somewhere else."

Hubbert's opposition to James also stemmed from his perception that James had united forces against him with Hubbert's biggest enemy—McCorquodale.

The feud between McCorquodale and Hubbert had developed long before James thought of running for governor. It deepened with each passing day, revolving primarily around the tough, but opposite, stances taken by Hubbert and McCorquodale on the earmarking of tax revenue.

McCorquodale felt that unearmarking taxes was one of the most important tasks the Legislature needed to accomplish.

Taxes were mainly earmarked for education.

Hubbert's professional reputation among his some 34,800-teacher membership rested on his being able to ward off the unearmarking of tax dollars.

Hubbert perceived McCorquodale as a tool of special interests, namely big land owners. He believed McCorquodale's insistence on unearmarking was insincere, that he wanted to unearmark only education money—not highway or docks or other non-education funds.

Animosity between the two was an ever-present force when James' programs were debated by the Legislature. Open warfare erupted as legislators were forced to choose sides between them.

"Joe basically wanted to shut down state government to force a major funding crisis in hopes of unearmarking state funds," one long time observer believes and a number of others agree. "For that reason, he was against any new revenue unless it was for roads, conservation or forestry. He liked to operate in a crisis. He lived to fight Paul Hubbert."

While James made it no secret that he worked closely with leaders of the Legislative branch of government, his instinctive mistrust of lobbyists led him to regard Hubbert with obvious reservations.

McCorquodale was a powerful House speaker. It was no secret on the hill that he used the experience he had amassed in two decades as a legislator to shepherd through the Legislature that which he supported and to kill that which he opposed.

"Hubbert and McCorquodale are not the best of friends and that's putting it mildly," Don Bryan said. "Often times the animosity that existed between them had a monumental effect on the governor's programs. We fell heir to old wars we did not start, wars we did not know of."

Bryan said McCorquodale often was opposed to something James proposed to do "simply because he thought Paul might benefit from it.

"At the same time I think Paul came to view us as being pawns of McCorquodale," Bryan said. "He thought that we were listening to what McCorquodale was saying and taking our direction from him."

That is indeed what Hubbert thought.

"Fob acquiesced to McCorquodale as speaker. He allowed himself to be put in the position that he got his programs through only when McCorquodale agreed," Hubbert said. "When Fob was fighting us, McCorquodale was on his side."

"When our relationship began to swing more and more toward McCorquodale, that wedge grew between Paul and Fob," Bryan said.

Said McCorquodale: "Paul and I did have our differences. They were not personal on my part. I am sorry they were on his. I have always been so strongly for education that when I ran for governor in 1982 I offered to withdraw from the race if a single person could be found in public service who had been more supportive of public education than I was during my 24 years in the Legislature."

James and McCorquodale differed greatly in their approach to working with legislators.

Hubbert describes McCorquodale's approach as a "combative" one which he learned from watching George Wallace.

Hubbert, who has admitted he would sit down to talk with the devil if he thought he could work out a compromise, said McCorquodale preferred confrontation and never wanted and never considered trying to work any situation out.

"You were either for him or against him, friend or foe," said Hubbert.

A number of James' former aides agree with Hubbert's assessment of McCorquodale. James, however, does not.

Former Rep. Tommy Sandusky of Mobile says that James, "wasn't afraid to challenge the legislature but his approach was not one of confrontation so much as an approach of reason. He said let's identify all the problems, put the problems on the table in front of the legislature in the form of legislative proposals, then try to sell them."

When the governor completes his budget, it passes from the executive to the legislative branch of government.

The first step in the legislative process is the House, where the budget is introduced as a bill and assigned to the House Ways and Means Committee. Public hearings are held and Ways and Means committee members thrash out differences or objections and may add their own special projects.

The governor is not officially involved in this process, though none of the participants loses sight for a moment that the budget after it passes the House and the Senate must return to the executive branch to be signed into law by the governor. He can, if he chooses, veto it. The budget then dies unless a majority of the Legislature votes to override the veto. It thus behooves all parties to work together in the legislative process to come up with a budget palatable to all.

"There's probably not a state in the union in which the governor's budget is not changed in some way. That's a legislative prerogative," Geddie said.

"Fob's budget bill would go through a committee hearing. Sometimes a substitute would have to be adopted, but the committee would always work from the governor's budget in drawing up the substitute," Geddie said.

After his education budgets were favorably voted out of Ways and Means, James' interest was obvious. He could frequently be found in the offices of various legislators while his proposals were being debated, or sitting next to McMillan or McCorquodale in the chambers keeping first-person tally on the process.

Many customs have taken root in the Legislature, allowing most reporters who have covered more than one session to predict with a great degree of accurately how legislation will progress step by step.

Legislative coverage in 1979 reflects that a few customs were broken that year.

One week into the 1979 Legislative session, Ted Bryant predicted that the coming week would "go a long way toward telling Montgomery prognosticators what to expect from the 1979 session of the Alabama Legislature."

"If there was a surprise from last week, it was the large number of bills reported out of committee on the first day of committee meetings," he said.

Predicting not one of the 69 pending bills would be acted on Tuesday "and maybe not Thursday," Bryant explained, "That's because the leadership doesn't want bills passed early in the session. Instead, the object is to allow bills to stack up on the calendar, creating a logjam as early as possible.

"Once the jam is created, it offers a ready excuse (to) adopt a special order calendar. That allows the (leadership-appointed) Rules Committee to determine which bills will be considered on a given day—giving the leadership control over which bills come up..."

The first bill on the House calendar was one to repeal the law mandating that "prevailing wages" must be paid on public works projects.

It was a McCorquodale bill. McCorquodale opposed the existing law because it forced small counties such as his home of Clarke County to pay the same wage scales as metropolitan areas, Don Bryan said.

Debate was "bound to tie up the House," Ted Bryant predicted.

If there was a truism during the James administration, however, it was that things did not normally happen as they had in the past.

On May 9, a *Birmingham News* headline read, "Unusual event as bill passes in Legislature before the mid-point."

"Legislative watchers are in for a surprise," wrote reporter Ralph Holmes. "This 1979 regular session is less than a month old and already general bills are making their way down to the governor's office for his signature."

The bills ranged from a simple one concerning bar pilots' fees in Mobile Bay to one pushed by James which prohibited the disposal of nuclear waste in Alabama.

The importance of the bills, Holmes wrote, "is that it is rare for a general bill to pass both houses of the Legislature before the mid-point in the session."

Legislation continued to move steadily throughout the session, despite iron-clad opposition to the budget every step of the way from Hubbert, and from other special interest groups to the gas tax or the constitution or other of James' reforms.

Soon after its introduction in April, however, James' War on Illiteracy bogged down, primarily because of opposition from Hubbert, estimated by reporters to have supported half the House with campaign donations.

James in a plea to legislators to pass it said he would scrap his highway program or his new constitution rather than see his education plans go down the drain.

The governor refused to take it seriously when aides told him that animosities between Hubbert and McCorquodale were interfering with his legislative programs. He remembers the conversations he had with Geddie, who politicked legislators after hours as well as during the work day, and with Don Bryan, longtime friend who constantly fought a weight problem.

"I knew all those forces were coming into play, but I didn't by design let my people know I was aware," James said. "I understood that it created a problem but I never accepted it as a fact that they couldn't get around the problem. I guess I played dumb. If I hadn't, what was already a big thing in their minds would have become bigger. I wasn't willing to say to Don Bryan, 'Now Don, I understand you're having a hard time and I realize you won't be able to get but 42 votes cause Joe don't like Paul and Jack don't like Jim.' What I told him was, 'Now look, Don, are you telling me that you're going to let a little feud between those two guys keep you from getting this piece of legislation passed? Come on, big boy. Get out there. Don't come back in here telling me that horse-uh that nonsense.' Or I'd say to Geddie, 'Look, ole blue eyes, you just ain't working hard enough. You're leaving here too soon. You want to get out and play a little bit too much, to take dear Paul or Papa Joe out to dinner. I don't care who likes who. We're going to be here four years. Then we're going to be gone. It doesn't matter."

It did matter. In late May, it was obvious that key James' bills were stalled.

The governor took to the stump to get grass roots support for what the AP described as his "three-pronged program," the War On Illiteracy, a new constitution and a gasoline tax hike to finance road and bridge repair.

"The governor said at a press conference last Friday that he would be willing to drop the gasoline tax hike if the lawmakers can come up with another tax to raise $100 million a year for road and bridge repairs," AP stated.

On the first day of his jaunt, James made stops in Huntsville and Birmingham. Two days later he hit the quad-cities area in northwest Alabama, then flew to Tuscaloosa.

"The governor's campaign will continue through June 13, with speeches or press conferences in most Alabama cities," AP wrote.

As James pleaded with the public to put pressure on their legislators to vote for his programs, the Senate took up one-by-one some 65 committee amendments to the proposed constitution, a process which the AP said "provides for almost unlimited debate."

House leaders, meanwhile, postponed voting on the education budget and its War On Illiteracy funding "for the past two weeks as they searched for additional revenue to provide teachers with a cost-of-living raise," AP wrote. "...the powerful Alabama Education Association has suggested the $20 million planned for the War on Illiteracy be used instead for salary increases."

A pattern was set in the first year of the administration. Hubbert opposed whatever James proposed. When James proposed pay raises, Hubbert fought them on the grounds that they weren't enough. When James proposed plans to battle illiteracy, Hubbert fought them on the grounds that the money should go instead for pay raises. When James' pay raises were approved, Hubbert took the credit in his Journal, which went to just about every teacher in the state.

James had set aside more than $40 million for teachers' pay raises in the first budget figures he worked with—the original $70-$80 million proposal for his War on Illiteracy. Lager said that James did not abandon his plans to give teachers pay raises when he removed them from his War.

"Pay raises belonged in the budget as a line item," Lager said, "not as a part of the War on Illiteracy." Instead of pointing this out to legislators and news media during Hubbert's harangue, James sat down with pencil and paper and budget figures to "find" the money for the raises. Each month he eagerly seized the reports from Revenue Commissioner Ralph Eagerton, searching for an indication that revenue would increase.

In June, he found some of the money for which he searched. Tax revenue had increased—proration could be cut from 6 percent to 3 percent. Because there was a gap of several months between the time the tax revenue increased and the time the increase became apparent, a surplus had built up for those months. James announced that the surplus could be used to fund a 7 percent pay raise for teachers. He added the pay raise to his Education Budget, which was in the House.

It was at that point that the McCorquodale-Hubbert feud flared.

The flare-up came after James accepted a suggestion made by McCorquodale, Don Bryan said. McCorquodale suggested that the pay raise be a "conditional" one, conditional upon the revenue being available.

"Joe knew the uproar it would bring from Hubbert, knew it would pit Fob as an adversary against Hubbert," Bryan said, "but Fob didn't see where the wording made any big difference. The revenue projections showed the money would be available. If it was available, he would fund the raise. If the money wasn't there, he couldn't fund it anyway."

A 25-year-veteran legislator, it is inconceivable that McCorquodale did not realize Hubbert would muster all his forces to fight against putting the restriction on the pay raise.

It is a tribute to Hubbert's genius that he could turn James' proposal for a teacher pay-raise into negative publicity for James.

"For a while there seemed to be a compromise that would work," the *Journal* wrote. "The governor would cough up half of the $20 million. It would have guaranteed that at least some of the conditional raise for the teachers would be paid. Hubbert, though, said no deal."

Hubbert would settle for only one thing, the *Journal* stated. He wanted to take James' entire $20 million War on Illiteracy funding for the pay raise.

James would sooner have given up every reform piece of legislation he intended to sponsor during his entire term than to think of abandoning his "war."

The battle raged on.

Meanwhile, James time and time again encouraged legislators to turn down proposals to spend money which he knew wasn't there.

The Judicial Compensation Commission recommended a 22 percent pay raise for judges. Under an unusual law, any increase recommended by the commission became law unless a legislative committee decided it should be put before the Legislature for a vote and it was voted against.

Under James' urging, that is exactly what legislators did. On July 13, both houses rejected the judicial pay raise. A compromise was worked out instead, linking a smaller hike for judges of $6,500 with an up-to-seven-percent increase to all state employees. The raises would be conditional upon the money being available. The compromise was approved by the House.

Reps. Roy Johnson of Tuscaloosa and Cecil Wyatt of Ramer admitted to reporters after reluctantly supporting the bill that employees might not get anything from the conditional pay raises. But, they said, it would be the only chance state workers had for a raise.

The state employees/judges pay raises were approved in the Senate in a stormy session which lasted until 3 a.m.

It was obvious when time came to vote on the conditional pay raise for teachers that Hubbert would defeat it in the Senate unless a senator could be persuaded to change his vote.

The lieutenant governor was firmly in control and at that time firmly in support of James' programs.

An observer describes how the "one senator" was convinced to change his vote: McMillan leaned from his chair on the dais and spoke to Sen. Richmond Pearson, who served in the prestigious position of chairman of the Finance and Taxation Committee at the pleasure of the lieutenant governor. He said, "Richmond, change your vote."

Pearson did. The conditional pay raise was approved in what writer Phillip Rawls called a "slightly different" form than the one approved by the House.

The Senate version was a victory for James. It left it up to him to determine quarterly "how much—if any—raises education personnel would get by judging the growth rate of state education revenues."

Hubbert, however, was successful in temporarily removing from the War on Illiteracy the funding which was to provide liability insurance for teachers.

"I can't predict the economy, but I think teachers can expect a minimum of 5 percent and hopefully 7 percent," James announced the morning after the bill passed.

"I will do everything in my power to make sure they get it," James said of the teacher raise.

James had won round one, but several opportunities awaited Hubbert in round two.

Because the Senate version of the education budget differed from the House-passed version, it had to be approved by the House.

The *Advertiser* predicted that House members aligned with the Alabama Education Association would try again to keep the budget from passing.

If the House refused to approve the Senate version, a joint conference committee from both Houses would work out a compromise budget which would have to be approved by the House and the Senate. If this happened, AEA forces would get another chance to kill the budget, the *Advertiser* pointed out.

Hubbert informed teachers that James would not give them their raise if it was conditional upon him finding the money.

"The money's not there. I don't know where he will find the money," Hubbert said. During House debate on the education budget, the Senate took up bills which had been held over, including one to give Medicaid a $9 million supplemental appropriation.

The bill was an obvious attempt to embarrass James, who after burning the midnight oil for months had announced cost-cutting measures he predicted would bail Medicaid out of its perilous financial condition.

"Gov. James is fighting the bill," the *Advertiser* wrote. "While agreeing that Medicaid is in financial distress, James is hoping the program will get by on 21 cost-cutting measures that (he will) institute Oct. 1. They are supposed to save $26 million, if they are all approved by the federal government."

When the last budget vote of 1979 had been taken, it was clear that James won, though he had to settle for $10 million for his War on Illiteracy. The other $10 million was to be put in reserve. Hubbert was unable to prevent James from providing teachers with insurance, however. From the time James signed the budget, every teacher in Alabama was provided at state cost a $128 per year liability insurance policy.

With only one day left in the session, Bryant wrote, "Alabama legislators will have plenty of work on the final day of the 1979 regular session today, but the conclusion of this session will be different from most in recent years.

"The major difference is that both budget bills, appropriating a total of about $1.5 billion from the general fund and the Special Education Trust Fund, have been approved before the final day."

Some 300 bills were passed by the Legislature that session and sent to James for his signature. During the legislative session a bill automatically becomes law if the governor does not veto it within six working days (Sundays are excluded.)

James vetoed a bill during the session which abolished the journal which annually listed all state salaries.

Legislators overrode his veto.

An aide to James said he vetoed it because "it conflicted with his desire for open government."

After the session, James talked to reporters at a news conference.

"James didn't get all he wanted, but as a freshman governor and a new politician, he probably got more than he anticipated," *Birmingham News* reporter Al Fox wrote.

"He was attired with coat and tie as TV cameras ran. But once he determined that the film was not rolling, he pulled off his coat, loosened his tie, rolled up his shirt-sleeves and accepted a cigar from a newsman and once again became the governor that reporters have come to recognize—although he is sometimes hard to find," Fox wrote.

"...James heaped praise on legislative leaders for guiding through part of his main programs. Defeated programs, such as the gas tax, served as an educational experience," Roy Summerford wrote in the *Advertiser.*

What happened to the constitution?

As recounted by UPI: "With Lt. Gov. George McMillan beating the drum, the Senate passed a diluted version midway in the regular session."

> But the House leadership made certain that time ran out before the House could consider three of the 15 articles a House committee approved.
>
> ...Recall, which some lawmakers viewed as a threat on their jobs, was rejected and initiative drew mixed reviews.
>
> Proposed home rule was controversial because it was broader than merely having constitutional amendments on local issues voted on by the areas affected, instead of requiring statewide votes.
>
> The AEA skillfully blocked James' plan to take earmarking of revenue out of the constitution and make...(it) a legislative decision...

Who, if anyone, was "to blame" for the failure to get a new constitution passed?

Hubbert blames McCorquodale, whom he says "sabotaged" its passage.

"It should have been updated," Hubbert said, "but McCorquodale didn't want it. There is nothing McCorquodale wanted passed which wasn't passed and nothing McCorquodale opposed which passed."

Waters commented in an article appearing at the time that McCorquodale was not "sold on a new constitution."

"In some ways it might have been too ambitious an undertaking. With a new governor and all of us new in coming in...with the education and the gas tax programs...that was a lot the first session," Waters said.

James took his defeats with a challenge flung at those responsible for its demise.

Over the next six months, he warned, the legislation he would introduce would put Goat Hill to a test as to "whether elected officials can listen and then look certain groups right in the eye and say no."

In 1989, James looked back on the fiasco as a learning experience.

"I went into office thinking the governor ought to save the state from wild goose chases," he said. "And the only wild goose chase in my administration—and I was the quarterback on that one—was that well-intended but wrongly conceived excursion into the new constitution."

With hindsight, James agrees with McCorquodale that he should never have asked the legislature to rewrite the entire document at once.

"That's not the way to do it. I was wrong," James said. "The way to do it is by amendments, to take it section by section and rewrite one section at a time, get each section passed and get it approved."

He does not waver from his view that a new constitution is needed, however.

And he is firmer than ever in his insistence that the new constitution must allow voters to kick an elected official out of office before the end of his term if the official isn't doing his job.

Initiative, referendum and recall, tools of good government available to citizens of other states since the twenties, should be in the hands of Alabamians, James says.

After the legislative session ended, James' aides sat down to figure out how effective they had been.

It was something they would do after each legislative session.

Geddie said that over the four years they got about 80 percent of everything they wanted passed.

"We had an amazingly high batting record," he said. "The press did not focus on the overall picture, however. They focused on things like unearmarking and the gas tax, which were big, but were only part of the picture."

Another reason for the misperception that James could not get his legislation passed was the fact that it took more than one session to pass most of his key bills, Geddie said.

"Many things took two years to pass, like the gas tax. We passed it the second time around, but the criticism from not getting it through the first time around had stuck in people's minds.

"What Fob did—and it's one of the great things about him but also one of his deficiencies—he plowed ahead in an attempt to solve every problem the state had in a four-year period," Geddie said. "He might in one session have 25 reform bills before the legislature when other governors would not have had a single one. Maybe a quarter of his reform passed, so Fob was labeled a failure. No matter that he accomplished five times what any other governor had ever done, in this view he was a failure."

The laws passed by James that first session affirm Geddie's contention.

James' bill to increase the gas tax was defeated in the House so solidly that Bryan remembers the occasion as "the most humiliating experience of my life." It would be brought back and passed the next year.

His bill also died to allow wine to be sold in retail outlets, such as grocery and convenience stores. It would be re-introduced in the future and passed.

James successfully passed a bill which would later be recognized as a milestone in his efforts to replace cronyism and favoritism in state government with good business practices. It put an end to liquor agents and off-brands which had dominated the state liquor business for many years. The bill removed a 3 percent distiller's tax on alcoholic beverages which had forced major distributors to remove their brands from Alabama's state store shelves in order to live up to a nation-wide agreement between major companies to sell to all states at an equal price.

James' successes that first session also included:

• A bill which allowed the substitution of generic drugs for brand name drugs, which *Alabama Journal* reporter Lou Elliott wrote "is expected to save consumers thousands of dollars."

- Game and Fish bills which increased the penalty for out-of-state residents caught hunting without a license from $10 to $25 and invoked stiffer penalties for persons convicted of buying or selling game birds or animals.
- A bill replacing annual vehicle tags with five-year ones to be updated yearly with stickers. Their purchase would be staggered alphabetically, ending decades of block-long lines for annual tag sales.
- A bill turning over the prison system to James, a formality since federal Judge Frank M. Johnson Jr. had earlier ordered the prison system placed under James as receiver.
- A bill increasing the fine for littering from a $10 to $100 range to a $100 to $500 range.

If James had given himself eight years to pass everything and had spread his legislation over those eight years, Geddie said, "I have no doubt he would have been very successful in getting the Legislature to approve every reform he wanted."

Hubbert after the first session was obviously chafing over his loss to James on the liability insurance and the entire War on Illiteracy. He immediately jumped on the new governor because the pay raise for teachers was conditional upon tax revenues bringing in enough money to fund it. News articles reflect that Hubbert used the issue to increase AEA membership through fiery speeches to teachers and through editorials in his *AEA Journal* which went to 93 percent of the teachers in the state.

Judges would get a raise, but teachers would not, Hubbert said.

There was not-so-veiled talk of a strike by teachers.

It was because of a suggestion from a long time merit system employee James had promoted to department head that James was able to come up with the first increment of the money for the pay raises.

Soon after James took office, Jan. 29, Phillip Rawls had written in the *Advertiser* that Revenue Commissioner Ralph Eagerton had suggested the state could pick up an extra $25 million a year in tax money if it actively checked out the inventories of out-of-state corporations which had Alabama plants. James immediately gave Eagerton the go-ahead.

On Dec. 10th the *Journal* observed, "The orchestration was a little spotty, but the timing was spectacular. Shortly before the AEA's Delegate Assembly was scheduled to vote on a resolution for a strike if the state teachers got no pay raise by January, Gov. Fob James resumed his role as resident magician and pulled another rabbit out of his capacious hat."

He had for some time made it clear state workers would get a raise, but was "pointedly noncommittal" about the conditional raise for teachers...there "was a rumor the governor wasn't going out of his way to find the money to teach Hubbert and AEA a political lesson..."

> Tuesday, Joe Dawkins, an advisor to the governor's Committee on Education, told the committee, "Chances for a pay raise are certainly slim this year."
>
> Then came the announcement, which left even Hubbert a little breathless. Of course, the AEA chief said, he was "elated" at the news, but at the same time he confessed to being "somewhat perplexed" about where the money was going to come from.
>
> But that, of course, was the real kicker. Instead of trying to reshuffle an already straitened budget, James hired a gang of 30 auditors to hit the home offices of out-of-state corporations that do business in Alabama for uncollected taxes. They managed to haul in $15 million worth, enough to pay for the teachers' raises...
>
> Since the state employees' raise is going to come from the $20 million James' cost-cutting drive has saved, it almost looks as though Alabama taxpayers are going to get a pair of fairly sizeable somethings for nothing. And if that's not magic in these inflation ridden times, it must be something even better.

# The Beginning

Toward the end of the 1979 school year, James was able to put in place the first phase of his education reform which Wayne Teague 10 years later would term the "shining light" of the James administration—his "Model Schools Program." After testing students to provide a benchmark in each school system on which to base future comparisons, teams of educators chosen from statewide applications were sent to fight the War on Illiteracy in school systems in which students' test scores were lowest.

After a two-week training session, the 29 teachers who made up the four basic skill teams fanned out into schools which had requested their help. Members of the skills teams had been selected from 375 who had applied. Each team had experts in math, language arts, reading, special education and teachers who could help classroom teachers in programs.

The skill teams received invitations from more than 30 schools in the state's 127 systems.

"The goal is truly and simply to find ways to assist those kids in improving academic achievement. This is a new concept," said Dr. William Berryman, coordinator for the Department of Education.

Team members could do demonstration teaching, but would not take over classrooms.

The state was divided into 12 districts.

"Those teachers will move into those districts. They will live in those towns," James said. "Where illiteracy reigns supreme, we're going to put more teachers in there from the Department of Education."

The skills teams were only one part of the War, Dr. Robert Lager reminded reporters. It was also in the plan to select 12 to 14 of the lowest-scoring schools in the state to include in the model schools program. A third thrust of James' War was the addition of 200 kindergartens which had been added in late August at a cost of $3.8 million. The fourth War effort was to provide money for emergency construction for the worst overcrowded schools. Millbrook's Robinson Springs School was the first school to receive $50,000 to relieve overcrowding.

There was increased activity in education statewide, including increased funding for K–12, and a new requirement by the State Board of Education that teachers had to pass a competency test before they could be certified to teach.

The chief opposition to James' War on Illiteracy came from Hubbert.

"The AEA 'School Journal,' one of the most acidic political organs published in this state, has already started reflecting Hubbert's strategy for the next five months," Elliott wrote on August 12.

She referred to an edition which included a cartoon of Lager, education adviser, with a Pilgrim hat on his head and a blunderbuss over his shoulder. Smiling in response were three men labeled "Lager's experts" who carried a variety of crude weapons and a sign reading, "teachers beware."

"The purpose of this cartoon is easy to understand—to create an atmosphere of apprehension and hostility toward the governor's program," the *Advertiser* wrote in an editorial. "Having battled the literacy program in the Capitol, and lost, the AEA now appears to be waging another battle in each and every classroom in the state.

> Despite the AEA's hostility, there is little for any teacher to fear. The experts who will be working in the literacy program are nothing more dangerous than experienced master teachers and administrators chosen from local schools, and their purpose — as explosive as modeling clay — is to record impressions and make suggestions about what can be done in the classroom.
>
> Few are the teachers who wouldn't welcome a visitor who might offer some helpful suggestions and that's the primary purpose of the governor's program. It's generally agreed that most school principals and teaching supervisors are too busy to spend as much time as they should helping others teach better, but the literacy teams won't have any other responsibilities. They'll be at liberty to brainstorm with teachers and be in an ideal position to spot problems that are never apparent when you're in the classroom day after day.

It was the new state-supplied liability insurance upon which Hubbert focused most intently, however.

To James, the issue was clear and was simple. He thought it "dead wrong for the state not to provide the liability coverage for teachers. particularly in this day of everybody suing everybody."

The October issue of Hubbert's *Journal* carried an ad which supposedly gave an objective comparison of AEA's teacher liability policy with the new policy provided by the state.

"The AEA policy clearly has the advantage in the ad," the Associated Press wrote in reporting that State School Superintendent Wayne Teague had asked Insurance Commissioner Hal Sumrall to do his own comparison of the two policies.

Sumrall made the comparison, then objected to Hubbert's ad as "misleading, incorrect and deceptive."

His report to Teague concluded that both policies were "virtually identical," AP reported.

The *School Journal* carried the ad again in November. No matter how strongly Hubbert opposed the state providing liability insurance, however, he was not able to do away with it until a few months after James' term as governor expired.

"Education had been the key pitch of his campaign," Ralph Holmes later wrote of the year of 1979. "So when he faced his first regular session of the Legislature, he came forward with what he called a "War on Illiteracy."

> He asked for money to put teams of teachers (into substandard schools).
> The Legislature agreed, after a good deal of lofty rhetoric. Though James didn't get as much money as the $20 million he asked for, he made a point: He was going to fight for better education, but he was going to do it his way.
> A lot of teachers didn't like that...

Holmes interviewed James at the end of 1979. The governor summed up his first year in office as one of "operations," a year of identifying what areas need attention.

James praised McMillan for the way in which he handled the State Senate. "No man has ever presided over a Senate fairer in the history of our state..."

> Of his Public Safety Department, James said it has made more drug arrests last year, working with local law enforcement groups, than in the past decade.
> The Highway Department has saved money, operated more efficiently than in the past. The Conservation Department is cutting costs and operating state parks more efficiently.
> Pensions and Security, James said, is first in the nation in tracking down fathers who are not supporting their children.
> A new law pushed by James aided the task of collecting delinquent child support by allowing the state to withhold tax rebates from those who are behind in support payments.
> James praised the state's National Guard for being tops in the nation in strength and for responding to emergencies during the last year..."The Guard is out of politics..."
> When he campaigned for governor two years ago, he rode a yellow and black school bus he called his "Reading, 'Riting and 'Rithmetic Special." The campaign pitch was to get back to the basics in education.
> The theme hasn't changed.
> He wants more emphasis put on the training of principals. He wants to know exactly the teacher-pupil ratio in each classroom. He wants to start at the kindergarten program and first build an educational foundation through the sixth grade, then go on to high school and then to higher education.
> James repeated his promise to run government on a pay-as-you-go basis.

"Debt indiscriminately passed on to the next generation is wrong," said James.

"In the second year, we meet the major issues and we meet them head on," James said. "We are going to bring this state face to face with reality."

One of those major issues, Holmes wrote, is the Medicaid program. It is ten years old and now costs the state's general fund $70 million a year and the federal government another $250 million.

"At the rate we are going it will bankrupt Alabama under its current structure," James said. "We have done everything to find a cost containment factor, but we are restricted by federal regulations."

One of the problems with Medicaid, according to James, is that no effort has ever been made to inform the public fully about how the program works and who pays for what. James plans to change that.

In the past, he said, only temporary stopgap methods have been used to deal with Medicaid funding.

"We are looking for a long-range permanent solution. That has never been done before. There have never been any permanent taxes passed...for the Medicaid program..."

With his first year as governor as a learning period, James is ready to launch his new programs.

"I feel like the upcoming legislative session is the most important in the history of the state," he said of the 1980 legislative session.

# — 7 —

# A Disastrous Year

No time is a good time for a major disaster. But for a state wallowing in debt and proration, the toll taken by a flood or hurricane is devastating.

James encountered all of these his first nine months in office. Two presidential disaster declarations encompassed one-third of the state's 67 counties, and damage occurred far outside the official boundary lines for disaster aid.

Major flooding hit west central Alabama after torrential spring rains.

By April 20, some 1,000 people in the Black Belt of Alabama had been forced to flee their homes as the Tombigbee River crested 24 feet above flood stage. At 72.4 feet, the crest was the highest water on record since the area was settled in 1818.

The flooding was caused by torrential rain for a 28-hour-period in which six people died in flood-related accidents in Alabama.

Flooding was worst around Demopolis, where the swollen waters of the Black Warrior merged with the overflowing Tombigbee. Alabama Air National Guard helicopters hovered for days as guardsmen scanned the countryside below for white sheets which were spread on the ground to signal distress.

Two National Guardsmen were injured when a trailer collapsed as they were loading cattle on barges to move them to safety.

James joined guardsmen aboard a helicopter, using a loudspeaker to urge citizens to leave the area before flood waters rose too high.

As the surge of flooding moved from north to south, National Guard, State Troopers and Civil Defense workers moved with them, opening armories for the homeless, feeding the hungry.

"As all this water moves into Mobile, the bay will probably increase in length by 20 miles," National Weather Service forecaster Sam Baker predicted.

By the time flood waters peaked at Bayou Sara just above Mobile Bay April 26, hundreds of Mobile Countians had been evacuated and county officials called the flooding the worst in 18 years.

James asked President Carter to declare 24 counties in west-central and south Alabama as disaster areas. Carter did, which made federal money available through the state for the aftermath.

The flooding was costly to the state.

In an article in the Birmingham *News,* Thomas F. Hill reported that Dallas County was hit hardest, with 4,711 forced by flooding to stand in food stamp lines. Other counties in which food lines formed included Autauga, Chilton, Elmore, Etowah, Greene, Hale, Jefferson, Marengo, Montgomery, Pickens, St. Clair, Shelby, Sumter, Talladega, Tuscaloosa and Walker.

By May 20, more than 10,000 flood victims in 17 Alabama counties had been fed with purchases made with more than $500,000 in food stamps. Pensions and Security Department Director Gary Cooper pointed out that 8,000 of the recipients would not have been eligible if not for approval of the disaster relief program by the U.S. Department of Agriculture.

Additionally, there were 1,213 applications to the department for emergency grants of up to $5,000.

"The Department of Pensions and Security responds whenever there is a disaster to assess what kind of welfare help the people need," explained a DPS spokesperson who estimated the flooding would cost some $1.3 million in welfare funds. The money was spent for repair work, temporary housing, clothing and in some cases automobiles.

## The Second Disaster

On the night of Sept. 12, 1979, Hurricane Frederic slammed its way into Gulf Coast history as it savagely battered tens of thousands of homes, uprooted trees by the hundreds of thousands and left 167,000 of the 170,000 customers in the Mobile district of Alabama Power without electricity.

Around 10 a.m. the morning of the 12th, James and a small group of aides and law enforcement officers flew in the state jet to the coast "white-knuckled" from being bounced around in the turbulence which preceded Frederic.

Alabama's governor of nine months rode out the hurricane in the Department of Public Safety command post trailer. It was securely lashed to the ground on a hill at Spanish Fort overlooking Mobile Bay, only a few miles from where the eye of the hurricane passed.

A central command post was necessary to maintain communications with local law enforcement officials, hospitals, emergency units, Civil Defense and the National Guard after the hurricane knocked out telephones and power and made roads and streets impassable.

James later talked about the night to Clarke Stallworth of the Birmingham *News*:

> "We knew that when that thing came over there, there would be no communications, so we put the trailer [there]...Well, the word leaked out that the governor was in a trailer at the top of a hill during the hurricane, and a lot of people questioned the governor's sanity. What they didn't know was that it was an all-steel piece of machinery, with a lot of sophisticated communications equipment and it weighed about 100,000 pounds.
>
> "But even so, the night the hurricane came in the bay, around 11 o'clock, that baby got to shaking pretty good. We put a tank retriever, a big heavy piece of equipment, on one side and a bulldozer on the other, and strapped it down with nylon rope.
>
> "It's funny now, but Gen. [Henry] Cobb and Col. [Jerry] Shoemaker had some anxious moments when that thing started shaking," James said. "You get into a situation like that and there are a lot of laws...the use of the Guard, calling for a state emergency...oftentimes decisions have to be made on the spot. [Shoemaker says what was worrying him was that he knew if anything happened to the governor of the state, he would be the one who had to take responsibility.]
>
> "We had questions to answer like: Shall the Guard go here or there? How many units do we bring in from Decatur? You've got looting over there, how hard are you going to hit it? Is it just a few kids or wholesale looting?
>
> "We had a closer feel for the situation. In that command trailer, we were in a lot better position to make the right decisions," James said.

In the early dawn light, James first heard of the damage by telephone, then took to the air by helicopter to see for himself, Shoemaker said.

The damage was unbelievable and impossible to describe unless you actually saw it.

Entire neighborhoods were blocked in by fallen pines, hickory and oak trees, many of which were aged trees which had resisted hurricanes for far more than a century. Power lines lay on the ground. Flies buzzed in the late summer heat as parents managed as best they could to keep children supplied with fresh milk and meat in homes in which refrigerators were useless without power.

The long water bridge to Dauphin Island was twisted and sections were missing. Debris cluttered waterways and turned the bay and the gulf into obstacle courses for marine traffic. The west end of the island, once a seemingly endless row of beach houses, was stripped almost bare of man's efforts.

On the other side of the bay, nothing, not even the foundation, remained of a huge two-story home next to James' house on the west beach of Gulf Shores. His house, which he had engineered purposely on deeply sunk pilings, still stood "but bleeding" as he put it.

Nowhere was the economic consequence to state government more visible than at the Alabama State Docks, where every roof on the giant sprawling facility was either knocked off or heavily damaged. Dock operations were paralyzed by the hurricane. The lack of electric power to operate port machinery—much of which could not be used until repaired—meant a massive backup of cargoes, docks director Robert M. Hope told news media.

Initial damage estimates to the docks topped $10.5 million.

All export-import shipments through the docks were halted. Barge traffic from upstream could not get past the sunken barges beneath Cochrane Bridge on the Mobile River north of the docks. Railroad traffic was at a standstill due to the presence of heavy power lines which had fallen on the tracks.

Two of the docks' three cranes which unload ships were destroyed at a $3 million cost. Before they could be replaced, however, a $3.5 million dock holding them up had to be replaced.

James took advantage of the constitutional powers invested in the chief executive to take charge of a coordinated emergency effort.

Within hours, the interstate between Mobile and Montgomery which had been jammed the day before with northbound traffic fleeing the hurricane was congested with southbound state vehicles and workers sent by James, each with a specific mission.

Even the air was crowded.

From the state military department came four small helicopters, three larger Huey helicopters and one "flying crane," as well as 70 Jeeps, 30 two-and-a-half ton trucks, 15 five-ton and up trucks, five 1,000-gallon water tankers, eight 450-gallon water trailers, 25 dump trucks, six front-end loaders and a large amount of emergency cooking equipment.

The public safety department sent two wreckers, two trucks and 200 trooper vehicles.

The Highway Department sent 40 dump trucks, 30 pickup trucks with radios, eight sign trucks and front-end loaders and four cranes and signal crews with cherry pickers.

State Highway Department crews were sent to Mobile to help clear roads blocked with trees, power poles and debris.

State Insurance Commissioner Hal Sumrall sent adjusters to set up temporary claims centers.

Mobile officials told news media that James had sent some 2,000 workers into the area to help, including 1,200 from the State Military Department, 250 from the Department of Public Safety and 140 from the State Highway Department.

The state Forestry Commission dispatched about 95 people equipped with truck and tractor units, power saws and communications systems, coordinating with James and Civil Defense personnel.

James R. Hylands of Forestry's protective division began an assessment of the damage to the state's forest resources. It was estimated the hurricane damaged 2.3 billion board feet of timber, more than was harvested in a full year in the state, for a $333.4 million loss.

The report prompted James to name a special committee of timber, wood products and paper mill officials to determine what could be salvaged. The 28-member Forest Disaster Recovery Council met in Jackson 11 days after Frederic.

The Forestry Commission, working with NASA and the U.S. Forest Service to make aerial photographs of the damage, was working on a deadline. Following on the heels of a pine beetle infestation, the storm had snapped many trees off at the ground. They had to be harvested in five to six weeks.

"If we have a drought in October, it will be extremely bad because of forest fires. They won't be able to get in to fight them because the roads are still blocked," warned Joe McCorquodale.

One week after Frederic, James took action not hitherto taken by a governor.

Taking advantage of an empowering section in the state code, James issued an emergency proclamation giving himself extensive power to deal with the emergency brought about by Frederic "without regard to the limitations of any existing laws."

The section of the state code allowing such a proclamation stipulates that the governor must call the Legislature into session upon issuing the proclamation, but James ignored the stipulation after a consultation with legislative leaders.

Later that day he went on statewide television to inform the rest of the state that south Alabama was facing a grave situation.

"We've just run out of food," James said. "...I believe if Alabamians have a way to make a contribution to this stricken area, they will. We're just trying to provide the logistics."

He appealed in the 6:30 p.m. broadcast to citizens to bring food to the state's 115 National Guard armories, explaining the emergency existed due to hot days, a lack of refrigeration and the fact that many grocery stores were still closed.

James also appealed to trucking companies and independent truckers, asking them to volunteer their rigs. A guard spokesman said the private response was "just tremendous."

Within 15 minutes, Warrant Officer Willie Barrow reported from one of three Montgomery armories, "There were so many people calling me they had to call me in extra help."

About 40 people arrived with food at the Huntsville armory before 9 p.m.

In Selma, donors provided "a good pickup truck load" within hours.

Three truck loads of food were collected within hours at a Montgomery shopping center.

Thousands of pounds of food were unloaded in Mobile within 36 hours, as 56 trucks from various state armories converged on the city.

It was not a moment too soon. Some 2,000 hungry people were waiting in line in Mobile when the food stamp center opened, making it impossible to serve them all in one day. Department of Pensions and Security Director Gary Cooper said in rural areas it was taking people two days to make it through the food stamp line.

National Guardsmen, guided by engineers relying on grid maps of

Mobile, had first worked moving trees which were blocking strategic roads. They then geared their efforts toward fulfilling requests from city officials.

In the first week more than 52,000 people obtained food stamps.

The state paid a direct price for Hurricane Frederic, a price which would be visible on the bottom line of ledger sheets for years to come.

It was visible immediately after the hurricane in the form of an announcement by Finance Director David Bronner.

The hurricane had paralyzed the second-largest tax-producing city in the state. Bronner projected a $15 million loss to the state in sales tax in September, which meant there would be no money for schools and education in the last month of the fiscal year.

Schools had been under 6 percent proration since March, which would have resulted in a $60 million cut in spending.

James had reduced that to 3 percent in June and to 2 percent in August.

It had been the hope that proration could be reduced further, Bronner said, but that hope blew out the door with Frederic.

Because of the flooding and the hurricane, James got the chance to work more closely with the state Civil Defense department in his first nine months in office than he otherwise would have done in his entire four-year term.

James found Civil Defense unprepared to cope with major disasters, disorganized and lacking equipment he had assumed would be basic. He also heard allegations of payoffs and kickbacks, of equipment which disappeared or was not used for the purpose for which it was intended.

James, not knowing if the allegations were true or false, was therefore wary of Civil Defense. He was, however, greatly impressed with the National Guard.

When James named 10-year veteran Civil Defense worker Sam B. Slone III as Civil Defense director, he announced that Slone would not report to the governor, as in the past, but to military Adjutant General Henry H. Cobb Jr.

"I am committed to support Gen. Cobb and Sam Slone in their efforts to develop a disaster response program second to none in the nation," was all that James said publicly.

He did not mention that he had asked the Department of Public Safety to quietly initiate an investigation into allegations which had been made.

The investigation culminated in early summer of 1980, when James decided the evidence uncovered by Public Safety should be turned over to a prosecutor.

Quietly, without a public announcement, James handed over to Montgomery District Attorney Jimmy Evans the results of his investigation into Civil Defense.

The matter came to public attention in June, when James suspended almost one third of the Civil Defense Department, "all of my key people," as Slone later put it.

The 10 people who were suspended had headed up and worked in the Mobile Disaster Housing Assistance Office.

News reports of the investigation surfaced when Civil Defense records filling several filing cabinets were taken into custody by Evans.

Evans confirmed an investigation of alleged kickbacks involving federal money spent to tow mobile homes to Mobile to house the homeless. He said James had asked him to investigate the allegations.

Among those suspended by James were Lee Killough, Civil Defense's southern area coordinator, and Toofie Deep Jr., his deputy.

Before the investigation was concluded, it spread across three states and resulted in prosecutions in state and federal courts. It was more than seven years before all aspects of the probe would be settled.

For two years, the public had no reason to believe the investigation's scope included more than the theft of a portable building.

In September of 1980, Deep was indicted and charged with stealing the portable building, which had been purchased with $1,684 in federal disaster funds. It was seized at Deep's residence by Evans.

Deep was convicted in November, 1980, and later sentenced to three years in prison.

At Deep's trial, Killough testified he had approved moving the storage building from Mobile to Deep's home.

Killough was indicted the next month, charged also with theft of the building. He also was convicted.

Two years later, in November, 1982, a federal grand jury in Montgomery spelled out the massive scale of the wrong-doing.

Deep, Killough and ten others including a state senator were indicted for alleged conspiracy to inflate the price of bids and contracts for mobile homes in order to provide $602,000 in kickbacks from Hurricane Frederic relief funds.

The kickbacks were said to range from $500 to $600 for each mobile home that was towed to the disaster area and hooked up to utilities.

The indictments stated eight Louisiana and Alabama contractors paid a total of $602,000 to Deep and that Deep paid $50,000 to Killough.

Deep and Killough pleaded guilty to conspiracy and filing false federal income tax returns and were sentenced in February 1983 to eight years in prison.

The contractors were sentenced to three years probation and fined $1,000 each.

Charges against the state senator were dropped after Montgomery U.S. Attorney John Bell announced a witness had lied about his involvement.

The sentencings did not end the saga of the hurricane money.

In September 1985 the Justice Department filed suit to recover $1.4 million from the defendants, which the government said was the total amount of the fraud involving some 1,100 mobile home hookups, the suit claimed.

State books were not closed on the affair until August of 1986 when an audit detailed the misspent money.

In addition to $685,800 in kickbacks, state examiners also criticized the payment of $430,603.59 to a contractor for building a 91-space mobile home park in Prichard. The contract had been only for $259,675.75. Additionally, examiners said problems had arisen from "poor workmanship."

In another incident, they also questioned the payment of $91,696.86 to a contractor for a 400-space mobile home park. He only built 308 spaces.

Also, two different contractors were paid for doing the same job, providing water and sewer service to certain mobile home spaces, examiners said.

In all, examiners said, more than $1.7 million of $13.8 million in federal disaster assistance to Frederic victims had been misspent.

Not once in the nearly seven years of investigations, trials, press conferences and audits was it mentioned that none of the above would have happened if the man sitting in the governor's chair at the time had not picked up his phone, called the man he named head of the Department of Public Safety and said, "Jerry, I want you to look into something for me."

# — 8 —

# Labor

James picked a union president to head the Alabama Department of Labor for a specific reason. Plants were closing nationwide. Workers were striking. James wanted a man who understood the needs of working men and women, who could work with both labor and management to mediate labor disputes. Jerry C. Ray, a plain-talking, even-tempered Marengo County man who had been president of Local 952 of United Paperworkers International, seemed to be the man he sought.

Ray took over an eight-person department with a $200,000 a year budget, charged with the task of ensuring fair labor laws. Ray would spend most of his time working with management and labor and coordinating with James. He had a tough job. Double-digit inflation deflated the buying power of paychecks while the recession made plant closings routine news.

The threat of strikes hung in the air.

In late April, the Birmingham City council voted to drop the Blue Cross insurance provided for city employees and replace it with a different policy.

City employees protested.

Police Sgt. Bill Gaut, chairman of the Fraternal Order of Police's job action committee, said current contracts under which city workers were employed called for negotiations with workers before any changes in insurance coverage could be made.

The city council voted the next week to reaffirm its earlier decision.

"Birmingham's police force went on strike Tuesday night...in a dispute over health insurance," the Associated Press wrote on May 2, 1979.

> A mass meeting of the four unions representing the various workers was held at the Fraternal Order of Police Lodge. The vote to strike was overwhelming.
> Policemen were told by their union not to report for the 11 p.m. shift. Members of the Laborers International Union and the Association of City Employees were not expected to return to their jobs Wednesday.

Jerry Shoemaker, then director of the Department of Public Safety, describes how the strike ended.

"Negotiations broke down. Neither side would talk," said Shoemaker. "Gov. James sent word to both sides that he wanted to talk to them, then he flew to Birmingham after dark. We met in a room at the airport."

Shoemaker said James brought along Ray, as well as National Guard Adjutant General Henry Cobb. Then–Birmingham Mayor David Vann met them at the airport with representatives of striking employees.

Shoemaker and Cobb were there as a show of commitment to provide police protection to Birmingham citizenry if necessary.

"If the strike could not be resolved, it would be up to my men and to Gen. Cobb's men to keep order," Shoemaker said. "I can't quote what the governor said exactly, but it went something like this: 'Okay, now, you boys have not been talking and that won't do. We are going to talk things over and work things out and we are going to stay here all night if we need to. If you don't work it out tonight, we'll stay here as long as you need. But we're going to talk.' "

Shoemaker said it was obvious from listening to the negotiations that both sides were concerned about the welfare of Birmingham citizens and both sides had good intentions. They just needed a catalyst to get them to talk.

They talked all night.

Bodyguard Gene Mitchell also remembers the incident: "We flew in to Birmingham at sundown and met with the mayor and a couple of commissioners and the leaders of various groups of firemen, police, etc. I handed the governor a cup of coffee at 6 a.m., he hadn't slept and nobody else had, and we headed back to Montgomery. The police or the mayor called a news conference after we left and announced the strike had been averted and nobody knew the governor had been there."

As usual, James kept a low profile, though some word seeped out that he had played some role in negotiations. When *Post-Herald* writer Ted Bryant, tongue-in-cheek, later searched for some reason to praise James in a column, he noted as praiseworthy James' "coming to Birmingham in the early morning hours and apparently laying some very straight talk on city officials and union representatives shortly before the city employee strike ended..."

No sooner had the Birmingham situation cooled off than a truckers' strike which had been brewing nationally heated to the boiling point.

In early June 5,000 truckers nationwide, members of the Independent Truckers Association, pulled their rigs off the highways protesting rising gasoline costs and restrictive laws.

The truckers had a long list of complaints, starting with the rising cost of diesel fuel and including imposition of the 55 mile-per-hour speed limit.

"The center for the independent trucking industry for the U.S. is in Birmingham," James Foy said. "The truckers' biggest problem was that they had signed contracts to move their loads for a certain amount. The price of gas had skyrocketed, which meant they were losing money every mile they were on the highway."

Dave Hammonds, president of the Independent Truckers Association of Alabama, zeroed in on two complaints: The need for all states to establish uniform weight and length laws for trucks, and the need to end federal "bridge" laws which require a certain length between front and rear axles to carry a certain amount of weight.

Truckers' gripes were not directed primarily toward Alabama. In most states, Hammonds told AP, the ceiling on truck weight was 80,000 pounds. The ceiling on Alabama bridges was legally 73,280 pounds, but long-haul truckers were not concerned because the law was not enforced on interstates. It was enforced on state bridges, however, which meant coal haulers, gravel haulers and others could not haul the 80,000 pounds they could elsewhere. The truckers' ire was directed toward a band of states which were enforcing the 73,280 pound limit on all roadways, including Mississippi, Iowa and Missouri.

Near the end of the first week of the nationwide "shutdown," a spokesman for independent truckers claimed 90 percent of all trucks in Alabama had been taken off the road.

A Georgia trucker's wife, Linda Pruett, was critically injured when a gunshot was fired into her husband's rig near Tuscaloosa.

James' response was to activate the National Guard, saying, "I will mobilize every resource in this state to protect all Alabama citizens and insure the safe passage of all traffic—private and commercial."

He called Shoemaker and Cobb to a meeting in his office. Guard spokesman Norman Arnold announced after the meeting that military police would join state troopers in organizing non-strikers into convoys of trucks which would be escorted with troopers and guardsmen at the front and rear. He did not reveal that James would ride with convoy.

Every segment of the state economy felt the effects of the strike. Farmers who feared to load their crops on trucks to take to the market suffered heavy losses as unharvested crops wilted in the fields in the blistering heat.

On June 20, James spoke to the Rotary Club in Opelika. The increasingly violent atmosphere of the truckers' shutdown was on his mind.

Guy Rhodes wrote: "'Plainclothes troopers are being used to drive some trucks,' James said. 'And if anyone tries to stop them from driving, we arrest them on the spot.'"

He was not without sympathy for the truckers.

> "They have some tough problems, some problems we are going to have to come to grips with," he pointed out. "Trucks with 13 to 17 gears are made to operate at 65 miles per hour, not 55 miles per hour, and contrary to what you may think, the 55 mile-per-hour speed is being enforced in most states."

Several hours later a Birmingham man, Robert Tate, was shot to death while driving down U.S. 72 near Tuscumbia.

James told Alabamians he would put the state "under full martial law" rather than see it paralyzed.

That night, James sent National Guard transportation units to North Alabama in Guard tankers to make gasoline runs.

James flew to the North Alabama cities hit hardest by the truckers' shutdown to meet with law enforcement and public officials and to hold news conferences to urge independent truckers to action.

The *News* wrote:

> "I advocate every man and woman defend themselves if their
> life or property is threatened — with everything at their disposal,"
> a tough-talking Gov. Fob James said grimly Wednesday evening.
>
> Gov. James was answering representatives of the trucking in-
> dustry who said their drivers were afraid to drive because of the
> independent truckers strike.
>
> James' statement came during a meeting the governor held with
> civic and other law enforcement officials and others in Birmin-
> gham...Earlier in the day the governor held similar sessions in
> Muscle Shoals and Huntsville.

James then flew from town to town in a National Guard helicopter
which landed at what reporters described as "troublesome spots"
where James "confronted angry truckers in person."

He also visited with poultry growers who had publicly stated they
were afraid to drive their chickens to market.

"After hearing reports of blockades by truckers at a certain inter-
section, James obtained a camper and followed a decoy truck to the
area to see what would happen," one reporter wrote. "There was no
incident and nervous security men were thankful."

Truckers nationwide halted the strike after five weeks, with James
praised in editorials for holding down further violence by his tough
stance.

Something good came out of the truckers' strike.

"The strike resulted in gasoline shortages in spots around the
state. Combined with the international energy crunch, the crisis focused the minds of state leaders on energy," wrote Jack E. Ravan,
head of the Alabama Department of Energy.

There was no such department at the time of the strike. The was
only the Energy Management Board, which existed as the vehicle
required by federal law to implement federally-funded energy conservation measures.

After the strike, members of the Legislative Committee on Energy
worked with James and the staff of the Energy Management Board to
come up with a state energy plan. Input was sought from public and
private agencies.

In May of 1980, James created the first cabinet-level Energy Department. It was placed under the governor and advised by a "broad-
based" committee of 27.

In 1981, the department received $350,000 "for ensuring Alabama's energy future through increased energy management, conservation, and resource development." It was the first line item ever included in the Alabama budget for energy problems, said Ravan, a former official of the Environmental Protection Agency who was hired by James to head the Energy Department.

The Energy Department grew. In 1982, it reaped a $1.1 million bonanza when the state in the settlement of a lawsuit against Chevron U.S.A. stipulated that the money be used for energy-related projects. State funding was nearly tripled, to $5.9 million in 1982. Employees were increased from 13 to 27.

The agency could point to unique accomplishments.

A toll-free hot line was put in service to provide Alabamians with information about the federal and state energy programs available to them. The biggest program was one in which the homes of the needy were weatherized to keep out the cold. Some 8,000 elderly and low-income citizens took advantage of the Energy Department's free offer.

A state energy policy was adopted.

Some 82 percent of the agency's budget was sub-contracted for energy research, mainly to universities, Ravan wrote.

The Energy Department won 13 advertising awards for its public information programs and won the President's Award for Energy efficiency.

By the time James left office, Alabama ranked 11th in the nation in the manufacture of medium temperature solar collectors and work had begun on two computer models which would be used for forecasting electricity price and demand, Ravan said.


## The Next Strike

On the heels of the truckers' strike came the Mobile police and firefighters' strike.

On July 17, 1980, then–Mobile Mayor Bob Doyle told a Birmingham News reporter, "I feel as though I were sitting on the edge of Mount St. Helens, waiting for the next rumble."

Doyle was getting ready to fire city employees who had walked off their jobs earlier that week after being refused a 20 percent pay increase. Firefighters had walked off first. Then sanitation and maintenance workers refused to cross picket lines, bringing all but essential city services to a halt.

Attorneys for the strikers admitted the strike was illegal as city secretaries prepared paperwork to fire some 400 workers.

James sent more than 100 National Guardsmen to assume firefighting duties. Tempers flared. News reports described shots fired at guardsmen.

The *News* wrote, "James has approved the use of National Guardsmen for firefighting but not for police duties, and given what city officials see as an ultimatum: Either the commission sits down and talks with police and firefighters, or, according to some reports, the Guardsmen will be withdrawn...It's the first mass walkout in any major Alabama city since Birmingham municipal workers staged a similar job action in May 1979."

The situation after 10 days was described by The Birmingham *News*:

> Striking employees wondered aloud in bewilderment why the commission "won't just sit down and talk with us."
>
> Commissioners with bags under their eyes from long hours without sleep grew angry when accusations were repeated to them that they refused to meet with strikers.
>
> They insisted they had met time and time again.

On July 24, about 600 firefighters, paramedics and police, and their children, took over the complex serving as Mobile's City Hall in protest of a settlement offered by the city.

Demanding to meet with city officials, the strikers parked their cars, pickup trucks and campers in front of the building, while others opened lawn chairs outside, giving the protest a fairground appearance," AP wrote. "...The City Commission stood firm on its refusal to withdraw suspensions meted to strikers (one day suspension for each day on strike).

"Strikers and their families...chanted, 'We want amnesty. We want amnesty.'"

James at that point repeated his actions of the previous year.

Headlines on July 25 stated, "Mobile firefighters, police end strike."

AP stated, "Gov. Fob James possibly was a factor in the settlement to end the strike..."

> The state plane arrived in Mobile around noon with James aboard, and a compromise on amnesty was announced within

hours.

James' role in the settlement which centered on the question of amnesty for strikers was not immediately clear. However, negotiations had deadlocked and firefighters occupied city hall demanding complete amnesty before James arrived.

The AP story stated firefighters would return to work accepting a one-day suspension for each day they were on strike, with a promise of no-firings because of the 10-day walkout. Police were expected to follow their lead.

James would not comment on his role, stating through his press secretary: "I just went down there to check out the situation."

The News reporter discussed the strike with Ray, described as "Ray, who worked night and day as a mediator representing Gov. Fob James..."

"The whole thing in Mobile just boiled down to a lack of communication," Ray said in a story with the headline, "Advice on strikes: Keep communicating."

Ray said neither side was lying. "The opposing sides just weren't on the same wave length, whatever the truth was."

During James' term, Ray would mediate in five major strikes, including strikes by United Mine Workers and employees of Alabama Power Company, Birmingham Water Works and Sanitary Sewer Board.

He would cut the department's personnel budget by one-fourth, $55,000, by handling the mediation himself with his assistant rather than hiring labor consultants and conciliators as had been done in the past.

Ray wrote that the Labor Department's role in the strikes minimized "both the destruction of property and losses to the employees and employer, as well as tax revenues."

James says, "Jerry really did a great job in preventing situations from getting violent. There's no telling how many strikes that man averted."

After his stint as labor commissioner, Ray would return to private life in Linden and serve as president of the Alabama Paperworkers Council.

# — 9 —

# Public Television

## Handshake Ends Seven Year Court Battle

In many departments of state government, James found problems which had existed for years with no apparent serious attempt to resolve them.

Such was the case in Alabama's Educational Television Commission.

Four years before James took office, the Associated Press on Jan. 8, 1975, wrote that the Federal Communications Commission refused to renew the license of Alabama's eight educational television stations because of "pervasive neglect" of the state's black population.

FCC also refused a construction permit for a ninth station.

AP wrote, "Noting the public stations had decided not to broadcast black-oriented programming in a state where blacks comprise 30 percent of the population, the FCC declared, 'A history of disservice of the magnitude disclosed by the evidence of record in this proceeding makes it impossible for us to find that renewal would serve the public interest, convenience and necessity.' "

Acknowledging a need for public television, however, the FCC authorized the state to continue operating the stations while FCC sought competing applications to begin new operations. Thus the state's stations were allowed to continue broadcasting on a temporary basis.

Incredibly, the situation remained the same when James took office. No steps had been taken by the state to resolve it except to pay attorneys for the on-going court battle to fight the decision.

James, when first informed of the status of the situation, called Opelika attorney Jacob Walker, whose ability to get people together he respected, and asked Walker to solve the problem without further court action.

He appointed Walker president of the Alabama Educational Television Commission.

The first publicity the issue received was Nov. 10, 1979, when the Birmingham *News* revealed, "...In Montgomery, a seven-year court battle over who will control public television in Alabama has ended with handshaking in the basement conference room at the Capitol..."

The *News* wrote of the key players: State Sen. U. W. Clemon of Birmingham was involved as chairman of Alabama Citizens of Responsive Public Television Inc.; George Drain of Montgomery was involved as chairman of Montgomery Citizens, which intervened in the case.

"A month ago, Gov. James called Clemon and Drain and asked them to meet with Jacob Walker," the *News* wrote. "After the meeting, this agreement was reached:

> • James would ask the Legislature to expand the commission from five to seven members, one from each of the state's congressional districts.
> • In each of the districts, citizens committees will be appointed, with James appointing two-thirds...AETC and Clemon's group will appoint one-third.
> • The committee will advise the commission members...as to the desires of the various communities as far as programming is concerned.

Two days later, the *News* wrote in an editorial:

> After seven years of stalemates and court dates, the two sides at odds with each other over the management and programming of the Alabama Educational Television Network have come to terms. Certainly this is something everybody interested in quality television in Alabama can applaud. Gov. Fob James should be commended for using his good offices to help bring it about.

But, the apparent ease with which the compromise appears to have been reached and the reasonableness of its terms makes us wonder if something could not have been done to end all the hubbub long before this. Though neither side wanted it, the end result of the seven-year confrontation between the Alabama Educational Television Commission and the Alabama Citizens for Responsive Public Television has been the loss of substantial federal monies which could have been used to upgrade the system.

Two months later, AP carried a story out of Washington, D.C. which stated, "The Alabama Educational Television Commission regained control of all nine public television stations in Alabama yesterday, five years after a regulatory agency refused to renew their licenses on grounds of racial discrimination..."

# — 10 —

# The ABC Department

## Money-Making Changes

James early on in his term in office decided that the single most important function he could perform as governor was to keep an eagle eye on the daily running of each department. The results of that decision are reflected in the bottom line of the account books of each of the departments under him.

James' cabinet members from 1979–1983 would now engage in heated arguments for days if asked which department could best be used to illustrate his hands-on philosophy of running state government.

None of them would disagree, however, that a study of the four-year history of the Alcoholic Beverage Control Agency under James is a lesson in basic management.

The state of Alabama got in the liquor business after national prohibition was declared a failure in 1933 and the Al Capone era of bootleg and shoot-outs ended. The federal government assumed regulation of all imported alcohol and of alcohol which was shipped between states. Each state assumed control of alcohol sold within its boundaries.

Twenty-two years of prohibition ended officially for Alabama when the Legislature overrode the veto of Gov. Bibb Graves to pass the Alcoholic Beverage Control Act on Feb. 2, 1937, allowing voters in each county to decide whether booze would be sold in their county.

Graves was actually a supporter of the act and had his floor leaders working actively to override his veto, says a man whose father was in Graves' cabinet at the time. He vetoed the act because there was at the time great opposition to it from church groups throughout the state.

The next month, simultaneous referenda were held in all 67 counties. Voters in 24 voted "wet," to allow the sale of liquor.

The first state-operated liquor store opened May 5, 1937, on a site now occupied by the Montgomery Civic Center. ABC stores quickly became known as "green fronts" because all were painted with a batch of government surplus green paint that was purchased at bargain-basement price.

By the end of the first year, there were 52 state-run stores in business. Customers selected merchandise from options displayed in a glass case. A store employee then filled his order in a back room, wrapping the liquor in the anonymity of a brown paper bag and handing it to the customer "over the counter."

The Alcoholic Beverage Control Board was the vehicle created in Alabama (and in 18 other states and Montgomery County, Maryland) to enforce the laws for sale of alcohol. The act creating the ABC board was written in the stern language of prohibitionists, bestowing on the board the duty "To promote temperance and suppress the evils of intemperance; to regulate and control the manufacture, purchase, bottling, sale, distribution, transportation, handling, advertising, possession, dispensing, drinking and use of alcohol..."

Thus the three ABC board members, appointed by the governor to six-year terms, have awesome powers. Board regulations carry the weight of law unless successfully challenged in court.

The board serves as judge and jury when charges are brought against those licensed to sell alcoholic beverages, with power to revoke or suspend a license as well as levy a fine.

The James administration successfully pushed legislation (the Administrative Procedures Act) which imposes requirements on the board which Joe Broadwater says cause it to be more responsible than it was in the past.

The board also gives thumbs-up or thumbs-down to the hundreds of brands of whiskeys and wines which must be approved prior to being offered for sale in the state-operated stores.

Day-to-day operation is handled by the ABC administrator, who is officially appointed by the board but is actually named by the governor. He serves as a member of the governor's cabinet.

A 1987 review by the ABC Department of "significant events" during the ABC Board's 50-year history listed only two items prior to James's term:

- Juke boxes were allowed in licensed establishments, 1948.
- George Wallace's 3 percent distillery tax was passed in 1964, changing the purchasing procedures of the ABC Board (which resulted in the withdrawal by liquor companies of major brands from state stores).

"Significant events" from James' four years in office were:

- In 1979 the ABC Board ended the requirement that establishments must open and pour for each drink a full "miniature" (1.67 oz.) bottle of liquor, allowing bartenders instead "free pour" of liquor. The move was fought by some of the liquor industry.(Broadwater says it was necessary because some brands were not available in the miniature size and distilleries which could bottle miniatures did not have the capacity to meet the retail demands of an entire state. Thus the ABC Department had been allowing licensees to pour from large bottles when miniatures were not available. "This caused absolute chaos," Broadwater said.)

- A law was passed allowing table wine to be sold statewide for the first time in grocery stores and other non-bar, non-state store establishments, and,
- A law was passed allowing non-state operated package stores for the first time since prohibition to sell liquor, which were the first moves toward getting the state out of the liquor business.

It was obvious in 1979 that the Alcoholic Beverage Control Agency would receive close scrutiny from the new governor.

As a candidate, James questioned the very existence of a state agency set up for the sole purpose of monopolizing the sale of something. Logic insisted that alcoholic beverages should be treated the same as other commodities, allowed to sink or swim in the marketplace of a nation founded in support of the private enterprise system.

"We were very skeptical that the public was best served by the state selling liquor as a monopoly," James said.

James and Broadwater worked well together. Their relationship dated back to college, when they first met as freshmen at Auburn. Their wives had been friends since childhood and the two families had kept in touch through letters and Christmas cards during years apart which included a Latin American stint for Broadwater in his CIA work as well as a South East Asia assignment where in Laos he acquired experience in dealing with corruption in government.

The history of the agency over which James put Broadwater was rife with scandal and exposés.

The green front stores in which liquor was sold were leased from private individuals. It would have been difficult during any gubernatorial administration to locate even one green front store owner who did not have direct political connections to the incumbent administration. When administrations changed, there was always great jockeying among store owners to get close enough to someone in power in the new administration to get their leases renewed.

Thus it followed that Broadwater discovered the state stores were not necessarily chosen by the dictates of the marketplace. He found they were frequently in the worst parts of town, had poor lighting and peeling paint and some were located in low-traffic areas where only winos and derelicts ventured out at night.

There was evidence that the agency was, to be kind, stagnating. Management of the department had at times been run by strict administrators. But the laws which governed the department were archaic, and board members had most often been appointed by prior administrations at the behest of friends who were engaged in the liquor business.

"The ABC board was still operating as they had in 1937, 1938 and 1939," Broadwater said. "State stores were continuously out of products though the state kept far too much inventory on hand.

"There was gross inefficiency," he said. "There had been no real period of reduced tax revenues to cause any administration to be cost conscious for quite a number of years. There were a lot of accusations and innuendoes about illegal behavior and there was some, of course, but very little. The majority of what we found being done wrong in state government was using too many people to do a job, not adapting to newer methods, and a reluctance to use new electronic equipment, cash registers and computers."

For example, the state was paying some $5,000 to $6,000 each year for bottles which had broken during shipment. Why? Because the seller was not made responsible by the state for delivering liquor to

Alabama. The state was in the trucking business. The state picked up all liquor from the manufacturer.

The arrangement, Broadwater said, was "almost unheard of."

Worse, the state was sending empty trucks to pick up the liquor.

"The ridiculous trucking situation, as well as the problem of having too much inventory and too much of the wrong product was brought to my attention by John Harbert and Gov. James," Broadwater said. "Nobody can afford to go one way empty today."

Harbert, a respected Birmingham businessman, was appointed chairman of the ABC Board by James, who also named two other "astute business people," Broadwater said. They were John Blue and Mrs. Freida Coggin.

Harbert had been a member of the board under Wallace but "had not been able to get the bureaucracy to do anything," Broadwater said.

"The past administration preferred that the ABC Board keep a very low profile and not attract any attention," Broadwater said. "Gov. James and the board he appointed were willing to take the flak we knew would come from many different directions as these long needed changes were made."

Broadwater now heads a division of a mammoth Huntsville computer software company, Integraph, which James calls one of the greatest success stories in Alabama industry.

Broadwater, in a 1988 interview, said in his position he frequently buys large quantities of goods which are shipped to Integraph.

"When I buy something here I let the seller get it to me, that's part of the sellers' burden," he said.

He did not have to convince James, who had been featured in newspaper articles for his innovative two-way use of Diversified Products' trucks when shipping merchandise to stores and returning with raw products for his manufacturing process.

One of the first actions Broadwater took was to get the monkey off the state's back for delivery of products purchased from the liquor industry. Proving once again that private enterprise could in most cases operate at less cost than governmental bodies, Broadwater's successor, Floyd Mann, noted in his report that requiring the companies which sold the product to haul it "results in the consumer getting the same product at a cheaper price."

"When we put the burden on private enterprise to do the hauling," Broadwater said, "many of them even rented warehouses in Montgomery to keep it handy. Since they could get it to us faster, this helped in our efforts to reduce the inventory we had to keep on hand."

James charged Broadwater with multi-faceted goals: bring the ABC Agency into the computer age, run it as a business; revamp the existing network of state-leased stores to make them responsive to the market; upgrade and revamp the employee system; and devise a plan to begin turning over the liquor business to private enterprise.

It went without saying that Broadwater would investigate the department from top to bottom and rid the state of the cronies and hangers-on of the Wallace years who had profited greatly through control of the liquor business in the state.

Broadwater was eager, as were other James appointees. But he had to learn the ABC set-up from the ground up.

The biggest problem faced by James' appointees, Broadwater said, was that "We had absolutely no links in Montgomery, no organization in place, no connection with anyone who knew what was going on. It took us two years to find out how they kept the books."

Some goals were obviously easier to accomplish than others. Broadwater immediately began working on the two tasks which would dominate much of the James administration's efforts in the liquor industry: relocating state stores to high traffic, low-crime commercial areas with adequate parking and converting the stores to self-service.

Broadwater discovered state stores were tremendously overstocked by conducting a poll of private companies which sold liquor in other states.

"Albertsons turns its inventory approximately 26 times a year. I believe Jacks in Florida turns 24 to 28 times a year. You should be turning every two to three weeks. Alabama, when Fob took office, kept such a big inventory on hand that we went for nine weeks at a time without turning our inventory over. This is a waste of state dollars you've put out which could be spent for better things, or could be earning interest in a bank," he said.

In many cases, simple lethargy had taken its toll. Broadwater points to the fact that the ABC Board had made only feeble attempts to audit the records of beer and wine wholesalers who sold to private retailers, though the state tax collected on such sales generated more than $40 million a year. The state simply accepted the word of the wholesalers that they were paying as much state tax as they should.

When James took office, only two of the state's 129 stores were self-service, yet in neighboring states like Florida it was difficult to find any other kind.

The brands of liquors and wines chosen by the ABC Board were ridiculed openly by patrons who comparison-shopped in other states. Top-selling brands available nationwide were not available in Alabama. Shelves were filled with unfamiliar brands not found in other states.

There appeared to be no rational basis for some of the decisions made. For example, the ABC Board prior to James routinely bought wine, placed it on the shelves and watched it sit gathering dust. The state was losing $ 1/4 million annually on its sale of wines in state stores, ABC figures showed.

Why the big difference from other states?

Because in Alabama, the ABC Board had for years relied heavily on "liquor agents" to influence their choices on which brands to stock.

Liquor agents were people who had little if any experience in the liquor industry; they were members of the existing political machine. They were hired by out-of-state liquor companies for the sole purpose of influencing the ABC Board to stock state stores with their brands. Liquor agents did not have to work long hours for their pay. Most times, a simple lunchtime conversation with the "right" person could accomplish their task. Liquor agents historically had political or family relations with the governor.

Or, as Broadwater puts it, "The liquor agent moves his product by who he knows, not what he knows."

Liquor agents should not be confused with legitimate liquor salesmen, Broadwater said. "Liquor companies do have salesmen who can be very helpful in providing information about their brands, sales in other states, etc."

When Wallace took office, he made a big show of getting rid of liquor agents by having legislators pass a distiller tax.

"It looked good and sounded good," Broadwater said.

But it did not work that way.

A lawyer who has long represented liquor companies in the state explained what the tax did:

"George Wallace knew the major liquor companies would have to pull out of the state. They had formally agreed after prohibition was repealed to treat all the states controlled by a liquor agency the same. That means they could not pay Alabama 3 percent more than other such states. When the major companies took their brands off the state store shelves, that left little distilleries with all the business. Little distilleries soon found that it was taking the state of Alabama months to pay them. They couldn't afford to operate that way. It would bankrupt them. At that point they were approached by a few of Wallace's friends and relatives and told they could discount their Alabama warrants with a certain Chicago bank. The bank would pay them, say, 75 percent of what the state owed them. That was okay with the distillers because they were told it was okay to charge the state a little more to make up for it. A funny thing, when the Chicago bank presented its warrants to the state for payment, it got paid the same day."

Some major liquor companies got around the distillery tax.

"Some of them concocted special brands," Broadwater said, "special products for sale in Alabama. They might, say, sell 86 proof to Mississippi and 80 proof to Alabama. For years what was available in other states wasn't available in state of Alabama."

Then again, a liquor company might do what Seagram's did, Broadwater said. "They sold liquor to a carpet store owner in Mississippi who in turn sold it to the state of Alabama. He did not have to pay a distillery tax. Obviously, he had a few Alabama partners, just as legal as could be."

Another way Wallace's friends profited through liquor sales to the state was by marketing liquor under their own labels.

"You can come up with a label for anything that is manufactured, get the label approved by the federal government and you can get any distillery to bottle it for you," Broadwater said. "This is the way certain people have gotten in to the liquor business."

A man who sold such "rotgut" to the state tells of discovering upon opening a bottle of it that the cap had rusted because the liquor was still fermenting.

One thing was understood from the start in the James administration, Broadwater said. "There was one main thing Fob James did not do that other governors did. He didn't allow friends and supporters to go get their own label printed and start selling liquor to the state."

"When the liquor industry saw that it was not going to have to operate through agents, but were going to be treated as a business, they became very helpful," Broadwater said.

The history of the ABC Agency under James is one of change.

The bookkeeping system in the ABC Agency left much to be desired, Broadwater said.

When James took office there was no "standard" record-keeping among the various state agencies, which meant the individual who had authority over all the agencies (the governor) could not compare how they spent their money. The same expenses might be lumped together in one account in one agency and scattered among several in a different agency.

Auditors employed by the state Examiners of Public Accounts had taken exception repeatedly to many of the ABC Board's practices. James ordered all departments of state government to adopt the "standard" bookkeeping system which is today in use statewide. By assigning uniform specific numbers to each expense in state government, the system makes it possible at a glance to discover how much is being spent on anything from paper to overtime in any department.

Management procedures were also suspect, Broadwater said. It took the entire four years of the term to wise up to some of the problems.

"We were closing the stores once a week and letting the ABC employees take inventory," Broadwater said. "I finally realized that in doing it this way the state was letting the keeper of the henhouse conduct the audit and we sent the auditors in for our last quarterly inventory. You might say, therefore, that we had a good count only once during the entire administration."

Meanwhile, Broadwater attacked the problem of shelves stocked with unpopular brands.

"We decided to offer a choice in each category of the most expensive item available and the cheapest item available, as well as two middle categories," Broadwater said. "We didn't try to make the cheapest and the most expensive to have the same track record. We had a performance level we expected for each of the categories. If a brand didn't move according to the time frame we had set up, we de-listed it and substituted another brand."

"For the first time, the state required liquor companies to show how they were going to promote a particular product, not in order to sell more liquor but to convince people to buy that brand instead of a different brand," Broadwater said.

In addition to reducing the amount of state money tied up in liquor inventory, Broadwater said, "We tried to reduce the amount of time between the point at which money from sales was deposited in a bank and the point at which it started drawing interest in the state treasury. Banks, of course, didn't like this because they had been in many cases using this money for five days interest-free."

A banker who admits to having had accounts from several state stores deposited in his banks over the years explains that the proceeds from just two state stores can result in a bank being able to use $5 million a year interest-free.

There were rumors of investigations and of threats made against the James administration by those being investigated.

"That were a lot of people running around talking big," Broadwater said. "But there weren't any licks passed while we were in Montgomery. Nobody was going to hurt anybody. There wasn't anybody up there with guts enough to hurt anybody."

During James' term, the department was completely reorganized. The reorganization was described in a four-year-end report to James written by Mann, who was named ABC chief when Broadwater was named Finance Director for the final six months of the administration. In 1981 the 10 operating divisions were combined into three divisions and one staff unit which all reported to the administrator, Mann wrote. "This change was to reduce the amount of day-to-day management which must be accomplished by the administrator, to increase coordination and to smooth transitions during changes of administration."

In the spring of 1982, James merged the department's two enforcement divisions, issued them uniforms, purchased riot shotguns and gas masks for them, and made them available to help state troopers when needed.

He also equipped their cars for the first time with radios which allowed them to communicate with each other and with other enforcement agencies. The cars were also equipped with jumper cables, siphoning hoses and fire extinguishers to enable them to help motorists in need.

Training programs were established for all officers in the use of weapons and in "pursuit driving," the high-speed chase in which most officers sooner or later find themselves engaged. They were also trained in first aid and in various ways in which they could help the public, from changing flat tires to giving emergency medical help. The agents were given formal training in the laws, rules and regulations pertaining to the sale of alcoholic beverages.

The equipment and training were costly.

But Mann wrote in his four-year-end report that the changes addressed "the total picture of regulatory problems."

The 103 agents, now combined in a single unit, had as "primary responsibility...the enforcing of intoxicating liquor and licensing laws in wet areas, as well as the enforcement of prohibition laws in dry areas...(and) the enforcement of legal drinking age," Mann wrote.

He said the ABC regulatory divisions had been upgraded in capability and equipment to make it "a more integral and proficient part of the overall law enforcement effort in the State."

Mann enumerated other changes.

A decision was made to stop selling wine in order to halt the 1/4 million dollars-a-year loss from wine which did not sell. "This line [wine] is being replaced by extending our selection of liqueur, ceramic decanters and high-profit specialty items," Mann wrote.

The liquor on the shelves was cheaper at the end of James' term because the state wasn't paying for its delivery anymore, Mann wrote. He said there was also wider array of brands from which to choose, with customers in the 83 self-service stores able to browse at will.

Self-service stores require fewer man-hours, hence the state saved money on salaries, he wrote.

Mann was enthusiastic about self-service stores, which he said allow a better chance for the customer to compare prices, brands, sizes, etc. Because customers are served more quickly, the number of sales increases, Mann wrote.

"For instance, in the new store in Muscle Shoals, there was a customer served every 16.7 seconds the first day the store opened," Mann wrote.

Conversion of the stores to self-service translated to a $4.4 million annual savings in personnel costs, Mann wrote, which was projected to increase to an annual $5.6 million savings when conversion of all stores was complete, Mann stated.

When James left office, the written goals of the ABC Agency included conversion of all ABC stores to self-service by the summer of 1983 with a corresponding reduction in staffing by attrition.

The conversion to self-service continued after James left office, but the benefits to the state in savings did not continue. At the end of Wallace's term, though more stores were self-service, there were only three fewer employees than there had been in 1982.

Broadwater took James' campaign promise of "fiscal responsibility" seriously, a term James once defined as the practice of spending each tax dollar with the same care with which a dollar from the church offering plate would be spent.

He set up an audit division to check the books of wholesale beer and wine distributors in the state. The move paid off—auditors discovered that significant sums of additional tax money were owed.

"This [audit] division designed and implemented a tax reporting system for these two taxes and is auditing all wholesalers on a rotating basis," Mann wrote. "In its first full year in operation [1981], the Audit Division collected almost $400,000 in additional taxes. In 1982, an additional $230,000 in taxes was collected."

Money was also saved when Broadwater discovered the source of theft which had plagued the department for years.

"We thought customers were stealing the whiskey," Broadwater said. An investigation revealed the theft was being done by some clerks who were taking advantage of the paperwork system in which two sales slips were issued at the time of a sale.

One slip was given to the customer and one became part of ABC records.

"If a customer happened to leave his sales slip on the counter, and many apparently did, the clerk could mark it as returned merchandise and take a bottle of the same brand home," Broadwater said. "It was simple, but it took us two years to discover what was really happening to the bottles in those situations."

Broadwater, who heads the security division of Integraph, used his knowledge of security procedures to cut drastically the amount of losses which had resulted from burglaries of state stores.

"Burglar alarm systems, mirrors and other security surveillance mechanisms are being used. As a result the losses through burglaries, robberies, and so forth, have been decreased from about $45,000 in 1978 to some $22,000 in 1981 and some $11,000 in 1982," Mann wrote.

Broadwater eliminated $350,000 in salaries and benefits when he rescheduled the physical taking of inventory from once a week to once a month. This, along with some reporting changes, saved 38,000 man hours, Mann wrote.

The savings could be accomplished thanks to the purchase of a system-wide point-of-sale computer system which among other duties kept track of each sale and fed the results to Montgomery daily.

The computer network also allowed the ABC Agency to transmit pricing information to all stores and made it possible for the central office to know immediately when a reorder was needed. It also greatly reduced paperwork, Mann said.

An article in *Computer World* bragged on Alabama's ABC Agency computerization, pointing out that its installation cost less than $100,000 in the initial seven stores in which it was placed in operation.

The total cost of the system would be less than $2 million, compared to $2.5 million spent by another state on a system which the magazine described as "largely outdated, unworkable and inoperable."

Alabama's computer system would save between $1.5 and $2 million a year, Mann wrote.

The computer-based inventory control system allowed the ABC Board to decrease inventory from $21.2 million at the end of fiscal year 1979 to $16.7 million at the end of fiscal year 1982, a 22 percent inventory reduction.

Not only was the inventory reduction done without reducing the selection to the customer, Mann wrote, "In fact, warehouse outage [being out of a product] has been reduced from an average of 26 percent in 1979 to 6.56 percent in 1982...a dramatic increase in the Board's ability to fill orders from the stores."

The dozens of such "small" savings in 33 departments of state government added up to tens of millions of dollars by the time James left office, Bobby Davis said. His assertion is documented in the "final reports" which James directed all department heads to file.

James was quick to send teams of auditors to trace state dollars in order to cut expenses or to make sure taxes were being paid as provided by law.

If state auditors were already overworked by his demands for audits, he did not hesitate to hire a private audit firm, Davis said.

The ABC Agency participated with other departments in cooperative ventures. One such effort was combining ABC efforts with those of the Departments of Mental Health, Public Health, Highway & Traffic Safety and Education to initiate a campus alcohol awareness program. Mann wrote that it was "the first such effort in the U.S. and is being watched by many other states."

In summing up accomplishments of the ABC Agency, and noting the smaller number of employees, Mann wrote, "So many times people criticize government and its bureaucracy. Here is just one example where our administration has reduced bureaucracy while increasing service to the public."

The sweeping changes wrought through legislation and administrative fiat were not heralded, however.

The James administration did not present them to the public or the news media as the tremendous financial and political accomplishments they were.

# — 11 —

# Law Enforcement

**A** James 1978 campaign commercial which aroused much comment was one in which he stood on the porch of an elderly citizen, knocking on her door. She was afraid to open it. "It's okay. You can come out. It's Fob James," he said.

Crime was not a political issue, James said. It was an issue to him personally and he meant to get personally involved in coming up with solutions.

James researched it in his campaign by taking advantage of every occasion possible to talk to prosecutors and judges and to listen to victims of crimes who approached him to talk about their experiences with the system.

He also studied carefully the new Criminal Code of Alabama which had first been approved by the Legislature in 1977. The Legislature voted to postpone the implementation, however, because so many "holes" had been discovered in it. The Legislature revised it in 1978, but more revision was needed. James said he was astounded at what he read, at what had been left out or at the penalties which had been lessened for major crimes.

After he took office, he commissioned one of the few "task forces" in his administration, naming professionals in the judicial system, law enforcement and citizens to undertake a study of what was wrong with the criminal justice system in the state. The Governor's Commission on Crime was headed by Montgomery Circuit Court Judge Joe Phelps.

It differed in composition from the "blue ribbon" task forces for which James has little use. It was composed of people like Mobilian

Manson Murray, an attorney who knew first hand of the violence of street crime. Murray survived a gunshot wound when mugged on the streets of downtown Mobile. But he lost an eye.

The commission included people from every walk of life.

It included Dothan District Attorney Tom Sorrells "who had a good reputation as a prosecutor," and Mobile Judge Cain Kennedy, whom James appointed.

James asked the group to research, to hold public hearings throughout the state, and to submit a written report on its findings. That report would form the basis for legislation which James would get passed in several sessions of the Legislature.

When James took office, according to an article written by Bill Berkeley, Alabama had "the smallest trooper force in the Southeast" and the situation was not expected to improve.

"The department's most recent budget report states that the number of state troopers has declined in the past five years, despite the fact that statistics show overall crime has risen dramatically."

Violent crime had increased 32 percent, while the number of troopers decreased 5 percent.

In presenting the department's budget in January of 1979, then-Col. Jerry Shoemaker told legislators: "We don't have the manpower, we don't have the equipment, we don't have the money to fight crime, patrol the highways, license the drivers, weigh the trucks, inform the public, inspect the vehicles, control the disturbances, or assist the motorists—to do all the things the public has the right to expect. We need help."

They got it, records show.

The top item on the agenda was recruiting new troopers. Shoemaker described a cadet program to James which had been used successfully by the state to recruit troopers for many years. It had been shut down eight years before, though Shoemaker was not aware of the reason why.

Shoemaker talked from a very personal perspective.

"In 1959, while a student at the University of Alabama," Shoemaker told the Birmingham *News*, "I read a news article which described a new program which was going to be started...I looked into the possibility of becoming an Alabama Highway Patrol cadet. It was probably one of the best programs Alabama has ever started."

Shoemaker had opted for the cadet program rather than other enticing programs offered by the armed services. So had others who by 1979 were majors, captains, lieutenants and so forth.

"We can look through our organization today and see the cadets from that program are the supervisors of today," Shoemaker said.

James gave Shoemaker the go-ahead to start the cadet program up again. Shoemaker got permission from the personnel board and cranked it up.

In October, Shoemaker was astounded when 200 young men and women signed up for the 30 slots available in the first cadet class.

There were several reasons the program was so appealing. Without the training, one had to be 21 to be a trooper. The cadet training made a graduate eligible to be put on the payroll at three-fourths of a trooper's starting salary until age 21 was reached.

The training took place at Selma, where an old airstrip was used to teach the cadets about such things as high-speed pursuit and riot control.

"This is a new breed of trooper," their teacher, Cpl. James Jackson, told the *Birmingham News*. "They want to believe that they're going to be the best."

Equipment was next on the list. Getting to a riot scene or a drug bust as quickly as possible was important. Two Army surplus helicopters and an aging Aero Commander plane were replaced with a Jet Ranger helicopter and a twin-engine Beechcraft Baron.

Evidence that would stand up in court was just as important. Color photo processors were bought to aid investigative efforts and to meet what Shoemaker termed "the increased demand for color photographs used as court evidence."

The funding was found through the same means as in other departments—cost-cutting measures and legislation to place fees on special services which would pay the costs of performing those services.

All Dothan troopers were moved into one building and elsewhere in the state there was "a continuing effort to bring area DPS officers under one roof," Shoemaker reported to James at the end of the term. "Central offices have been built or acquired in Dothan, Selma and Huntsville and bids are being accepted for Tuscaloosa."

Legislation is but one of several avenues available to a governor to make an impact on the criminal justice system, James says. "The criminal code ought to be protective of the public. It is up to the governor, as it is the responsibility of others in certain professions, to ensure that the code does that," he said.

He includes the state's attorney general and the news media as "others" who share the responsibility for informing the public if they discover that laws do not accomplish the purpose for which they were intended or were misrepresented to the public.

"I can't believe there is a newspaper editor in this state who has not taken the time to read the criminal code, who has not been angered at what he finds and has not assigned reporters to do stories which inform the public," James said. "What do they do with their time? I used to ask editors if they had read the code and they would sit there and stare at me as though I had lost my mind."

In addition to legislative action, the governor should make a strong impact on the criminal justice system "by the signal he sends," James says. "If every police officer in the state is aware that he has the aggressive support of the governor, you're going to see things happen."

James sent his "signal" by specific actions. Perhaps his strongest message was not sent to the general public, but to law enforcement. And law enforcement officials say he came through loud and clear.

Zeroing in on the immense drug traffic problem in Alabama, James used his administrative power to create a State Narcotics Unit to draw all state-level narcotics investigators into what Shoemaker called "a cohesive force." James transferred agents from various departments to the Department of Public Safety.

"The State Narc Unit was formed in 1979 with personnel of the ABC Board and Department of Health working with the Department of Public Safety narcotics investigators under the leadership of a state trooper captain," Shoemaker said.

To facilitate the work of both the Narc Unit and the White Collar Crime Task Force, the Intelligence Unit was transferred from the administrative division to an investigative division, the Alabama Bureau of Investigation, Shoemaker said. A central intelligence file was started.

Periodically, James sat in on meetings of the Narc Unit, joining the scruffy-looking crew which sported the beards and casual dress mandatory for undercover agents. It was an off-the-record coffee-drinking session in which everybody let down their hair and the governor got filled in first-hand on every covert operation in the state.

Jerry Shoemaker, still with Public Safety in 1990, though not director, has under glass on his desk a color snapshot of the biggest haul of marijuana ever made by state and federal officials in Alabama, eight tons seized in Hurtsboro moments after a plane flew it directly in from Colombia.

It is not the record-setting size of the load which makes the picture a keepsake, however. The seizure set another record—it was the only one in the history of the state in which the governor of the state participated as an undercover agent.

"For weeks Gov. James had been bugging me to go along on an actual operation," Shoemaker said. "I stalled as long as I could, then I said okay. But I let him know that once we got into the situation, he would not be governor—he would just be another citizen who had to take orders. He said okay and asked what he should wear."

James showed up in jeans and an old hat. Shoemaker handed him a bullet-proof vest.

"He looked at me like I was trying to pull something on him and said, 'Is everyone else wearing one of these?' When I assured him we were, that he was not being handled with kid gloves, he put it on," Shoemaker said.

Shoemaker, learning when the pot plane would arrive, said he again stalled getting on the helicopter which would take them to the scene as long as possible. The plane had landed but the bad guys had not been arrested when James arrived. The bad guys were just getting ready to eat a few dozen doughnuts when the arrests began, in fact.

"They were not aware the governor was there. We had so many officers on the scene that he was thought to be just another one," Shoemaker said.

FBI agent Pat Mitchell said all the enforcement officers were busy, ignoring James, as they took care of the legal technicalities of arresting the entire group of smugglers.

"Gov. James wandered around until he heard radio traffic coming from one of the bad guys' trucks," Mitchell said. "He kept after us until someone checked it out."

The conversation on the radio was between two stake-outs who had not heard from anyone and were wondering what was going on. A state or federal agent got on the radio, pretended to be one of the smugglers, found the location of the stake-outs and sent a crew to arrest them, Mitchell said.

"We were trying not to crack up at the idea of the governor getting involved in the bust," Mitchell said.

When word got around as to James' identity, Mitchell said one of the prisoners asked to meet him.

"It turned out he had played football for the University of Florida at the time the governor had played for Auburn and they had played against each other," Mitchell said. "The guy's hands were too big for the handcuffs to fit and we had to make him pretend the handcuffs were locked before we let him meet Gov. James."

Admittedly, a few state and federal agents had a rosy glow for a few days when their routine was broken and egos were stroked with a little attention from the governor. But did James' excursion have any real effect on law enforcement?

Shoemaker and Mitchell both are vigorous in their insistence that it did.

"It was a morale booster like you wouldn't believe," Shoemaker said. "The governor cared. The governor was interested enough to get involved."

Law enforcement has the best grapevine around, Mitchell says, "and the word spread all over the state by the end of the day."

The Narc Unit in its first year of existence seized more than $5 million in cocaine and $44 million in marijuana.

James also got directly involved in the investigation of white collar crime. He did so only after being convinced by prosecutors over the state, members of the Department of Public Safety and the head of the Ethics Commission that Attorney General Graddick was not prosecuting white collar crime.

For months there had come to James' office a steadily increasing procession of law enforcement-linked visitors asking his help in prosecuting offenders, says Gene Mitchell, who at that time was deputy director of the Department of Public Safety and chief of the governor's security. Mitchell's office was within the governor's suite. Most of the time, however, the bodyguard/aide sat on the other side of an open door as James received his visitors.

"District attorneys would try to get Fob to intercede with Graddick, to force the attorney general to get off his stool and prosecute cases which required the resources of the office of state attorney general," Mitchell said. "We heard story after story of how Charlie wouldn't prosecute."

Ethics Commission Director Melvin Cooper appealed to James for help in prosecuting ethics violators. He said Graddick had refused to prosecute some 50 to 60 cases which the Ethics Commission had referred to him for prosecution.

James was insistent upon giving Graddick another chance. He

called the attorney general to his office in 1980 for a friendly but to-the-point chat, Bobby Davis said.

Davis said James told the attorney general: "Charlie, all of us have a job to do. I'm the governor and my job is to do the things the governor is supposed to do. You're the attorney general. You're supposed to prosecute. Now, if I ever don't do my job, I expect you to tell me. Folks have been telling me you're not doing your job, Charlie. So I'm telling you. If you don't do it, I've got no other choice but to name a special prosecutor who will."

Mitchell was also present. He said Graddick turned pale and assured James there would be no further problems.

There was no significant increase in the prosecution of white collar crimes after James decided not to form his own task force, however. In fact, such prosecution in Montgomery County apparently decreased.

The Montgomery *Advertiser* wrote: "District Attorney Evans'... own successful prosecutions of top state officials slowed sharply when state funding for his investigative staff dwindled."

The *Advertiser* wrote, "That came after Gov. James met with Graddick and announced he had been assured by the Attorney General himself that he would pursue white collar crime."

Different segments of law enforcement had different reasons to be unhappy with, or suspicious of, Graddick, including members of his own department.

Not long after Graddick took over as attorney general, a secretary who had worked for the Attorney General's Office for several years was alone in the office, except for a telephone repairman, who was checking a nearby phone. When the repairman heard the secretary making flippant comments on the phone, he warned her to be careful about what she said. He had been working in the basement on the main telephone system, he said, and it had been tampered with. He warned her that others could be listening in on her conversation.

She told several long-time top prosecutors in the office what the man had said. One of them crawled around examining the telephone equipment in the basement long enough to become convinced that what the telephone man had said was true. Another of the attorneys approached a federal prosecutor with the story. Graddick denied it when questioned by the FBI, and the matter officially ended there.

James, prodded by the Department of Public Safety, began to seriously consider forming his own task force.

"Gov. Fob James is reviewing the role his office should play in bolstering state investigations of white collar crime," AP stated. Press Secretary Jon Ham was quoted as saying James had received reports on several "continuing investigations" but "has not addressed" a proposal to name a special prosecutor as he had been urged to do by district attorneys.

The task force he named was headed by Securities Commissioner Tom Krebs, and included Capt. Johnny Hendrix, head of the Department of Public Safety's Division of Intelligence and Investigations, Mitchell, and representatives of the Alcoholic Beverage Control Board and the Revenue Department.

"Our job was to provide support services to district attorneys. We never went into a county unless the district attorney asked us to," Mitchell said.

The team also included Evans.

The *Advertiser* described James' formation of the task force thus: "Gov. Fob James declared Attorney General Charles Graddick 'legally incompetent' and appointed State Securities Commissioner Thomas L. Krebs to head (the governor's task force on white collar crime) ...James noted that with an office of 57 lawyers and 17 investigators, Graddick had managed to bring just 29 criminal cases in two years while other agencies found Alabama a gold mine of major prosecutions.

"Besides Tom Krebs and his pet Leviticus Project which tracked interstate corruption in the coal industry, U.S. Attorney Barry Teague's series of prosecutions halted corrupt purchase practices by commissioners in counties scattered all over South Alabama."

James also used funds at his disposal to assist Evans in his wide-ranging investigation of white collar crime.

"The hard-nosed attitude that James had for law and order was clearly shown soon after he was in office," Ralph Holmes wrote. "Following a shootout between blacks and the Ku Klux Klan in Decatur, the governor promised there would be no more "Wild West Antics" if he could help it.

"Later demonstrations by both groups went peaceably, as James sent hundreds of state troopers to Decatur on one occasion to maintain order.

"A bitter and sometimes violent strike by independent truck drivers broke out in North Alabama," Holmes wrote. "Promising safe passage on the highways for the motoring public, including those truckers who wanted to operate, James beefed up the trooper force in the northern area of the state and called out specialized units of the Alabama National Guard."

James also beefed up law enforcement through administrative action, through his reclassification plan which upgraded salaries of law enforcement, and through a uniform raise for deputy sheriffs.

Whereas in the past the term law enforcement usually referred only to the Department of Public Safety, James included all facets of enforcement in his directives to upgrade and provide training.

The ABC Agency had two separate enforcement arms when James took office. One group of agents focused its attention on illegal sales, going after moonshiners and bootleggers, who sold liquor without the stamps which signified state tax had been paid on it. The second group of agents, under the Beer Tax & License Division, conducted the investigations required by law before licenses could be issued to sell liquor by the drink. They also checked operating establishments to make sure all liquor laws were complied with.

James combined the two. At the end of James' term, then-ABC administrator Mann wrote in his four-year-end report that the changes turned ABC enforcement into a "more integral and proficient part of the overall law enforcement effort in the State."

Equipment and training were also provided to the Marine Police in the Department of Conservation.

One simple, but important, act in enforcing security in prisons, Montgomery attorney Rod Nachman said, was issuing uniforms to officers. "Before that, Nachman said, "it was hard to tell the guards from the prisoners."

James was aware that each and every action of a governor on law enforcement issues sends a signal to the enforcement community, to the people, and to the criminal element on how tough he really is when it comes to crime.

The thought was ever on his mind as the April 5, 1979, execution date drew near for convicted murderer John Louis Evans III. Evans and his partner, Wayne Ritter, coldly executed Mobile pawn shop owner Edward Nassar as his two young daughters sat nearby watching television. Evans and Ritter confessed also to a 73-day crime binge which included nine kidnappings, two extortions, 37 armed robberies and one murder.

Both men laughingly begged for the death sentence at their trial. Evans changed his mind about wanting to die and launched a last-minute appeal. If the U.S. Supreme Court refused to postpone the execution or did not answer in time, it would be up to James to decide Evans' fate.

Mike Waters, James' legal adviser at the time, remembers the intensity of the hours on April 5. It is easy to say what you would do in such a situation, Waters said. But it is a different matter to do it.

"The governor spent hours reading about the case. He knew there was only one decision he could make. When we walked out the door, Evans' mother was waiting for him. She was upset. She begged him not to let her son die. Gov. James was very gentle with her, but I think she knew what his decision was. When we walked off, his knuckles were as white as his face. I've never seen him like that before or since."

Waters was ready to announce to news media that James would not give Evans a reprieve when U.S. Supreme Court Justice William Rehnquist issued a temporary stay of the execution. The appeals process stretched beyond James' term in office. Evans was eventually executed.

James spent more time planning his law enforcement program than any other endeavor in office except education, Mitchell said.

Agents of the Department of Pardons and Paroles were included in his planning. Specialized training was provided to them in the new criminal code. A computer link was established between the department and the Law Enforcement Data System, making information on probationers and parolees instantly available to all of law enforcement.

James was the first governor to realize that an increase in the number of people being supervised should mean a corresponding increase in the number of parole officers, Director Warren Gaston said in 1989.

On July 25, 1981, the federal court in Montgomery released 277 state inmates because of overcrowding. Sixty of these were not released from supervision of the state. They were added to the workloads of parole officers.

To handle the load, James sponsored a supplemental appropriation bill to hire 30 new probation and parole officers and 17 clerical personnel. Four new field offices were established at Ashland, Athens, Tuscumbia and Lafayette.

In every department of state government which employed enforcement agents, those men and women who carry badges and are charged with the responsibility of maintaining law and order, the four-year-end reports noted attention had been devoted to these officers for the first time.

James' efforts in law enforcement were directed toward producing a well-equipped, well-trained group of professionals who operated as what Shoemaker termed "a cohesive force."

Law enforcement, obviously aware of James' interest and involvement, responded. The esprit de corps which developed is perhaps best evidenced in 1982 when the national and the state economy bottomed out in recession. The General Fund Budget faced 15 percent proration, or cutback.

"Extraordinary measures were taken to prevent the loss of vital manpower," Shoemaker said. "More than 98 percent of the employees of the Department of Public Safety volunteered to take one day without pay each pay period to reduce the departmental budget, which was about 76 percent personnel costs."

# — 12 —

# Prisons

Perhaps no situation in Alabama enraged citizens at the time James took office as much as the daily spectacle of court-convicted criminals turned away from prisons because federal judges had ordered the overcrowded prisons not to accept any more inmates.

For four years the prison overflow had been housed in local jails, which in time were also bursting at the seams. In early 1978, there were 2,800 state prisoners housed in county jails.

The public was inundated with media interpretations of the ramifications of the federal orders. The public was thus aware that convicted rapists and murderers were packed in the same jails with prisoners who under the American system of justice had to be regarded as innocent—people awaiting trial who for some reason could not get out on bail.

There were also in the jails inmates convicted of lesser offenses and in some cases there were juveniles. Sheriffs in eight counties were enraged by federal judges who ordered them to reduce an inmate population they were powerless to reduce. They held press conferences and threatened to sue the state.

With the increase in number of prisoners came a corresponding decrease in patience among both inmates and guards. Shorter tempers meant an increase in the number of fights and stabbings which always rise in crescendo with the thermometer of an Alabama summer. Their jails were time bombs waiting to explode, the sheriffs knew.

All facets of the criminal justice system were affected.

Judges, keenly aware of the overcrowding, were under pressure to put criminals on probation who would have been sent to prison in the past.

Members of the Board of Pardons and Paroles, aware that attempts had been made before and might be made again to place their agency under federal jurisdiction, were under pressure to step up the number of inmates released monthly. A chart of parolees would have shown an upward spiral, though a similar chart on the number of parole officers who supervised them would have remained constant. The parole officers knew they were only able to give cursory supervision to the newly-released criminals. They were also aware state officials turned deaf ears to their pleas for more officers.

The crises had developed in the seven-year period prior to James taking office.

On Oct. 4, 1972, U.S. District Judge Frank M. Johnson Jr. issued a ruling in response to a lawsuit charging the state violated the U.S. Constitution by not providing the proper medical treatment for its inmates. He ordered the state to improve medical care of its inmates, terming the state's neglect of inmates' medical needs "barbaric" and "shocking to the senses."

The response of Gov. George Wallace was to hire attorneys to challenge Johnson's ruling.

Three years later, Wallace's appeal process ended when the U.S. Supreme Court refused to overturn Johnson's 1972 order.

On the heels of the Supreme Court's action, a class action suit was filed on behalf of inmates charging that the overcrowded conditions of Alabama prisons violated the constitution. The suit was jointly heard by Johnson and U.S. District Judge Brevard Hand of Mobile. During the trial, attorneys for the state admitted that the conditions in Alabama's prisons constituted cruel and unusual punishment and agreed to sanctions imposed by the court, thus tying the hands of any future governor who would have argued otherwise.

In January, 1976, the judges ruled that in housing 3,700 inmates in four prisons which were built to hold 2,212, the state prison system was in violation of the Eighth Amendment to the U.S. Constitution, which prohibits cruel and unusual punishment. They issued a joint order that no more inmates could be admitted until the overcrowding was alleviated.

Johnson issued orders that inmates had to be provided with meaningful work and educational opportunities, protected against violence from other inmates, provided with rehabilitation and that there be changes in housing and discipline.

Citing filthy conditions and a "jungle atmosphere of violence," Johnson ordered changes in inmate personal hygiene, food service, classification methods, mental health treatment, visitation privileges and the space available for the individual inmate. He named a 39-member Human Rights Committee to monitor compliance with his order.

Wallace responded by accusing Johnson of trying to create a "hotel atmosphere."

Within a year, county jails were overflowing with state inmates. In February of 1977, as James was setting out to run for governor, Houston County officials in settling a federal suit agreed to improve the county jail and build a new jail within two years. Houston was the first of eight counties which would eventually be operating under federal court orders.

This was the situation when James took office. Within weeks he was met with a threat from the corrections department that 363 people would be laid off by March 15 if prisons weren't given $3.5 million in emergency funding.

Prison officials, holdovers from the previous administration, had no way of knowing their request violated one of James' most basic convictions. Whatever the problem, he felt pumping money in should be the last step in the process, not the first. Before resorting to monetary aid, James wanted to know for a fact that every technique known to good management had been applied and that money was really needed.

A second firm belief came into play in the meetings with various corrections-connected officials which he quietly initiated soon after the November election: James believes money spent on lawsuits is money poured down the drain, unless all other alternatives have been explored.

James attempted during his transition period to work through the appointed Board of Corrections to come up with a realistic plan with which state and federal officials could agree upon, Bobby Davis said.

However, James soon decided the Board of Corrections was a hindrance, not a help, Davis said. "He decided the only way he could get the prison system straightened out was if he was in direct control."

So the governor-elect asked advice from House Speaker Joe Mc-Corquodale and from incoming Lt. Gov. George McMillan, who as a senator had headed the legislative task force on prisons.

McMillan steered him to Montgomery attorney Rod Nachman. Nachman had three years before headed Judge Johnson's 39-person human rights committee, McMillan said. The committee had been dissolved but Nachman was well regarded by Johnson because of his knowledge of prison matters.

James called Nachman for an appointment to meet with him. In that meeting he outlined the steps he wanted to take to put the prison system on a good management footing. He asked Nachman if Johnson would give him the power to implement the plan he had outlined. He wanted Johnson to remove the control of the prison system from the Board of Corrections and give it to him as court-appointed receiver. That designation would give him far more power in solving the prison problems than he would otherwise have.

"I was delighted with his suggestion," Nachman said, "because I had long preached that the primary problem was mismanagement. I got hold of Judge Johnson, who was in Florida fishing, and he said he would do it if the request were made by James as governor, Graddick as attorney general, McMillan as lieutenant governor and McCorquodale as speaker of the House."

The four men filed a formal request, which Johnson granted two weeks after James took office. Johnson made it clear he wanted Nachman to remain involved. James named him as special counsel. In granting James' request, Johnson noted that "Time does not stand still but the Board of Corrections and the Alabama prison system have for six years. Their time has run out." Thus James became the first governor since reconstruction to hold both state and federal authority over a public institution.

Johnson would only retain jurisdiction of the case for the next seven months, when upon being sworn in as a member of the 5th Circuit Court of Appeals he turned over the prison case to U.S. District Judge Robert Varner of Montgomery.

James named a search committee composed of Nachman and corrections consultant George Beto to find the best man possible to head day-to-day operations of Alabama's prisons. Beto had been a consultant to Johnson's human rights committee.

A newspaper article quoted an unnamed friend of James describing the qualities which James demanded in a prison commissioner:

"What Fob wanted was a guy who'd get the [federal] court satisfied, who'd rehabilitate the prisoners that could be rehabilitated, and squash 'em like bugs if they started trouble."

"We recommended a fellow named Robert Britton, a top flight guy, and the combination of James and Britton turned the entire management of the prisons around," Nachman said.

Britton was a member of the first graduating class of the school for corrections at Sam Houston State University.

Britton in October of 1979 announced that the state had taken the first major step toward complying with the 1972 court order. He said a four-year, $13.8 million contract with Brookwood Health Care Systems of Birmingham had been signed to supply medical care in state prisons.

The most important item on James' agenda was building prisons.

A Nov. 27, 1979, memo to James from Mike Waters, his legal adviser, capsuled the problem. It was written seven months after Britton was named Commissioner of Corrections:

The state prison system was under federal court order not to admit more inmates to state prisons. Judges in two federal districts, Montgomery and Birmingham, had ordered all state prisoners removed from county jails.

The Legislature had appropriated bond money to build new prisons, stipulating that the prisons could not be built in Escambia, Elmore or Montgomery Counties, where existing prisons were located.

"Hence, the Legislature has limited the flexibility in building prisons where prisons already exist," Waters wrote.

Though the existing prisons were in South Alabama, 52 percent of the prison population was sentenced from North Alabama, Waters wrote.

"As a practical matter, locating prisons in North Alabama should help the rehabilitation of state prisoners. Many of the prison inmates come from low-income families, and these families can hardly afford to take off from work in order to drive from North Alabama to South Alabama to visit them. This creates a real hardship on the families...It also helps breed an attitude within the prison inmate that hinders rehabilitation," Waters wrote.

More than half the state's inmates were housed in the two prisons near Atmore, close to the Florida state line. For many years, state prison authorities had candidly agreed with national penal experts that any additional prisons should be built in North Alabama.

State officials, however, had been rebuffed time after time in efforts to find North Alabama sites for new prisons. A prison had been planned in Boaz until the city in May of 1977 withdrew its offer of a prison construction site to the state. The move, AP noted, was "typical of the public opposition the Board of Corrections faces in finding a prison site."

Only one prison had been built since the 1972 court order. Six months before James took office, the $3 million Staton Correctional Center opened in Elmore County with 448 beds for inmates. Elmore is a central Alabama county which adjoins Montgomery.

Voters five months prior to James taking office approved a $15 million bond issue for prison construction. In the last months of the Wallace administration, three sites were picked and land purchased at Wadley, Heflin and Union Springs for prisons to be built with the bond money.

These were not the sites prison officials knew were needed, however. Union Springs was in Bullock County, a South Alabama location. Neither of the other two was north of Birmingham.

James told Britton to base his guidelines for picking the prison locations on criteria that were best for the entire state.

The first prison site Britton announced was in St. Clair County, near Jefferson County, which has the biggest population of any county in the state. The site was only minutes from Jefferson County by interstate.

There was local opposition when the site was announced, with the company which had provided the land for the prison backing down on its offer when faced with the threat of local retaliation.

A seven-month standoff occurred. When St. Clair residents expressed fear for the safety of their community, James brought them to Montgomery to see for themselves that posh subdivisions thrived only miles from existing prisons.

Suits were filed. Nachman filed suit in federal court in Birmingham to force Kimberly-Clark Corp. to go through with its offer to sell the state the site for the prison. In March of 1980, James announced that the company had agreed to sell the state the property.

Britton began searching for land on which to build a second prison in the Birmingham area, with plans in the mill for a third prison to be built in the Tennessee Valley.

"We had similar litigations in Limestone County when we picked a site there and in Hamilton when we rented a place in which to house aged and infirm inmates," Nachman said. "It took great courage on the governor's part to look at the issue from the standpoint of what was best for the entire state. He knew how essential it was to build the prisons and he never backed off."

James played a time-clock hopscotch with the federal court his entire term in office as he attempted to meet federally-set deadlines for improvements.

He was constantly in court to defend his actions as receiver as inmates sued to have him removed. One news article notes such an appearance in early 1980 as the second time inmates had tried to have him removed from the position.

One of James' primary goals was to develop a classification system. He said, "This was the backbone of the prison system. It told you what every inmate was there for and where he was."

The court had decreed that a computerized classification system had to be in place by March 1, 1980.

That was also the deadline for other improvements, such as adding space for 130 additional prisoners.

Britton also took decisive action in running the prison system.

Newspaper articles of the day relate how Britton, faced with a rampant drug problem, unhesitatingly banned all outside packages to inmates, even packages from their mamas.

Twelve inmates in the Holman Maximum Security Prison near Atmore staged a "hunger strike and peaceful demonstration" in protest of what they said was brutal treatment and tightened security.

Within 12 hours, Britton transferred the leaders of the hunger strike to Kilby Prison at Montgomery.

Four of the group announced they would launch the protest from Kilby.

Britton shipped them out again, this time to a federal penitentiary in Atlanta.

State and federal officials told reporters they had never heard of anything like it. The four convicts complained that it was illegal.

Britton was unmoved and made his feelings clear: "In prison, something like that can lead to a dangerous situation in a hurry. We're not going to put up with any type of mutiny at all. To me, any type of demonstration at all is mutiny."

As in other state agencies, there was an effort directed by James to make the prison system as self-supporting as possible.

Alabama's prison system owned more than 10,000 acres of land in which produce was raised and hogs and cattle were grown.

Britton introduced "a new work ethic."

He said, "I want each inmate to do a full day's work. If you work 'em, they'll be too tired at night to cause trouble." He therefore ordered guards to haul prisoners off to the fields and prison shops at daybreak.

Efforts to make prison land self-supporting were successful.

In some cases, production nearly doubled, reporters wrote after the first year. Prison farms were producing all the vegetables needed by the prison system and plans were being made to provide the food for Alabama mental institutions and reform schools.

Operations were streamlined at a cattle ranch near Montgomery.

At Tutwiler Women's Prison, a canning plant which had been dismantled years before was hauled out of storage and rebuilt.

The canning operation returned such immediate dividends that James gave Britton $750,000 in federal revenue-sharing money to build a canning/freezing plant at nearby Draper Prison.

Two hundred inmates were put to work operating the State Highway Department's furniture plant.

When critics complained that Britton's methods were inhumane, Britton countered by listing the improvements made by the administration in medical care and diet.

Before the James administration, inmates had hardly ever had fresh eggs and never got milk, he said. Their food was served cold.

"It was a month before I could find a piece of meat," he said.

For every problem solved, a new one appeared. A drop in the bond market in early 1980 delayed the closing of the $15 million bond issue which was partially to finance the new prison.

Every way James turned there was someone with his hand out for money, most often backed up in his pleas with a federal court order. Where would he find the money?

Some $1 million was obtained from the Law Enforcement Planning Agency to improve prison electrical systems and heating, a drop in the bucket compared to what was needed for the entire system.

The money would be hard to find. A newspaper in 1980 put the downwardly spiraling state economy in perspective: Prison funding came from the General Fund. Taxes which fed the General Fund had dropped to such a degree that the state had lost $27 million in federal revenue sharing funds. And the taxes were continuing to drop.

Taxes which fed the Special Education Trust Fund were also dropping, with one newspaper noting that the projected shortfall of $40 to $50 million in taxes made proration "inevitable."

James needed roughly $15 million to continue efforts toward complying with the federal court order, the newspaper stated. Another $15 million had to be found for the state's mental institutions to continue their snail's pace toward compliance with similar federal orders to upgrade.

Sheriffs in the state continued to fume and to sue or to threaten suit as inmates filed successful suits to order local officials to do something about overcrowded jails.

In May of 1980, Britton sent corrections official John Hale to tour the Madison County Jail at the request of Madison County Sheriff Joe Patterson, who wanted to show prison officials firsthand how crowded it got when you put 256 inmates in a jail built for 176.

It was, said Patterson, "a time bomb waiting to explode."

"The jail is as crowded and conditions are as bad as any I have seen in the state, but Madison County has to get in line behind other county jails that have court orders to reduce their state prisoner populations," Hale said.

He said the overcrowding could not be relieved until a new prison was built.

Patterson said he had considered filing a lawsuit against James and the prison department to force them to remove some state inmates.

"But if we did that they would only take the men from this jail and put them out in other crowded jails and make situations worse in eight or nine different places, so we will try to cooperate with them for right now," Patterson said.

Five days later, despite Britton's objections, James signed into law an act which made it far more difficult for inmates to earn early release from prison through "good time" behavior.

Its toughest provision eliminated the possibility of such early release for inmates sentenced to more than 10 years.

Britton warned that the law could result in a mushrooming of the state's 5,800 inmate-population, one fourth of which was housed at the time in county jails.

Nevertheless, James said, he agreed "in principle" with the tough new law.

In July, 1980, James was criticized (again) by prison reform groups after it was learned that Britton for three months had been locking inmates who refused to work in an open pen in the sun. They were left in the pen, he said, until "they got their thinking straight."

The concrete-floored pen was "absolutely necessary to discipline inmates who refuse to work," Britton said.

Southern Poverty Law Center attorney John Carroll said the pen was "considerably harsher" in the July heat wave than the treatment afforded those inmates who worked in the fields.

James responded that it was "reasonable confinement" if the inmates refused to work. He expressed confidence that prison wardens were being "fair" in disciplining inmates.

The practice was, after all, one which was used commonly by the nation's armed forces, James said.

In October of 1980, Varner gave the state an eleven-month timetable to remove all state prisoners from city and county jails.

Three months later, Britton told a 1981 legislative committee the state could not meet the timetable because for too many years the state had done "too little too late." News articles noted the state failed to meet each step of that timetable as the Sept. 1, 1981 deadline drew near.

James in May of 1981 got the Alabama Legislature to approve his plan to spend $45 million of the state's $449 million oil-lease windfall on prison construction.

A few hours later, AP reported, Varner threatened to free 1,000 prisoners to relieve overcrowding in county jails and ordered the Department of Corrections to provide him with lists of prisoners "least deserving of further incarceration."

Later that same month, Varner ordered the Montgomery County Jail to free 18 state prisoners and six county prisoners to relieve overcrowding. It was the first time a federal judge in Alabama had freed state prisoners, although county inmates had been released from the Montgomery County Jail on four previous occasions.

James said he would oppose any mass release, AP wrote on June 4. He announced that temporary barracks to hold 500 prisoners would be in place within two months. He also formally announced plans for the 600-inmate prison in St. Clair County and the 600-inmate prison in west Jefferson County. AP called them "the first full-scale prisons in north Alabama."

One week later prison officials signed a letter of intent putting in writing that 500 modular units at a cost of $394,720 would be constructed. The money would come from the $45 million James took from the oil-lease monies.

Those units were completed in July when James announced 500 inmates from crowded county jails were being moved into modular units.

Varner announced four days later that he would release some 400 state inmates.

By that time, the summer of 1981, it was no secret to political insiders that Attorney General Charles Graddick was quietly planning a race for governor the next year, contingent of course upon neither James nor Wallace running for reelection.

In July, after James had worked intensely for nearly three years on prison problems, Graddick jumped into the situation.

He announced that James had not pursued alternate means of housing the inmates and that he would appeal to the U.S. Supreme Court to stop the release of the "bad dangerous people."

When reporters asked Graddick what "alternate" housing he would pursue, he replied, "Tents."

Commented James: "He's out of his cotton-picking mind."

James not only had been pursuing alternatives, his attorneys answered, he had provided alternatives in the past and was building prisons as quickly as humanly possible. His attorneys filled in the court on efforts which had been publicized and efforts which had not, such as his attempt to purchase or lease federal prison space at Talladega. Federal officials had refused because they too had more inmates than space available.

Federal judges refused to take Graddick's arguments seriously. Six hours before the inmates were to be released, Justice Lewis F. Powell Jr. removed the temporary stay he had issued in order to hear Graddick's appeal. The appeal was rejected.

Rebuffed in federal court, Graddick took the unprecedented step of appealing to a state court to intercede in the federal court ruling. The suit, obviously filed for the publicity it generated, charged that James was trying to let criminals loose on the streets.

James commented that Graddick "doesn't mind jumping on a 72-year-old lady who got $22.10 too many food stamps" but has shied away from "the big boys who can fight back," the *Advertiser* stated.

It does not take an attorney to know state courts don't have the power to tell federal courts what to do. A student in a civics class should be aware of the fact. A reporter who covers federal or state courts is aware of the fact. That is, in fact, what Judge Sam Taylor told Graddick when he refused to seriously consider the suit: "State courts don't have jurisdiction over federal cases."

Varner was not the only one concerned about the overcrowding. Prison officials knew the inmates packed like sardines in the August heat could erupt in a matter of moments into violence. They worked with parole officials to come up with what Pardons and Paroles Executive Director Gaston refers to as a unique list of inmates to give to Varner. Gaston said every inmate on the list was either eligible for parole in a matter of weeks or was to be released to officials in other states in which they had committed crimes. The list was further combed to weed out any other than non-violent offenders. On July 25, 277 of these state prisoners were released a few weeks early or handed over to law enforcement officers from other states.

Varner set a September 1 deadline for the state to remove 1,600 of its remaining prisoners housed in county jails.

When Graddick held press conferences and charged that hordes of violent criminals were being turned loose on the citizens, James fumed aloud that it was "inexcusable" for any official to distort facts as Graddick did.

Prison officials also directed intense effort toward reducing the number of state inmates in county jails, prison spokesman Hale said. Twice since September 1979, Judge Varner had ordered the release of inmates from overcrowded county jails. His third such order released 37 inmates from the Montgomery County Jail.

Britton the next day put in effect a "pre-release" program to relieve county jails by allowing state inmates within 90 days of release to leave prison early under the supervision of a sponsor.

As 400 inmates were released to sponsors, Hale said, 400 county-held inmates would take their place.

"State prison officials are moving inmates into the system from county jails this week while...James continues his search for surplus money to fund construction of metal buildings to ease overcrowding in violation of federal court orders," Frank Blanchard wrote in the July 15, 1981, Montgomery *Advertiser.*

A number of county jails as well as state prison facilities are under federal mandates to control overcrowding. State facilities are already packed and prison officials are scrambling to find more space for large numbers of state inmates building up in jails.

Press Secretary Windy Leavell said James was searching for money to construct metal buildings to house another 600 inmates as Hale announced the state successfully used its early-release program to meet a federal court deadline in moving 110 inmates out of the Jefferson County jail.

However, Hale noted, the state now faced similar deadlines for moving state inmates from jails in Montgomery, Mobile, Houston, Tuscaloosa and Choctaw counties.

In August of 1981 Brice Building Company of Birmingham submitted the $21 million low bid for construction of the St. Clair prison. Because only $15 million had been provided in the 1978 bond issue, James had to come up with the additional money (which he did).

On Aug. 29, 1981, AP outlined steps James was taking to temporarily reduce overcrowding:

- Install modular units for 500 prisoners similar to the 500 installed in July.
- Transfer 100 prisoners to federal prison in Atlanta, with another 100 to follow as space became available. Federal officials had agreed.
- Sign a contract with Houston County to use the old county jail for 600 state inmates.
- Transfer state inmates from overcrowded county jails to lesser crowded county jails.

Graddick's grandstanding cost the taxpayers dollars.

On Aug. 23, Bessie Ford of UPI noted James had dipped into his contingency fund to pay four law firms $54,336 for litigation involving prisons, mental health, and the U.S. Department of Education.

Why had the attorney general not provided attorneys to represent the state?

Jimmy Samford, who succeeded Waters as legal advisor when Waters left to go into private practice, commented that James and the attorney general did not always agree on how to handle things.

James disagreed with Varner when the judge ordered a second release of prisoners in December. Conditions in Alabama prisons had improved, the court order had been met in everything except overcrowding and that was being taken care of with the construction of the additional prisons. Prior to his administration, the state had made no effort to take the tough steps necessary to deal with the situation. James had taken those steps. He did not believe the court had any reason to further interfere with the state's running of the prison system.

"James was to confer with legal adviser Jimmy Samford today, then probably ask him to challenge a U.S. District Court order to turn 352 prisoners free just three days before Christmas," Ralph Holmes wrote.

How did the situation differ from the summer release?

In several ways, James said.

"We satisfied ourselves that the 200-odd inmates getting out a little bit early wouldn't jeopardize the public safety," James said.

The same was not true of the December release.

"Also, the legal aspects of the case were different," James said.

In December, James said there was a good chance he could prove the federal court should release the tight grip it had on the state's prison system.

"I think we've got a chance to win, and that's where we're coming from," James said.

"Fundamentally, we think the Alabama prison system is sound. If there is a problem, it is with overcrowding. We are building prisons as fast as humanly possible," said the governor.

"James doesn't want the issue to become a political football, but he plans to fight the release in court," Holmes wrote. "'We'll fight it. It is our desire to win. We plan to go to court.'"

James said crime and prisons "are emotional problems and should be because people are getting beat up, robbed and raped. But the way to solve that is to have adequate prison space and to correct parts of our criminal code that haven't made crime as painful as it should be for the criminals."

While James worked on the presentation he would make to prevent the prisoner release, Graddick held news conferences and took credit for "convincing" the governor to finally do something about the prison system.

James' appeal of the planned release of prisoners in December was successful after his attorneys presented evidence of his accomplishments to the 11th Circuit Court of Appeals in Atlanta.

"Graddick didn't say a word during the hearing," Nachman said. "But he held a press conference on the steps of the courthouse afterward and told reporters how he had stood up to the federal courts."

James in his four years put into effect the most ambitious prison-building program of this century, though there was opposition from varying opponents every step of the way. He built the 1,000-inmate West Jefferson Facility in Jefferson County, the 1,000-inmate St. Clair Facility, the 936-inmate Limestone County Facility and the 500-inmate Staton Annex. Additional space was renovated or leased to house another 1,000 inmates.

In his term, James brought the system to 95 percent compliance level with the federal court order. As he left office he negotiated a settlement in the long-standing federal oversight of the prison system. Graddick had no part in the settlement and did not participate in any of the proceedings.

In his four years in office, James routed more than $321 million to the managing, upgrading and staffing of the prison system, including:

- More than $237 million in appropriations.
- $3.8 million supplemental appropriation in 1978–79.
- $2.2 million Revenue Sharing in 1978–79 for farm equipment, canning equipment, Cattle Ranch construction, grain bins, a classification system and renovation at Draper Prison, Kilby Prison and other facilities.
- $1 million in 1979–80 matching funds for renovation.
- $6.7 million conditional funding for operations in 1979–80.
- $45 million for temporary housing, renovation of the heating, ventilation and electrical systems at three prison facilities, construction of the prison in West Jefferson ($28.8 million), and construction funds for the prison in St. Clair County ($13.8 million).
- $550,000 for work at Staton Annex in 1981–82.
- $25.6 million for a three-year contract to provide medical services for inmates system-wide.

James increased the capacity of existing prisons, adding or finding space for 179 more inmates at Kilby Prison, 20 at Tutwiler Prison for Women, 34 at the Cattle Ranch, 317 at Draper Prison, 80 at Fountain Prison, 25 at Fountain Trusty Barracks, 116 at Holman Maximum Security Prison, and 6 at Staton Prison.

All told, though he served as governor during the worst recession of modern times, James added 1,079 employees to the Department of Corrections and increased the funding 159 percent, from $30.2 million in 1978 to $78.1 million in 1982. He increased the number of corrections officers by one-third, from 774 to 1,031.

He doubled the capacity of the state's corrections' system with the prisons he built and the facilities which he upgraded, leased and renovated. There was space for 4,241 inmates when he took office, more than 10,000 when the facilities he funded were completed.

Because of the vast changes wrought by James, the court released the all-powerful control it had exerted through the position of receiver. Control of the prison system reverted to the state, to be monitored by a four-man implementation committee.

There were subsequent consent agreements. In November of 1984 the court ruled that because of the vast improvements in the system which James had put in place, the case would be de-activated and go off the docket at the end of 1987. This was conditional upon no valid objections being presented by the oversight committee to such action.

The committee did object to ending federal oversight of the system, however.

"The number of inmates was again climbing in the prison system and we were concerned about overcrowding," Nachman said. "We were also concerned that the Pardon and Parole Board was not fulfilling its role, and considering the possibility that the parole process should be put under receivership as had been done with the prison system."

In 1987, the Oversight Committee reluctantly agreed to officially close the books on the suit which provoked Johnson's original ruling.

In 1989, however, Nachman and federal officials watched warily as the same situation developed which originally inspired Johnson's action.

In May, 1989, prison officials announced the prison system was full and could admit no more inmates until there was space available.

In June, 1989, Mobile County Sheriff Tom Purvis in frustration watched the number of inmates in his jail grow to dangerous proportions. He threatened to take 42 state inmates to Montgomery and dump them at the prison gates.

Sheriffs in other counties waited, watching as the number of state inmates in their jails swelled to more than 700 in December.

The Pardons and Paroles Board stepped up its release drastically, combing the prison records of every non-violent offender in the state, letting offenders out who would otherwise have waited until 1994, at the earliest, to be considered.

Judges, aware of the growing crises, put inmates on probation who normally would have been sent to jail. The number of convicted criminals who never set foot in prison swelled to more than 20,000.

Law enforcement officials acknowledge that the grapevine among the criminal element is second to none in disseminating information. Surely the word has passed. There's no room in prison except for violent offenders. Burglarize a house, but don't wave a gun. If you get sent off, you'll get out in a few months.

In 1989, with a stable state and national economy, a new 600-inmate institution sat empty in Barbour County because no money was provided to run it. In fact, Prison Commissioner Morris Thigpen stated at 1990 budget hearings, unless the Legislature provided $7.7 million in emergency funding, there was no money to operate either the Clio facility or a new prison in Clayton.

The 700 inmates in county jails would more than fill the new Clio prison, Thigpen acknowledged. The state's inmate population had swelled to 13,700 and is increasing by 150 inmates per month, Thigpen said. Three new prisons per year would be needed to take care of the increase.

Does the Hunt administration intend to build new prisons?

"It's obvious the kind of struggle we are going through right now to try to get the necessary funding to operate these two new Barbour County prisons and the shape the General Fund is in...I think the answer is very clear. I just don't see any way," Thigpen said.

# — 13 —

# The 1980 Legislative Session

James' "top goals" for the 1980 legislative session, the Associated Press wrote, were passage of a package of Medicaid bills designed to put the Medicaid system in the black for the first time in six years and finding a way to finance his highways and roads program.

Reporters prepared the public for the coming session.

"When the Legislature ended its session last year, it was generally praised by Gov. Fob James, Lt. Gov. McMillan and House Speaker Joe McCorquodale for being one of the most responsible lawmaking bodies to meet in Montgomery for years," Ralph Holmes wrote in the Birmingham *News* prior to the 1980 legislative session.

The nation's downward spiral into recession was continuing, taking with it Alabama and other states which relied heavily on the manufacturing industries for employment. Tax revenue was decreasing as the need for money for welfare and unemployment increased.

Despite the record high unemployment in textile, steel, shoe and auto factories, some $27 million federal advance money which had been borrowed from the Unemployment Compensation Fund prior to James' taking office had been repaid in 1979, the Industrial Relations Department reported.

Political writers warned the state that the 1980 session would be a tough one.

Kendal Weaver in an AP story wrote, "The Medicaid program, facing an estimated $75 million deficit, is under orders to curtail services April 1..."

"This year [James] must decide whether to cut back on state Medicaid or find a way to fund [it]," the *Alabama Journal* noted.

Lt. Gov. George McMillan said the funding of Medicaid, highways and education were the three biggest problems facing the Legislature.

Weaver wrote, "The Mental Health Department, under federal court order to make massive reforms, needs perhaps $50 million more than budgeted for the next fiscal year, and perhaps $100 million in new construction funds to comply with the court's mandate."

Gas tax revenue had dropped while roadbuilding costs had spiraled, Frank Bruer wrote in the Birmingham *Post-Herald.*

"The federal government has threatened to cut all money unless the highway maintenance program is improved," Lou Elliott and Jeff Woodard wrote in the *Journal.*

Weaver stated, "James, who spent his first year seeking spending cutbacks and more efficiency in state government, has given all a fair warning: The budget, for his second year, will be a 'bitter pill to swallow' for more than a few."

The governor's legislative package for 1980 included many proposals which, by themselves, "in any other year, would be top-drawer issues," Weaver wrote. However, this year they would be overshadowed by James' other undertakings.

There was media speculation that James would try to create a new State Department of Environmental Services; also, that he would seek to open the door to private enterprise in the retailing of liquor.

Relentless in his determination to find money for roads and bridges, James did his homework. He worked quietly behind the scenes getting input from the Legislature.

McCorquodale, meanwhile, was also seeking answers to the problem. He polled the 104 other House members, listing eight revenue-producing measures and asking which they favored. The eight proposals ranged from a four-cents gas tax increase to a $10 or $20 increase on license tags. If House members did not support any of the measures, McCorquodale asked them to come up with their own solutions.

McCorquodale explained to a reporter the financial quandary faced by legislators: "The public often views the Legislature as dealing with a bottomless pit of money. This is not true. We cannot deficit-spend like the federal government. Many legislators made campaign commitments not to increase taxes, but the only place the money can come from is new revenue sources."

It is a matter of record that legislators split ranks on just about every issue which faces the Legislature. Nowhere is this split more evident that when legislators face the task of increasing taxes.

A joint House-Senate Highway Committee was also looking for money for highways. Though a flat rate tax had been proposed by some legislators, the committee endorsed a bill sponsored by Rep. Rick Manley to impose a five-percent fuel tax which at 1980 fuel prices would raise $100 million.

The petroleum industry opposed the percent-hike. Bob Geddie explained why: the price of gasoline was expected to increase nationwide. A percent-hike would increase the amount of tax paid by retailers.

Rep. Alvin Holmes of Montgomery opposed an increase in gasoline tax and proposed instead that 10 percent of the needed money come from a new tax on cigarettes and 90 percent from a new tax on beer and other alcoholic beverages.

When the issue of taxes arose, Dr. Paul Hubbert was sure to get involved.

In January, *Post-Herald* columnist Ted Bryant explained why as he answered a question asked of him by a letter writer: "Does the political power of the AEA come from bloc voting by teachers based on instructions from AEA headquarters?"

Bryant wrote:

> The base of a lobby organization's power naturally lies in its membership and the threat of not only a bloc vote, but of those members working for or against a political candidate. But there are any number of other factors that figure into building an organization's power. By far, the most important of those other factors is the person or persons who head up an organization and deal directly with the politicians.
>
> In the case of AEA, that person is Dr. Paul Hubbert, the trim, 40ish, cigar-smoking executive director of an organization that includes more than 50,000 members. Before Hubbert became director more than a decade ago, AEA represented little more than a spring vacation for students and a convention where politicians could say what wonderful things they're doing for education.
>
> In the last 10 years, however, Hubbert's fingerprints have been on more pieces of legislation in Montgomery than most members of the Legislature. Almost every tax bill, whether it raises or lowers taxes, affects the Special Education Trust Fund—which AEA is sworn to protect—in one way or another. So Hubbert is involved...
>
> So how does AEA get its power? First with a group of lobbyists who maintain personal contact with legislators and check bills.

Hubbert is not the only lobbyist AEA has working the second floor of the Capitol.

...usually Hubbert himself testifies before legislative committees...if AEA doesn't get its way in committee, or if it appears a vote in the House or Senate is going wrong, Hubbert is a master of the old "show of force" trick...

To pull this off, a number of teachers are called to the capital from over the state, first to show solidarity on a given issue, then to buttonhole legislators from their districts. Legislators who can tell Hubbert and his lobbyists where to get off find themselves in a different position when confronted with constituents from their home districts...

As for AEA's political contributions, the money comes mostly from something called A-Vote, a political action group to which teachers make voluntary contributions. Most of the money does not come from membership dues...it is significant that more than a dozen legislators are school teachers or affiliated with education...

Hubbert was ever-present to run down James' proposals.

When James released a "working draft" of his budget in January, it was hailed by legislators as the first time a governor had ever given them a budget before they began budget hearings. His budget increased the funding for elementary and secondary schools by some $32 million and asked for a seven percent raise for teachers.

Hubbert, in a manner reminiscent of television commentators who follow presidential speeches with explanations of what was really said, immediately held a news conference to give his own version of James' budget. Hubbert contended that James' budget cut the funding for elementary and secondary schools and increased by $26 million the amount available "for university presidents to do with as they please."

He arrived at this bit of misdirection by ignoring James' reform measures which accompanied the teacher pay raises to provide the money for them. The AEA chief then subtracted from existing revenue sources the $39 million needed for the teacher raises and announced James was cutting the education budget by $6 to $7 million.

Reporters asked Hubbert if he was not happy that James was proposing a pay raise for teachers. Shrugging it off, Hubbert said he still did not know where James would find the money for implementing the rest of the 1979 pay hike. There wasn't money available for that, Hubbert said. Besides, he said, seven percent wasn't enough. Teachers deserved more.

News reports do not reflect that anyone challenged Hubbert's contention that he did not know where James would find the money for the teacher pay raises. James proposed legislation to enable the raises to be paid by using the surplus in the General Fund. Hubbert and State Superintendent of Education Teague called a news conference to fight this and other legislative proposals by James.

Hubbert continued in the same vein in the Jan. 15, 1980, edition of his *AEA Journal* in an article with a headline which stated: "K–12 Suffers in Governor's Budget."

Even on the pages of the anti-James *Journal,* it was obvious that James forged ahead with the heart of his War on Illiteracy despite the cuts he was forced to make as the economy of the state and nation continued to decline.

"The governor recommended cutting his War on Illiteracy funding from $10 million to $2 million," the *Journal* stated. At the same time, James asked for "a $3 million appropriation for a program to attract higher qualified educators into principals' posts."

Hubbert appears relentless in his efforts to discredit James to teachers. On Feb. 1, 1980, a front page headline in the *AEA Journal* stated, "James Budget Bad News." There were other articles or editorials echoing Hubbert's anti-James theme in the same issue. One was headed, "M-O-N-E-Y Spells Relief." Another head stated, "Retired Teachers Impatient for Raise."

News clippings reflect that Hubbert's game-playing accomplished what he intended. It planted the belief in the minds of teachers and even reporters that James was slashing education funds. For example, one reporter soon afterward wrote in an analysis, "The governor also has made a 'war on illiteracy' the chief theme of his education program—but educators in the early grades say his preliminary budget plans would actually cut back funds for classroom basics."

The allegation was repeated in headlines and on the television news. It gradually became the common belief, anchored in memory as firmly as the cement of which the sidewalks outside James' office were made.

It was no secret that Hubbert planned to pack the House gallery with AEA members on February 5 in a show of lobbying muscle for James' State of the State address. He had done it every year.

James may have acted oblivious to the use of such tactics, but it was obvious his supporters were not.

On Feb. 4, the *Alabama Journal* revealed that Grassroots, an organization formed to stimulate public support for James' programs, was also asking his supporters to sit in the gallery for his speech the next night. This "is a switch," the *Journal* observed.

James' supporters staked out their seats in the gallery as early as noon on Feb. 5 for the 6:30 p.m. speech. Hubbert's group, arriving at the normal early time, were crowded out of the gallery and forced to mass outside the House chamber door.

Hubbert and AEA members obviously perceived the incident as a staged confrontation designed by James to "one-up" them. The perception was probably reinforced by smug looks on the faces of James' supporters and cabinet members. The perception was wrong.

To James, each participant in state government (or any level government for that matter) has a role to play. Elected officials play the highest role. Joe McCorquodale was not only elected by the people in his House district to serve as a legislator—he was elected by his peers to serve in the highest leadership role in the House. George McMillan was elected by the majority of all those who voted to serve in the highest leadership role in the Senate. The same was true of Charlie Graddick as attorney general and of the other constitutional officers. In carrying out his duties as governor, James believed he should work with these elected officials, assuming fully all responsibilities and powers given him as governor, respecting all responsibilities and powers given them in their respective offices—and expecting them to do the same.

Hubbert and other lobbyists also had roles in the governmental process in James' view, but they could never vie for power in his eyes with elected officials whose powers and duties emanated from the constitution and the people. James therefore not only did not sit around and plot how to defeat Hubbert, he did worse in Hubbert's eyes—he appeared to ignore him in the decision-making process. James corrects that assessment: "I treated him the same as any other Alabama citizen." That would have been the same in Hubbert's eyes as to be ignored. The two were motivated by different agendas: Hubbert's every step was taken with the sole purpose of pleasing his bosses—the AEA members in the state. James saw his duty as "playing no favorites," giving everyone a fair hearing. Department heads tell of numerous times when James instructed them to make decisions based solely on the merits of an idea, the facts involved and "how the overall issue related to the public good."

It was a jubilant James who began his 1980 State of the State address with an announcement that the cost of state government had been cut by $50 million during his first year in office. "Yet, in many areas, services were improved," he said.

"We have just touched the tip of the iceberg in streamlining this state's government, using your tax dollars to advantage," he said.

He put it officially on the record that he had found the money to fund the first-quarter of the "conditional" teacher/state employee raises which legislators had approved in 1979.

He also introduced the bill which was his solution to funding the rest of the seven percent pay raises. He asked legislators to allow him to use any reserve of the General Fund (which had an annual surplus every year at the time) and the SETF "interchangeably" to insure that teachers and state employees continued to receive their increases, as they had for the first quarter of the year. The reserves would also be used to "insure either fund against proration."

James asked solons to pass a number of bills.

His legislative requests should have sounded familiar as he outlined them in his speech. The words came straight from his campaign and from his 24-paragraph inaugural speech.

"The greatest injustice in this country is the inflation imposed upon us all, but, more severely, upon those citizens living off fixed retirement incomes," he said. "These citizens, the generation of my parents, through their hard work and sacrifice, have provided us with great opportunity. It is not their fault that as farmers, as housewives, as working men and women, as school teachers, as businessmen, that we suffer extreme inflation.

"NO," he emphasized, and on his copy of the speech the words were underlined, "it is the expedient politics of government at all levels, the deficit spending of the federal government, and the flagrant printing of U.S. dollars.

"It is right for us to remedy this injustice as best we can, meager as our actions may be," he said, asking legislators to pass a bill which eliminated the utility tax on electricity for citizens 65 years of age or older.

Medicaid had claimed much of his time in the preceding months and it took up much of his speech.

"Medicaid was intended to provide medical services for those who are unable to secure such services through their own efforts or that of their families," he said. "The idea is noble, but like so many government programs, the implementation is ill-conceived, ill-designed, and, if allowed to continue on its present course, will either break the State of Alabama or necessitate new taxes on a continuing basis.

> In its first year, 1970, just ten years ago, Medicaid cost the taxpayers of Alabama $12 million. This year, $94 million...
> Medicaid has been in the red for the past five years and threatens to bankrupt your state government. This practice is prohibited by our constitution and is against the law.
> This problem must be solved. We can and should provide medical care for those who genuinely cannot help themselves and whose families genuinely cannot help them either. But unless both these conditions are fully met, it is a disgrace to penalize the hard-working, taxpaying citizen in order to subsidize a cost created by the irresponsibility of others.

He asked legislators to pass a comprehensive Medicaid reform package.

As a short-term solution, James asked the Legislature to authorize him to transfer $25 million from the State Insurance Fund to the General Fund to meet Medicaid obligations for the coming year. As a permanent solution, he asked the Legislature to petition the federal government to modify regulations "so that we can make Medicaid efficient and at the same time improve the service and stop the abuse."

The petition James presented the Legislature asked the federal government:

- To permit the state to set reasonable co-payment requirements on all Medicaid Services.
- To allow the state to purchase medical services and supplies on a bid basis to insure maximum quality at an economical cost.
- To allow the state to deny eligibility to recipients because of proven abuse.
- To permit the state to impose reasonable financial assessments on the families of recipients.

If the federal government did not respond to "these reasonable, common-sense requests," James said, the Legislature would either have to come up with new revenue or "I have no choice but to eliminate the optional programs of Medicaid" as of Oct. 1, 1980.

"Public education in the broadest sense is an essential function of government," James said. "It is not so stated in the Alabama constitution. My fourth request...is to pass legislation proposing a constitutional amendment establishing education as an essential function of government."

Ira Harvey commented that it was the first such proposal since 1936.

James continued, "Alabama does not have an education policy. My fifth request...is to pass a bill setting in concrete a policy designed purely for the most precious, special group of all, our children, a policy to win the 'War on Illiteracy.' "

"Gov. James completed his package for education by presenting proposals for the broadest and most far-reaching restructuring of the governance of education since 1935," Harvey wrote.

This included:

- An improved minimum-program law to lower teacher/student ratios in the basic skills. "This is not happening despite declining enrollment and increased funding for the past five years. The money is not getting through to the classroom, and it must," James said.
- Expansion of the kindergarten program by 200 new units per year until available for every child. James asked that local boards be allowed to double-shift kindergarten programs if they so desired.
- A three-tier diploma system in which graduating seniors would receive either an academic diploma, a vocational diploma, or a certificate of attendance.
- A restructured and stripped-down State Department of Education with six basic missions for grades K–12:

    1. To monitor teacher/pupil ratios grade by grade. "Averaging by a statewide basis leads to false conclusions," he said.

    2. To establish standard fiscal accountability in all schools, including full disclosure of the relationship between federal, state, and local funds. "Alabama ranks 11th in the nation in federal expenditures per-student; we rank 46th in the nation in local expenditures," James said. "I urge the Legislature to pass House Bill 41, which raises the minimum level of local participation from 7 to 10 mills. Underlined in James' copy of the speech was the next sentence, "This is a step in the right direction."

    3. To accurately assess student performance by testing and on-site inspection. Underlined on his copy of the speech was, "Problems are never solved by sweeping them under the rug."

4. To require a basic-core curriculum for grades K-12, with all other programs optional and determined by local school boards.

5. To provide continued training to improve the skills of teachers, principals, and superintendents with compensation that is competitive in the job market, and commensurate with the qualifications, the performance, and the responsibility of the individual.

6. "And, last but not least, to develop a standard set of rules that students must follow to insure a level of discipline conducive to learning," James said. "We must never forget the ultimate responsibility for a child's learning lies first at home, and then [underlined] right in the lap of the classroom teacher — and that responsibility is awesome."

"In the War on Illiteracy," James told legislators and listeners, "the teachers are the infantry, the principals are the master sergeants, the superintendents are the captains, and the [underlined] mamas and daddies are the generals—and, too often, we mamas and daddies have been absentee generals, and that won't work. To every parent in Alabama, I ask your support of this amendment, this policy, and House Bill 41."

"I have been in your State Capitol one year," James said, switching subjects, "I have looked, I have listened as to how your tax dollars are spent. I am convinced that the earmarking of all your tax dollars is a cancer that needs immediate removal."

Earmarking hurts the very people it was intended to help, because in any given year, when there are extra dollars, the government will swell like a bloated hog; and when dollars are scarce, that hog will continue to feed at the expense of the children, the poor, and the general public.

"I understand the history of earmarking, but this is a new day. Let me show you what earmarking is like—a tire tube with a thousand patches," he said, holding aloft an innertube.

Earmarking won't stand up when the rubber hits the road. It won't carry Alabama into this decade viable, efficient, sensitive to the needs of the people. I have no desire to add another patch and play the politics of appeasement and expediency...

Earmarking is foolish and unwise. Suppose that, today, your family decides to budget your income; the right amount for food, for house payment, for utilities, for clothes, for insurance, for education, for a car payment. Then, next year, you sit down to budget again. Suppose you are made to budget exactly the same as the year before. Even if your income changes, up or down, your car stops running, your roof leaks, or your child gets sick. What could you do if your income was already earmarked and you could not use it as needed?

Each year the Legislature budgets your tax dollars, and as long as we have earmarking, your state government will be in the same fix as the family I just described...I ask you to let your legislators know if you want your tax dollars spent with the same care and discipline with which you spend your own money.

James asked lawmakers to pass a bill eliminating statutory earmarking of all state revenue and to enact legislation to be approved by the voters eliminating constitutional earmarking. The legislation had been part of the new constitution which had failed the year before.

On James' copy of the speech he had marked out "Now, big bosses of the special interest groups will pitch a fit" and substituted a comment provoked by the new tax limitation law in California. "Unearmarking can be Alabama's Proposition 13," James said.

"Transportation is fundamental to the economic, social, and recreational well-being of every man, woman, and child in Alabama," James said, turning to highways. "We are derelict in our duties if we allow our roads and bridges to deteriorate. Yet, it is only fair that state government be efficient before we speak of new revenue."

His administration's Highway Department was efficient, James said, noting that cost of running the Highway Department had been cut by 8.7 percent.

"Revenue for highways is declining as Alabamians buy less gas with a fixed state tax that hasn't changed in 20 years," he said. "But, the cost of fixing roads and bridges has gone up like everything else.

The Highway Department, together with Public Safety, are actively weighing trucks and enforcing our weight laws. Eleven teams of highway and law enforcement personnel, each with a set of portable truck scales, are being put in the field. This costs money, but will pay off big in preventing overweight vehicles from destroying your roads.

Last year there were approximately two billion gallons of gasoline purchased in Alabama at an increased cost of 40 cents per gallon, which equals $800 million. No rational mind would think the price of gas will not increase another 40 cents per gallon this year as the price rises to match world levels. This is another $800 million leaving Alabama. All told, one billion six hundred million dollars over a 24-month period. This [underlined] is economic disaster.

"Mississippi and Georgia both have a higher gas tax than Alabama, yet pump prices remain virtually the same in all three states," he said. "The price of gas will continue to rise to match world levels and we do ourselves an injustice if we don't take a few cents to fix our roads. I stand ready to support and work with the Joint Highway Committee and other members of the House and Senate in finding the best way to correct this injustice and meet our obvious responsibility."

"We have other needs," James said. He listed them:

1. "There are elementary and secondary schools to be renovated and in some cases it's time to build new schools. Further delay will result in greater costs." James in the budget he gave to the Legislature requested $20 million absolute and $15 million conditional funding for capital outlay to build new and improved elementary and secondary schools.

2. "There is good reason to employ additional state troopers in order to safeguard our highway passengers, enforce truck weight laws and speed limits, 24 hours a day, seven days a week.

3. "Then, there is mental health, the prisons, and our poor, especially the young and the elderly. All need attention.

To pay for these services already places a heavy burden on Alabama taxpayers. I will try to the best of my ability to do what is right. Until our house is in order, I think it is wrong to seek additional revenue, with exception of highways for the unique reasons I have already outlined. I will support another revenue measure that is fair and progressive only when our house is in order.

There can be no new beginning unless there is an end to what has been happening in the past.

"The biggest problem I have is that a lot of people want to continue the mistakes of the past. They don't want a new beginning because they liked it the way it was," he said.

I say we must learn from the mistakes of the past. I say we need a new beginning that has meaning to every man, woman and child. It is not my new beginning. It's the people's. I will make a lot of politicians, bureaucrats, wheeler-dealers and those who desperately cling to the past angry as a swarm of hornets, but so long as I know I am helping to bring about that new beginning for the people of Alabama, that's all that matters.

The important thing is to give the people good state government. I'm not worried about politics. I am worried about Alabama next year, in 10 years, in 20 years. That's what has meaning to me.

I have tonight proposed solutions to our problems for the short-term and the long-term. I will work day and night to make Alabama a better place to live for every man, woman and child. However, a governor must work within the framework of laws set by the Legislature.

...I ask that grass-roots Alabama make their views known, loud and clear. Tonight I ask for your support and your prayers.

There were also numerous other bills pushed by James which he did not mention in his speech.

News accounts noted that James spoke "...above the shouts of teachers and school employees protesting in the hallway outside the House chamber."

Commented House speaker McCorquodale of the commotion, "It's very regrettable and I think it's an utter disgrace for this to occur while the governor is attempting to outline his program before the people."

Commented Hubbert on the speech, "There are no bloated hogs in the nursing homes and no bloated pigs in the classrooms."

Sen. Don Harrison of Montgomery, perhaps Hubbert's strongest ally in the Senate, was asked by reporters to comment. Harrison said his overall reaction was, "Blah."

The 1980 legislative session would set precedents as feuding factions sparred and tempers flared.

In obvious retaliation for the catcalls of Hubbert's group on opening night, "somebody" closed the Capitol's rotunda between the House and Senate, restricting visitors to the gallery on the floor above. The move was obviously to prevent Hubbert from buttonholing legislators, though no one among the House leadership openly took the blame or credit.

A columnist for Hubbert's *Journal* complained that the "heavy-handedness" of the legislative leadership in closing the rotunda "smacks of undemocratic right wing tactics similar to those used in Germany prior to World War II."

"He wasn't calling Joe McCorquodale a Nazi, mind you," one newspaper editorialized. "But don't be deceived by these feints of independence. The Legislature has never threatened to outlaw Hubbert's checkbook."

The rotunda was reopened.

The 1980 session might live up to its advance billing as "possibly the toughest in history," Frank Bruer wrote after the first week.

> It took only two days for tempers to grow short, finger-pointing to start and a rash of name-calling to break out.
>
> By the second day two members of the House of Representatives were calling each other liars.
>
> This is a rarity. It hardly ever happens before the last two or three days of a session and mostly only on the final day...Legislators in both chambers claimed James was "too idealistic" last week in his call for unearmarking...and a new highway revenue source.

Bruer wrote at length of earmarking: "...Alabama has more earmarked funds than any state in the nation.

> Thirteen sources involving currently more than $1.2 billion are earmarked for education.
>
> That's only part of it. In all, 70 revenue sources are earmarked, with only 10 of those going into the general fund.
>
> It's even more complicated than that. The various revenue sources are split in numerous ways.
>
> For example, specific portions of the 12-cent tobacco tax are earmarked for the general fund, education, mental health, conservation and welfare.
>
> The income tax is earmarking within earmarking. Except for an amount necessary to replace the homestead exemption...all of the income tax is earmarked for the Special Education Trust Fund and further earmarked only for teachers' salaries. It cannot be used to pay for salaries of janitors, cafeteria workers...[etc.]

Hubbert's tirade against James never let up. A Feb. 22 editorial in Hubbert's *Journal* was headed, "Why Can't Teachers Have a Raise?" A second editorial, headed "Teachers, Look Out For Hatchet," stated, "Rumor has it that very soon the James program calls for the elimination of P.E. as a required subject. So, if you're a P.E. teacher, on your guard!"

Such scare tactics were obviously meant to incite teachers and to induce those who were not already members of AEA to join.

In March, AEA authorized its Board of Directors to call a strike if the Legislature removed earmarking or if legislators did not give teachers at least a 10 percent raise.

"By laying the foundation for a statewide strike, Alabama teachers last week showed the extent of their anger over...James' proposals to provide a 7 percent pay raise for teachers and unearmark tax money...," wrote Jean Lufkin Bouler in the Birmingham *News*.

By the time of the annual AEA convention, teachers were ready to lynch James.

At that convention, James' education adviser, Lager, responded to the allegations tossed around by Hubbert's camp that James was "anti-education."

"I've been a teacher for 21 years," Lager said. "Any teacher who has lived in Alabama for 20 years who calls Fob James anti-education is a fool or a charlatan. Fob is honest-to-God committed to getting education out of the mess it's in."

Lager then made a statement that echoed James' disbelief that anyone would take seriously the distortions made by Hubbert, "I don't think teachers will be fooled by a bunch of propaganda from AEA," Lager said.

He was wrong. And James was wrong.

James accepted the invitation to speak to the AEA assembly which was issued annually to every governor. Depending on which road he took into Birmingham, James probably passed by the billboard which stated in giant letters, "Fob: Teachers must eat too. 7% is not enough."

"Dear Ann Landers," James began his speech to the 4,000 AEA members at the convention. "About one year ago I got a new job. At that time I thought I had lots of friends in the state of Alabama."

After the laughter subsided, James for an hour and forty minutes explained his plans for education and answered teachers' questions.

Explaining his views on unearmarking, James promised teachers he would not support "any kind of unearmarking unless education were declared an essential function of government under the constitution," Harvey wrote. Designating education as an essential service would prevent education funds from being prorated when revenues fell short of expectation.

In making the promise, James probably sealed the fate of his legislation to declare education "essential," for it suddenly became part of James' "unearmarking" fight. James never intended it for any but the purpose he explained—to give education its rightful place at the top of state priorities.

Education should be based on a pyramid, with primary and secondary learning forming the base for higher learning, he said.

"In this state we have somehow got an inverted pyramid," he said.

He told teachers his administration the previous year had held four-year colleges to the same level of spending for the first time ever, while increasing by 10 percent the funding for primary and secondary education.

The hostility of his audience prior to his speech was noted by reporters. Quotes from several teachers indicated the hostility had lessened after they listened to him. One teacher commented on the "courage" it must have taken James to appear before them. Another commented that he handled the hostile questions well and without becoming angered.

Did Hubbert find it discomforting that James might have achieved a little rapport with the teachers? Possible. The *AEA Journal* a week after James' speech to AEA carried a prominent article which was obviously intended to dispute the facts James had presented to teachers: "The most glaring error is that Alabama is not 5th in state dollars for schools," the article stated. However, "It is true we rank 5th in the proportion of dollars that come from the state."

With a dearth of fact to dispute, Hubbert apparently had no qualms about resorting to innuendo. An editorial in the same issue had the headline, "Retirement Cuts Rumored".

James never at any time during his term in office introduced legislation to cut retirement benefits which had been earned by teachers. The damage was done in the eyes of teachers who read the headline, however. Hubbert's message was clear: teachers needed him to protect them against James.

The year before, in the spring of 1979, teachers had massed on the steps of the capitol, demanding that James come out to speak to them.

James had refused, instead inviting them inside to talk in more comfortable surroundings.

A year later, James had learned a lot. He knew by this time teachers did not just happen to show up on the steps of the capitol. He knew exactly who to call if he wanted to talk to the instigator of that rally.

In the spring of 1980, he invited Hubbert and the AEA Board to the mansion for breakfast.

In the April 4, 1980, *AEA Journal* the state AEA president warned teachers that "nobody should get their hopes up" about the breakfast meeting. In perhaps an unintended slight, the president also indicated disdain for James' education program. The governor had invited teachers inside the capitol to talk the previous year, the AEA president reminded readers: "The results of that meeting were minimal at best. The governor went on to push his *so-called* 'War On Illiteracy' through the Legislature, while only securing a 'conditional' pay increase for teachers."

At the breakfast meeting, the president wrote, "The morale of teachers was also discussed with the governor, as was the necessity of AEA being provided input into the education decisions governing public education in the state."

The *Advertiser* wrote, "No decisions were made at the three-hour meeting, but AEA Executive Director Paul Hubbert said it provided a chance for 'good dialogue'...and opened up some lines of discussion for the future."

"We indicated at that meeting that we felt very strongly that he needed to reconsider some of the statements he had made about unearmarking," Hubbert told reporters at the time. Hubbert said most states designate certain tax monies for highways and education. "That seemed to be something he had not considered before."

An argument can be made that the meeting was a milestone in the relationship between Hubbert and James, maybe not a turning but a starting point. Lager had left his position as education adviser, moving to Mobile to work in international trade. For the first time, the governor and the AEA chief communicated directly.

They engaged in conversation long enough to discover they shared important goals. More and more often after that, the two men talked.

Soon after the breakfast meeting, the *AEA Journal* on the editorial page wrote as part of an editorial: "FACT: According to the results of the governor's California Achievement Tests, two-thirds of Alabama students scored at or above national level. FACT: Alabama is getting as much per dollar expended as any state in the country when one compares low expenditures against achievement tests."

James used knowledge gained in his first legislative session to make his second more productive.

Whereas James had set out to communicate equally with all legislators, he soon learned this was impossible.

"I was bad, early on, to write letters to them," James says with a laugh. "I'd send up short, double-spaced letters to be put in their mail boxes keeping them informed on what I thought was important. Two weeks later the letters would still be sitting there in those boxes, unopened."

"When we decided we needed floor leaders we began identifying people who were supportive of Fob's programs," said Bob Geddie, James' Senate liaison.

"I sat down, Geddie sat down, and we began to identify people who were team players," said Don Bryan, House liaison for James. "That was no problem."

The list was given to James for his input. There was no problem there either.

"Then I showed our list to Joe McCorquodale," Bryan said. "He took two names off our list, Reps. Roy Johnson of Tuscaloosa and Jimmy Holley of Elba. Then he added some folks he said were supportive of Fob and that's why we wound up with McCorquodale's people for most of our floor leaders, like Rick Manley, Jack Biddle of the rules committee, and Jim Sasser.

"They were all the speaker's men. They carried the speaker's water," Bryan said. "To think they were going to be floor leaders who thought first of Fob was asinine. Floor leaders ought to say to hell with everybody else. They can't be working for the governor and the speaker at the same time."

James refused to remove Johnson from the list of floorleaders even though McCorquodale considered him a "Hubbert" man. James' faith in Johnson never wavered. Johnson later (to the astonishment of many) introduced unearmarking legislation. Still later, he stood with James in the fight to pass a voluntary prayer law.

Bryan said he made it a point to pull the floor leaders aside before they met with James to discuss legislation and tell them, "I don't want a one of you in here if you're not going to support him. Period."

But that wasn't the way James felt, Bryan said. "He's changed his mind today. But back then when he addressed the maybe 20 floor leaders we had, he'd tell them 'Now gentlemen I want your help, your support, but all I'm asking is that you give me a fair hearing and come down on the side of right.'

"It didn't mean anything for me to tell them they had to support the governor. The boss was telling them that was not the way he was going to operate," Bryan said. "Today, I suspect he feels differently. In fact I know he does."

Geddie said James did not want floor leaders at first because he was inexperienced and did not know their value.

"We should have had floor leaders selected before our first legislative session, and we should have instilled a sense of loyalty in those selected," Geddie said.

Even after James picked floor leaders, he did not use them as effectively as they should have been used, Geddie agreed.

The effective way, Geddie said, is to get them together in a room and hammer out a legislative program. "They should have been told up front, here are my rules. Can you live with them? If you can, you're a floor leader. Floor leaders can disagree among themselves, but when they leave that room they must have an agreement all will live up to," Geddie said.

"It's okay to differ in that room. But when you walk out that door as a floor leader of the governor, you should be a supporter of his bills," he said.

Even when Bryan felt strongly that James was completely wrong in how he went about something, however, Bryan did not necessarily confront him with it. There was a line over which he did not step.

"There's something about the governor, about being the governor. Fob the governor and Fob my friend are two different people," Bryan tried to explain. "There are bounds you are limited to. He's the governor of Alabama and you don't forget it."

Bryan said James "knew what he wanted. He knew why he wanted it. Often times we didn't articulate what he wanted well enough to the public and we all knew that. Most of us knew at the time we were doing a poor job of communicating, but frankly we didn't know how to correct it. We went in and got caught up in what we were doing and we forgot how essential public relations is. Why, all of us with our business backgrounds knew you had to politick every day of your life in business. At Diversified Products there wasn't anybody there Fob didn't know by name, a thousand and something employees and he knew their wife, their grandfather and grandmama's name and knew their children, where they were, when they were sick, what grade they were in. He was out in the plant and he talked to them. We were in state government and we knew to do those things but we didn't do them. He didn't get out and talk to state employees and tell them what his goals and objectives were. That can be done. We were too caught up in trying to move ahead quickly and get everything done in four years because he had told everyone four years was it. Fob told everyone, hell, we won the second world war in four years. Surely we can straighten state government out in four years."

Rep. Leigh Pegues of Marion sponsored James' comprehensive package of bills providing for a complete overhaul of Medicaid. It was first on the legislative agenda.

The gas tax increase never got off the ground in 1979 when it was shot down by a two-to-one margin, Ralph Holmes wrote in the Birmingham *News*. "By the time the next regular session of the Legislature came around, James had carefully done his homework and proved that he had learned some politics along the way."

The tax, James said, was necessary to keep Alabama's highways up-to-date, to repair old bridges and resurface roads.

"So, with the help of roadbuilding lobbying organizations and after telling his story over the state," Holmes wrote, the tax increase began its way through the hazardous route bills must take which includes some 16 points at which they can die.

The Ways and Means committee was chaired by Rep. Walter Owens, who had promised James that the committee would approve a bill to provide highway money and send it to the full House for a vote.

To garner support for his highway bill, Pegues revealed results of a legislative study of pump prices in Georgia and Mississippi where state gasoline taxes were higher than Alabama taxes but the price charged consumers for gas was not. He said, "There's no rhyme or reason for pump prices. They're not affected by taxes."

Ballots were taken by voice votes on whether to approve or kill a bill sponsored by Rep. Nelson R. Starkey Jr. of Florence which levied a five-percent increase on wholesale fuel. It had the endorsements of the Joint Highway Study Committee, the Association of County Commissioners and the governor.

"Vocal response from committee members seemed equally divided," Bruer wrote. "But Owens swiftly declared the committee's favorable report. He informed the committee the vote had been 9–6."

Right behind Starkey's bill was a package of bills sponsored by Manley to provide highway money by removing some exemptions on the existing fuel taxes.

James at this point was working quietly, without fanfare, with legislators. This is evident from various news articles written at the time, though maybe only through brief references to such.

It only takes a few hours in the archives reviewing what columnists wrote of James to learn that he was dismissed by many as ineffectual in dealing with the Legislature.

Why did James so firmly come to be perceived as a governor who was unable to get his legislation passed that columnists blithely use the "fact" as background eight years later?

Perhaps insight can be gained from reviewing the news coverage of the waning days of the 1980 session.

In 1980, all legislation stalled for three months as divisive factions performed exactly as reporters had predicted prior to the session.

Meanwhile, revenue figures for the first months of the year revealed an unexpected downward trend and budget analysts accordingly revised their predictions downward for the next year. There would not be as much increase in tax money as had been predicted. James rewrote his education budget to conform to the smaller amount of money anticipated to be available.

Legislators were so embroiled in fights over the original budget that neither the Education Budget nor the General Fund Budget was given much hope of passing by reporters.

Reporters three months into the session prepared their readers for the flop which the 1980 session was sure to be. No significant bills would be passed, they wrote. Both budgets would probably flounder around and die.

Frank Blanchard in a May 4 column whimsically compared the session to college terms in which students "majored in parties and minored in studies."

> They set a pattern...nine weeks on the party circuit, cutting some classes and otherwise enjoying the extracurricular diversions of campus life, and one week of feverish cramming for final exams.
>
> You could spot these free spirits instantly on exam day. Eyes at half-mast, bloodshot. Clothes so wrinkled they must have been slept in, breath reeking of coffee...

> For the past three months...lawmakers have faced issues rang-
> ing from a bill to designate the wild turkey as the state game bird
> to budgets...
> Few bills have passed, and even fewer of the vital revenue and
> budget measures have cleared both houses...
> And now, with the end of the session upon them, the lawmakers
> are cramming for finals.
> The calendars of bills are bulging; some of the legislation is
> vital...New taxes needed to fund those budgets await action.
> In a last minute sprint...will they get their sheepskin or return
> to Goat Hill to make up an "incomplete?"

*Advertiser* writer Jeff Woodard wrote, "McCorquodale said Monday he does not expect the education budget to be considered by the
House at least until Thursday, which will leave the lower chamber with
two days to take final action on the money bill...

"Because the session is about to end, House committees no longer
are handling House bills and are concentrating on Senate-approved
legislation."

Frank Bruer wrote, "Neither the general fund nor education budget for the next fiscal year has passed. If both do in their present form
they each likely will be in proration early next year. State government
is somewhere between $60 million and $100 million short of the revenue needed to carry it through 1980–81.

"There are growing indications nothing of earthshaking significance will get through the maze of political tangles."

Sprinkled throughout news reports are predictions by unnamed
observers and anonymous sources that the session is doomed and that
James is to blame.

An unnamed person identified only as a "lobbyist" is quoted as
pronouncing, "This session has been something like a ship without a
rudder...Nobody knows where the hell they are going."

Also sprinkled throughout the articles and columns are references
to James which by nuance cite him as backup source for the pronouncements of his ineptitude, such as, "James, who admits readily to being
a novice in politics..."

James, who happened to feel he would be batting at least .700 that
Legislative session, obviously had "admitted" no such thing—unless in
jest.

Another reporter wrote, "The governor—still not demagogueing
it but his voice at least rising now above an inaudible whisper—says

the Legislature shoots down everything he tries to get through..."

Really? Neither the words nor the image bear any relation to the Fob James described by cabinet officials and close friends or on view to the public.

Aides say they were confounded at the time when they read such attributions because they never heard James voice similar sentiments. James says he could never have made such a statement because he never believed it.

The session did not end as lobbyists or unnamed sources had predicted daily in news reports.

Faced with a desperate financial shortage, momentum grew within the Legislature to increase the state sales tax. James was adamant in his opposition.

Excerpts from these reports describe the frenetic activity as the clock ticked away the session.

> ...the House (in passing nine tax measures) has provided the Senate with a potential new income of less than $60 million — some $40 million less per year than the Senate leaders claim is necessary.
>
> The position with only three days left in the session is that a majority of the Senate still thinks [raising] the sales tax — with exemptions for food and drugs — would be the simplest and perhaps fairest way of getting the $100 million which is claimed to be needed.
>
> James has repeatedly said he would veto a one percent additional sales tax, claiming it is regressive and hits the poor people the hardest...

There were indications that James was not sitting idly by waiting for the session to end in ignominy, that he was wheeling and dealing in age-old political tradition.

Ralph Holmes wrote on May 6, "As far as late night hours go, Gov. Fob James, hoping for legislative settlement of money matters by the end of this session, is telling lawmakers his office will be open until 11 p.m. each day for the convenience of the Legislature."

Sam Duvall on May 7 reported the machinations employed by James to convince the House to send to the Senate his bill which gathered all of the state's environmental services under one director appointed by the governor.

"It had been passed by the House the week before but James lacked the three-fifths votes needed to suspend the rules to send the bill to the Senate," Duvall wrote.

Some House members objected to the bill because they said it did not conform to federal guidelines.

Duvall said James worked all weekend with federal authorities to rework the bill, however, bringing it into compliance with federal guidelines.

Under pressure from the governor's office, the 37 votes against suspension of the rules did not hold up, Duvall said.

> One House member who voted against transferring the bill said he had been asked to reconsider his vote on the promise that the governor would not veto a favored local bill which he wanted passed...

On Tuesday night, Duvall reported, "...the James administration... had the necessary votes to send the bill to the Senate...by one vote.

The bill will create a huge 'umbrella' agency which will control strip mining, air and water pollution and certain operations of the state Health Department."

The bill died in the Senate.

The House had to choose which, if any, gas tax would be approved: a bill sponsored by Rep. Larry Keener which levied a flat 4-cents-per-gallon tax or Manley's bill to impose a five percent hike.

After fierce lobbying by the petroleum industry against the percent-tax, Keener's bill began to look more attractive to legislators.

"Keener contended that a 4-cent-per-gallon tax would be constant and not rise with the anticipated jump in gasoline prices at the pump and would be more fair to the consumer."

"The second year on the gas tax, we were down to two or three critical votes," Geddie said. James met with Baldwin County Sen. Bob Gulledge and Gulledge agreed to vote with James after learning the Highway Department planned to widen Highway 59 to Gulf Shores in his district.

"There was a lot of bargaining," said Don Bryan. "I never got chewed out by Fob in my life like I did when Roy Johnson told him he had sold me his vote to get some road paved. I thought Fob was going to have a damned heart attack. But the road needed paving. The Highway Department had it down to be paved at some point in the future. What difference did it make when it was paved?"

"There was a water project in their district that Bobby Denton and Charlie Britnell wanted," Geddie said. "We addressed that need also. One by one, we picked up the votes we needed."

Keener's bill passed in the House and was sent to the Senate, where it was approved, with amendments, 18–15. It was returned to the House, where opposition was expected.

"But in an unexpected move, the House, at Manley's recommendation, quickly concurred with the Keener substitute and sent the bill to the governor who has said he will sign it," one report stated.

The House voted 48 to 41 to agree with the Senate changes.

"Although unpopular, Keener said that the people of his district had indicated that the state and county road programs needed more money now and not later," one reporter wrote.

James supported the tax for two reasons. He argued that the tax would not make gasoline prices in Alabama increase more than in neighboring states and that the tax was desperately needed to repay Highway Department debt from prior years which totaled $40 million a year. Prior governors had passed the bond issues and not provided for the pay-back, thus the majority of highway money had to go to debt service rather than current needs.

It was obvious from the beginning of the session that the Senate and the House had totally different views as to how the state budgets should be written. Neither accepted the other's versions.

When the Senate substituted the House-passed Education Budget with one which all parties admitted spent more than the state would take in, James hit the roof. It would put the state in proration for the third year in a row. James said he didn't think the Senate was serious in passing the budget. He once again took an opposite stand from Hubbert, though Hubbert admitted the budget would throw education in the red by 1.2 percent.

"The head of the state's teacher lobby said yesterday he generally supports the Alabama Senate Education Budget that has been called 'irresponsible' by Gov. Fob James," UPI wrote. "But Dr. Paul Hubbert, executive secretary of the Alabama Education Association, acknowledged the $1.37 billion budget should be reduced by about $15 million to keep it in the black."

The Senate budget was returned to the House Ways and Means Committee, where Owens substituted it with one which, UPI wrote, reflected the anticipated drop in revenue estimates made by state Budget Officer Jimmy Raiford. Tax money would be coming it at a 9.4 percent increase, not the 11 percent upon which original budgets had been figured, Raiford said.

Harvey describes the ending of the session: "With the clock

stopped at midnight once again on the last legislative day, the education appropriation bill and pay raise bill finally were rewritten into an acceptable compromise."

The compromise Education Budget was a blend of earlier budgets, scaled down but not enough to adequately reflect the continuing decrease in state tax revenues. James' more realistic figures in his substitute budget had been ignored, but his influence over the final budget was obvious in other ways.

Worked into the compromise was the $11.4 million which James had requested to fully fund the teachers' pay raise from the previous year. Harvey wrote that teachers were given a 16 percent pay raise to be funded over the next two years.

Because the budget did not contain the surplus required by House rules, it took a three-fifths vote to approve the compromise. "Passage by an 81 to 20 vote narrowly avoided a special session," Harvey wrote.

The final $1.372 billion education budget was based on a projected growth of 9.44 percent, Harvey wrote. The General Fund budget was $296.8 million.

"Because of the recession that is making itself felt in state revenues, James could veto the budget," Ted Bryant wrote, "and call legislators back in special session." He quoted James saying the Legislature in approving the budget "is not relying on realistic figures."

The budgets "...leave little or no room for an expected reduction in state income," Bryant wrote.

When the session ended there were some big wins for James.

One of his big victories in the face of decreasing revenue was the addition of another 200 kindergarten classes, his annual goal. He also kept intact the $2 million for his War On Illiteracy despite efforts from House and Senate forces to decrease it or cut it out.

One newspaper summed up, "Gov. Fob James, who risked making last-minute changes in his legislative program, has claimed success in the 1980 Alabama Legislature in at least two critical areas: Medicaid and highway funding.

"The six controversial bills give the state more control over the administration of the Medicaid program," the *Advertiser* wrote.

> Both were named top goals by the administration and legislative leaders at the outset of the 1980 regular session in February.
> Both the health-care program and the state's ailing roadways emerged at the close of the session Tuesday morning with the financial boost they need...Medicaid...threatened with a complete

shutdown June 1 for lack of funds, will survive through the end of
the fiscal year on Sept. 30.

Medicaid serves more than 300,000 persons, including about
10,000 in the intermediate nursing home program and 200,000
receiving medicine. The program has weathered four financial crises since December.

It had taken two years, but the "Excellence in Local Education
Bill" James had urged legislators to pass in his State of the State was
approved. Sponsored by Sen. Jim Bennett, the law amended the basic
financial provisions of the "Minimum Program" for the first time since
1939, Harvey wrote. It required counties to provide at least 10 mills
in local revenue for education. The reason education funding was
among the lowest in the nation in Alabama was lack of *local funding*,
a fact which James noted in most of his speeches on education. The
*state* ranked fifth in the nation in percentage of funding it supplied.

The bill was named for Bennett by joint resolution of the Legislature in recognition of his tireless effort to improve basic education
in the state.

A bill supported by James, which completely revised the Alabama
Banking Code, also passed. Sponsored by Rep. Eric Cates, the overhaul in the banking system had been given very little chance of passing
by legislators quoted in news articles.

Several bills to aid law enforcment were approved, including one
to set minimum salaries for deputy sheriffs and one to outlaw the sale
of items used for "inhaling, injecting or ingesting" illegal drugs. James'
legislative aides had worked closely with the State Council of PTA to
get this one through.

The 4-cents-per-gallon increase in tax on gasoline and diesel fuel
approved by the Legislature should provide an anticipated $91 million
a year for the Highway Department, Frank Bruer wrote. Counties
would get 55 percent. The state's 45 percent would just about cover
the annual bonded indebtedness of the department, freeing funds for
James' highway program.

Faced with downwardly revised revenue figures after the session
began, legislators had appeared firmly headed toward increasing the
state sales tax, until James almost single-handedly stood them off by
threatening to veto it. Instead of the sales-tax increase, James supported a variety of innovative revenue-producing measures which affected only certain segments of the population.

An estimated $15 million a year was produced for the General

Fund by diverting refunds from a 13.5 cent coal severance tax from coal producers to the state. Levied in 1973 to pay off bonds which had financed a high speed coal-handling facility at the Alabama State Docks, the tax before the law was amended in 1980 was to revert to coal companies after the bond issue was paid off.

In lieu of the sales tax hike, legislators increased taxes on cigarettes, liquor, and gummed cigarette rolling papers and on the sale of cars between individuals.

The best news for state employees and teachers was the two-year pay raise schedule which had been worked out by James and legislators. Depending upon the economy, James would be empowered to give to state employees up to a 14.5 percent increase in salary and to teachers up to a 16 percent increase.

This headline appeared after the session in giant letters in the *AEA Journal* on a two-page spread: "AEA...Wins Salary Increase of 16 percent for You." It further stated, "Thanks to AEA-ESPOs lobbying efforts, you will be making 16 percent more next year."

"For state employees, the raise works this way," Holmes wrote. "The 7 percent conditional raise for this year was locked into the plan for next year and another 7.5 percent was added."

Administratively, James got through the Legislature a bill which was proclaimed by editorial writers to be the most significant change in ABC operations since prohibition. It allowed the sale of wine in grocery stores and convenience stores—a step toward getting the state out of the liquor business.

News articles quoted grocers and small shop owners predicting a boost in their retail sales after the appearance of wine on grocery shelves. Greg Taylor wrote in the *Advertiser* that food store executives and distributors predicted, "Customer traffic...will increase, and store sales will jump 3 to 6 percent a week; convenience stores will make room in coolers for 15 to 20 brands...prices will average as much as $2 less than state-store wine price; and the new law will create new sales, some jobs and expanded warehousing for Montgomery beverage handlers."

James' legislative failures were obvious, such as the death of his bill to eliminate utility taxes for the elderly. Hubbert had announced opposition from the day it was proposed unless an equal source of revenue could be found to replace the revenue lost. Geddie said statistics were also introduced by opponents indicating such an action would be almost impossible to carry out administratively.

The most important reason for its failure, Geddie said, was that legislators faced with sinking revenues could not justify more than one such exemption—they approved James' legislation exempting sales tax on medicines prescribed for those over 65. James had campaigned on a pledge to remove sales tax on all drugs. He would come back again the next year with legislation to broaden the exemption.

James' bill to centralize all environmental agencies under one roof died, but he would bring it back again the next year. He had abandoned his unearmarking fight in expediency when it became apparent that all legislative efforts had to be focused on legislation to bail out Medicaid and other underfunded state agencies, a reporter wrote.

Another James' proposal which died was the one to make education an essential function of government by constitutional amendment. The seemingly motherhood-and-apple-pie legislation was opposed by the same people who opposed unearmarking because James had vowed not to fight for unearmarking until education was under the constitution an essential function of government.

However, James considered passage of his other bills great victories, especially the Housing Authority bill which had died each year since it had been introduced in 1973. Approved in the last hours of the session, the legislation created an authority which would issue bonds to provide low-interest loans for low and middle income families to buy homes. The bill was named "The Mitchem-Kelley Act" in a resolution commending Sen. Hinton Mitchem and Rep. Phil Kelley for their work in passing it.

Other James-supported measures which passed included:

- A bill giving "full police power" to enforcement officers of the State Forestry Commission.
- A bill clarifying the Alcoholic Beverage Control Act which increased license fees for establishments which sell alcoholic beverages.
- A bill making it a felony to falsify Medicaid claims or to take Medicaid kickbacks.
- A bill providing for restitution to victims of crimes by offenders and for establishment of local restitution centers.
- A bill reestablishing and defining the duties of the State Toxicologist.
- A bill establishing safety standards for production of mobile homes.

- A bill creating a revolving fund in the Finance Department "for purchases of all office supplies, janitorial...[etc.]"
- A bill stipulating that a minimum of 75 days constitutes the first four scholastic months of a school year.
- A bill sponsored by Rep. Larry Dixon to provide for a State Parent Locators Office in the Department of Pensions and Security to locate parents who failed to support their children.

"Key leaders in state government called the session an unqualified success," Holmes wrote. "Both presiding officers said a sudden shift in the economy, the decrease in sales and income taxes, forced the Legislature to shift gears in mid-session...

"Walking in the Capitol office the day after the session, James, tie pulled down, coat over his shoulder, grinned and said, 'Man, I like this job,'" Holmes wrote.

James told a news conference that the Legislature gave him about 80 percent of what he requested.

He predicted it would be a "struggle" to make it through 1981, however, because of the economy's downward plunge. He predicted revenue would fall about $60 million short in 1981.

He was right.

"Even as the 1980 Regular Session ended, revenue collections into the ASETF continued to dwindle," Harvey wrote. "This guaranteed that the newly-passed budget would be in proration."

In July, State Superintendent of Education Teague predicted proration could reach 10 percent.

At the start of the new fiscal year in October, James did not hesitate. After studying reports of revenue coming into the SETF, he declared 7 percent proration in the Education Budget for the coming year.

Each day James waited to declare proration would have made it worse, would have called for a higher percentage of proration to be declared.

As it was, because October checks were already in the mail, when proration was actually imposed in November it was eight percent.

# — 14 —

# Halfway

**J**anuary of 1981 was midpoint in James' term as governor.
State newspapers graded his "report card."
Ralph Holmes wrote in the Birmingham *News*:

> James took over the ailing state prisons and the Mental Health
> Department as receiver, abolished the Board of Corrections, and
> put his staff to work trimming the soaring costs of Medicaid and
> Pensions and Security.
> James' answer to money problems in the Highway Department
> was a controversial 4-cents-per-gallon tax on fuels.
> When it was time for the first round of budget hearings, James
> sat in with the legislative committees. He told his department
> heads to cut back 10 percent on their budget requests. Most of
> them complied. Those who didn't asked for level funding only to
> avoid a cut in services.

Of the hiring freeze and layoff of temporary and probationary
employees, the *News* wrote, "Figures from the state Personnel Department show, however, the total number of employees now, as opposed to two years ago, has shifted by less than 2,000. Almost all of
that came from cuts in the Highway Department.

> Two main taxes support the Special Education Trust Fund:
> Those on sales and income. For the last fiscal year, sales tax fell
> $21 million short of the projected $479 million. Income tax fell $18
> million short of its $508 million projection.
> "People are not spending. It's that simple," said Finance Direc-
> tor Sid McDonald.

Proration for the SETF continued for all of the last fiscal year.
Last week, McDonald and Budget Officer Jimmy Raiford reported the condition of the fund is worse than had been anticipated.

Besides more money for mental health and prisons, James is
asking the Legislature for $75 million for improvements in the
State Docks in Mobile. That, he feels, will more than pay for itself
in docks revenues and new jobs.

James, commenting on the two years, told the *News,* "Growth in
government has been stabilized. The Highway Department has been
stabilized. The National Guard has been strengthened.

> Jerry Shoemaker [Public Safety Director] is the unsung hero of
> this administration...The big thing has been the drug business.
> I think we struck a major blow to the drug smuggling business
> when we created one agency to deal with that. We have no desire
> to fill the jails with kids using marijuana. We want those who bring
> it in.
> ...Our school kids have for the first time met the national aver-
> age in testing. Every kid is tested every year. We know how to rate
> a school...We are looking at the very rudimentary level. We are
> looking at teacher-pupil ratios, the number of hours teaching basic
> skills, discipline...

The story continued: "Still, James isn't ready to give himself an 'A'
for his effort in education. That, he said, will come when the school
system is tops in the nation. And that is coming, with a continued
interest in education and with a focus at the community level rather
than money, he said.

> When it comes to jobs, James is high on his plan for prepared
> cities. Prepared cities is a creature of the Alabama Development
> Office (ADO). Staffers from that office visit towns in need of new
> industry, working with city fathers to sell the cities to prospective
> industry.
> "We're getting there in tough times," James said. "We get the
> industry to the state, then it is up to the cities to sell themselves.
> We give them their checklist."
> James has been selling Alabama in Europe this year and he
> plans to go to Japan later this year.
> "The other states don't have the vast waterway resources we
> have," he said. During his campaign, James talked about the po-
> tential of the State Docks in Mobile. Now at the halfway point he

is asking the Legislature to expand the facilities by $75 million or more.

"It is a gateway to the central part of the United States, to South America. We have a keen interest in agricultural exports. World trade can be our salvation," he said.

...Medicaid is a problem James feels he has a handle on.

Every druggist, every nursing home is being paid current...

Liquor has traditionally been a dirty word in politics...One of the first things...Broadwater did was to put big signs over the liquor stores, so they can be found.

The *News* gave a department-by-department rundown of major agencies under James.

> Mental Health had been under court order since 1972 to upgrade programs, staffing and facilities for the mentally ill and retarded.
>
> James in January of 1980 asked U.S. Circuit Judge Frank M. Johnson Jr. to put him over the Mental Health system as receiver. Johnson did. Since then James has run it instead of the appointive board.
>
> James' mental health commissioner, Glenn Ireland, said the system is close to complying with the federal court order. Some 30 general practitioners and psychiatrists were recruited in 1980 and extra money from the state Legislature and from the federal-state Medicaid program was spent to upgrade and expand many buildings.
>
> Ireland was gloomy about the future, however, noting some of the year's appropriation was "conditional," which he said meant conditional "on the money appearing from out of the blue."

The department needed an $85 million bond issue to comply with the court order. James would fund much of what was needed in his Public Works Project in 1981.

Concerning highways, the *News* wrote that James "set two major goals for the state's highway department as he campaigned in 1978.

> He said long range planning was needed. And he said he wanted to take politics out of the Alabama Highway Department.
>
> Highway Department Director Bobby Joe Kemp, in the job just six months though a career department employee, said..."The governor has never called me and asked me to pave a road for anybody. We base work on priorities. We do the work where it is needed."

The job rolls were cut. When James took office, the Highway Department had 5,812 employees. It now has 3,938 on the payroll. For comparison, the agency had a peak of 8,464 employees in July 1970...

"We had a lot of fat in the Highway Department," he said. "This has built up over the years. It was nobody's fault. We had things like the photo lab and carpenter shop we really didn't need..."

The savings in salaries alone, Kemp said, are about $24 million a year.

As to long range highway plans, "We've got plans. We have a 20-year plan, a 10-year plan and a five-year plan."

The key plan is to finish Alabama's interstate highway system... it is projected everything will be completed by 1987.

James says he opposes highway bond issues...he called them "borrowing on your children's future."

The payback on bonds borrowed for highway construction in past administrations is plaguing Kemp now. The bond payments are just about the proceeds of the 4-cent per gallon gas tax...

Another of the accomplishments [is the] equipment pool.

Rather than have unused bulldozers and other equipment scattered all over the state, Kemp has put it in two pools at each end of the state. The result is a savings of about 150,000 gallons of fuel each month.

In the prisons, James faced the results of decades of neglect — unsanitary and rundown facilities, lack of properly-trained staff, and overcrowding in the county jails.

He also faced the stern orders of the federal court in Montgomery to carry out a long list of reforms to eliminate what the court had called cruel and unusual punishment to the convicts.

Unlike the Wallace administration, which had fought the federal court, James asked...a chance to run the system as he saw fit.

As receiver...he soon put that power to effective use when he battled local citizens in St. Clair County over the proposed location of a major prison...and hand-picked Robert Britton as prison commissioner...

Holmes capsuled the following accomplishments:

- A contract was signed with the Brookwood hospital management group for professional medical care to inmates.
- A new cannery and freezing plant in Elmore County has processed a half-million pounds of food at a savings to taxpayers of a quarter-million dollars since it opened last summer.
- Inmate classification has been computerized, a move de-

scribed by the federal court as "key" to effective prison reform.
- A staff training program has been put into effect which has
  been called by American Correctional Institute experts one
  of the most aggressive and progressive training programs in
  the nations.
- Overcrowding has been reduced in county jails by 400 with
  plans to move another 400 state inmates from county jails
  within a few weeks.

Asked to size up James' performance, Birmingham industrialist
John M. Harbert III was quoted in the *News* article as saying, " 'If
James has a weakness, it's that he's not communicating well enough
with voters about what he's doing. And he's not quite as accessible to
the people as he could be.' "

# — 15 —

# The 1981 Session

The 1981 legislative session was one in which James once again tackled every problem on the state horizon and then some.

For the third year in a row, state tax revenue increases had not been great enough to offset the overspending of the 1978 Legislature. When it was apparent that not enough money was coming in to pay the 1981 bills, James in October of 1980 declared proration of the Special Education Trust Fund for the fiscal year just beginning.

Between then and the Legislative session he found a way to reduce that proration by what turned out to be a $65 million chunk—Rep. Eric Cates of Greenville sponsored James' bill stepping up the collection of business income tax from quarterly to monthly for a one-time bonanza.

Despite the money crunch, there is evidence that legislators were aware that state government was being run more efficiently than it had been in the past. When Hoke Kerns resigned as Medicaid director to take a job in private enterprise, a resolution of commendation passed by legislators noted that Medicaid had "operated at a deficit for more than eight years." This deficit had been "rapidly reversed," the resolution noted, from "a delinquency in accounts payable into one which now operates on a sound basis, paying all bills currently and as due."

James wrote a letter to legislators as a preface to a booklet detailing his legislative package. In it and his Feb. 3 State of the State Address, he called attention to legislation which was urgently needed to strengthen law enforcement. "We need a new capital punishment law. We have included it in a tough new anti-crime package which also contains legal weapons to crack down on illegal drugs," he said. "It's time to take the handcuffs off our police, sheriffs, state troopers, ABC agents and other officers, and put the handcuffs on the criminals."

Alabama's death penalty statute had been struck down by the courts. Reinstatement of the death penalty was top on the list of crime bills because, "It is a deterrent to vicious crime, period," James said.

"Mental health, prisons and earmarking are issues of vital concern. They must be dealt with by this Legislature," he said.

He also called attention to a bill he was introducing as a second attempt to consolidate environmental agencies. James asked legislators also to approve his reform of the state merit system as well as his legislation to require two-year budgets to be passed every other year.

"Go back to biennial budgeting and you'll stop a lot of pork-barrel, monkey-business with the budgets," he said.

He also said he would present a plan to restructure the state retirement system.

James proposed legislation "to challenge the absurdity of the Supreme Court banning voluntary prayer from public schools," and asked again that tax revenues be unearmarked.

It was the War on Illiteracy, however, which formed the heart of his legislative package.

James' $1.3 billion Education Budget, based on a projected 5 percent increase in revenue, increased elementary/secondary funding by $48 million and reduced higher education funding by $12 million, Ira Harvey wrote.

James explained why in his State of the State address: There was a declining enrollment at all levels of education. Alabama had one four-year college for every 230,000 people, compared to the national average of one four-year college for every 400,000.

"We need few, if any, new buildings on our college campuses," he said. "We are seventh in the nation in gross dollars spent on medical education. The number of two-year schools...exceeds that of most other states including many states with populations larger than ours. There are duplications of programs in higher education from one end of this state to the other—and everybody knows it."

For two years, James had concentrated on improving the education of kindergarten through 12th grade. The results of that concentration proved that extra money to K–12 could be justified.

James held high in his hand concrete evidence which proved that his plan worked, that his War on Illiteracy was succeeding—charts and graphs showing that students in the lowest-scoring school in the state had improved test scores after his Skills Teams worked with their teachers and principals, after administrators of those systems attended seminars put on by his management-improvement teams.

He was ecstatic.

"I can say for the first time in this state's history, our children have met the national average on basic skills achievement tests. I thank thousands of dedicated teachers, support personnel, principals and superintendents for their good work," he said.

"This is one small step in the right direction, realizing national averages have been declining for a number of years and that averages are a poor substitute for sure knowledge of whether an individual child is learning or not."

He presented legislators with copies of the information packet he held in his hands. It revealed how students were performing in every school in the state.

"Our public schools are among the first order when we ask what are the essential services of government," James said. "You will appropriate this year over $750 million to 127 school systems. It is by far the largest appropriation you make and it should be...You have the right to demand performance in each and every one of our school systems and to know exactly how your taxes are being utilized."

The information packet James termed "about 40 years overdue" included:

- A comparison of achievement test results in each school system, or systems, in each legislative district.
- The teacher/pupil ratio of each school in each district and, "more important," in each and every classroom.
- The amount of local funds, state funds and federal funds received by each school system, how the money was being spent, the cash balance at the beginning of the year and the cash balance at the end of the year.
- The ranking of each school system as to the money it received per child.
- The share each county and city government would get in 1982 of the $100 million from federal court-ordered property reappraisals. "There is no reason the great bulk of this new money should not go to local school systems," James said.

- A comparison of teacher salaries and benefits in Alabama and other southern states for 1980–81.

"You now have tools from which to make sound financial and sound educational judgments," he said.

In the past three months, he announced, he had released $60 million to build schools for K–12, and soon would release another $30 million.

The additional money he requested in his budget for K–12 would allow even greater improvement in the education level of the states' children, he was sure.

James in his first two years in office had demonstrated a tendency to encourage people on all sides of issues to get together and talk it out, whether it was people on opposite sides of a lawsuit or legislators who couldn't agree.

Continuing in this vein, his next request was an effort to bring legislators and educators closer together.

Having observed that State School Board members had their hands too full to spend time with the Legislature, and having observed that legislators were too loaded down with every problem in the state to devote full time to education, James proposed what he saw as a way to ensure that each understood the problems of the other: he asked legislators to add the speaker of the House and the lieutenant governor as members to the state school board.

"There must be clear and concise communication between the school board and the Legislature. The school board needs to understand the financial resources of the state. The Legislature needs to understand the priorities, the policies, the problems, the progress and the funding patterns of our public schools," he said. "...You appropriate one-third of our total tax revenue through the state school board."

Additionally, James asked legislators to create a second board to manage the state's two-year colleges.

No board, no matter how capable or hard-working, could guide the policy and management of the public school system and of 21 junior colleges and 28 technical colleges, he told legislators.

He also asked the Legislature to remove the two-year colleges and technical schools from the supervision of the state superintendent of education and create the position of chancellor to manage them. He asked legislators to allow more oversight of the four-year colleges by strengthening the role of the Alabama Commission on Higher Education from one of coordination to one of administration.

"...It is impossible for our great schools to pursue a mission of excellence, a mission of quality not quantity, unless they build on their strengths and eliminate their weaknesses. This has not been done. Therefore I recommend that the role of the Alabama Commission on Higher Education be changed from one of coordination to one of administration, and that the commission be restructured and given the authority to carry out that role," he said.

James blamed the earmarking of funds for the overbuilding of the higher education system in the state.

To illustrate, he explained that in a number of growth years in the last two decades the Special Education Trust Fund unexpectedly got more tax revenue than had been anticipated. The surplus funds were used to expand post-secondary education to a level far exceeding our realistic needs, James said.

The Highway Department and the Mental Health Department also received earmarked funds.

Earmarking was responsible for "2,000 employees too many in the Highway Department in January, 1979," James said, and for a "brand new $7.5 million dollar maximum security hospital in Tuscaloosa still standing empty."

Yet, "the Department of Corrections receives no earmarked funds, and we have today 1,400 state prisoners in city and county jails, and the federal courts are threatening to let dangerous criminals out on the streets," James said.

He asked legislators to approve the unearmarking of tax revenues.

James spent no time on other bills his administration would push. One such bill, which was approved without fanfare, allowed local school boards more fiscal authority by giving them the authority to shift up to 40 percent of their funds from one budget item to another.

Effective budgeting was foremost on James' mind.

He asked legislators to isolate the budget every two years in a return to biennial budgeting. "When you throw the budget into the midst of hundreds of other pieces of legislation, the budget can be held hostage, leveraged and an orderly analysis of all elements within the budget becomes very difficult," he said.

Effective budgeting required getting costs in line.

"It is my desire for all state employees to receive salaries and wages that are competitive to salaries and wages paid in the private sector for the same work. This is fair to the state employee and to taxpayers. This is not the case in Alabama today," he said.

A survey of Alabama companies accounting for more than 250,000 employees revealed that some state job classifications were high, some were low, he said.

There was no fixed procedure for salary increases. The Legislature periodically awarded pay increases. In addition, "The state merit system includes four different pay raises that are given by the administration. Last year over 60 percent of our employees received such raises," James said. "Obviously, if the Legislature mandates a pay raise on top of the existing pay raises already in the system, inequities are locked in and compounded for another year. I believe this is a serious mistake.

> I am therefore recommending that the Legislature by joint resolution instruct the governor and the personnel board to adjust the basic pay of each job classification within the merit system to a level competitive to the private sector within the state of Alabama. In situations where state job classifications are unique to the public sector, we should adjust to a level competitive to the average level of pay within our 12 sister southern states. I welcome a legislative project oversight committee to work with us on this project.

> Job classifications that are determined to be high should be held level for the period of time necessary to bring these classifications into line. And job classifications that are determined to be low should be increased to the proper level. These adjustments should be made effective Oct. 1, 1981.

James also wanted to bring fringe benefits more in line with those enjoyed by private enterprise.

He said Alabama gave 13 legislative holidays and the governor traditionally added Christmas Eve, New Year's Eve and the Friday after Thanksgiving. This was compared to an average of 9 similar holidays given the private sector.

"It is wrong for the state to give 50 percent more holidays," James said, recommending state holidays be cut from 16 to 12.

He also recommended bringing sick leave and vacation leave into line with the private sector, though current employees would retain all benefits earned under the existing system.

To offset reductions in these benefits, he proposed new fringe benefits—life insurance and long-term disability. He also recommended that state-provided medical insurance be "improved and perhaps expanded."

For the state not to do so, James said, was "not only wrong. It is a non-competitive personnel policy." He asked legislators to provide, at no cost to employees, life insurance benefits equal to one to two times the employee's annual base salary at time of death. The disability insurance would protect against loss of income from sustained injury or illness.

Alabama "substantially exceeds retirement benefits provided by the other 49 states and also substantially exceeds retirement benefits provided by over 90 percent of the employers within the private sector," James said. "Contributions from taxpayers to the retirement systems for the fiscal year 1981–82 will be $235 million. This does not include social security. When you combine social security paid by the state in the amount of $111 million, you have a grand total of $364 million. This is about 17.5 percent of total state taxes...Money for the retirement fund is paid off the top, before one state service can be rendered.

"The present situation is not sound, because if the state continues to increase its payments into the retirement fund, the state—not the retirement fund—will either go broke, cut services or raise taxes," he said. "Another danger faced is that the retirement benefits already earned by thousands of dedicated state employees and teachers will be jeopardized."

James said it was "unfair to state employees and taxpayers alike to continue this trend." he said "experts in the retirement field" would present these findings in detail to a joint session Feb. 17 and remain in Montgomery for three days to answer questions.

Any changes in retirement benefits, he emphasized, would have "no effect whatsoever on retirement benefits" earned prior to October of that year.

James closed by saying firmly that Alabama's "so-called" financial crisis "is a myth."

He said, "I have in the last 20 minutes recommended to you plain, concise and exact measures to solve [it]...Government, by and large, doesn't know what belt tightening is. The housewife does. The farmer does. The employees of Chrysler Corporation do. Our retired people do. But this government is fixing to learn if you pass my proposals and the sooner the better."

It was obvious even before James finished speaking that lobbyists for the major power lobbies in the state would unite against him—AEA, the State Employees Association and the dozens of legislators who were either on the payrolls of education institutions, had family members on the payrolls, or were linked in some other way with Alabama's junior colleges, technical schools or universities.

Lobbyists for state employees would admit to news media a year later that they had used James' proposed changes to increase membership in the State Employees Association. It was a simple matter to scare employees into joining by telling them James was destroying their benefits and their retirement system.

James, meanwhile, postponed introducing his retirement legislation until the next session in order to be able to enlist the support of state employees and teachers.

There was no precise figure given on how many legislators had received monetary contributions and/or campaign help from AEA. Columnists clearly believed Hubbert had contributed to more than half the Legislature and Hubbert did not deny the reports.

The major opposition to James' legislative package came from higher education forces, however, who apparently did not care how badly K–12 needed funding if even a small percentage of that funding was diverted from money they considered theirs. Neither did higher education take kindly to James' efforts to increase oversight.

Stephanie Wolfe Bell partially described in the *Advertiser* the clout wielded by higher education—many liaisons are of the type which do not have to be listed on ethics disclosure statements. She wrote:

> Sen. Bob Hall of Pinson and Rep. Hugh Boles were on the faculty of Jefferson State Junior College. Sen. James Lemaster of Scottsboro was a part time college instructor. Sen. J. Richmond Pearson of Birmingham was adjunct associate professor at the University of Alabama in Birmingham, where his wife was also employed. Rep. Bill Bolling of Hanceville was chairman of the extended day program at George C. Wallace State Community College. Rep. Joe Ford of Gadsden was administrator at Gadsden State Junior College.
>
> Rep. George Harold Grimsley of Columbia was vice president of George C. Wallace State Community College. Rep. Seth Hammett of Andalusia was head of administrative affairs at Lurleen B. Wallace Junior College. Rep. Yvonne Kennedy of Mobile was administrator at Bishop State Junior College (soon to be president). Rep. J. David Stout of Fort Payne was a junior college instructor.

James' unearmarking bill was killed early in the session by the Senate Finance & Taxation Committee—chaired by Pearson.

The House approved James' bill which strengthened ACHE and gave it control over two-year colleges. The victory occurred despite the opposition of two two-year college presidents, Rep. Wayne Cobb of Hamilton, president of Northwest Technical College, and Rep. James Sasser of Ozark, president of Alabama Aviation and Technical College.

It was killed by the Senate Education Committee, however— chaired by Sen. G.J. "Dutch" Higginbotham of Opelika. The Mont- gomery *Advertiser* wrote that Higginbotham resigned as financial aid director at Chattahoochee Valley Community College just before his committee killed the ACHE bill, but that he was "looking for another job in education." Also a member of the Education Committee—and voting against the bill—was Sen. Charlie Britnell of Russellville, presi- dent of Northwest Alabama State Junior College in Phil Campbell.

James saw no reason why legislators who divided their attention among every aspect of state government should decide down to the penny how each college and university in the state would spend its portion of state tax money. That task could be better decided by the people appointed as trustees for that purpose and by those who worked full time for the institutions. His education budget appro- priated lump sums to each institution according to a formula and left it up to them to decide how it should be spent.

Of this, Frank Bruer wrote in the Birmingham *Post-Herald* on July 6, 1981: "...James is back at it again, coming up with some of those weirdo ideas. Right now his revolutionary idea is that education mon- ey should be spent where it's needed...simply appropriating a lump sum to a university or system."

For example, Bruer wrote, James would have given the University of Alabama Board of Trustees $141.7 million and told the members, " 'here 'tis. You know where it's needed on those three campuses..Go spend it how you think it should be spent..'

"The idea was too much for everyone concerned. It was way too much for the Alabama Legislature, which has been in a well-worn habit of saying exactly where the money goes for what..."

Bruer wrote that the idea was tossed in the trash by a legislative committee "cheered by the university officials" who were obviously so intent on opposing James that they ignored the fact that it would have given universities greater freedom in administering their programs.

The House approved a General Fund budget similar to the one proposed by James.

When the Education Budget came up, however, the House split firmly along McCorquodale/Hubbert lines as the two squared off over Hubbert's efforts to create a statewide medical insurance program for teachers.

Harvey backgrounds the situation: "With proration and gloomy economic predictions awaiting the 1981 Legislature in February, there appeared little chance that teachers could receive another pay raise for the second year in a row."

Therefore, "AEA demonstrated interest in establishing a hospital-medical insurance program for teachers [which AEA] considered to be feasible. State employees had come under a self-insured plan administered by Blue Cross in 1979 with a cost to the state of only $43 per month or $516 per year. Teachers, as employees of local boards, however, received only a state supplement of $247.20 yearly plus the local boards' contributions. Initial projections indicated that setting up a statewide insurance plan for teachers would add an additional $20 million to the $15 million already provided by the state." The $20 million figure was revised to $21 million.

When James' Education Budget hit the House floor, Ways and Means Chairman Walter Owens tried (and failed) to substitute a budget which increased elementary/secondary funding to $61 million, Harvey wrote. The hitch was a proposal in Owens' budget by Speaker McCorquodale which reduced the state's contribution to the retirement system for any teachers hired above the number mandated by the state to the local systems. It was perceived as "a blow to hiring more teachers," Harvey writes, because local systems would either have had to pick up the difference or cut the number of teachers.

Owens then handed out copies of a second substitute which tied the House up in debate nearly four hours, Harvey wrote, because it did not contain any of the $21 million Hubbert was insisting upon for the insurance program. It contained instead a $24 million reserve as a hedge against proration and was approved 81–20.

The House version of the Education budget was similar to James' in one respect—it contained a reserve as did the General Fund budget approved by the House. That reserve was designed to ward off proration if revenues did not live up to expectations.

The Senate immediately appropriated $21 million of the House's projected $24 million surplus for the insurance program and spent the rest as well.

House and Senate budgets varied considerably. The Senate Education Budget was based on a five percent growth in revenue; the House version was based on four percent. The Senate removed from the House version of the General Fund budget some $15 million in line items.

James labeled both Senate-passed budgets deficit ones.

"I will not sign a proration budget," he said.

A $363 million General Fund budget passed in the final moments of the session, which officially ended at midnight Monday. It actually was passed Tuesday morning, however, because legislators stopped the clock at a few minutes before midnight and instructed clerks keeping the records to record all legislation approved Tuesday morning as passing before midnight Monday.

A legislative conference committee finished rewriting the General Fund budget only a few hours before its final passage, which meant legislators approved a budget they had not read.

"With the many differences, it was almost certain that no compromise could be reached," Harvey wrote of the possibility of a joint House-Senate conference committee agreeing on an Education Budget.

The conferees "brought with them the sharp ideological split" so clearly demonstrated during floor action, Harvey wrote. After deliberation lasting through May 18, the last day of the session—with the clock stopped until 6 the next morning—the Legislature adjourned without an Education Budget.

AP writer Phillip Rawls wrote that "a shootout between the various elements of education" stopped passage of the 1982 education budget.

More than 120 bills were adopted in the flurry of activity on that final night and morning.

"The Legislature ended the 1981 regular session Tuesday morning (without an education budget) because lawmakers could not agree over funding for a $21 million medical insurance program for school teachers," Rawls wrote.

"James said...the education budget didn't pass because people who have had their snouts in the trough too long were looking out for their own interests."

Also dead was James' biennial budgeting bill which would have switched the state from one-year to two-year budgets and required the Legislature to devote itself solely to the budgets for 15 days every other year.

Almost lost in the loud uproar over failure of the education budget to pass was the success James had in passing legislation, some of which would in other administrations have been hailed as major reforms:

- The first total revamp of the state personnel system in 30 years was approved despite fierce opposition from the State Employees Association. Long pushed by James, it passed with an amendment setting up a legislative oversight committee.
- James fulfilled his campaign promise to exempt all prescription drugs from state and local sales tax.
- He got his $45 million to build new prisons, with the money to be taken from the proceeds of the sale of leases of offshore oil and gas-rich bottomlands.
- He also got his $65 million for major construction and renovation of the Mental Health system.
- A law was added to the books allowing the state to withhold state income tax refunds from people who owed money for child support or student loans.
- A bill passed to provide money to pay court-appointed attorneys for indigents by raising court costs $5.
- A bill was approved allowing local school boards to shift funds from one budget item to another (excluding teachers' salaries).

After James had a chance to study the General Fund budget, he indicated he was upset enough about the errors and mistakes in the hastily thrown-together document that he might not sign it. But he did.

For example, the budget instead of appropriating $3.5 million to the Public Service Commission made a $1 million error and gave it $4.5 million.

A $ 1 million grant intended for the Cystic Fibrosis research center at the University of Alabama in Birmingham went instead to the University of Alabama in Tuscaloosa. The budget also failed to give a $3 million conditional appropriation to the prison system. Not by coincidence, a $3 million conditional appropriation which had not been requested was given to Mental Health.

Columnists had differing versions of why the education budget failed.

Bob Ingram wrote "...the real hang-up was a hard-line stance taken by the all-powerful AEA in support of a costly new medical program for teachers. The House of Representatives, to its credit, took a look at existing and anticipated tax revenues and said 'no'...But across the rotunda, where the AEA is in firm control, the Senate insisted on the new program. Neither side would budge. The education budget died."

Ted Bryant wrote:

> The fact is that the rank and file legislators have very little to do with the budget process. It is tightly controlled by a few leaders...
>
> Now here's why the Legislature didn't approve the $1.3 billion education budget on the last night of the session:
>
> The budget was in a House-Senate conference committee that was appointed by the House and Senate presiding officers, Speaker Joe McCorquodale and Lt. Gov. George McMillan.
>
> Conference committee members told other legislators they could not reach agreement on a $21 million appropriation for medical insurance for teachers.
>
> That $21 million had very little to do with the Legislature's failure to adopt a budget.
>
> What happened was that the House leadership decided that no education budget would be adopted unless the Senate approved a "current use" bill designed to give a property tax break to large landowners, at the expense of education.
>
> A filibuster killed that bill in the Senate.
>
> The $21 million appropriation was just a ruse, particularly by the House leadership, to disguise the real game that was being played.
>
> Concerning the "current use" bill, James said, "Somebody ought to ask some of those striped-suited boys down there how in the hell they could support that piece of legislation."
>
> Intentionally or not, that remark embraced the House leadership. The sponsor of the bill was Rep. Richard Manley of Demopolis, speaker pro-tem, and the measure had strong support from Speaker McCorquodale. The nattily dressed Manley even wears striped suits.

The current use bill was defeated for the moment. But the issue would not be dropped by big landowners in the state—a great deal of whom were corporations and trusts administered by banks.

Commented James of the antics he had observed taking place with the education budget: "The people back home don't come to Montgomery and stick their nose in their own state government like they ought to," Bryant wrote.

"Meanwhile, the governor is sitting down and talking with the 124 legislators who are not a part of the leadership, patiently explaining what he wants them to do (in a special session)."

James was incensed that the Legislature would fail to do the one major thing for which it existed, appropriate the taxpayers' money in a careful, deliberate manner. He was further incensed at the politics behind the fiasco.

In his newspaper column written for weekly newspapers, James blasted legislators he accused of having conflicts of interest.

Records of the Secretary of State reflected that key opponents of his education reform had received donations from AEA, he said, citing Sen. Earl Hilliard of Birmingham ($1,500), Sen. Cordy Taylor of Prattville ($4,850), Charlie Britnell ($4,000), and Dutch Higginbotham.

"You decide who voted how and for what reason. If you feel these senators voted in the public interest, you should feel good about the votes to kill the bill. If not, draw your own conclusions."

Taylor responded to reporters, "I think it is somewhat sickening that the chief executive officer would use this type tactic to put pressure on me as a legislator to support his program."

James also took to the road to let the public know what was going on.

"Should 45 bankers be allowed to vote on something that directly affects them?" the governor asked news media. "Should 45 barbell manufacturers be allowed to vote on bills that directly affect them?"

In Mobile at the end of May, James made a plea to the news media.

"The governor wants newspaper and electronic media to provide reporting teams with expertise, legal aid, accountants, people who can get in there and find the real issues through all the smoke and demagoguery," the Birmingham *News* wrote.

" 'Never in the history of the state has there been more of a need for good reporting,' he said."

The key thing on James' mind was the state budget, both Education and General Fund. He would call a special session, in due time, to pass the Education budget.

But first, he wanted to do a little thinking, and a little homework.

# — 16 —

# The Isolation of the Budget

James' August 4 State of the State address for his first special session in 1981 was soul-searching in nature, a stern lecture in tone.

Special sessions of the Legislature were not unknown to the state. There had been special sessions in 1971, 1975 and 1978.

"In each case, like tonight, it was necessary to call a special session in order to pass a budget. The education budget was not passed in the 1981 regular session, even though the session consisted of 30 legislative days within 105 calendar days," James said.

"We should ask ourselves why we failed...Surely we agree the appropriation of tax dollars is the most essential function of the Legislature and that using tax dollars to provide education for our children, Medicaid for our elderly, law enforcement for all, and other essential services, are the principal reasons the voters sent us to Montgomery in the first place," he said. "Why, then, should we accept failure in the budgetary process when it is within our power to improve the way we spend two billion dollars taken from the hard-earned paychecks of over one million Alabamians?"

During the past 90 days, James said, "I have talked with practically every member of the Legislature. A large majority of you have told me you would support strong action to make the way we spend tax dollars more efficient and open, strong action to make the budgets top priority.

"In government, the strongest action of all is a constitutional amendment," James said.

He proposed a constitutional amendment which would change the system which "tolerates a budget of one billion three hundred million dollars popping up for a vote at 3 a.m. on the last day of the regular session."

The amendment required the governor to submit his budget to the House and Senate no later than the second legislative day.

In turn, it required the House and Senate to pass both budgets and those budgets be signed by the speaker and the lieutenant governor, before one single bill, local or general, could be transmitted from one house to the other.

It would from that day hence be referred to as "the budget isolation amendment."

"For the first time in this state's history, when it comes to spending tax dollars, all cards will be on the table, face up," James said.

James acknowledged legislators' concerns that such a budget isolation amendment would bring to a screeching halt all legislative functions until the budgets were passed. But he disagreed.

James said committees would continue to meet and bills could proceed as normal until they reached the point at which they would come before the full house for debate.

To ensure that the budget isolation amendment would not "create a condition whereby the Legislature cannot address an emergency situation such as Hurricane Frederic," James included in the bill a provision by which a three-fifths vote of the House and Senate could set aside the mandate for budget isolation to take up a particular piece of legislation. (He originally proposed a four-fifth vote be required).

Turning to the education budget, James said tax revenues had grown more than had been predicted. He increased the estimate on which he figured revenue from the 5 percent of his revised regular session budget to 5.5 percent, which allowed him to increase funding for all postsecondary education to "near level funding."

However, said James, "I strongly urge you not to exceed these projections for fear of another proration year."

James otherwise stayed with his original budget appropriations from the regular session, except for a 25 percent increase in the money going to local school boards "for the sole purpose of compensating teachers and support personnel for any increase in their insurance premiums."

"Tonight, I hope the stage is set for your rapid passage of the isolation reform measure and for the education budget," James said.

The governor also strongly urged legislators to approve legislation known as the "co-employee bill." Until it was approved, Alabama remained the only state in the southeast in which employees of a company could sue one another for on-the-job injuries.

"Fob James may have done his homework in talking to legislators," Al Fox wrote Aug. 5 in the Birmingham *News*. "Most legislators feel that the skids have been greased for early passage of a budget."

Fox noted that James' State of the State address to the joint session was the shortest speech ever given by a governor, only 14 minutes.

"He received applause only once and laughter another time, and both were led by Rep. Roy Johnson of Tuscaloosa, a junior high principal and outspoken supporter of AEA."

Hubbert immediately termed "totally unacceptable" James' $1.337 billion budget because it didn't include the full amount Hubbert wanted included for the teachers' statewide medical insurance program. (James included an additional $3.72 million conditional appropriation for the teachers' health insurance program which, added to the $14.9 million already in the budget, would bring the total state contribution to $18.6 million.)

James' budget for 1982 gave four-year schools what they were getting under the prorated 1981 budget plus 4 percent in additional money. He proposed that "flagship institutions," Auburn, Alabama and UAB, get an additional $1 million each.

James' budget gave $41.5 million to junior colleges and $34.9 million to technical schools.

Roy Johnson leading the applause for James?

Ted Bryant wrote of some stranger alignments revolving around the $14.9 million currently provided by the state for teachers' medical insurance and the additional $21 million requested by Hubbert.

Wayne Teague proposed his own budget, Bryant wrote, one which projected $16 million more revenue than James' budget—with that $16 million earmarked in his budget for teacher insurance.

> Speak to me of politics and strange bedfellows.
> What a difference a few weeks makes. Just look under the sheet here. Take a peek.
> That's Wayne Teague, state superintendent of education. And who's under there with him?
> Paul Hubbert? Yep. The one and the same, Paul Hubbert, executive director of the Alabama Education Association.
> But isn't this sort of a labor-management situation? Hubbert represents the teachers, so he's labor. And Teague represents the

State Board of Education, so he's management. Now what are they doing in bed together?

And look in this other bed. It's kind of full.

There are the leaders of the state House of Representatives, several of 'em.

And who's that in the middle? None other than Fob James.

But didn't the House leaders throw out the governor's education budget back in the regular session ? And adopt their own? What are they doing in bed together? And where are the senators?

Well, it looks like a bunch of them are over there sneaking into the bed with Hubbert and Teague. That one's going to get crowded too.

It looks like Lt. Gov George McMillan is leading the way.

The question is: Who's going to have the most people in their bed by this time next week?

It was a short session.

On August 4, the first day of the session, bills providing for budget isolation were introduced in the House and the Senate. Both called for constitutional amendments. Several days later, the House bill was substituted with a bill which contained almost identical language but imposed budget isolation on the Legislature for the upcoming 1982 session. The purpose of the substitution appeared to be self-evident— unless there was such a bill, there would be no budget isolation until at least 1983, because the amendment would have to be ratified by voters.

HB 38 became known as the "trial run" budget isolation bill. It self-destructed after the 1982 session. One more thing, thought to be unimportant at the time, it was not a constitutional amendment. It was a statute.

The trial run isolation bill was passed by the House and sent to the Senate.

The education budget was also moving along smoothly. An Aug. 16 AP story stated: "A conference committee of three House and three Senate members, meeting in James' office Thursday night, worked out a compromise on the budget...to add $3.7 million in absolute funding and $3.7 million in conditional money to the teachers' health insurance program."

"On the 6th legislative day, the conference committee sent a report to James," Ira Harvey wrote. "Meanwhile, questions arose concerning a $3.7 million appropriation for hospital-medical insurance. James returned the conference committee report with an executive amendment for the insurance and both houses concurred. The $1.3 billion required rethinking on the part of House leadership about funding distribution and an increase in revenue estimates by the governor from 5 to 5.5 percent."

The education budget which passed differed from James' original budget only in the additional insurance money, deletion of his $3 million for the "flagship" universities and about $2 million cut from the amount needed to fully fund the teachers' retirement system. It also gave each four-year college an additional $100,000 in conditional funding.

On Aug. 19, the Legislature approved the trial-run isolation bill. It also approved the bill providing for a statewide vote to amend the constitution to provide for permanent budget isolation.

Tim Funk of the Anniston *Star* wrote of the last night of the session: James, "in the Senate...leisurely shook hands while the upper chamber debated a co-employee bill he had endorsed.

> In the House, he sat next to...McCorquodale. When he wasn't shaking hands, he gazed out at the representatives busy with his education budget. He puffed contentedly on a cigar.
>
> The co-employee bill passed. His education budget passed. And, earlier in the session, both houses had approved his proposal to isolate the General Fund and Education Budgets.
>
> "I like these special sessions," a smiling James said the next day at a press conference ...
>
> James refused in the early days of his administration to follow gubernatorial tradition and handpick the speaker and House and Senate committee chairmen. He said the tradition violated a greater tradition — the separation of powers among the branches of government.
>
> But there was James during the special session, playing mediator for the House and Senate conferees as they sat in the governor's office outlining possible compromises.
>
> When the conferees later disagreed about whether they had agreed to conditional funding for teacher medical insurance, James corroborated the Senate members' version and sent an executive amendment to the Legislature including the funding. Despite fierce opposition in the House, the governor again prevailed.
>
> Before the special session, James went on the road to sell his budget and education reforms to the voters. Along the way, the governor met behind closed doors with legislators to see what they would support and what they wouldn't.
>
> He found wide support for his budget isolation plan.

> James next recruited two floor leaders—Sen J. Richmond Pear-
> son of Birmingham and Rep. George Clark of Eutaw. The gover-
> nor agreed to drop an unpopular provision—that the Legislature
> would adjourn automatically after 15 days if the budgets weren't
> passed by then.
> The governor also showed flexibility in the early negotiations
> over his education budget. He agreed to push his revenue-growth
> projections upward—to 5.5 percent.
> ...(Wayne) Teague predicted James' budget wouldn't make it
> out of the House Ways and Means Committee. It did. Paul Hub-
> bert...called the James budget "unacceptable."
> In the end, even the strongest AEA allies in the two chambers
> accepted it...James called the final document "absolutely excel-
> lent," saying, "It puts a strong priority in the way K–12 is funded
> and the needs of the postsecondary sector are fairly addressed."

James signed the budget and the budget isolation amendment. In
addition, Harvey wrote, the Legislature concurred in an identical statutory requirement for budget isolation to be in effect for the 1982
regular session of the legislature.

"From here on, it will require a three-fifths vote of each House to
agree to pass any single measure before the budgets," James said.

Harvey also hailed the passage of James' education budget as a
victory for the governor. He wrote: "While the [Wayne] Teague coalition had presented a substitute budget to the special session, the governor's bill was found attractive to the coalition, which accepted it."
Harvey said the budget did not include a $16 million increase for
insurance. An executive amendment added by James did increase the
total allotment to each teacher to $309 annually, however, Harvey
wrote.

James talked of the successes of the session:

"The co-employee bill means Alabama is no longer the only southeastern state that allows employees to sue one another for on-the-job
injury. It was a liability. Some of our sister Southern states used it
against us in recruiting industry," James said.

The Legislature also approved a redistricting plan based on the
1980 census dividing the state into seven congressional districts.

"Fresh from his biggest legislative victories in more than a year,
Gov. Fob James apparently is ready to strike again while the fire is
hot," AP wrote Aug. 20 in predicting a second special session soon.

Meanwhile, the news media picked up where James left off in
pointing out the need for some central control over institutions of

higher learning in the state. Articles revealed: The University of Alabama had two planes that cost over a half-million dollars each and
Auburn had six smaller planes. The chancellor of the University of
Alabama lived in two substantial houses owned by the school and
junior colleges spent five times as much on athletic scholarships as on
academic scholarships, spent nearly a million dollars on public relations and "offered a host of bogus physical education courses that,
depending on your mood, comprise a laugh or a scandal." The University of Alabama in Birmingham spent $22,000 on "housekeeping" at
one of the chancellor's homes and $13,800 at the other and asked for
a 21 percent increase in "administrative support."

James called a news conference to say he would call later special
sessions to try again to rework the Commission on Higher Education,
the coordinating authority for four-year colleges and universities
which had no authority to control them. Legislators would also decide
how to spend a $449 million oil lease windfall—and James had plans
for the money.

"And if his legislative victories weren't enough to cool his critics—
particularly those in education circles—James announced he is cutting
proration of the current state education budget in half, freeing $60
million for schools, reducing proration from 10 percent to 5 percent..."
AP wrote.

The reason James could release the money to schools, Ralph Holmes wrote when the fiscal year ended Sept. 30, was legislation James
pushed and the Legislature approved in the regular session which
changed the way business income tax was collected.

Sponsored by Eric Cates of Greenville, the bill requiring the state
to collect income tax monthly rather than quarterly brought in to the
treasury an extra $65.7 million in 1981.

The fiscal year ended with a surplus of $6.3 million in the general
fund and the SETF short $40 million. The Legislature appropriated
$1.37 billion but the education fund only received $1.33 billion in
taxes.

Holmes wrote: "Alabama is ending this fiscal year in far better
shape than some thought, but still not as good as many had hoped."

The $40 million shortfall, he wrote, was "brighter than expected.
The predicted shortfall was 10 percent or about $137 million. The final
figure is 3.6 percent."

Equally good news was that James could report a turn-around in
Medicaid under his management.

The Medicaid Department was $34 million in the red when James took over. It "finished the 1981 fiscal year with a $6 million surplus," Holmes wrote.

James credited Hoke Kerns and Rebecca Beasley with the turn-around.

As the *Advertiser* wrote: "During the James administration's first year, when the state's Medicaid program was bankrupt and unable to pay bills, the then-director would always bring to legislative hearings a quiet, unassuming woman who commanded great respect in the legislative chambers for the simple reason that she seemed to know what she was talking about. She's the aide the director turned to when legislators asked about money."

Legislators asked, "Who was that woman?" the *Advertiser* wrote.

> "We call her Wonder Woman" says Gov. James, who officially gave her control of Medicaid in January, then added Pensions and Security in April and then the Commission on Aging in May. Mrs. Beasley now does the work of three cabinet members.
>
> The impressive aspect of Medicaid's fiscal recovery is that it was accomplished the way James contended it could be done, through sound management instead of more infusions of money. Medicaid rolls were computerized for the first time, for example, and Mrs. Beasley bird-dogged private insurers and the federal government's other health program, Medicare, to pay up when paying up was their responsibility—not the state's.
>
> While the governor credits Mrs. Beasley, she is just as insistent to credit him, but in a way uncommon to the governor's image. What he has done, according to Mrs. Beasley, is give hard-working, success-oriented career state employees an opportunity to make contributions unencumbered by political pressures...

Holmes quoted James as commenting on Medicaid, "Alabama will be one of the few states in the country that won't have to reduce services to meet new federal spending targets in the next fiscal period."

AP pointed out that James had indicated he would cut proration a month before he actually did so, which non-coincidentally happened to be one day after the Legislature passed a new education budget "almost identical to the one he recommended."

"Asked about the possibility of another prorated school budget, James said, "I would be very, very surprised. Of course, I was surprised when interest rates went to 20 percent."

The *Advertiser,* in writing of the success of the session, said that James' "short barnstorm jaunt in July" reinforced pressure from home on legislators.

James was aware of the public image of him which had been so carefully nurtured by AEA and the State Employees Association.

On Aug 25, UPI quoted him telling a Montgomery civic club that he was "puzzled" at people saying he was inept at making politics work. He was puzzled, he said, because the Alabama Legislature had responded favorably to many "gut reform" issues he had hurled at it.

"James said he has tossed at the Legislature since he took office in 1979 more tough propositions than the lawmakers have been asked to pass in 100 years...," UPI wrote.

Near the end of 1981, AP reported another first.

"When Alabama's state tax forms are mailed in a few weeks, they will tell you more than how to pay money to the state. They'll tell you where your tax dollars have gone."

James mailed the "special report" to every taxpayer in the state. It was detailed—eight pages long. It was also, conforming to the dictates of the Jamesonian system of management, a lightweight grade of paper which the wire service reported did not require any extra postage.

Gov. James with his predecessor, Gov. George Wallace.

Gov. James speaks to Legislature; at right, Lt. Gov. George McMillan and House Speaker Joe McCorquodale.

Gov. James and former Gov. "Big Jim" Folsom, a
supporter.

Gov. James with Frank
Thomas Jr., chairman,
Governor's Private Industry
Council, and Lynda Hart,
CETA director.

The governor teaches
school.

The governor with executive secretary Bobby Davis, left.

The governor with Pensions and Security Director Gary Cooper and Cooper's family.

President Reagan, Gov. James.

Gov. James signs legislation to protect abused spouses; from left, State Rep. Mary Zoghby; Barbara Crysel, Montgomery DA's office; Mobile tax collector Freda Roberts, Penelope House board member; Ellen Brooks, Montgomery DA's office.

The governor at work.

The governor as commander-in-chief with Adjutant General Henry Cobb.

Oscar Adams, appointed by Gov. James as Alabama's first black Supreme Court justice.

Taking the prayer case to the U.S. Supreme Court.

Legislative liaison Bob Geddie with his children.

With students at the Alabama Institute for the Deaf and Blind.

With the Hee Haw gang.

With conservation group.

Braxton Counts II and his wife, Linda Lee, James' cousin.

The James family. Seated: Tim James, wife Angela holding Fleming, Fob IV,
Bobbie James, Betsy (on floor); standing: Betsy, Fob III, Fob Jr., Pat.

James' grandchildren: Betsy (upper left), Fob IV (above), Fleming (lower left), Tim (below).

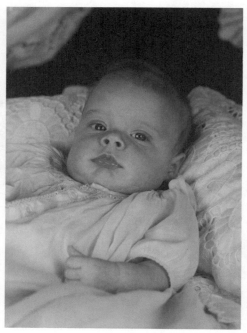

# The Second Special Session

James called the second special session of 1981 at the request of the Legislature.

In 1980, the United States government sent census takers door-to-door to gather statistics to paint a numerical picture of the nation, as has been done every ten years since 1790. When the information from each census is put together, we know how many residents there are in the United States, what they do for a living, how many children they have and, most importantly, where they live.

The distribution of citizens is most important because only with such knowledge can state Legislatures reapportion state lawmaking bodies and draw new districts for Congress to ensure that each citizen is equally represented when decisions are made as to how to spend tax money and to enact new laws or amend old ones.

In the first special session of 1981, a redistricting plan for the seven U.S. Congressional seats in the states was approved Aug. 18. The task of reapportioning state legislative districts was a tougher one, however.

Reapportionment is a sticky task at best, with the fate of current officeholders and even the balance of power between factions hanging in the balance. In 1965 the Voting Rights Act was approved by Congress in the wake of racial violence when blacks tried to march from Selma to Montgomery. Affecting mostly the Southern States, the legislation gave the U.S. Justice Department far-reaching authority over activities which formerly were under the sole jurisdiction of the states. Any change in election laws must be pre-cleared with the Civil Rights Division of the Department of Justice.

The first census taken after the Voting Rights Act was in 1970. It was clear that any redistricting plan would have to create districts in which blacks formed the majority and thus would elect black representatives. Thus any such plan would pit incumbents against each other or force white incumbents to run in newly-created black districts.

After the Legislature repeatedly was unable to agree on a plan in the seventies, the federal court stepped in and imposed a redistricting plan on the state, and ultimately something of the same fate awaited the efforts of legislators in 1981 and 1982.

Legislators were aware in the 1981 session that a similar fate loomed on the horizon if the Legislature did not quickly draw new districts to conform with the 1980 census.

On May 17, 1981, the Legislature approved a resolution sponsored by Rep. Rick Manley to replace the decade-old committee on reapportionment with a new one and to increase the number of legislators who served on the committee. Obviously expecting the worst, Manley included in the resolution the phrase, "Whereas, the U.S. Government will *all too soon* complete the 1980 census..."

Two days later Manley sponsored another resolution: "To state the Legislature's resolve to reapportion itself and to suggest to the governor that a special session be called exclusively for reapportionment purposes."

He noted the Legislature was "firmly resolved to make every effort" but also noted that "certain population figures of the 1980 census are presently in dispute."

The Legislature wanted a special session to hear the report and suggestions of the Legislative Interim Committee on Reapportionment.

Legislators in the first special session of 1981 approved a plan to redraw congressional lines in the state.

When James complied with the Legislature's request for a special session to reapportion state legislative districts, he included a pet project of his own—a request that legislators take $7.5 million from a recent oil-lease sale for seed money for a $200 million bond issue to provide homes through the Alabama Housing Finance Authority for middle and low-income families. It was the first portion of a planned $600 million project. Repayment of the bond issue would come from mortgage payments; it did not require the use of state tax revenue.

The mechanism had been set up in the regular legislative session through which the bonds would be issued. All that was needed was the money. James planned to introduce an overall plan for spending the oil-lease windfall in November. But Legislative approval of the low-income housing bonds was needed quickly or federal regulations could prevent the bonds from being issued in 1981.

James did not get involved in the redistricting, which was clearly designated as a duty of the Legislature.

A revised plan was haggled over by legislators, and finally approved Oct. 26 despite protests from blacks that it discriminated against black voters. It still did not have black support. Blacks said the district lines were drawn in a manner which protected incumbent whites and made it as difficult as possible for blacks to increase their numbers in the Legislature.

The Alabama Housing Authority legislation was sponsored in the House by Rep. Phil Kelley and in the Senate by then-Sen. H. L. "Sonny" Callahan.

Ralph Holmes described what happened to the housing money:

> House Ways and Means buried the home-building bill Tuesday, prompting an effort by supporters to resurrect it Wednesday with a rarely used parliamentary procedure to force it out of committee.
>
> But the House, refusing to take an almost precedent-setting vote to override the committee's refusal, delayed the fight until the next special session."

McCorquodale talked proponents and opponents into postponing a fight over the issue until James called the next special session. James said he would call the Legislature into session one day early, with that day to be devoted to the housing issue.

News stories announcing the third special session of 1981 quoted James as saying that his proposals for the next special session would include a request for $19.5 million to provide seed money for the total $600 million in bonds which would provide housing for low and middle income families and stimulate the stagnant building trades economy.

On the eve of the special session, James was told in a meeting with his advisers of the bankers' solid opposition. The Independent Bankers were ready to fight his plan. The Modern Bankers, which had just been formed, were also lined up against him.

"Fob got on the phone on a Monday morning to call the chief executive officer of most of the major banks in the state," Geddie said.

His strategy was to simply outline what he wanted to do with the money and rely on their understanding of finance to induce them to support him.

Bankers profited directly because proceeds from the bond issue would be deposited in Alabama banks.

The first banker James called was John Woods, who supported James' plan after he heard it because he supported the principle on which it was based. When he hung up, Woods started calling other bankers in James' support, Geddie said.

Within 24 hours, the Independent Bankers and Modern Bankers announced they were supporting the governor.

There were few holdouts, Geddie said.

"One particular banker continued to resist the plan. By Friday, when he discovered all ABC accounts were about to be withdrawn from his bank, he came around," Geddie said.

On Nov. 3, 1981, James called the Legislature into its third special session of his administration to vote on what to do with the windfall.

In his State of the State Address James explained his windfall plan with an analogy.

> Let us suppose that one day a rich uncle gave you $1 million and you knew this was a one-time shot, non-recurring, and you had a little girl or little boy one year old and you wanted to use the money for the total well-being of you and your child.
>
> How better could you use the $1 million than to put it all in U.S. Treasury Notes with a guaranteed income stream into your bank account that would allow you to go to your banker and borrow $1,100,000? You see, you have made yourself and your son or daughter 10 percent right off the bat. Then you take the one million dollars plus the $100,000 and buy a home, a farm, a shop, a factory, a store, machinery and equipment, or other things of value that will grow in value which you and your child and your future grandchildren can use to make a living—all the while knowing beyond any shadow of a doubt that 20 years later, when your child is 21 years old, the original one million dollars will be released to him intact, guaranteed, and that your banker will be fully paid off,

guaranteed.

"We have a heavy responsibility to be good stewards," James said, to insure "that every penny is used to the public interest."

He said his plan met the three conditions necessary to being good stewards.

It preserved the principal for future generations.

It maximized the buying power.

It insured that, with one exception, "not one dime" would be used to enlarge or enrich the operating costs of government.

That one exception was prisons, "where we must have additional capacity if we are to lock up all the criminals that ought to be locked up," he said.

Some $57 million in interest had accrued since the state got the money, giving James a total of $506 million with which to work. James recommended using all but $46 million of this to set up a trust fund which could never be spent. He asked legislators to approve spending the $46 million immediately on emergency needs, including:

- $19.5 million seed money for the Alabama Housing Finance Authority which would take advantage of the last three years of a federal program in which $600 million in bonds would be issued over the next three years to finance low-interest housing for low and middle-income families. The $600 million would generate 6,000 construction jobs, James predicted, "which will impact very favorably on Alabama's economy."
- $6 million to repay Alabama counties for feeding and housing state prisoners which, added to the $6 million appropriated in the 1981 budget "should clear the obligation," James said.
- $10 million to create a research fund for higher education to use in the development of services for high-technology industry in order to attract higher-paying jobs to Alabama.
- $10.5 million to cover construction debts of prisons and mental health through March 1, 1982.

The windfall money would be invested in the Heritage Trust Fund.

Money for a mammoth public works program would come from the proceeds of a bond sale, with interest from the Heritage Trust Fund going into the state's General Fund, which would pay off the bond issue.

James asked the Legislature to adopt a five-year construction schedule during which time the money in the fund would earn interest until the moment it was needed, netting approximately $150 million in interest and bringing the total of construction money available to $657 million.

A list of construction projects was detailed in the legislation, "so everybody will know what they are getting. This list has been given to the press to inform the public of all projects. Nothing is left to the political whim of tomorrow. The people should not be asked to buy a pig in a poke for the next 20 years," James said.

James recommended buying "the following assets for all Alabama citizens":

- $150 million for education, the majority of that to be used in the 127 local school systems for renovation and construction of classrooms in kindergarten through 12th grade. The first $75 million would be divided up immediately, equally, based on the number of students in the system.

  James acknowledged that postsecondary and higher education schools "certainly" had capital needs. He said some $70 million would be made available to them totally unrelated to the oil bonus money, to come from existing bond capacity.
- $300 million for widening, repair and construction of bridges and highways. He named six major bridge projects: the Tennessee River Bridge at Scottsboro; Tombigbee River Bridge at Pickensville; Coosa River Bridge at Childersburg; Coosa River Bridge at Wetumpka, Chattahoochee River Bridge at Phenix City North Bypass; and Alabama River Bridge at Claiborne.

  James also named some of the major highway projects, including: the four-laning of Highway 98 in Mobile County; the four-laning of Highway 59 in Baldwin County; work on U.S. 431 in the counties of Henry, Lee, Randolph, Marshall, and Madison; work on U.S. 80 in the counties of Dallas, Hale and Marengo; the four-laning of U.S. 280 in Tallapoosa, Shelby and Talladega Counties; work on Alabama 157 in Cullman and Colbert; the four-laning of Alabama 20 in Lawrence and Lauderdale Counties; the four-laning of U.S. 82 in Bibb County; work on Alabama 134 in Dale County; and work on Alabama 35 in DeKalb County.
- $30 million to county governments to fix county roads.

Legislators had by approving previous bills already appropriated:

- $65 million for Mental Health.
- $45 million for prisons. "Let me report that a 1,000-inmate prison is well under construction in St. Clair County, and construction of a 1,000-inmate prison in Jefferson County is getting started," James said.

  James requested another $20 million to build a third 1,000-inmate prison in the Tennessee Valley, saying, "Only then will the State of Alabama be able to lock up all the dangerous criminals that ought to be locked up. When it comes to fighting crime, let us be men and women of action, not words."
- $50 million to initiate a joint venture with the federal government to deepen the Mobile ship channel to 55 feet, enabling the port to become the only deep water port on the Gulf Coast. "These funds will also be available for the construction and improvement of up-state docks facilities."
- $10 million for a new Highway Department building at the old Kilby Prison site, enabling the state to renovate the present Highway Department and move into it the state agencies which were renting space from private landlords outside the Capitol complex.
- $12 million to restore the Capitol.
- $7 million to the Conservation Department to acquire public hunting and fishing lands; and for capital improvements too long deferred in the state parks, as well as for shell planting and oyster improvement, for enforcement equipment with which to monitor oil and gas development, for providing adequate water access for industrial development with emphasis on seafood and marine industries, and for the continuance of the public fishing lake development.
- One-half million dollars to purchase new equipment for the Alabama Public Television network, "our educational television."

"I believe the people of Alabama deserve these projects," James said. "Out there across the state I ask the people to let me know if this is right. Let Speaker McCorquodale know. Let Governor McMillan know. Let your legislators know if you need renovated or new classrooms for your children's sake, roads and bridges for your cars, trucks and school buses to travel on; prisons to safeguard the public, the women, the children and the elderly; the only deep-water port on the Gulf Coast to bring industry, trade, commerce and jobs to Alabama; and over 12,000 new construction jobs for Alabamians..."

There were people who opposed his plan, James said.

If it were not approved, he said, "then I would propose we take the full $449 million dollars and equally divide it among the some one million households in the state and send every Alabama family a cash Christmas bonus of $449.

"There are those who say leave the money in the treasury and let the people take pot luck on what they get. Well, you have heard that for forty years but where are the roads and bridges and school houses?"

Opposition came from various directions, including the rumor mill. Harvey wrote that "rumors" went out, upsetting education, that James was supposedly planning on giving all the money from the bond issue designated for education to K–12, leaving out higher education.

James called legislators into his office and explained that 21.34 percent of the bond issue would go to education. $75 million would go directly to K–12, based on enrollment. The remaining money would go to the Alabama Public School and College Authority (which consisted of the governor, the finance director and the state superintendent of education) to be divided as follows: $22 million to universities and junior colleges; $8 million to technical schools; and $45 million to be alloted among all segments of education on a priority basis.

The Nov. 11 *AEA Journal* asked, "Is building a bridge, resurfacing a road or constructing classrooms more helpful in getting reelected than providing a cost-of-living adjustment?...The answer...by House vote of 61–4 is 'yes.' "

Headlines in the *AEA Journal* Nov. 15 stated, "Pork barrel bills glide through House re: oil-lease windfall." The article stated, "The administration's machine is moving with strength through the upper chamber with only a couple of senators voicing opposition."

The Legislature approved James' windfall plan, which had to be okayed by voters in a referendum. From the moment the Legislature approved it, James geared his efforts toward a massive public relations campaign to solicit voter approval.

"He treated it just like you would an election," Geddie said. "We paid for an advertising campaign with money solicited from private donations and Fob campaigned for it statewide."

The *AEA Journal* headline stated on Dec. 1, "James' oil plan goes to voters—teachers and support personnel ignored in disbursement of millions."

Voters approved the windfall plan.

In the final accounting: Interest had hiked the original $449 million to $506 million; investing all but $46 million of this in the Alabama Heritage Trust Fund would provide enough income to pay off a $520 million bond issue; the construction money would earn interest until needed to pay for stages of a five-year public works issue, adding another $137 million, bringing the total public works project to $657 million.

In 20 years, when interest from the trust had paid off the bond issue, the state would still have the $460 million.

The *Advertiser* wrote that the last bill to be approved in the session was the one giving the go-ahead for the $600 million in housing money.

The Legislature also approved a bill sponsored by Rep. Eric Cates of Greenville and endorsed by James which divided the first $100 million of the housing bond money equally among the 67 counties, with the rest to be divided by population.

One of the many departmental bills which were quietly approved each session established the Alabama Game & Fish Endowment Fund, with money for the fund to be derived from the sale of lifetime hunting and fishing licenses. It was introduced in the special session because James was particularly interested in passing it.

There was also a resolution which was approved and signed into law by James that would be forgotten by 1989, when a federal court ruled that it was unconstitutional to pray before school athletic events. Act 81–1123 requests all inter-collegiate sporting events of state-supported schools in the state of Alabama to start with a public prayer.

With all of James' bills dealt with, the *Advertiser* wrote, Sen. Doug Cook of Birmingham introduced a resolution to call the nine bills the "Fobonomics Program for the Economic Recovery of Alabama."

When James received a breakdown for what would be the costs of the closing of the windfall bond issue, he discovered $280,000 entertainment costs.

"He called New York demanding to know what the $280,000 was for. They said that's for the parties we have at closing," Executive Assistant Bobby Davis said. Following long-established custom, the closing was scheduled to take place in New York. More than three dozen legislators were planning to be there, as well as others from

Alabama who had some role to play in the signing.

"Fob wanted to know why they couldn't send the papers to Alabama and hold the closing in Montgomery," Davis said. "He told them to forget about the parties. They told him not to worry about the parties, that the state didn't pay for them."

The costs were under "administrative costs," which under tax laws at that time could be included in the bond issue.

"Fob had me call them back and tell them he had rescheduled the closing for the Senate chamber. I called and the bond attorneys told me we couldn't do that, that there were 181 things to sign and forty legislators were all set to go to New York."

James uttered a one word exclamation of disapproval and told Davis there was no way the closing would be held in New York as long as he was governor.

The frugal closing was held in Montgomery.

After James left office, however, bond closings reverted back to the former days of wine and roses—or very expensive brandy, anyway. In a succeeding administration, a $240 bottle of brandy was consumed at a New York closing. At another, an investment banker rented a yacht for more than 200 people and hired a band to play while the party cruised New York harbor. The costs will be paid by the state of Alabama over the years as the bond issue is paid off.

Two or three years after James left office, interest rates had dropped and it was time to refinance.

James said he read stories of the refinancing with amazement.

"I couldn't believe the fees which were paid when the state brought in another whole bunch of lawyers and paid them huge sums of money. It seemed to me that most of the work had been done the first go-around, that they should have been able to cut costs by putting some of the paperwork from the first bond issue on a copying machine," James said.

Several aspects of James' windfall plan did not turn out exactly as he intended.

One involved something the financial world and the IRS call arbitrage.

Arbitrage is, in laymen's language, the difference in the amount of profit between selling tax-exempt bonds and non-tax-exempt bonds. It was within the power of the IRS to declare that James' plan took advantage of the bonds' tax-free status to make a profit to spend on state projects when that profit should have gone to the IRS.

If IRS labeled James' plan arbitrage, he would have been unable to issue tax-exempt bonds, which would have killed the entire transaction.

Tax-exempt bonds can be issued by the state or other legally-empowered bodies. Because investors pay no tax on the interest of the bonds, the bonds are attractive to buyers. Therefore, buyers will settle for a lower interest rate than on non tax-exempt bonds. The state of Alabama benefitted monetarily (more than $400 million, North's figures show) by paying a lower interest rate to bond holders on the money borrowed for James' public works projects.

Enter the IRS, which had issued guidelines limiting the use of "arbitrage."

The arbitrage issue arose, North said, after the City of Denver, Colo., prior to James' windfall plan, came up with a "creative" method of financing which allowed the city to build a $10 million facility at no cost to Denver taxpayers. This was accomplished by selling $100 million in tax-exempt bonds, then while paying less-than-market interest on the money it borrowed, investing the $90 million it did not need at high interest rates. The interest Denver received on the $90 million was enough to pay for its $10 million facility without spending a cent of taxpayers' money.

Obviously, North explained, somebody paid for the building. The IRS determined that the U.S. government, through loss of taxes on interest paid on the tax-exempt bonds, paid for the building. The IRS ruled the profit Denver made was arbitrage, that arbitrage was a no-no. Financial journals buzzed with speculation. What would IRS declare was arbitrage in the future?

James saw no similarity between the Denver case and his plan. Comparing the two made him angry. He insisted the money invested belonged to the people of Alabama and had no legal connections with the government's desire to sell its general obligation bonds. The IRS suggested that if he waited a year, there would be no problem. This confirmed his belief even more that IRS's convoluted logic was wrong.

North, Slaughter and other financial advisers were aware that IRS was watching closely any situation in which the issuance of tax-exempt bonds resulted in profit.

"Initially, IRS ruled that private corporations could not profit from arbitrage," North said.

What James did was technically different. The money he invested in the Heritage Trust Fund did not come from the tax-exempt bond

issue which was approved as part of the same package. The Heritage
Trust Fund money was the oil-lease bonanza. Every penny of the bond
issue was spent for the public projects for which it was issued. North
and Slaughter, however, were afraid that IRS would view James' investment plan as a variation on what Denver had done and disallow
it because figures compiled by Slaughter showed the state would profit
by $436 million over the 20-year period.

Because of this fear, they carefully separated in the legislative
package the Heritage Trust Fund from the $540 million bond issue.

No wording in the legislation linked the two. Interest earned by
Heritage Trust Fund investments did not go to pay off the bond issue.
It went to the state's general fund. The legislation approving the bond
issue did not refer to the Heritage Trust Fund as collateral. Repayment
of the bond issue was made a "general obligation" of the state. Maturity dates for investments of the Heritage Trust Fund were timed
carefully to mature near the date that bond payments had to be made,
but not on the same dates. The Heritage Trust Fund was a constitutional amendment, approved by the voters.

Establishment of the Heritage Trust Fund directly benefitted the
state in a manner obvious to the bond expert but not as obvious to
most laymen. Each time the state issues bonds, which is borrowing
money, the rate of interest is determined by Wall Street based upon
the state's credit rating. The higher the rating, the better deal the state
gets.

"The rating services were obviously aware the state had a new
source of income," North said, which ensured a triple-A rating for the
bonds.

As the state was preparing to issue the bonds, after the special
session and after the constitutional amendment had been approved,
an article appeared in the Wall Street Journal on Alabama's "creative"
new approach to financing. It stated Oklahoma and Texas and several
other states were watching it to see if it got past IRS or if IRS declared
it arbitrage and refused to allow Alabama to go through with it.

"We were not happy, to say the least," North said.

Then the notice arrived from IRS that it was conducting an informal inquiry into the matter, which could bring the entire process to a
screeching halt. As bond attorneys, North and Slaughter would be
required to inform the financial world of the possibility that IRS would
not let Alabama go through with James' windfall plan.

"Fob spent days finding out everything he could about arbitrage,"

Bobby Davis said. "His lawyers told him what he wanted to do was legal, but that IRS wouldn't let him do it because every state in the union would fall in line behind Alabama if they did."

With the help of First District Cong. Jack Edwards of Mobile, James arranged a meeting in Washington with top IRS officials.

"We arrived in Washington on a Sunday afternoon and worked essentially around the clock through Friday morning," North said.

"There was a battery of lawyers, IRS on one side, our attorneys on the other," Davis said.

"It was really a negotiation between IRS computers and our computers," North said. "They would say they didn't like this or this and we would go to the hotel and work that night. Then we'd come back again the next day and do the same thing."

"After three days," said James' bodyguard, Gene Mitchell, "Fob walked in and said, 'I don't understand all you lawyers but let me ask a question since y'all aren't getting anywhere.' "

Mitchell related the exchange.

"Are we illegal?" James asked.

IRS said, "No, governor."

"Then we want to do it," James said.

IRS said, "You can't."

James said, "Are we not following your guidelines?"

IRS said he was.

"You show me where we're wrong and we'll pack our suitcases and go home," James said.

Finally, Mitchell said, James told the IRS attorneys, "You get Roscoe down here. If it's right, we want to do it."

Roscoe L. Egger Jr. was chief of the IRS.

James asked Egger, "Do I understand this correctly? We could do this if the trust fund money didn't come from the oil-lease windfall?"

Egger said yes. He said if James were not able to issue tax-free bonds, the interest rate on the taxable bonds would be too high to be able to pay them off with the trust fund interest. Therefore James was taking advantage of the tax-free status. It was arbitrage.

To back up his contention, Egger spread news articles from across the United States on the table which labeled James' plan arbitrage.

"That won't fly," James told him, motioning his people to leave. In the hallway he told them what he wanted them to do before the next morning's meeting with IRS.

When James arrived the next morning, he spread on the table

news articles from across the United States. All were negative articles on Nancy Reagan, criticizing her for the money she spent on clothes or for her lifestyle or her influence on the president.

"Now, hoss, are you going to tell me you believe everything you read in the newspapers?" James asked the IRS chief.

Egger said, "Hell, no, I don't believe everything I read in the papers."

"We said great. Then let's start all over again with a clean slate," James said. "From that point things got better."

IRS ruled that Alabama could go ahead with its plan, except for a slap on the wrist. They ruled that $50 million of the $540 million had to be invested in low-interest government securities for six years.

This resulted in a profit which was some $25 million less than it would have been without IRS intervention, but North termed the amount insignificant compared to the hundreds of millions of dollars by which the state profited through James' plan.

Interest from the perpetual trust would allow the state to pay off in a 20-year period a $507 million bond issue. Construction money would draw interest as a five-year construction plan was put in effect, which James calculated could earn another $150 million if interest rates did not sharply decline.

IRS also ruled no other states would be allowed to follow James' lead.

"I disagreed with the IRS ruling as it related to other states, but I was not governor of any other state," James said.

James had been warned that publicly linking the perpetual trust and the bond sale might invoke an IRS penalty, Geddie said.

"We knew that from day one," he said. "But we had no choice. The only way we could rally public support for Fob's windfall plan was to lay the whole thing out before the public."

"They closed the door to the other states and caught our shirttail in the door," James said.

James said he never ceased to be amazed at the manner in which "politics" popped up when least expected.

"After all of this had been settled, the final document required the signature of the state treasurer as well as the governor," he said. The treasurer was Annie Laurie Gunter.

"I called Miss Annie Laurie who was at some convention out west, I think, and told her we had received clearance from the IRS and everything was set but the final signing of the documents," James said.

"The lady stalled and as the conversation continued, I realized she wanted my assurance that I would approve some appropriation or authorization for an expenditure for her office."

Mrs. Gunter got the approval.

"Here we were at the end of a long hard journey, uphill all the way, to purchase over $600 million of assets for all Alabamians and she threatened the deal over something for her office," James said. "I think I told our people to give her the capitol if necessary, but do it quickly before IRS changed their minds."

Though it was not a matter of public knowledge, financial precedent was also made the day the state of Alabama raided Wall Street to get the best deals investing the windfall money.

Dr. David Bronner, who worked with the Heritage Trust Fund board in Montgomery against a deadline to put together a portfolio of investments, explains why:

> The fixed income [government] market was kind of holding its breath to see which vehicles would be used. Normally, you go to someone you know or a couple of people you have done business with and trust and ask them to put together the best package. In this case, with $540 million, I wanted to do it on a bid basis to make sure no one could accuse me of showing favoritism. So I asked the heads of all the big brokerage houses to meet in one room and give us prices. We knew what we wanted to get for our money and once we started hearing prices we would know which way to go to get it. Everything depended on the prices holding firm. It is difficult to get someone to hold firm on a price on Wall Street for four or five minutes, even on a $100 million deal — if they guarantee you 15 percent for an hour and during that hour the market moves to 14 1/2 percent, they've lost a bundle. And here we were asking the senior people of every firm to hold firm long enough for us to determine what would work for us and what wouldn't. What we had to do, basically, was kind of hold the market at a standstill. It was unrealistic if not totally mind boggling.

Regardless, Wall Street went along. "There was literally a room full of people bidding on everything from house mortgages to plain old governments to ships [a type of mortgage] with everyone talking at once," Bronner said. "It was a zoo. After I heard a few bids I knew what to listen for. Everybody was talking at once and none of them were really happy to be there doing it that way. I had to ignore extraneous talk and sift through the bids mentally to zero in on the ones which sounded good for the state.

"It was highly unorthodox, the way we did it," Bronner said. "Contrast that room of noisy irritated people to the way we usually do it, in a quiet office. The way we did it, coupled with the size of the deal meant that everyone was looking at it. The governor's reputation was on the line."

"When it was over, I felt real good," Bronner said, "We screwed up the market for a couple of hours. But it worked."

The $540 million bond issue which funded James' five-year public works program was the third-largest general obligation bond issue in U.S. history.

Some nine months later, James accepted the "Distinguished Service Award" from the Alabama Conference of Black Mayors for his foresight in getting the oil lease windfall plan approved in a statewide referendum.

Speaking for the 24 mayors who were members of the organization, Tuskegee Mayor Johnny Ford explained, "Many of the towns of which these men are mayors, such as Tuskegee, have been able to pave some streets, we've gotten assistance for our schools and other things since he's been governor."

At the end of 1981, AP wrote that James "bids good-bye to 1981 with no special ringing of the bells—not for his own political achievements.

> It was a year in which his political stock, near bankrupt in the first quarter, closed with a rush as he won passage of his multimillion-dollar oil lease windfall package.
>
> But as he looked back, he says the oil-lease windfall success should not be viewed as any political milestone. Indeed, he says, political popularity is no measure of public performance.

"I'm trying to give the taxpayers an insight," James said. "For a politician to be praised for handling the public's money prudently is like your company giving you an accolade just for showing up at work on time."

The year ended on an upbeat note for the James administration, a fact which seemed to challenge James' chief foe to new heights of negative oratory.

At the December delegates meeting of the AEA, Hubbert worked the group into a cheering, standing ovation with his anti-James diatribe.

Hubbert's remarks to teachers were repeated in his *Journal*: "How can a millionaire know what it's like to live on a school person's salary?" he asked.

Send the pied piper from Opelika back to his sporting goods company and elect officials who will put public education back on the top of the priority list where it belongs, Hubbert told them.

As teachers cheered, Hubbert told them he was ready to meet "the challenge" head-on.

"I'm raring and ready," he said. "Bring on 1982!"

James was probably unaware of Hubbert's tirade. If aware, the AEA chief's words caused no chill of foreboding. In convincing the Legislature to lock the revenue produced directly and indirectly by the oil lease sale into a long-term $657 million public works project, James had defeated three major foes all at the same time—a few hold-out bankers, the Internal Revenue Service and Dr. Paul Hubbert.

# 19

# Roads and Bridges

**F**rom the day James was elected, he zeroed in on the Highway Department as the department of state government which most needed reform.

The department was submerged in debt and that took a huge bite out of its operating funds. Fewer and fewer dollars were getting to the roads.

James' relationship with the agency dated back to his student days at Auburn, when he worked for the Highway Department.

He served as a lieutenant with the U.S. Corps of Engineers 926 Reserve Unit in Montgomery. Many of the unit's officers and men worked for the Highway Department. Many of the civil engineers who worked for the state were former classmates of James.

"I was proud of the tradition and esprit de corps found within the department," James says.

In other words, he loved the department and the people in it and felt at home when he was with them.

As a civil engineer, James' first jobs were in highway construction. He understood the industry. He knew costs. He knew big money could be saved by restructuring the department.

In 1974 James had become deeply involved in what turned out to be a year's project. He chaired the Alabama Citizens for Transportation, a task force dedicated to coming up with a long-range plan for roads in the state.

In January of 1975, James reported to ACT that he had worked for 12 months on the project with highway department officials and research teams from Auburn University and the University of Ala-

bama. A lot of the help James received with the project came from
Rex Rainer, head of the Department of Civil Engineering at Auburn.
James presented to ACT what the Birmingham *News* described as "a
complete plan describing in detail our road and highway needs during
the next 20 years" and how much they would cost.

ACT's 20-year plan was presented to the governor, the Legislature and the Highway Department. It was not adopted, but it gave
James a working, in-depth knowledge of the state's highway needs
which he would use later as governor.

It also added to the growing feeling James had within that he
might have to serve in a bigger role than chairman of a task force if
he wanted to change things.

James took office as governor with a single thought governing
every action taken on the Highway Department: Great sums of money
would be saved by getting the state out of the construction and maintenance business and concentrating on engineering, design, inspec-
tion, and material testing. At that time, there were nearly a dozen
construction divisions within the department.

It took him several years, but by the time James left office the
overall management of the Highway Department reflected the plod-
ding stubbornness with which he worked to restructure it from top to
bottom.

Don Bryan in retrospect puts the situation James encountered in
the Highway Department in perspective: "...the 4-cents-a-gallon gasoline tax, people never understood why we got that passed. We never
sold our story on that. But then, we never sold our story on a lot of
things. For years Wallace had been floating bond issues, and prior to
Wallace, Folsom, saying they did it because people in this state had
been taxed enough. So they floated bond issues? To keep from taxing
the people? There's only one thing bad about a bond issue, it's a loan.
It has to be paid back.

"The problem was that nobody prior to Fob had ever passed the
revenue provisions to pay back bond debt as it occurred. In 1978, the
debt amounted to $400 million. The principal and interest was $40
million a year. When you realize the total the state was spending for
resurfacing highways was only around $25 million a year, you begin to
see the problem. There had to be some method of repaying that
money. If you took $40 million away you simply could not maintain
our road system. If you look at the 4-cents-per-gallon tax, it generated
about $40 million a year for the state after you pay the counties and

cities their share."

"I knew the Highway Department was misdirected in 1979," James said. "I knew the job they could be doing and I knew how many people it would take to do that job. There was no way to justify the Highway Department's being heavy into construction and maintenance."

It was the Highway Department more than any other that James was thinking of when he issued the executive order soon after his inauguration to lay off "provisional" employees who had been on the job less than six months. The order also froze hiring.

To oversee the job of revamping the Highway Department, James turned to Rainer.

He directed Rainer to undertake as highway director a complete review of the Highway Department's mission and organizational structure for long range action.

He also directed the Highway Department to identify the narrow 20-foot-wide highways in the state which could be widened to 24 feet in conjunction with routine state maintenance resurfacing projects.

Bobby Joe Kemp, who succeeded Rainer, stated in a four-year-end report to James that the directive resulted in 600 miles of two-lane highways being widened to 24 feet during his term.

James charted a methodical course and stuck to it, Bob Geddie said of the manner in which he and Rainer ran the Highway Department.

"He also drew upon excellent leadership within the ranks of the department," Geddie said.

James' first action was to "re-evaluate" the budget that had been submitted by the Wallace administration, Kemp wrote.

James slashed the budget drawn up by the outgoing administration by $17 million, Kemp wrote, by such things as abolishing several departments which "were not contributing to the mission of the department." These included the photo lab, cabinet shop and public information department.

"Other units were combined to eliminate duplication...," Kemp wrote.

As in other departments, the Highway Department was studied from a business standpoint as to what legislation needed to be passed to update or modernize procedures.

In 1979 legislation was passed to allow the department to carry over maintenance funds at the end of a fiscal year. Prior to that, unspent funds were returned to the general fund. The money was thus lost to the department unless re-appropriated by the Legislature, which the administration explained to legislators resulted in a "hurry up and spend it" mode of thinking.

In 1981, legislation was passed to allow the Highway Department to replace vehicles "on a timely basis" without requiring separate appropriations each year. Prior to that, the condition of the vehicle was not the primary factor in deciding when to buy a new car. There were wholesale replacements of automobiles when the Legislature provided money for it.

The department was also reorganized. Kemp wrote that the reorganization was directed toward establishing more efficient lines of communications, "thereby reducing time required for decisions."

James did not talk publicly at that time about the rank political influence which permeated the Highway Department when he took over as governor and had been present for years before he took office.

He was quoted on the subject in newspaper articles four years later, however.

Just days before the 1982 Democratic Primary, when citizens would vote on whether to give Wallace a fourth term in office, James spoke up.

"...Gov. Fob James has attacked the 'garbage' and 'corruption' that he says he found in state government when he took office in January 1979," Dave White wrote in the Birmingham *News*.

> The governor says he found "sheer fraud and corruption" in the state Building Commission and "mismanagement and political patronage" in asphalt deals in the Highway Department.
>
> "There's a vast difference in the way business has been done in Montgomery the past 3 1/2 years," said James. "The way it used to be cost taxpayers tons of money"...
>
> But James didn't criticize Wallace by name...
>
> "That may have been standard practice in Montgomery," [James] said, "...But what we did was different...We changed the business practices because we thought they were wrong. We tried to get all the garbage out. People elected us to clean up the mess, not complain about it..."
>
> "Where you could clean up an operation by changing management and direction, that's what we did...Where we found corruption we prosecuted," James said.

When James took over as governor, he found that asphalt was bought by the state through purchase orders issued by the department head, not by soliciting bids, an example of "mismanagement with ample opportunity for political patronage," the *News* wrote.

With its power to buy cars, trucks, heavy earth-moving equipment, parts, materials, etc., the Highway Department is "the biggest means of patronage a governor has if he wants to use it," James said.

James spoke not from hearsay but from personal experience.

A quarter century ago, Braxton Counts II called James to ask if he would ride to Montgomery with him. Counts was married to James' first cousin, Linda Lee. He was also a good friend. He was excited.

"I had started a new asphalt company and someone called from the Highway Department to ask if I wanted to sell asphalt to the state," Counts said.

After waiting with other asphalt producers and contractors, Counts and James were ushered in to see the then-highway director and the state finance director.

"The finance director told us, 'A $50,000 contribution to the governor's campaign is normal for getting a state contract, but since you're new in the business $25,000 will be fine,'" Counts said. "I'll never forget Fob's face. It went beet red. I could see he was about to blow up so I got him out of there fast."

Counts did not make the contribution and did not get the state contract.

James, when he took office, made it clear that such shake-downs were a thing of the past. He ordered that all work, including maintenance and resurfacing that could be done by private contractors, be let by competitive bid.

One reason the state saves money by taking bids is because the state would buy and maintain a huge volume of equipment and beef up its payroll in order to do a few jobs. Between those jobs, much of that equipment and personnel would sit idle.

James, to illustrate his point, draws a chart of ups and downs showing work-intense periods punctuated by periods in which machinery and operators sit idle waiting for the next job.

When James left office, Kemp was able to brag, "Cost-underruns have become the rule and not the exception..."

Toward the end of James' administration, his highway director estimated the department would save some $4 million in 1982, or about 15 percent of its $25 million road resurfacing budget, by putting the resurfacing work out for bid.

James said, "The Highway Department is there for the purpose of determining the priority of roads and that should be based on traffic density, safety and economic impact."

In the 1980–81 fiscal year, the first year the 4-cents-per-gallon gas tax was in effect, it provided about $80 million in revenue. City and county governments reaped 55% of the tax. The rest went to the State Highway Department, offsetting the huge annual sum owed for principal and interest on past bond issues.

Kemp wrote of changes in the department:

- The Highway Department owned 4,800 vehicles at the beginning of James' term. According to need, cars and trucks were assigned to motor pools in Montgomery and in each division office. Annual, continuing review of the needs of the department resulted in a reduction of some 500 vehicles the first year, 1,200 the second year and 300 the next. Kemp said the fleet reduction saved some $2.5 million annually.
- Small but effective steps were taken to save money, such as a change in the departmental policy requiring all employees to fill out time cards routinely. Under the new policy, time cards were filled out only when there was a deviation in normal work schedule, such as illness or vacation. Instead of disposing of old road signs, they were recycled at a central sign shop in Montgomery.

Other actions brought larger savings.

- Several district offices were consolidated, which Kemp said saved $300,000 a year. $61 million was saved through participation in the federal Advance Interstate Construction Program which speeded up the letting of many interstate projects by as much as five to ten years through the sale of short term bonds.
- Some $900,000 a year was saved by developing a self-insurance program for workmen's compensation, Kemp wrote.
- Another $100,000 a year would be saved because the Highway Department took over operation of the state welcome centers, Kemp said.

When James took office there were 5,838 employees in the Highway Department; there were 3,621 when he left. Kemp said the savings in personnel costs totaled $49 million per year. Wallace added 910 people to Highway Department payrolls during his four-year term following James.

The Highway Department budget increased only from $344 million to $387 million during James' term.

When James persuaded the Legislature to approve his mammoth public works program made possible by the $449 million sale of oil and gas leases, the Highway Department came in for $270 million to build projects specifically listed in the legislation. Another $30 million was channeled directly to counties for local road work.

Not written into the legislation, but depended upon by the Legislature, was James' promise that the $270 million in projects would to the greatest extent possible be placed under some phase of construction by the end of calendar year 1982, the month before a new governor would take office. The work was also to be done using the existing work force.

"The department has fulfilled both...commitments...with a work force some 2,200 less than in January, 1979," Kemp wrote in his four-year-end report. He noted that a "cash forecasting system" had been instituted to maximize the oil lease funds.

Every county in the state benefitted from road work which was completed or set in motion during James' term.

James publicly stated his intention to complete the interstate system in Alabama. This involved opening 50 miles of interstate including the Alabaster-to-Hoover portion of I-65 and the 12-mile section of I-65 between U.S. 43 and Alabama 225 north of Mobile, which included the $85 million Mobile River Bridge linking Mobile and Baldwin Counties. Construction had begun on I-359 (Tuscaloosa) and I-759 (Gadsden) spurs, and federal approval had been given for the $21.4 million I-565 spur (Huntsville).

Bypasses were let to contract, including those in Cullman, Courtland and Enterprise. The Courtland bypass completed the four-lane highway between Decatur and the Quad-Cities.

When James left office, all of I-59 was completed and all of I-459, I-10 and I-65 were either complete or under construction or scheduled for contract lettings.

Through James' Public Works Project:

- The Decatur Beltline was four-laned.
- The Scottsboro bypass was four-laned.
- The contract was let to bid for the four-laning of Alabama 157 between Alabama 20 and the Colbert-Lawrence counties line.
- A section of U.S. 280 in Shelby County referred to as "The Narrows" was four-laned. Work was scheduled to begin on the remaining two-lane portion of U.S. 280 near Childersburg, which completed the four-laning between Birmingham and Alexander City.
- Construction was nearly completed on a 45-mile stretch of four-lane between Selma and Demopolis.
- U.S. 84 between Dothan and Avon, a five-mile stretch, was four-laned.
- U.S. 43 was four-laned in Washington and Clarke Counties, with work scheduled to begin on an additional eight miles of four-lane between McIntosh and Sunflower.
- U.S. 82 was four-laned between Reform and McShan in Pickens County, "eliminating hazardous driving conditions in the area," Kemp said.
- Alabama 59 between Interstate 10 and Foley was being four-laned.
- U.S. 82 was four-laned between the Tuscaloosa County line and Eoline, with money provided to extend the four-lane from Eoline to Alabama 5 north of Brent.

Also:

- The job was contracted out to add passing lanes, widen and resurface U.S. 431 between Phenix City and Abbeville.
- Money was set aside to complete the remaining six of ten scheduled projects to widen and upgrade U.S. 98 in Southwest Alabama, dubbed "Bloody 98" because of frequent traffic deaths. The first four projects were under construction.

An extensive program of new construction had been completed, including:

- A five-mile stretch of new highway extending U.S. 280/431 to a point six miles north of Phenix City, where it connected with a

new six-mile stretch under construction from Salem to Motts.
- The relocation of U.S. 431 in Randolph County between We-dowee and Swagg Road, extending the two-lane road an additional five miles north to Foster's Crossroads.
- The relocation of Alabama 24 in Franklin, Lawrence and Morgan Counties.

Money had been set aside to complete and work already begun on:

- A five-mile section of U.S. 78 in Walker County between Sumiton and Union Chapel.
- A new two-lane location of U.S. 431 between Abbeville and Headland.
- Range Line Road in Mobile between I-10 and Hamilton Boulevard (Island Road).

James also replaced 19 bridges in Childersburg, Scottsboro, Phenix City, Cullman, Marion, Lillian in Baldwin County, south of Troy, and in the counties of Monroe, Pickens, Autauga, Cullman, Lauderdale and Mobile. Federal funds were obtained to replace the Claiborne-Murphy Bridge in Monroe County and Cochrane Bridge in Mobile County.

A January, 1983, editorial in the Birmingham *News* stated, "When all the pluses and minuses of the four years of the James administration are tallied, one particularly bright spot that will have to be considered is the ambitious road-building program carried out by the State Highway Department over the past four years.

> All told, Alabama spent about $1 billion on completion of its interstates and other road construction or planning, with a sizable chunk of that money going for interstate building right here in Jefferson County.
>
> And that tremendous outlay of money not only produced better transportation in the state, but also jobs—some 130,000 of them plus, if estimates by economic experts are correct.
>
> What's more, the record amount of road-building carried on by the James administration was accomplished by a less than record-sized staff in the Highway Department..."

James is well aware of what was accomplished in the Highway Department during his term. However, he has learned the public is not aware. It is his own fault. Back in 1981 and 1982 when various projects were being dedicated or announced, he refused to allow staffers to publicly give him credit for any project built with public money.

"It's not my money. I didn't pay for those roads and bridges. It's the public's money," James said.

In 1986, Jack Miller said, James was campaigning in Scottsboro when he commented on the massive bridge crossing the Tennessee River.

The bridge had been needed for years, but the Highway Department had put off the construction until James included it in his public works project.

"When Fob commented on the bridge, somebody spoke up and said, 'Yes, that's the bridge George Wallace built,'" Miller said.

# 20

# Three Forgotten Agencies

The Department of Pardons and Paroles was one of three areas which James said he discovered had been pitifully neglected by the state for years.

The other two were the Department of Youth Services and the Alabama School for the Deaf and Blind at Talladega.

"Pardons and Paroles doesn't grab your heart the way the other two do," James said.

But it was the department which had suffered the most in the years of confrontation over the prison overcrowding between the federal judiciary and the state of Alabama.

James gave Pardons and Paroles the attention it had lacked. In his four years, he added 47 people to the staff and increased the budget from $3.9 million in 1979 to $5.6 million in 1982. He also provided supplemental appropriations for 30 additional employees which were added after he left office.

In turn, he used the department to implement campaign promises to get tough with criminals and to assert the rights of victims.

In 1981, new guidelines were adopted for setting up initial parole consideration dates for prisoners to insure that less serious offenders got reviewed first and that career criminals and heinous offenders served longer periods before initial parole review.

In 1982, policies were adopted to ensure that the victims of crimes were not forgotten in the parole procedure.

Legislation was passed requiring the Pardons and Paroles Board to notify the trial judge and district attorney that a parole was pending at least 30 days before acting on that parole.

The board added to that requirement one which stipulated that written notice would be sent to victims of serious crimes when paroles of the perpetrators were to be considered.

The sheriff was also to be notified.

Additionally, staff members were directed to notify news media of pending parole consideration and of actions of the board.

A victim impact statement was devised by the board for inclusion in each pending parole file. The statement would fully inform the board of the impact of the inmate's criminal acts on his or her victims.

Restitution, the act of a criminal reimbursing his victim monetarily for his crime, appealed to James as reasonable and logical. During his term the Legislature passed a law requiring restitution as a condition of parole if ordered by the sentencing judge.

The board formally adopted a policy allowing it to impose restitution as a condition of parole if a judge had not.

As one method of relieving jail overcrowding, a restitution center was opened in Montgomery under contract with the county commission to provide an alternative to jail for certain non-dangerous offenders.

Prisoners assigned to the center by the board, or a judge, were not only required to pay money to their crime victims but to pay child support and other family obligations. Twenty-five percent of their gross earnings went to operate the center.

James, through legislation, levied a $15-a-month supervision fee on people on probation or parole.

Alabama was one of the first states in the nation to adopt supervision fees and the plan has since been copied by other states, then-executive director David H. Williams wrote. The fee in 1986 was increased to $20 per month.

The department was in desperate need of attention when James took office because it was the agency which bore the brunt of workload increase when criminals were released early due to prison overcrowding.

Though the number of parolees had increased drastically as prisons grew more overcrowded, there had been no corresponding increase prior to James in either parole officers or funding.

The officers were spread even thinner when a law passed prior to James took effect, expanding probation jurisdiction for the first time to the District Courts of the state. Prior to that time it had rested solely with circuit judges.

James approached management of the department in the same manner as other departments, starting with the administration. He made two appointments to the three-man Pardons and Paroles Board: Jack C. Lufkin, a merit-system employee who had worked for the department since 1956; and Ealon M. Lambert, a 12-year veteran board member.

The department was "extensively reorganized" into five major divisions, 12 geographical districts and 40 field offices. Williams said in his four-year-end report.

"The 1979 reorganization has resulted in improved communication, greater administrative control over field operations and more effective operations," Williams wrote.

"All management was assigned investigative, supervisory and/or hearing officer responsibilities in addition to other duties," he stated.

James treated the Pardons and Paroles Department as one member of the family of state departments, all of which should be working together cohesively. He perceived its parole officers as units of the state's overall "law enforcement" corps.

In September, 1979, a disaster-relief team was assembled from the P&P department and sent with sister-teams from other state agencies to assist in recovery operations after Hurricane Frederic. They disbursed emergency supplies and funds and also provided security.

"Inter-departmental relationships were particularly strengthened with the Mobile County Sheriff's Department which furnished housing for the team," Williams wrote.

Some legislation solved longstanding problems.

There had been difficulties for years in setting up hearings for prison inmates, Williams wrote. The law required that prisoners be brought to the Board of Pardons and Paroles or that two of the three board members had to travel to where the prisoner was. There were logistics problems in transporting prisoners and it was difficult for two of the three board members to arrange the time required traveling together to different prisons.

Legislation was passed allowing one board member to hold a hearing on prison grounds, solving the problem.

# Youth Services

The Department of Youth Services exists to rehabilitate delinquent youths committed to the custody of the state by the 67 juvenile courts.

When James took office, the department had never in its existence been given one penny by the state for capital outlay.

A chronicle of that existence would have been filled with frequent pleas for monetary help for the young·people committed by law to its care.

James' attention in his first months in office was riveted to the problems which stared him in the face daily, from Medicare's shortage to the money he had to find to deal with the prison situation.

It was only a matter of time before he added Youth Services to his "must" list, after being alerted to its plight by Birmingham Sen. Pat Vacca, the department's biggest booster.

On May 24, 1980, the Birmingham *News* stated, "Gov. Fob James has eased a funding crisis for the Alabama Department of Youth Services by releasing a $500,000 conditional appropriation...DYS Director George Phyfer...said overcrowding in the state's three reform schools had reached near-crisis proportions...With the conditional funds released Friday, this year's operations budget totals about $9.4 million. Next year's total would be only slightly higher at $9.6 million— almost certainly less than enough to cover inflation...On the overcrowding question...the board did not set a ceiling on the number of youths which can be accepted...Instead, internal policies were changed to permit youths to move through various programs faster..."

A four-year-end report to James from Phyfer highlights the agency's accomplishments in that period, ranging from opportunities offered its students to administrative reform.

There were significant new programs made available to Youth Services students. Perhaps the most significant was the chance to complete a basic education at an accredited school. James backed legislation which recognized the educational system of the department as a separate school district, which allowed the department to get its share of the annual funding rationed out to state school systems by the Department of Education.

In addition, special education classes were provided by three teachers hired with federal money which became available after Youth Services was brought into compliance with federal mandates of the

Education of All Handicapped Children Act.

Vocational training for older youths was begun at Mt. Meigs.

Other departments under James worked with the Youth Services Department to provide services at lower costs and to provide training to rehabilitate the youthful offenders incarcerated in the department's facilities.

An architectural/engineering study of all buildings was done with cooperation of the State Finance Department, Phyfer wrote. It revealed the department needed $17 million to renovate and update its buildings. A five-year-plan was developed and an "overall push" was begun to direct the DYS activities. A bond issue was authorized to build an intensive care treatment unit.

After a flood damaged the Roebuck facility in Jefferson County, a campaign was undertaken to solicit private donations which resulted in "major repairs done on the academic building" in 1982. The campus was renamed by the Legislature for its leading advocate in the Senate, Paschal P. "Pat" Vacca.

A citizen group was formed which raised money for a new chapel on the Mt. Meigs campus near Montgomery, which was nearly completed by the end of James' term. Construction was begun on a maximum security unit at the same location.

When two greenhouses were donated to the Roebuck campus, horticulture classes were begun and a contract was signed by the Finance Department with Youth Services to provide flowers and bedding plants for the Capitol complex. The contract would provide income to pay for supplies needed in the classes, such as fertilizer and seeds.

It took the cooperation of several state departments and a $150,000 grant to establish the wilderness/camping/work project. Based on the need for renovation at the state parks and created with the intent to employ Youth Services students, Phyfer predicted the modern-day version of Franklin Roosevelt's work corps would provide a model for the nation.

At Oak Mountain alone, he said, students had restored everything from cabins to bridges.

At the same time, there was an emphasis put on the health of the students. A nutrition program was begun which reduced the intake of refined sugars and white flour and stressed the healthful aspects of fresh fruit and vegetables instead of candies and cookies. The food service contract was switched from a private vendor to a food service operated by a government-training program which provided food for all the campuses and set up a food service training program for 40 students.

Phyfer wrote that maximum capacities were set for overcrowded dorms to reduce hazards. "Behavioral incidents were substantially reduced with this policy," he said.

As in other departments under James, Youth Services was reorganized administratively and records were computerized.

Phyfer said reorganization utilized a "a regional concept" in which the state was divided into four regions with four specialists over them who provided consultation and training in juvenile courts and licensed facilities.

The reorganization resulted "in streamlined administrative structure...regionalized consultation and technical assistance to juvenile courts...more direct access to the executive director by division managers," Phyfer wrote.

An expanded central office was completed, allowing all administrative personnel to be placed under one roof.

A micro computer was purchased with federal money. All budget and financial procedures were automated. The computer provided all financial reports, monthly spending reports and financial status information as well as personnel reports and juvenile court statistics, Phyfer stated.

The same emphasis was placed on the training of Youth Services personnel charged with law enforcement responsibilities as in other agencies under James. Phyfer said 36 training sessions were held for 760 juvenile justice personnel in 1979, followed by 40 in 1980 and 46 in 1981.

When James' system-wide new classification and pay plan was implemented in the Department of Youth Services, it resulted in the downgrading of 20 positions and the upgrading of 40 positions, Phyfer said. The pay scales for two job classifications, youth services aide and youth services child care worker, were raised to a competitive level with similar positions in the departments of corrections and mental health.

Youth Services felt the pinch of recession. In 1982, Phyfer noted, federal funds "continued to diminish." The hiring freeze continued as in other agencies, though not as strictly enforced in Youth Services as in some agencies. Phyfer noted that new employees were hired only to take the place of departing staff members who were considered "critical"—security, nurses and teachers.

James increased the Youth Services budget from $8.8 million annually in 1979 to $11.2 million in 1982. The increase was actually more than the figures indicate, because expenses were cut significantly when dozens of food workers were transferred from the payrolls of the department to other payrolls.

In 1982, James included $6 million for Youth Services in his public works construction windfall bond issue.

Phyfer at the end of James' term wrote of this in his four-year-end report, "For the first time since the creation of the agency, $6 million in capital outlay funds were appropriated to improve student housing and other facilities."

# Alabama Institute for the Deaf and Blind

When Dr. Jack Hawkins took over as president of the Institute for the Deaf and Blind in the fall of 1979, he was appalled at what he found.

No attempt had ever been made to renovate the pre-World War I buildings. They were dilapidated, steamy-hot in the summer and cold in the winter. The school was in dire financial straits.

"We had a deficit of $300,000," said Hawkins.

He appealed to James, who took him up on an invitation to visit the campus.

James was also appalled at the living conditions for the children who were sent to the campus to learn how to overcome the disadvantages given them by their blindness or deafness.

"Gov. James took a very personal interest in the institute," Hawkins said. "The first thing he did was make some changes in the Board of Trustees, which introduced a new element of interest. He managed to increase our budget by almost 39 percent during a period when the state was experiencing extreme economic difficulties."

For additional money, James turned to Lynda Hart, who headed the CETA program.

"Lynda assisted us in capturing federal grants through some creative methods; that was when the tide began to turn," Hawkins said.

Watching the red ink turn to black on the institute's books was a good feeling.

But the children still lived in and studied in "horrendous" dorms and classrooms in which the furnishings were World War II surplus furniture.

In 1981, James allotted $3.75 million from his windfall public works program to renovate the buildings on the Talladega campus.

"It was the biggest shot in the arm we'd ever had," Hawkins said. "It allowed us to get in there and get started."

In 1981, James asked Hawkins to get together a delegation of students from the institute to fly on the state plane to Washington, D.C., to attend the National Prayer Breakfast.

"On the way, the subject of a chapel came up," Hawkins said. "There hadn't been a chapel on campus since around 1917. I told Gov. and Mrs. James we were considering starting a private fund-raising campaign to build a chapel."

Hawkins said before he made it back to the campus, Bobbie James called and left a message. She said she and her husband had discussed it and wanted to contribute the first $5,000 donation, "seed money," for a new chapel.

"That kind of committed us," Hawkins said. "We undertook to raise the money and eventually raised $675,000."

When the chapel was dedicated in 1985, it was the first building in the history of the institute to be built entirely with private funds.

The keynote speaker was former Gov. Fob James.

"In my estimation Gov. James made more of a difference to the Institute than any other governor ever made," "Hawkins said. Today the classrooms are air-conditioned, the buildings have been renovated and there is a different spirit on the campus. I trace it all back to Fob James and his determination and commitment."

# — 21 —

# The 1982 Legislative Session

In an AP interview by Kendal Weaver which was published three days into the last year of his term, James mused a bit on how it felt to be governor.

> "I don't feel any different than the day I took office or the day before. I'm the same guy I was. Politics has not changed me. I hope I have changed politics some.
>
> "If you get caught up in the trappings of office, if you develop a keen ambition to perpetuate yourself in office, then you start wondering and probably start hesitating in making decisions.
>
> "...If you ever start wondering, 'Well, now if I do this, that big special interest group is going to be against me in the next election, and I'm not going to get any campaign funds from this group,' I think at that point you ought to quit and go home," he said.

James admitted that he might seem harsh but argued that the alternative was harsher.

"...The problems of the state and nation over recent decades were caused largely by those who took the path of least resistance," he said.

The big question: Would he run for re-election? The question was an issue to the news media and the general public, though James had told close associates from day one that he would not. Most, from Joe McCorquodale to Bob Geddie, had begged him not to let the fact be known, not to let legislators or other officials think of him as a lame duck.

Weaver wrote that James commented, laughing, "I'm campaigning for the next regular session right now."

He added, however, that whether or not he would be a candidate would not affect his actions.

"I would not act any differently either way...We will be totally consistent in the fourth quarter, same as we were in the first," he said.

James talked statewide of the broad range of legislation he intended to ask legislators to pass in the '82 session.

An editorial boiled down his legislative program after he met with editors to explain it:

To avoid a piecemeal approach, James said he had compressed the legislation to address three issues:

- Employee compensation. He recommended a 14 percent pay raise for teachers and a 10 percent hike in the salary of state employees.

Hubbert's response, as quoted in newspapers, was to demand a 25 percent increase for K–12 teachers and for the post-secondary teachers employed by the two-year colleges. A spokesman for the State Employees Association demanded a 20 percent increase. The *AEA Journal* wrote of James' proposed 14 percent raise under a headline which stated, "Governor's proposed budget called insult to educators." The article used the word "damnable" in reference to James' plans.

- Education reforms. James proposed the creation of the position of chancellor to oversee the two-year colleges and measures which would give enforcement teeth to the Alabama Commission on Higher Education. He also sought to impose a uniform system of accounting in all schools which would make it possible to compare the spending patterns of schools in which students scored low on achievement tests with those which scored high.
- Criminal Code revisions. Drawing on recommendations made by a commission appointed to draft reforms and get input from the public, James proposed several dozen changes in existing law. His package included bills allowing prosecutors to turn down (strike) the same number of prospective jurors as defense attorneys. allowing judges to try juveniles charged with felonies as adults, and strengthening laws aimed at syndicates or organized groups involved in pushing drugs and illegal gambling.

State Superintendent of Schools Teague termed Hubbert's 25 per-cent pay hike "ridiculous." But he did not support James' 14 percent raise. He endorsed instead a 15 percent pay increase—for K–12 teach-ers only. The State Board of Education should decide the amount of any post-secondary raise, Teague said, just as the boards of trustees did for four-year colleges. He also felt that any raises for lunchroom workers should come from local school boards.

James and Teague had other basic disagreements over the budget. When Teague presented his budget request to the Legislative Fiscal Oversight Committee in early January, he asked for money for an-other 500 kindergarten teachers and another 133 driver's education teachers. James, riveted to his program of basics, said the state would do better with 150 fewer driver's education teachers and 150 more kindergarten teachers in their places.

Bob Ingram, writing of the reforms James would push in regular and special sessions, quipped, "If James can achieve any or all of this during an election year, it will be little short of a miracle."

Ingram, recalling that Hubbert called James' proposed 14 percent pay raise for teachers "an insult, a slap in the face," noted that Hub-bert had no such response to Teague's proposed 15 percent increase. "It seems improbable that the extra one percent offered by Dr. Teague would make that much difference...," Ingram wrote. "[Dr. Hubbert] insulted and slapped the face of the governor and at the same time widened the gap between the teachers of Alabama and their em-ployers—the taxpayers of Alabama, most of whom would rejoice at the prospect of a 14 percent pay raise."

The 12th of January, 1982, was a day of bitter cold. It was also the day of James' last State of the State address to a regular session of the Legislature.

Snow had begun falling on the icy capital that morning and roads were closed throughout the state, leaving legislative leaders in a quan-dary as to whether the session's opening should be postponed.

The decision was made to proceed on schedule, though the empty chairs in the Legislature outnumbered the ones in which legislators sat. House Speaker McCorquodale found a bright spot. "Nobody wants to go out on a night like this," he told reporters. "The governor will probably have more people watching his speech on television than under normal conditions."

The weather was bad, James told listeners in his speech. And so was the national and local economy.

Unknown to James or the public, it would get much worse in the next few months.

"We were listening to what economists were saying," says then–State Budget Officer Rebecca Beasley. "They had us coming out of the trough of recession when actually we were going deeper. The major impact of the recession was on our two main taxes, sales tax and income tax. What this means is that we were making decisions on the notion that the economy was going up and it was not."

Bobby Davis echoes her remarks: "During all that work on the bond issue we had talked to the top financial advisers in the country. They all felt the recession was bottoming out in 1981."

At the time James spoke to legislators, inflation had drastically reduced the buying power of the dollar. The automotive industry was the one affected most by the recession. In Alabama and elsewhere in the nation, employees were being laid off and plants were closing down. Chrysler Corporation remained in business only because of a massive federal government bail-out. Alabama, heavily dependent upon its plants which produced tires, steel and parts for the automotive industry, had the number two highest unemployment rate in the nation—11.4 percent. Because Alabama was one of the states which received more federal dollars than its citizens paid in federal taxes, the state's budget had become over the years heavily dependent upon federal funds. News stories were written pointing out that the state's unemployment compensation fund had been depleted by the increasing number of people drawing unemployment checks. As the Legislature burrowed in for the election-year session, the word came from Washington that federal unemployment funds to Alabama were being cut.

James prepared legislation which would boost the contributions made by employers and employees, tighten eligibility requirements and increase the maximum weekly unemployment benefits from $90 to $115.

He philosophized in his speech on the situation.

"Tonight there are 32,362 fellow citizens out of work in Jefferson County, 7,397 in Etowah County, and 8,120 out of work in Lauderdale and Colbert Counties," he said.

The automotive industry which 10 years before had been the strongest in the world "is now struggling to get its house in order to survive in a world market," he said.

Who was to blame?

Echoing sentiments which had induced him to run for governor five years before, James said, "I believe we have been victims of a federal government that failed to discipline itself, that ran up a tremendous deficit, and that made up the difference by printing bogus dollars. This caused high inflation. Our paychecks lost value. Our retirement checks lost value. If it had happened in one year, there would have been total chaos. But it happened gradually over two decades."

Had Congress called for a constitutional amendment mandating a balanced budget to remedy inflation? He answered his own question: "No."

James questioned the "basket-case" economic policy dictated by the international banking community and a few others who "profit billions without hitting a lick at a snake or taking any capital risk whatsoever.

"For two decades we have marched to the guillotine of high interest rates under the subterfuge of stopping inflation," he said, with nothing but high interest rates and a one-trillion-dollar deficit "to show for 20 years of selfish special-interest politics in Washington, D.C."

Economic recovery would not come quickly to a nation in which the treasury had been ransacked for 20 years.

So what could Alabama do as a state government to help the unemployed?

"We can help those laid off to find new jobs, and if additional training is necessary, provide such training," he said. "This is being done.

"And if any company wants to reconsider a decision to close a plant, we can make sure every alternative is explored. This, too, is being done, as was the case with U.S. Steel in Birmingham.

"Then, we must continue to seek new industry to give Alabama a more diversified industrial base."

The state's home-building industry had almost come to a standstill because of high interest rates, James said. However, in December the Alabama Housing Finance Authority had issued the first third of $300 million to be available that year for low-interest mortgages for low and middle income families, which would include many young first-time home buyers.

"The impact on unemployment will be tremendous," James said, "not only from direct construction jobs which will run in the thousands, but for men and women who work in industries providing supplies, materials, home furnishings, real estate services, financial and insurance services, and transportation to the home-building industry. In terms of jobs for Alabamians, it will run into the tens of thousands, all in the private sector."

Additionally, over 12,000 direct construction jobs would be created by James' $500 million public works plan, financed with proceeds of the oil lease sales the previous year.

The 1982 session was a unique one, James reminded lawmakers. It was the first one operating under his budget isolation reform. No legislation was to be voted on until the budgets had been approved.

After legislators approved budgets, James urged, they should approve his reclassification plan for the state merit system which was "long overdue."

He also outlined a proposal "to insure that when a state employee or teacher retires that their money will be waiting for them."

Noting that his job as governor "is to deliver quality public services at a fair price to the taxpayers of Alabama," James reassured Alabamians that no new taxes were needed if the state's expenditures were brought into line.

> Taxpayers send more than enough money to Montgomery to run state government and run it well. State employees have greatly improved many departments during the last three years.
>
> The Highway Department is one example, Medicaid another, Prisons another, Mental Health another, the National Guard another, and the list goes on.
>
> Our school children have shown marked improvement on competency-test scores, thanks to thousand of dedicated teachers.
>
> But the facts clearly show we still have some areas where our costs are out of line – badly out of line – and can only be brought back into line by acts of this Legislature.

James said his reclassification plan for the state personnel system was long overdue. He said, "It is performance oriented. It cleans up the mess in which our job classification system has fallen since its inception 30 years ago. It is fair to employees and fair to taxpayers. It offers state employees far greater opportunities for advancement. It deals fairly with promotions, dismissals, salaries, and working conditions..."

Over 15% of every tax dollar sent to Montgomery was spent on retirement and social security, an extremely high percentage when compared to other states, James said. This was unfair not only to taxpayers but to public employees because it created a cost too high for the state to guarantee that it could be met in the future, too high for the state to promise state employees or teachers that their money would be waiting for them when they retired.

James had the previous session prepared legislation to halt the ever-increasing drain on the General Fund by the Retirement Systems, which did not earn enough income on investments to fund the pensions of teachers and state employees.

"Last year James had little support for his pension proposal and didn't even introduce it," Kendal Weaver wrote for AP.

Sen. John Teague of Childersburg, who in 1988 became lobbyist for State Employees, said at the time that James' pension plan had been opposed the year before because it affected future benefits of current state employees.

His retirement plan in 1982, however, affected future employees and should receive approval, Teague said.

"'Everyone is cognizant of the fact that we're going to have to do something with retirement because of the rising costs,' Teague said."

James' proposal for strengthening the retirement system was to change the formula by which retirement was figured. To determine benefits, the number of years the employee worked for the state is multiplied by a formula which differs from state to state. Alabama's formula, 2.0125, was the highest of all 50 states. As an example, an employee starting to work at age 25 who retired at age 55 would receive 60 percent of his regular pay plus social security and other benefits.

To get the support of state employees, James' legislation grandfathered in all benefits current employees had earned. They had two choices of how their future benefits would be figured.

One, they could opt to continue earning retirement benefits under the same formula, but contribute six percent to the fund instead of the five percent they currently contributed.

Two, they could opt to continue contributing five percent, with future benefits figured under a formula of 1.6.

Employees hired after Oct. 1, 1982, would not have those choices. They would contribute six percent and benefits would be determined by the 1.6 formula.

The bottom line was that James' retirement reform ensured that new employees when they retired in the future could take home (including social security) 100 percent or more of their average salary for their top three years. Current employees would do better.

James' research into the teachers' retirement systems revealed what obviously was known to the education community but little known by the general public—the state paid for not one but two retirement plans for the faculty of four-year universities. One was the state retirement plan with which most people were familiar, the one other geared toward college faculties, called the TIAA.

"I recommend we make this optional," James said. "In other words, the employee may choose one or the other, but not both.

"These 'positive revisions' provide excellent retirement benefits and put our retirement systems on solid ground for today and for the future, and it gets our costs in line," he said.

AP wrote that his revisions would reduce the state's financial obligations by some $35 million a year.

AP stated that Lt. Gov. McMillan said in support of the retirement revamp, "I want us to reach a point where ... to fulfill a commitment to meet a salary we don't have to terminate any people."

James' reform package included bills to modify the state's policy regarding holidays, vacation schedules, and the practice of paying accumulated sick leave as severance pay upon retirement. In each case, if his legislation was approved the state would pay less than it had but still be well above the fringe benefits provided by private industry.

James recommended adding two benefits which private industry commonly provided but the state did not—life insurance and disability insurance. He explained, "I have proposed the necessary changes to give state employees a balanced, highly competitive package of fringe benefits."

James said the 14 percent pay raise he recommended for teachers would cost $85.9 million, which "leaves little or no reserve in anybody's education budget for contingencies or a shortfall in projected revenue."

Neither would there be a reserve in the General Fund after his 10 percent raise for state employees was approved. It would cost $36.4 million.

"However, if the Legislature will pass my proposals for 'positive revisions' on fringe benefits, they will create a $27.4 million reserve in the education budget and a $10 million reserve in the general fund," he said.

This would provide money for a six percent raise for retired teachers and state employees and still leave a $21.4 million reserve in the education budget and an $8.2 reserve in the general fund to guard against proration.

If legislators okayed his programs, James promised, "You will not have proration. I repeat, You will not have proration."

"It is right to maintain a reserve and it is right to position our retirement funds on solid ground once and for all," James said.

James next addressed an emotional subject—the rumors which had engulfed his reform plans.

State employees had been told the governor was "against" them, he said.

That was a lie, he said.

"Sure I want an honest day's work for an honest day's pay, but can one state employee out of 28,000 name me one time during the last three years that cronyism or political influence was imposed on his work? No. I have placed more merit system workers as department heads than any governor in Alabama history..."

James' package for higher education called for a change in the "mission, authority and name" of the Alabama Commission on Higher Education "so we can get a handle on the costs of two-year colleges and four-year colleges and universities."

He cited a vacuum of fact, an absence of role and scope, a total lack of accountability and control within some elements of higher education. Until remedied, he said, "raw politics will prevail as the key ingredient of how the tax dollars are used."

James' next reform proposal "has to do with the ultimate responsibility of government to protect its citizens...against the ravages of crime. Some give lip service to this responsibility. I say action is all that counts. Major state penitentiaries are under construction on accelerated schedule...Now it is time to correct in a sane, sensible manner those laws on our books that tilt the scales of justice toward the criminal...It is time to correct a system of justice that is soft on white-collar crime. It is time to recognize that our penal system must rehabilitate and turn back into society, sometimes under pardon or parole, those inmates that are reformed and deserving and that have paid their debt to society. But above all, we must keep locked up those criminals who are dangerous..."

The 32 recommendations he presented had been put together by the members of his Governor's Commission on Crime, which was chaired by Montgomery Circuit Court Judge Joe Phelps.

So firmly did James believe that all functions of government could operate with less money that he testified in support of President Reagan's tax cut before the U.S. Congress the week before the legislative session began.

Cut income taxes, he told Congress. But when you do, cut spending across-the-board by 10 percent.

James referred to that testimony to legislators in a pep talk at the end of his speech.

There were those who said the Legislature would quit the field of responsible government in this fourth quarter, a quarter led by a lame-duck quarterback, he said.

"On many occasions I have said that this Legislature, this Senate, this House, has a mark of greatness in it. I testified in Washington last Friday that I believe the federal government, in sending money back to the states, should make one requirement only; that not one dime could be spent until appropriated by the state Legislature.

> Far and wide I have reminded people that the state Legislature is the fountainhead governmental body of this country. It is the essence of the rights of states. I have pointed out that not too many decades have passed since legislators elected our two U.S. senators. I have pointed out that every single element of Alabama citizenship is represented right here.
>
> I absolutely refused to usurp the prerogative of the Alabama House and Senate to organize themselves. I have stood by that principle without flinching...

Of those who believed the Legislature would cop out in the fourth quarter, James said, "I say they are dead wrong."

It was, however, an election year.

Since the budget to be considered would take effect during that election year, efforts were made by legislators to push the revenue estimates as high as possible, Ira Harvey wrote, "as in 1978."

The major difference between 1982 and 1978, Harvey pointed out, was that the national and state economy was in worse shape in 1982 than it had been in 1978.

Also different, Harvey pointed out, was that the Legislature was forced by James' isolation law to consider the budgets first. Budget isolation was in effect.

AEA's announced legislative agenda, Harvey wrote, was "to go to work to elect politicians who will place public education rather than big business at the top of the legislative agenda."

A resolution was approved by the AEA board calling for such actions as a march on the capitol during the session, invoking sanctions against the State of Alabama for its failure to properly fund education, a media campaign to inform the public of the plight of education employees, picketing, a one-day protest, and monitoring the proposed teacher pay raise.

Three weeks into the session, Ralph Holmes wrote an article on how the budget isolation amendment was working. Or, rather, how it was not.

"Both the state House and the Senate appear confused about the procedure to be used as long as isolation is in effect," Holmes wrote.

> And that caused Gov. Fob James...to suggest that possible gubernatorial candidates...McMillan and...McCorquodale get their acts together.
>
> "Isolation is sound," James said after watching the Legislature in its first two weeks of the session. "Isolation won't work because the House and the Senate won't get their rules together..."
>
> The statute blocks any bill...from passing from one house of the Legislature to the other until the two budgets have reached the governor's desk for final approval.
>
> However...with the consent of three-fifths of the members of the house in which the bill is being considered, it may be transmitted from one house to the other...
>
> McCorquodale told his House members that means the House can pass any bill with the routine simple majority, but to transmit the bill to the Senate, it must have a minimum of 63 positive votes...
>
> McMillan told his Senate members that before any bill can be considered by the Senate, a resolution must be introduced and then go to the Senate Rules Committee. Upon Rules Committee approval and approval of a minimum of 21 senators...a bill [can] be considered by the Senate.
>
> So far the House has passed about a half-dozen bills and the Senate has passed only one...

Commented James to the 10th annual Legislative Prayer Luncheon: "The speaker and the lieutenant governor signed off on it six months ago. Now they say [they] can't interpret it. That's pure raw monkey business."

Hubbert, meanwhile, scaled his 25 percent pay raise request to 16 percent, with Ingram noting he probably did so in the wake of violent anti-AEA sentiment from the public. It is more probable he intended to do so all along.

"The House leadership and the governor held to the 14 percent, and the ASETF appropriation bill passed out of Ways and Means at that level," Harvey wrote.

In the Senate, competing bills proposed 14 and 16 percent pay increases.

Senators, learning that the Teachers Retirement Fund would need $7 million less than was in the budget, regarded the $7 million as "found" money.

House members dug in their heels for a long debate on the teacher pay raises. As is true with much of the legislative action on the floor, there were amendments and substitutes to those amendments offered which were prompted by different motives than those apparent at first glance. For instance, State Rep. Bob Gafford successfully amended Rep. Jimmy Holley's motion to give a 16 percent pay raise to all education personnel. Gafford's substitute, approved in an 81–5 vote, was for the apparent purpose of including more folks in the pay raise than Holley's motion did. Gafford's amendment gave all education personnel a 16 percent raises, all state employees a 14 percent raise, and threw in all judges in the state for hefty raises also.

What was the unstated motive? Gafford stipulated that the money could be taken from anywhere it needed to be taken from. If there wasn't enough money in the SETF to pay teachers' raises, it could be taken from the General Fund. If there wasn't enough money in the General Fund to pay state employees' raises, it could be taken from the SETF.

It was diversion, plain and simple, the word which transformed Paul Hubbert from a complacent cigar-smoker in the front row of the gallery into a frothing-at-the-mouth activist.

The amendment revitalized the McCorquodale/Hubbert feud which plagued most legislative happenings.

Phillip Rawls wrote for AP: "State Rep. Roy Johnson, a proponent of 16 percent raises, said Gafford's plan, which was supported by the House leadership, attempted to pit teachers against state employees...Rep. Charles Adams of Phenix City said Gafford's parliamentary move had trapped the House members 'neck deep in quicksand.' "

Two weeks later, with the House still deadlocked over the pay raise issue, McCorquodale in an unusual move left the speaker's platform to take the House microphone and urge his colleagues not to inflate the budgets.

"McCorquodale says some lawmakers 'playing election year politics' want to grant big raises to teachers and state employees because no one will know until after the election if such raises were ruinous to the budgets," AP wrote.

"'The sins of the Legislature will not be known until after this year's election is over,' McCorquodale said."

The situation existed because of the change from biennial to annual sessions of the Legislature, McCorquodale said.

Overspending by the 1978 election-year Legislature had resulted in three years of budget proration, he said. He referred to the fact that the 1978 Legislature had spent the "cushion" which a surplus provided from the year before and had indebted the next Legislature by spending an anticipated surplus which did not materialize. Each year thereafter in James' term, decreasing revenues failed to produce the projected revenues.

The Senate on Feb. 4 approved a $1.46-billion revised version of the Education Budget which included a 16 percent raise for teachers. Where had they found the money for the extra 2 percent? They hadn't. Yet. Exactly. What they did was take out of the education budget some $17 million for what they described as "quasi-educational" agencies. When they got the General Fund budget from the House, senators explained, they would find money in it for the agencies. More than half of the money involved was the $9.6 million appropriation for the Department of Youth Services. The department had been funded with education money in the past because it is responsible for educating juvenile offenders. State Sen. Dewey White of Birmingham was unable to convince the Senate to hold off until they had the General Fund budget in hand in order to determine the effect of such action on such agencies as prisons and mental health.

Though the House was stalled, the Senate acted on several of James' proposals.

In mid-February the Senate Governmental Affairs Committee approved James' legislation creating a new environmental agency to police air and water pollution more effectively and enforce regulations for coastal areas and water wells. It was the third year in a row that James pushed the legislation.

At the time the bill was introduced there were seven different agencies and boards charged with overlapping authority to issue permits and enforce regulations affecting the environment, including the Alabama Water Improvement Commission, Water Wells Standards

Board, Board of Certification of Water and Wastewater Systems and Environmental Health Administration, as well as divisions of the State Health Department which dealt with hazardous waste management, public water systems and solid waste disposal.

White's bill merged these agencies and boards into one umbrella agency, the Alabama Department of Environmental Management (ADEM). News media dubbed the legislation the "one-stop permitting" bill because it consolidated permitting authority as well as regulatory oversight. ADEM would be monitored by a commission which drew its members from the panels it replaced, including experts from the various environmental fields—a doctor, an engineer, a lawyer with an environmental background, a chemist, a biologist and one member certified by the Water Well Standards Association.

Controversy continued to revolve around the budgets.

Both chambers, using the $7 million not needed by the Teachers Retirement System and removing a $9 million appropriation to the Youth Services Department from the SETF budget, approved a 15 percent raise for teachers in the final budget.

James said the $433 million General Fund budget passed by the House would put the prison system $11 million in the red. The Senate was "irresponsible" in shifting education agencies to the General Fund in order to come up with a 16 percent teachers' raise, he said. The state could not afford any more than 14 percent.

The Senate Finance and Taxation Committee in late February got the $433 million General Fund budget, approved it and sent it to the full Senate. The ploy of transferring "quasi-educational" agencies to the General Fund in order to increase teacher raises left the General Fund short by millions of dollars. The money had to be made up by stripping essential state agencies of desperately needed funding. Even after these cuts, the Senate's version of the General Fund budget still overspent the House version by $236,000.

A Birmingham *News* editorial noted James was threatening to veto either of the two major budgets "if he doesn't believe they're based more on fiscal reality than politics and wishful thinking. He is absolutely right to do so. Not only could the threat put pressure on the lawmakers to stick closely to dollars-and-cents reality, but if ultimately used, it might also save state agencies...from [the] fourth straight year of proration—the cumbersome, haphazard approach the state uses to straighten out its finances when revenues coming into state coffers are not equal to the amount of money budgeted to be spent.

The primary reason that sort of situation arises has been politics. Lawmakers, faced with a barrage of lobbyists wanting more money, more benefits or higher wages, have found an avenue of escape from turning them down in the budget in recent years by simply upping the estimated amount of money the state will collect...

By the end of March the Legislature was more adamantly split down the middle than ever before. The issue was the current use bill.

In 1978, a "Lid Bill" approved by the Legislature to place a cap on property taxes included a "current use" provision allowing property to be taxed on current use rather than market value. The State Revenue Department was instructed to prescribe rules and regulations for the "current use" provision.

In 1979, before the Revenue Department issued its rules and regulations, the Legislature in a resolution defined current use in a manner which tax experts agreed would lower considerably local funding to schools.

Because the formula was complex, legislators attempted the next year to pass another bill which Harvey wrote simplified the procedure for gaining the tax advantage. Its passage would "result in a loss of tax money to education and other government functions," Harvey wrote. The attempt failed.

In 1982, Harvey explains, there was a "further legislative attempt to provide additional exemptions through expansion of the definition of 'current use' approved in 1979."

Because the majority of large parcels of land is owned by large landowners and corporations who already pay one of the lowest property taxes in the nation, these large landowners would be the ones to benefit most by the bill. The biggest losers would be the school children; AP wrote that the current use bill would cut some $18 million a year in funding for local government and schools. Local funding for education was so low it was an already an embarrassment. The revenue for local funding was derived from property tax.

Legislators passed the current use bill. James could veto it, but McCorquodale was believed to have the votes to override a veto. James made a futile attempt to gain time to change a few votes by closing up the governor's office when the bill was delivered to him. Then he vetoed it. The Legislature overrode his veto.

"The addition of exemptions to the already low property tax meant fewer tax dollars for public schools," Harvey wrote.

In late March the Alabama Supreme Court struck down James' temporary budget isolation act.

"The Alabama Legislature, now free of 'budget isolation,' reaches the midpoint of its 1982 session Tuesday, with both chambers focusing on the budgets simultaneously for the first time," AP wrote. "The House has before it the $1.46 billion education budget, while the Senate's agenda includes the $433 million General Fund budget. The bills are to run schools and state government in the fiscal year that begins Oct. 1."

While the temporary budget isolation act was on the books, AP wrote, the House did not get to either of the budgets. The Senate approved an education budget "after a spree of amendments guaranteed that the budget would be reworked later.

"The education budget before the House closely follows Gov. Fob James' recommendations. It is not the measure approved by the Senate, which would shift some $17 million worth of programs out of the school budget, making the General Fund budget obligated to pay for them," AP wrote.

To pay for the programs which had been transferred to the General Fund budget, the Senate Finance and Taxation Committee "decided to strip money from other departments—$8 million from the Department of Public Health, $6 million from the Department of Corrections and $5 million from the Department of Mental Health," AP wrote. The money would be restored to them if the funds were available.

"The budgets before each house are based on James' recommendations that state employees get a 10 percent cost-of-living raise and that teachers get 14 percent increase," AP wrote.

Still pending, however, was competing legislation that would boost pay raises to 14 percent for state employees and 16 percent for teachers.

On the 15th day of the 30-day session, the Senate approved a $433 million General Fund budget, having added a total of $539,000 in amendments and spending all but $129,161 of what had been projected to be the growth in revenue for the next year. Not all senators were happy with the budget. State Sens. Ryan deGraffenried Jr. of Tuscaloosa and Sonny Callahan of Mobile argued that transferring the Department of Youth Services and other "quasi-educational" agencies to the General Fund would destroy the state's mental health system, which was operating under court orders mandating improvement.

Others argued that "any problems" could be resolved in a joint Senate-House legislative conference committee.

Meanwhile, the House approved the education budget—minus the 16 percent teachers' pay hike. That fact came as a surprise to most House members, however.

It was another case of legislative sleight-of-hand. AP wrote that it was not until after the budget had been approved that it was discovered that the raise had been deleted from the budget through an amendment which had been added. Most House members believed when they voted for the amendment that its sole effect would be to add school cafeteria workers to the list of those getting the 16 percent raise.

"State Rep. Roy Johnson of Tuscaloosa, who proposed the 16 percent raises, said the House leadership deceived the majority of the House," AP wrote.

Speaker Pro Tem Rick Manley of Demopolis said, however, "That's nothing but strategy."

AP described House action on the General Fund budget: "The $433 million budget that covers the cost of day-to-day government sailed through the House Ways and Means Committee Wednesday in a form closely resembling the governor's recommendation."

There was a key difference, however: Ways and Means allowed for a 12 percent state employees' raise, with Chairman Walter Owens of Centreville explaining that the extra money would come from $11.8 million no longer needed by the state Employees Retirement System for fiscal 1983.

The James team in four years had learned to "use" the Legislative rules when they needed to, as witnessed by the handling of the one-stop permitting bill.

As a senator in the previous term, McMillan had watched the powerful clique which ruled the Senate, a newspaper story reported, "hold bills hostage that all people agreed were meritorious. Then the sponsor of the meritorious bill was coerced to vote for something he did not want to vote for simply to get his own bill passed. McMillan took office intent upon reform. One innovation he introduced was the 'consent calendar.' "

A bill that had virtually no opposition could be put on the consent calendar and acted on quickly, virtually free from threat of filibuster or legislative logjam. The bill could not be changed on the Senate floor in any way—thus avoiding any devious move to alter its contents—and had to be voted up or down after no more than 30 minutes of review. Each senator was allowed to place three House bills and three Senate bills on the consent calendar each session.

In mid-March, Sen. Dewey White placed his one-stop permitting bill on the Senate consent calendar. Under Senate rules, senators had two working days (usually 10 calendar days) to file a written objection to any bill they didn't want on the consent calendar.

If five or more senators objected, Kendal Weaver wrote, "It is yanked off the consent calendar and placed on the Senate's regular, slowpoke work agenda."

The one-stop permitting bill was approved, though some senators objected after-the-fact.

"I didn't think the bill should have been on the consent calendar at all," McMillan said, commenting to news media. He said the problem was that some senators had gotten "lax."

For most of James' term, McMillan was found by James' legislative team to be helpful, efficient, and most importantly, a man who could be counted on to do exactly what he said he would do.

Toward the end of James' term, there was a noticeable difference in McMillan's attitude. After Bob Geddie watched what had to be deliberate stalls by McMillan of James' legislation, he sat down with the lieutenant governor and asked what was wrong.

McMillan was honest. He said both he and McCorquodale were aware that James was not running for re-election and both of them intended to run for governor. McMillan felt James' personal friendship with McCorquodale was giving the speaker an unfair advantage in the governor's race.

"George was honest and I appreciated it," Geddie said.

In mid-April James was successful in getting his legislation approved to revamp the state merit system.

AP wrote, "The Alabama Legislature, after months of feuding, voted Tuesday for the first major revision of the state merit system in three decades. With the Legislature's vote, Gov. Fob James and the State Personnel Board are free to implement within two weeks a new pay and classification plan for state merit system employees.

"The plan would provide an average pay raise of 1.5 percent for state employees, although some would receive nothing and some would get much more," AP wrote. "The pay raise would be in addition to the 12 percent cost-of-living pay hike that is now before the Legislature."

In his last year in office, Bobby Davis said, James fought unsuccessfully to tag as conditional the pork barrel legislation added by legislators.

"But the Legislature was up for re-election. It was a losing battle," he said.

McCorquodale said the same thing at the time.

"House Speaker McCorquodale predicted a 'tremendous tax increase' for the public next year as well as proration for both schools and state government if the Legislature does not curb its 'Santa Claus' impulse where budgets are concerned," Vivian Cannon wrote for the Mobile *Press Register.*

"'The General Fund budget is already a good $11 million in the red and they don't care,' McCorquodale said of the legislators, most of whom are running for their seats again. 'You try to talk to them and tell them the facts and they just don't listen.'"

Revenue was coming in to the state at only a 5.3 percent increase over the previous year, though the budget had been planned on a 5.5 percent increase.

"'And that's dropping,' McCorquodale said."

There was a lot of compromising before the session was over. The Legislature stopped the clock at 11 p.m. on the final night of the session and approved and sent to James a $1.4 billion education budget and a $433 million General Fund budget which contained 12 percent pay raises for state employees, 16 percent pay raises for teachers and up to 31 percent pay increases for judges.

Neither budget, however, contained money for the Department of Youth Services.

"Repeated efforts by House leadership failed" to provide the funds for Youth Services, Cannon wrote.

The Senate had initially taken $9.6 million from Youth Services for the teacher pay raise, substituting a $12 million "conditional" appropriation. The Senate did the same for James' War On Illiteracy, reducing the appropriation from $2 million to $388,292, but including a $1.7 million "conditional" one.

James did not mince words. Shifting the Youth Services Department from budget to budget to come up with two percent more in teachers' pay raises than the state could afford was "irresponsible," he said.

The General Fund budget also included what James termed the height of budgetary irresponsibility—the 31 percent pay hikes for state judges. The raise was approved in the last days of the session as, Weaver wrote, "four state senators, three of them lawyers, blocked a bid to scale down the judicial salary boost."

Under what Weaver called a "unique" provision of the constitution, the salary of judges is set in Alabama by legislative inaction rather than action. The Judicial Compensation Commission recommends an increase. Then, unless the Senate Rules Committee votes to let the entire Senate decide the matter, the raises go into effect.

"The controversial pay raises, starting with Supreme Court Justice C. C. 'Bo' Torbert and moving down to district judges in every area, become effective immediately," Vivian Cannon wrote. "They do not require any action from Gov. Fob James and he has no authority to veto them."

The salary increases ranged from a $9,000 hike for Torbert (from $49,500 to $58,500) to an $8,900 hike for district judges (from $29,500 to $38,400)

With the judicial raises removed by law from his purview, James offered his compromise: a 15 percent teachers' raise and the full $2 million for his War on Illiteracy, balanced with $1.8 million in cuts made in other segments of education.

If legislators were unwilling to compromise, James warned, he would call a special session in this election-year in which to focus attention on the subject.

Sam Duvall wrote in the *Advertiser,* "Gov. Fob James' 'hell-for-leather' approach to state government was never intended to endear the former Opelika businessman to the other segments of state government."

Weaver wrote, "The governor's compromise plan, which didn't reach the Legislature until about 11 p.m., set off a round of debate in the House and put the Legislature in a clock-stopping mood."

During the next five hours there were four compromises between James and legislators, as each finally gave in one percent on the pay increases, agreeing to an 11 percent raise for state employees and a 15 percent raise for teachers. The $5.5 million pay raise for judges was a "done deal."

It was left to James to come up with the funding for Youth Services by taking it from other departments under him.

"Some legislators who supported James said he came in too high with his recommendations and should have anticipated the move of the teacher and state employee lobby to up the ante on whatever raise was proposed," Duvall wrote.

"But James said he'd decided to offer all he felt could be adequately funded..."

What happened to the retirement overhaul? Duvall and Cynthia Smith wrote in the *Advertiser,* "The AEA and the Alabama State Employees Association closed ranks on the plan and the election-year Legislature simply hid behind...two weaker issues and refused to give James' retirement bill the opportunity for a final vote."

In his third attempt, James passed his bill consolidating environmental regulatory and permitting agencies into the umbrella agency of the Alabama Department of Environmental Management. He was also successful in passing a key education reform—the bill removing the two-year college system from control of the State Superintendent of Education and putting it under a separate chancellor.

Asked how he felt he fared in the regular session, James said he was pleased with the overall outcome, Duvall wrote.

"We got two major bills through this time, one setting up one-stop permitting, we've had that up there for three years; and the chancellor's bill..." James said.

"The one-stop permitting bill forms an umbrella agency (ADEM) incorporating all of the state's environmental control agencies into a single agency. Businesses and individuals seeking permits for work in areas of environmental concern will have to make only 'one stop' to receive permits...

"The chancellorship bill, again, is a fundamental restructuring where you separate kindergarten-12 totally from the junior colleges, in their management and administration."

The *Advertiser* wrote that James was basically satisfied with the state funding budgets.

"'We also got the one-for-one jury strike bill, probably the major bill in the crime package,' he said. Phil Rivers, assistant legal adviser to James, said, 'There really was no priority attached to the bills other than the one-for-one strike. That was the big one.' It gave prosecutors equal leverage with defense attorneys in picking juries.

James said his state merit system pay-reclassification plan was also an important item approved by joint resolution of the Legislature," the *Advertiser* wrote.

James was also successful in passing a bill which increased the penalties on crimes involving the use of sawed-off shotguns and sawed-off rifles, and his bill was approved giving judges rather than defendants the discretion of deciding whether jurors needed to be sequestered during non-capital trials.

Among his losses were the rest of his criminal code package and bills which restructured the Commission on Higher Education.

James said, "...We resisted very strongly the 'current use' bill and lost that one..."

James' reclassification plan was aimed at taking politics out of the pay-raise process for state employees. He thought it ridiculous that state workers were dependent upon legislators periodically finding money for pay raises.

A career employee in the State Auditor's Office says state employees were unaware at the time of one of the biggest benefits which would result from the reclassification. "Before the new plan was put in place, department heads routinely put women on the payroll as clerk typists, which was the lowest paying job, and then assigned them whatever duties they wanted to," she said.

Under the reclassification plan, however, there are written job descriptions for each position. Anyone who is hired to fill a position has to be paid for the skills involved in the position.

The *Advertiser* story continued:

> James said he's not very concerned that his legislative style has angered some in state government.
> "I'm going to make some more of 'em mad. We've treated every Alabama citizen fair," James said. Some of these spoiled ones "don't like that."

Reflecting on James' relations with the Legislature, Finance Director Rex Rainer told Duvall that James' "political inexperience early in the administration resulted in an organization that was not stable." But he said James had "learned how to deal with the Legislature in subsequent sessions."

Rainer said that, like James, he was surprised at the behavior of legislators in an election year.

Duvall wrote, "Asked how he would rate the overall performance of his administration, James said he didn't feel comfortable rating himself, but added: 'You have to look at any administration to see whether the governor is representing the people or special interests, and therein lies your answer.'"

James was particularly enthused about the passage of one of many departmental bills, one allowing taxpayers to check a box on their state income tax returns to contribute a dollar from their refund to support non-game wildlife programs.

Hubbert snubbed James his last year in office by not inviting him to speak as "governor" to the annual AEA meeting. James was asked to speak as a "candidate" for re-election on the same program with other candidates. The outgoing president explained that the decision was made because James had "nothing new or exciting to tell the teachers" and it would be "wasting our time." James, the outgoing president said, had "never come out and praised teachers for the job they are doing with limited resources."

"As governor, he has no inherent right to appear before AEA," the AEA president said.

Such obvious misrepresentation meant that Hubbert did not care whether he publicly insulted the governor or not.

Having promised when he ran for the office that he would be a one-term governor, James refused to speak as a candidate.

# — 22 —

# The First Special Session of 1982

The Justice Department in May of 1982 rejected the Legislature's 1981 redistricting plan, agreeing with blacks who had challenged it that the plan "posed a serious danger of discriminating against black voters."

News reports quoted the criticism of one obvious oversight by Assistant Attorney General William Bradford Reynolds, head of the civil rights division. Reynolds said the plan failed to assign to any district 6,764 residents of Montgomery who were 90 percent black.

The main issue, however, was how many blacks would likely be elected to the Legislature under the plan.

In the election which took place in 1972 after a three-judge panel divided the state into new districts, the number of black legislators increased from two to 13 in the 105-member House and from none to three in the 35-member Senate.

Black legislators who challenged the 1981 plan contended that districts had been drawn purposely to prevent any significant increase in black representation.

Legislators who supported the 1981 plan disagreed with the Justice Department, contending that while it would have no effect on the racial makeup of the state Senate, it would increase blacks in the House from 13 to at least 17. Black legislators submitted their own reapportionment plan, which would likely have increased the number of blacks in the House from 13 to 19 and in the Senate from three to six.

Aware that June 9 was the deadline for qualifying to run in the fall election, James at the request of legislators called them into special session May 24 for the specific purpose of coming up with another plan. Consistent with his firm belief that a governor should not interfere in any activity expressly delegated to another branch of government, James did not become involved in the Legislature's reapportionment.

Less than a week after the special session began, a reapportionment bill sponsored by Rep. Rick Manley was approved by the Legislature. It was signed by James. This was not to be the end of the story, however. As in the early 1970s, site of the action changed to federal court where Alabama's reapportionment would remain a key issue long past the 1982 election.

"Black legislators...voiced almost uniform criticism of the new plan, with some saying it was another attempt to check black representation at the statehouse for the next decade," AP wrote.

AP wrote that the Justice Department felt, after a "tentative" review of the just-approved reapportionment plan, that the legislation corrected problems "for the most part." Remaining questions centered around west Alabama districts and one Jefferson County district where there were high percentages of black residents.

If the Justice Department rejected the Legislature's second attempt, AP noted, it would be up to the three-judge federal panel to decide what Alabama would do about its elections.

The Justice Department appeared to waffle, neither rejecting nor approving the reapportionment plan.

Meanwhile, officials of the state's political parties fidgeted over the approaching deadlines for primaries for the upcoming November election, as did candidates, probate judges and county commissioners. State law required all precincts and wards to be in place three months before an election.

Aware of the upcoming election, the three-judge panel in June agreed to accept a modified version of the Legislature's second reapportionment plan temporarily—through December of 1983—leaving the door open for a major rewriting of the entire document.

In July, Kendal Weaver wrote for the AP that partly because of that reapportionment, 23 of the 105 House seats would have no incumbents in the Sept. 7 Democratic and Republican primaries.

The month before the election, the Justice Department officially rejected the plan, saying it diluted black voting strength.

The September election took place under federal court-ordered boundaries that were "virtually the same as those rejected by the Justice Department," Marie Prat wrote for the AP. "The panel, meanwhile, is reviewing the slightly modified plan to determine whether it should be implemented permanently."

It was not. A second election had to be held after legislators elected in November of 1982 had served for only months.

The reapportionment plan based on the 1980 census which was finally put into effect increased the number of blacks from 13 to 19 in the House and from three to five in the Senate.

Though the first special session of 1982 was primarily to deal with the reapportionment crisis, other legislation was also approved. New circuit judgeships were created.

Rep. Tommy Sandusky, a floor leader for James, sponsored successful legislation allowing education personnel who had no need of health insurance to instead choose dental insurance.

A cost-of-living increase for state retirees, sponsored by Sen. Ryan deGraffenried Jr., was approved.

Legislators also approved a resolution acknowledging the General Fund crisis which James had warned would result if expenditures were not scaled down to conform to revised revenue estimates in the regular session.

Senate Joint Resolution 22 noted that, "...the economy of the state and the nation...does not appear to be heading for any dramatic upturn." It noted a fiscal crisis of "unknown proportion" which had caused the finance director to threaten to halt state purchases and created a committee to study the fiscal crises in the General Fund "to determine the extent."

# — 23 —

# Prayer, Textbooks, and Stabilizing the Retirement System

## The Second Special Session of 1982

"**I** have called this Special Session of the Legislature to ask you to settle three issues that go straight to the heart and to the pocketbook of all Alabamians," James said.

He referred to passing a law allowing voluntary prayer in schools, adding parents to the committee which chooses the textbooks for public schools, and shoring up the state retirement system.

"A month ago in Mobile, three elementary school teachers were sued in federal court for having mentioned God in class," James said. "The man who sued them claimed that he and his children were caused severe emotional distress by the teachers' having led their classes in a blessing before meals, which went:

> God is great; God is good,
> Let us thank Him for our food.

It was sadly true that in the eyes of the U.S. Supreme Court those teachers had done something wrong, James said.

"But under the original meaning of our Constitution and the First Amendment thereto, those teachers have done something right.

"As Governor of the State of Alabama, the full authority of my office now stands behind those brave teachers in Mobile," James said.

"I am proposing to you a bill that will insure the rights of teachers and students to pray to God while at school. This bill encourages truly voluntary prayer, whether by teachers or students. No teacher is required to pray at all, and if a teacher chooses to invite a class to join in a prayer, no student need participate."

James' bill included a prayer "available to all, yet required of no one:"

"Almighty God, you alone are our God. We acknowledge you as the Creator and Supreme Judge of the world. May your justice, your truth, and your peace abound this day in the hearts of our countrymen, in the councils of our government, and in the classrooms of our schools. Amen." (The Legislature would later add the phrases, "in the sanctity of our homes" and "in the name of our Lord.")

James pointed out that the prayer was in the tradition and language of the Declaration of Independence.

He said every American should understand that the First Amendment was intended to prohibit government from establishing a state church, such as the Church of England.

"It is a bald-faced lie to say that when the people of the United States ratified the First Amendment to the Constitution they meant to remove God from the classrooms of our schools or from the halls of our Legislature," James said.

The second reason James called the Special Session was to ask the Legislature to "give the people of Alabama full and equal representation on the State Textbook Committee."

James said he had been unaware until he became governor of the fact that there needed to be a change in the manner in which textbooks used in the states' schools were chosen.

"I found out we needed to get a little parent input," he said.

"The governor called me to his office one day and quizzed me for hours," remembers Melvin Cooper, executive director of the Alabama Ethics Commission. "It was during that the time that the issue came to a head on legislators voting on legislation that affected their pocketbooks."

James was in the office he had set up behind the mansion, which his staff referred to as his "working office." It was where he went when he wanted to delve into an issue uninterrupted.

"On the floor behind him and on his desk there were stacks of what appeared to be school books," Cooper said. "Every book had slips of paper stuck between the pages marking places I suppose he wanted to remember. I couldn't help it, I said, 'Governor, if you don't mind me asking, I'm curious. What are you doing?'

"He was reviewing textbooks," Cooper said. "The governor of the state was sitting there reading all those textbooks. I couldn't believe it. I thought if I were governor I could have found something better to spend my time doing. He was upset about what he found, too. He picked up an economics book and showed me something and asked if I could believe anyone would put that in a textbook."

After the special session began, James held a news conference to explain why he was urging a Senate committee to approve new textbook laws.

"Gov. Fob James says he's disgusted with some of the textbooks he's seen proposed for use in Alabama classrooms and he wants the authority to appoint half of the people who pick the books," the AP wrote. "Currently educators outnumber non-education committee members 14–2.

> "The textbook screening process used now isn't working," James said. "I saw a lot of textbooks that were poorly written and that took prerogatives with children they shouldn't have taken."
>
> As an example, James cited a book that was "asking 11 or 12-year-old girls should they have an abortion or not..."

The textbook committee approved the books used in public schools. It was made up of 14 professionals recommended by the state superintendent and appointed by the state school board and of two laymen appointed by the governor.

James proposed adding 14 Alabama citizens to be appointed by the governor and confirmed by the Senate.

"...The closer you can move decision-making to the people, the better off you are," James said. "There is no substitute for the good common sense and judgment of the average Alabamian..."

The third reason for calling the special session was to address an issue "the politicians of the past have lacked the guts to address," James said, bringing back another plan to solve the problem of the growing cost of the Retirement Systems to the state.

The cost in 1950 was $4 million; in 1960, $9 million; in 1970, $34 million; in 1975, $75 million; in 1978, $158 million; in 1982, $225 million.

"Add the cost of Social Security to that and you have a total cost to the taxpayers of $340 million per year."

"How did your state government get in this shape?" James asked. "It goes back a long time ago when teachers and state employees were not paid competitive wages and the politicians would not face up to this inequity. So they came in the back door to make up the difference with extravagant retirement and fringe benefits."

Salaries and wages had in recent years become highly competitive with the private sector, "and this is right," James said.

On the other hand, the $40 to $50 million too much being spent each year "ought to be used for schools and kindergartens, to maintain roads, to fight crime, to insure Medicaid payments and to guarantee that state taxes will never need to be increased" to provide the basic services which Alabama tax dollars were required to provide.

The cost of the retirement systems should be reduced to insure the stability of the system, James said.

Severe funding problems had developed in Tennessee, Maryland, New York City "and just last week in the state of Michigan...17,000 state employees were given a choice of reduced salaries and benefits or be laid off."

James' proposal for new employees was that the present formula of 2.0125 be reduced to 1.4 and the 5 percent contribution be lowered to 3.5 percent.

He had three options for current teachers and employees. They could opt to continue as they were, not changing a thing. They could choose to be paid a lump-sum refund of one-half of the money they had paid into the retirement system (plus interest), with retirement benefits to be calculated at the old formula for service prior to the refund and at the new formula of 1.4 after the refund. Or they could choose to be paid a lump-sum refund of all money they had paid into the retirement system (plus interest) with retirement benefits earned prior to the refund and after the refund to be calculated at 1.4.

James proposed to increase the contribution of judges from 6 percent to 10 percent.

Of the two retirement plans in existence for the faculty of four-year colleges, James said, "I know of no other employer in the world, private or public, that has its costs this far out of line. Frankly, I'm ashamed to admit such a thing exists, but such have been the special interest politics on Goat Hill."

Current faculty could keep both plans under James' proposal. New faculty would have to choose.

James said retired state employees and teachers would not be affected, "except the state's ability to grant them cost-of-living raises will be improved."

James said his reforms would reduce the cost of the system by $40 million a year, but were "totally fair to all public employees. Reforms that are actuarially sound as substantiated in writing by leading actuarial firms, including George B. Buck and Company, the actuarial firm that has serviced the Alabama retirement system for 40 years."

James told legislators they had two choices; either pass his reform measures or tell folks back home they weren't concerned that state government was overpriced by $40 million a year.

James then told Alabamians listening that he had been told by legislators on occasion the only people they ever heard from were special-interest groups, that the average citizen never contacted them.

Recalling the overwhelming vote to "save oil money from a few special interests" James said, "I want to say right now to the people of Alabama that I believe you do care, but you need to stand up and be counted."

He explained that the House had 105 members and the Senate 35, that the lieutenant governor in the Senate and the speaker in the House presided and appointed committee chairmen.

"These two gentlemen, Speaker Joe McCorquodale and Lt. Gov. George McMillan, both announced candidates for governor, play the major roles as to what gets passed and what doesn't get passed.

"So if you, the state employees and teachers want these reforms, and I believe you do once you know the truth you will find my proposals to be 100 percent in your best interests. And if you, the taxpayers, want these reforms, which are certainly in your best interests, call or write" and let them know.

James then listed the phone numbers for McMillan, McCorquodale, the Legislature and his office.

Bob Ingram wrote what happened in his column:

> It may have been the best television show of the season...when James turned to the two men behind him [McCorquodale and McMillan], noted that both of them were declared candidates for governor, and then challenged them to take a stand on his proposed...reform legislation.
>
> The expressions on [their] faces...were something to behold.

> McMillan...as though his underwear were too tight; McCorquo-
> dale almost bit the stem off his pipe, then finally mustered a sheep-
> ish grin. All the while, James was enjoying himself immensely.
>
> Not content just to put the two on the spot, James then pro-
> vided the statewide TV audience with the telephone numbers...and
> urged the people to call...the switchboards lit up like a Christmas
> tree at the capitol...there was surely a rise in South Central stock.

The *Advertiser* noted that roughly 300 calls had been answered in McCorquodale's office by 8:30.

Legislators, vulnerable in an election year more than ever to AEA's threats of retaliation, once again turned a deaf ear to James' retirement reforms.

However, they approved his textbook legislation, which in final form added ordinary citizens to the committee of educators responsible for choosing the textbooks for the state's schools.

There was also a special appropriation made to crippled children and Rep. Dutch Higginbotham sponsored the bill which was approved which allowed the Armed Forces to recruit on the campuses of public schools.

Legislator Ted Little of Auburn sponsored the bill for James which established the Educational Television Foundation Authority, a public, non-profit entity which had to be created to allow statewide fund-raising for public television annually.

It was the passage of James' bill to allow voluntary prayer in public schools which riveted the attention of the state and the nation on the Alabama Legislature.

# — 24 —

# A Matter of Law

## The Prayer Case

$J$ust as educators today say James was a decade ahead of the rest of the nation in stressing literacy as the key to economic survival, there is an indication that he was also a decade ahead in legal thinking.

Four justices of the United State Supreme Court in the summer of 1989 echoed the arguments James made in 1982 to reverse the 1962 U.S. Supreme Court ruling prohibiting voluntary prayer.

*Time* Magazine wrote of the case:

The U.S. Supreme Court ruled in 1989 that the annual display of a Jewish Hanukkah menorah next to a Christmas tree outside Pittsburgh's City-County building was constitutional.

"Yet in the same decision," *Time* wrote, "they concluded that a Catholic-sponsored creche depicting the Nativity in the county courthouse one block away was not."

Far more than cradles or reindeer is at stake, *Time* warned.

The case "saw the emergence of an outspoken bloc of four conservative justices, just one vote shy of a majority, who are openly intent on challenging long-established views on the separation of church and state."

Time wrote that the four Justices—Anthony Kennedy, Antonin Scalia, Byron White and Chief Justice William Rehnquist—"favor a sweeping reinterpretation of what the Bill of Rights means by forbidding 'establishment of religion.' "

The magazine stated that Kennedy, in dissent, wrote that in effect a whole train of Supreme Court decisions " reflects an unjustified hostility toward religion.

"In his opinion, Kennedy proposed that the court apply two new tests to determine the constitutionality of links between government and religion."

First, Kennedy wrote, " government may not coerce anyone to support or participate in any religion or its exercises. "

Second, the court should outlaw only those " direct benefits that tend to create a state religion.

"Kennedy's position and his vehemence troubled liberal court observers," *Time* stated.

"One more vote—perhaps a Bush appointment to the court— would give these justices the clout to undo 40 years of church-state law on...school prayer..."

James' federal court fight to allow students to pray in the classrooms may have been the most misunderstood of any of his undertakings.

His effort was perceived by a great many people as something he was pushed into by his wife, a religious activist.

It was perceived by others as the well-meaning but totally ignorant efforts of a non-attorney to challenge something he knew nothing of, an issue which had already been challenged, ruled upon and laid to rest at the Supreme Court level.

It was neither. James disagreed with the legal basis on which a string of anti-religion decisions had been made.

The U.S. Supreme Court ruled in 1962 that a school board in New York had violated the Constitution of the United States by allowing students who wished to do so to join in this prayer: "Almighty God, we acknowledge our dependence upon Thee, and we beg Thy blessings upon us, our parents, our teachers and our country."

In 1963, the U.S. Supreme Court ruled against reading the Bible in schools, saying the Constitution made the religious function "altogether private."

In 1980, the U.S. Supreme Court ruled that posting the Ten Commandments on a schoolroom wall was unconstitutional.

After these rulings, federal courts in Texas prohibited students from meeting on school property before or after school hours for spiritual purposes. Arizona courts prohibited student-initiated prayer at school assemblies. In Illinois, a federal judge forbade a kindergarten class from reciting, "We thank You for the flowers so sweet."

The fight was simple to James, the issues crystal clear. The Supreme Court had wrongly interpreted the U.S. Constitution in forbidding voluntary prayer in public schools. The Court based its argument on the prohibition in the Constitution against establishing a state religion. It did not take a lawyer to interpret that allowing voluntary prayer in no way established a state religion. Furthermore, James believed the Supreme Court lacked jurisdiction to interfere in the running of state schools.

He disputed the contention by attorneys that only attorneys were qualified to interpret the constitution. There were attorneys among the framers of the constitution, but there were also planters, bankers and newspaper editors.

James did not dispute the courts' right to ban prayer on religious grounds, nor on moral grounds, nor on ethical grounds. He disputed that right on legal grounds. And he had a lot of company.

James' views were echoed in an article written by former U.S. Sen. Sam Ervin in the American Bar Association Journal in December of 1982. Ervin was also a former justice of the North Carolina Supreme Court.

"The Founding Fathers drafted and ratified (the Constitution) to secure to Americans the power of self-rule and freedom from governmental tyranny, whether legislative, executive or judicial," Ervin wrote.

> ...They undertook to make Supreme Court justices faithful to the Constitution by making it the supreme law of the land and by requiring them as well as all other federal and state officers to be "bound by oath or affirmation to support it."...Notwithstanding these provisions, two members of the Constitutional Convention of 1787, Elbridge Gerry of Massachusetts and George Mason of Virginia, opposed ratification of the Constitution by the states because it contained no provision sufficient to compel activist Supreme Court justices to obey their oaths or affirmations to support the Constitution or to prevent them from substituting their personal notions for constitutional precepts, while pretending to interpret it.

Ervin said he rejoiced because the Founding Fathers reposed in Congress the power to "define, limit, or curtail" the Supreme Court's jurisdiction.

"Juridical activists are judges who interpret the Constitution to mean what it would have said if they, instead of the Founding Fathers, had written it," Ervin wrote. "The moral inhibition of their oaths or affirmations...has not sufficed to restrain them. Life tenure and undiminishable compensation do not render them immune to the temptation to make themselves independent of the Constitution."

Ervin pointed out that Alexander Hamilton believed such activism constituted an impeachable offense.

"The tragic truth is that juridical activism has run riot among Supreme Court justices during recent years, " Ervin wrote.

> They have belittled the role of the states in the federal system of government...It is high time for activist Supreme Court justices to realize that the Constitution of the United States belongs to the people of America and not to them, and that their supreme obligation to our country is to obey their oaths...to support the most precious instrument of government ever devised by human experience and wisdom.

The Supreme Court in forbidding prayer in schools cited the First Amendment to the Constitution, which clearly prohibited the establishment of a state religion, such as in England.

President Reagan agreed with James and millions of Americans that the founders of the nation and the framers of the First Amendment did not intend to forbid public prayer.

He pointed out that the same men who drafted the Constitution and the First Amendment also established chaplains for the United States Congress who are paid with public money to begin each day of Congress with prayer.

Reagan in May of 1982 proposed a constitutional amendment which was not approved. It stated: "Nothing in this Constitution shall be construed to prohibit individual or group prayer in public schools or other public institutions. No person shall be required to participate..."

The President quoted Benjamin Franklin, who in requesting the observance of prayer by the Constitutional convention said, "I have lived, sir, a long time, and the longer I live, the more convincing proofs I see of this truth—that God governs in the affairs of men...I also believe that without His concurring aid we shall succeed in this political building no better than the Builders of Babel: We shall be divided by our little partial local interests; our projects will be confounded, and we ourselves shall become a reproach and bye word down to the future ages."

He quoted President George Washington's farewell address: "Of all the dispositions and habits which lead to political prosperity, religion and morality are indispensable supports...And let us with caution indulge the supposition that morality can be maintained without religion...Reason and experience both forbid us to expect that national morality can prevail in exclusion of religious principle."

James agreed with Reagan's goal. But he did not agree with the President's method of achieving that goal. James was firmly insistent that the Supreme Court had wrongly interpreted the U.S. Constitution and the amendments thereof. The solution was not to change the Constitution. Therefore, efforts should be directed toward the Court, not toward Congress.

The ruling against prayer by the Court was not unanimous. U.S. Supreme Court Justice Potter Stewart disagreed with the 1962 ruling. He wrote:

> I think this decision is wrong...the Court says that in permitting school children to say this simple prayer, the New York authorities have established "an official religion." With all respect, I think the Court has misapplied a great constitutional principle. I cannot see how an "official religion" is established by letting those who want to say a prayer say it. On the contrary, I think that to deny the wish of these school children to join in reciting this prayer is to deny them to opportunity of sharing in the spiritual heritage of our Nation.
>
> The Court's historical review of the quarrels over the Book of Common Prayer in England throws no light for me on the issue before us in this case. England had then and has now an established church. Equally unenlightening, I think, is the history of the early establishment and later rejection of an official church in our states. For we deal here not with the establishment of a state church, which would, of course, be constitutionally impermissible, but with whether school children who want to begin their day by joining in prayer must be prohibited from doing so.
>
> What is relevant to the issue here is not the history of an established church in sixteenth century England or in eighteenth century America, but the history of the religious traditions of our people, reflected in countless practices of the institutions and officials of our government.

"At the opening of each day's session of the Supreme Court, Stewart pointed out, "we stand, while one of our officials invokes the protection of God. Since the days of John Marshall our Crier has said, 'God save the United States and this Honorable Court.' Both the Senate and the House of Representatives open their daily Sessions with prayer. Each of our presidents...has upon assuming his office, asked the protection and help of God."

Stewart quoted:

President Washington on April 30, 1789:

> ...it would be peculiarly improper to omit in this first official act my fervent supplications to that Almighty Being who rules over the universe, who presides in the councils of nations...that His benediction may consecrate to the liberties and happiness of the people of the United States a government instituted by themselves for these essential purposes...In tendering this homage to the Great Author of every public and private good, I assure myself...No people can be bound to acknowledge and adore the Invisible Hand which conducts the affairs of men more than those of the United States.

President John Adams on March 4, 1797:

> And may that Being who is supreme over all, the Patron of Order, the Founder of Justice, and the Protector in all ages of the world of virtuous liberty, continue His blessing upon this nation and its Government...

President Thomas Jefferson on March 4, 1805:

> ...I shall need, too, the favor of that Being in whose hands we are, who led our fathers, as Israel of old, from their native land and planted them in a country flowing with all the necessaries and comforts of life...I ask you to join in supplications with me that He will so enlighten the minds of your servants, guide their councils and prosper their measures that whatsoever they do shall result in your good...

James had studied the Constitution and the Bill of Rights. He had read the thoughts of the founding fathers and of the issues which faced them.

What the Supreme Court had ruled, James believed, it could reverse. There was precedent. For many years the nation lived under the Supreme Court's pre-Civil War "separate-but-equal" doctrine of race. It was not until 1954, with different justices on the bench, that the court in the famous Brown vs. Board of Education ruling reversed that doctrine. Three justices were still on the bench in 1982 who had been members of the Court which banned prayer in 1962. Only one, Justice William J. Brennan, had voted with the majority. Justice Stewart had written the dissenting opinion. Justice Byron White had not participated in the court's ruling.

Who could say how the court would rule in 1982?

With this thought, Opelika Rep. Shelby Dean Ward introduced for James in the second special session of the Legislature in 1982 a bill entitled "Prayer in Public Schools."

Reporters took note that the only time Bobbie James entered the Legislative chambers during proceedings was when the prayer bill came up for a vote.

Her involvement should have come as no surprise. Earlier, with her husband's backing and encouragement, she ran unsuccessfully on the Republican ticket for the State School Board, with prayer one of the issues.

During the gubernatorial campaign she told a reporter: "I would like to see prayer put back in the public schools—it can be done."

Fob James III, a Duke Law School graduate, was made the attorney of record.

It would have been politically unpopular in Alabama to object to a bill allowing students to pray in school. Some opponents of the legislation therefore centered their opposition around the support of James' wife and the involvement of his son.

Regardless of any controversy surrounding the bill in the Legislature, there was no doubt that a majority of Alabamians supported it.

Dr. Fred H. Wolfe, pastor of Cottage Hill Baptist Church in Mobile, echoed the feelings of many Americans in a statement supporting James' prayer bill. Wolfe, as president of the Southern Baptist Pastors' Conference, stated: "I urge you not to be swayed by the idea that—hey, we are imposing religion on other people. This is not it at all. We are simply saying that we want to continue to have the freedoms we've enjoyed as Americans through the years...the right to pray voluntarily wherever we might be; whether it be in a classroom, the State Legislature or the halls of the Senate."

Rep. C. Howard Nevett, a black minister from Jefferson County, offered a substitute deleting the worded prayer and substituting the Lord's Prayer.

Rep. Roy Johnson of Tuscaloosa tried to explain to legislators why it was necessary to stick to the prayer James had included in his bill. He argued that in the court's eyes, the Lord's Prayer would slant the bill too much toward the Christian faith.

On June 29, the House refused to adopt Nevett's substitute.

When it was voted down, legislative liaison Bob Geddie turned to Bobbie James in the gallery and whispered with a twinkle in his eye, "Miss Bobbie, we just tabled the Lord's Prayer."

The House also voted down a substitute which would have deleted the suggested prayer and left it to students and teachers to make up their own prayers. Legislators supporting James' bill explained that deleting the prayer would have left it too open for interpretation and therefore would spark lawsuits challenging the prayers in classrooms.

The *Advertiser* wrote on June 30, "A number of House members objected to the 'suggested prayer' included in the bill, which was written by the governor's son...while he was a student, according to Rep. Shelby Dean Ward of Opelika, sponsor of the measure.

"First Lady Bobbie James, a major proponent of the bill, rode out almost three hours of sometimes stormy debate in the balcony of the House chamber before passage on an 81–8 vote."

There was a great deal of squabbling over the final version the House would endorse.

Bobbie James remembers the moment in the House when the pendulum began to swing from "anti" to "pro."

"When the debate started, there were six people lined up at one microphone against Shelby Dean," she said of the prayer vote. "Every now and then Joe McCorquodale would look up at me. Then Roy Johnson walked over to stand with Shelby Dean, and one by one others did."

It was approved by the House and sent to the Senate, which added, "In the name of the Lord" to the prayer and clarified the language to state clearly that teachers could lead classes in any prayer, not just the one used as an example in the bill.

When the prayer bill was sent back to the House for approval of Senate changes, it included the statement, "From henceforth, any teacher in any public educational institution within the State of Alabama, recognizing that the Lord God is One, at the beginning of any homeroom or any class, may pray, lead the willing students in prayer or lead willing students in the following prayer to God."

Opponents said the prayer in the bill would not stand up under judicial review.

A news account reported: "But Rep. Roy Johnson of Tuscaloosa, a high school principal who assisted Mrs. Ward in fighting efforts to change the bill, said the suggested prayer was there for a purpose.

"This bill doesn't mandate or give us a state prayer. It gives us a suggested prayer and the words and phrases in the prayer have been very carefully selected," Johnson said.

Other language in the prayer, that which recognized God as "Creator" and "Supreme Judge of the world," was taken directly from the Declaration of Independence.

The Legislature passed James' prayer bill, making Alabama was the first state to challenge the Supreme Court's ruling since it was issued in 1962.

On August 9, 1982, U.S. District Judge Brevard Hand issued a temporary ruling against the new prayer law pending a trial on the merits of the statute. Hand's ruling was in response to a lawsuit filed by Mobile attorney Ishmael Jaffree against three teachers who led students in saying the blessing at mealtime. The suit was amended by Jaffree to include James and state and county officials.

James received a letter from Washington attorney Hermine Herta Meyer, a former justice department lawyer who was an expert in Constitutional law.

"Alabama now has an opportunity to draw attention to the true constitutional situation by defending the Alabama law on the basis of the Constitution and its sources" rather than on the basis of "former Supreme Court decisions," she wrote James.

He hired her to prepare a petition to the U.S. Supreme Court in support of the prayer law.

The Birmingham *News* wrote in September of 1982 that James said people may misinterpret what he is doing, thinking him in opposition to federal courts' rulings in civil rights cases.

"The federal government and the Justice Department rulings on 'equal protection' are totally right; they are totally right on the one-man, one-vote concept," he said.

"James said he takes issue with the role that the Supreme Court has carved out for itself—one in which he said justices have taken powers never given them by the U.S. Constitution."

On his 48th birthday, September 15, 1982, James was in Washington, D.C. to petition the U.S. Supreme Court to instruct Hand not to take jurisdiction over cases involving school prayer in Alabama.

The 1962 decision banning prayer was based on the ruling that prayers in the schools "violate the establishment clause of the First Amendment to the Constitution as 'reinforced' by the Fourteenth Amendment."

The establishment clause of the First Amendment states that "Congress shall make no law respecting an establishment of religion."

Meyer, the lawyer for James, contended in the Supreme Court petition that Justice Hugo Black, in relying on the establishment clause as basis for the court's ban on prayer, did not research the First Amendment.

"On 14 printed pages, he [Black] gave an historical view of the quarrels over the Book of Common Prayer in England...and of the early...official churches in the American states," Meyer wrote in a petition to the U.S. Supreme Court in the prayer case. "But the one thing he did not do was to look into the history of the [establishment] clause in the First Amendment in order to find out its intended meaning, and tell us where in the provisions of the Fourteenth Amendment that 'clause' had been 'reinforced' as he said it had."

Meyer was a legal scholar and author of a book on the Fourteenth Amendment. The thesis of her book was that the U.S. Supreme Court had routinely used the "due process" clause of the Fourteenth Amendment to assert federal jurisdiction where none existed in the constitution. The due process clause states, "Nor shall any state deprive any person of life, liberty, or property without due process of law."

The late William O. Douglas, who was a supreme court justice for more than 30 years, is quoted by *U.S. News and World Report* in an invterview as saying, "Due process, to use the vernacular, is the wild card that can be put to such use as the judges choose."

However, Meyer argued that the true meaning of the due process clause was to prevent mob violence, or other corruptions of the trial and punitive process by state officials.

Meyer's legal argument convinced Watergate prosecutor Leon Jaworski and U.S. Senator Sam Ervin.

After reading her petition, Jaworski wrote to James, "I have long felt that leaning on the Fourteenth Amendment for support in depriving the States from determining the propriety of religion in public schools is an abomination. It distorts the meaning of the Fourteenth Amendment and prostitutes its use."

Ervin, a constitutional scholar, had been a supporter of the Supreme Court's decision. He had voted against the late Sen. Everett Dirksen's proposed constitutional amendment to allow prayer in schools. Meyer's legal argument made him change his mind.

Upon reading Alabama's petition, Ervin wrote that the Supreme Court's jurisdiction to decide the prayer issue "seems to rest in large measure upon a rather flimsy assumption of Supreme Court Justices." He said he hoped the Supreme Court would not "dodge the point" raised by Alabama's petition.

The petition quoted Levi Lincoln, attorney general to President Thomas Jefferson, who advised the secretary of state regarding Supreme Court decisions:

> The Constitution does not require that a Supreme Court decision must be blindly accepted as precedent by the Executive or other courts...while (the court opinions) deserve great deference... still greater deference is given to (public officials acting on) their own conviction of the meaning of the laws and the Constitution.

James' brief agreed that the advice was especially true now, "when the court openly ignores the relevant historical record surrounding the...constitution...and apparently rests its decision on the personal speculation of the justices."

James quoted the 1957 Supreme Court decision which stated that "outside of the U.S. Constitution no federal power can legitimately exist," then challenged the justices to show him anywhere in the Constitution where it gave them power to interfere in church-state matters.

How could the Supreme Court decide religion has no place in American schools "when the same Congress that drafted the First Amendment provided for chaplains for the House and Senate?" James asked.

"The governor's brief scoffs at Justice Hugo Black's 1962 decision against school prayer which relied on a 14-page history of 'the quarrels over the Book of Common Prayer in England and of the history of the early establishment and later rejection of official churches in America,' " the Birmingham *News* wrote.

"What Black did not do, James charges, was base his ruling on the First Amendment or the Constitution."

Pete Cobun, a reporter for Mobile and Huntsville newspapers, wrote from Washington, D.C.:

> At a press conference this morning, James said "I am today encouraging all Alabama school officials, as well as the people of Alabama, to stand on their constitutional rights to ignore this federal court injunction and to proceed with prayer in the classrooms, with blessings at mealtimes, and with any other heart-felt prayer which the citizens of Alabama may wish to say."

The decision outlawing prayer in schools was "a dangerous usurpation of power," James said at the press conference, "a tragic error."

The proper response for him as governor, James said, was the petition he was filing with the Supreme Court.

"...Common sense tells us that if the judges can ignore [the] Constitution and create a new one by judicial fiat, we are a government of men and not of laws, a government by consent of the judges rather than by consent of the governed," he said.

James felt not only free to challenge the Supreme Court but bound to do so. He quoted Abraham Lincoln's admonishment that a Supreme Court decision should not be given the same weight as the Constitution. Lincoln said:

> ...the candid citizen must confess that if the policy of the government, upon vital questions affecting the whole people, is to be irrevocably fixed by the decisions of the Supreme Court the instant they are made...the people will have ceased to be their own rulers, having...practically resigned their government into the hands of that eminent tribunal.

"Lincoln understood that the Supreme Court was capable of error and that unless other institutions of government were willing to challenge (the Supreme Court)...the people would live 'under the despotism of an oligarchy,' " James said.

"Until the Supreme Court faces this Constitution it is sworn to uphold, and addresses the legislative history of the constitutional provisions in question, which it has never done, I will ignore the lower court order," James said.

Asked by reporters to explain any difference between his calling on Alabamians to ignore federal injunctions and George Wallace years earlier calling on them to ignore federal court orders, James said, "the difference is that due process was denied by state law to black citizens in Alabama under Wallace. There's not one scintilla, one iota's similarity philosophically, politically or operationally between myself and my predecessor."

James "dared" the federal courts to fine him for ignoring Hand's ruling, the *News* stated.

The Clerk of the Supreme Court, citing "common law of the clerk," refused to accept the petition.

Meanwhile, Alabama became the center stage for James' legal challenge. A November hearing was scheduled by Hand to determine why James should not be held in contempt for urging Alabamians to pray in defiance of the federal restraining order.

It was in that hearing that the first indication appeared that James might have found a federal judge with a kindred spirit.

Hand refused to hold James in contempt.

After viewing a videotape of James' news conference, Hand said, "I am not going to slap the governor up side the head on this.

"This court doesn't take lightly the statement that was made...I sometimes wonder if the governor read the opinion [court injunction] before he made the statements that he did make."

Janet Gresham wrote in the Selma *Times-Journal* that James' attorney, Maury Smith, explained to Hand "that the governor meant no disrespect or contempt of the federal court...Smith said James' opinion is that federal courts do not have jurisdiction over prayer.

> Hand's ruling was a surprise to Mobile attorney Ishmael Jaffree and his attorney, Ron Williams of Mobile. Jaffree called the decision a "shocker." He said he will no longer pursue a contempt ruling against James, that the decision was "a matter of discretion" and that Judge Hand evidently felt this was "not a matter of severe contempt."

Smith commented that Hand's ruling was "splendid."

Meanwhile, U.S. Sen. Jesse Helms (R–N.C.) attached to Congress' debt ceiling bill an amendment doing what James wanted to do, but based on a different rationale.

The debt ceiling bill had to be passed by Oct. 1 for the government to stay in business. Helms' amendment prohibited the Supreme Court from overturning state laws which had been passed reinstating prayer in public schools. It accomplished this purpose by stating "the Supreme Court shall not have jurisdiction [over]...any State statute...which relates to voluntary prayers in public schools..."

Helms' proposal sparked a filibuster which, ironically, was fought by those Helms described as "liberals who have characterized the issue as a constitutional one."

The Washington *Post* wrote, "Attorney Gen. William French Smith, the American Bar Association and other legal experts have said the so-called court-stripping bill may be unconstitutional, an encroachment of the legislative branch on the authority of the judiciary. President Reagan has come out in favor of a constitutional amendment to reinstate voluntary prayer in the schools; the White House has been noncommittal about the Helms proposal."

"The issue is not school prayer," Sen. Daniel Patrick Moynihan (D–N.Y.) was quoted in the Washington Post as saying. "This is a court-stripping bill. If we pass this legislation, there is no limit to the legislative tyranny that will follow."

Helms' proposal failed.

James' last words in the prayer case were written to Hand in a letter dated Dec. 15, 1982. Referring to Justice Douglas' statement that the due process clause was the court's "wild card," James wrote, "Your honor, the constitution of the United States is not a wild card: It is the supreme law of the land."

James concluded, "Your Honor, I ask you, for the sake of the people of this country, to dismiss the school prayer cases for lack of jurisdiction, and in so doing, to reaffirm the rule of law and bring to light again the Constitution of the United States."

On Jan. 14, three days before James left office, Hand in a ruling which made front pages from California to Maine ruled with James. He ruled that the Constitution of the United States clearly left the issue of prayer to the states.

"It is not what we, the judiciary want, it is what the people want translated into law pursuant to the plan established in the Constitution as the framers intended," Hand wrote.

It is wrong to treat the Constitution as "a living document, chameleon-like in its complexion, which changes to suit the needs of the times and the whims of the interpreters."

"Amendment through judicial fiat is both unconstitutional and illegal," Hand wrote.

"We must give no future generation an excuse to use this same tactic to further their ends which they think proper under the then political climate, as for instance did Adolph Hitler when he used the court system to further his goal," Hand wrote.

The Eleventh U.S. Circuit Court of Appeals overruled Hand and was upheld by The United States Supreme Court.

James knew when he left office the fight had just begun. It would have to be carried on by governors who followed him.

There was no one elected after James, however, who chose to carry on his fight.

# — 25 —

# The Third Special Session

The third special session of 1982, which began Aug. 9, was one in which James introduced a package of 21 crime bills and a constitutional amendment to strengthen the Alabama Commission on Higher Education by placing it within the state constitution on a level of authority equal to the boards of trustees of the universities of Auburn and Alabama. An accompanying statutory bill defined the scope, role and authority of ACHE and established qualifications for its members.

He also pushed a reform bill sponsored by Sen. Richmond Pearson to halt the long-time abuse by state officials of the far-flung "fleet" of state aircraft which were owned by any agency which had found the money to buy one. James' bill established a Department of Air Transportation, described as "a central controlling authority to ensure the safe, efficient operation of aircraft." All planes belonging to the state were to be transferred to this department, which was charged with "maintaining records of all flights," initiating proficiency progress for all state pilots, and "establishing priorities for the use of" state planes. The department would be audited by state examiners.

Geddie told reporters James did not see any need to address the Legislature—he was introducing nothing new.

James' package included a bill increasing the penalties for drivers arrested for driving under the influence of alcohol and other bills which James felt he could pass in a special session in which he could focus attention on them.

The ACHE measures failed, but James got 20 of his 21 crime bills approved. The bill which died would have imposed stringent penalties for racketeering.

"Minutes after the House and Senate ended the session Friday night after churning out scores of bills in the constitutional minimum of five working days, James said he was delighted," Ralph Holmes wrote.

"All of the major bills recommended earlier this year by the Governor's Crime Commission passed Friday evening. Only two hit snags—one to allow more than one defendant in the same case to be tried together, and the other to abolish insanity as a criminal defense—and they passed after limited debate.

"'Without any question, the soft spots in the Criminal Code have been eliminated in the main,' James said in a post-session news conference."

One reporter wrote, "Gov. Fob James got all he sought in anti-crime legislation in this week's special session."

The DUI bill, sponsored by Rep. Duane Lewis of Bessemer and Sen. Bill Smith of Huntsville, passed. It increased from $100 to $200 the fine on a first DUI conviction. It made attending a school mandatory. A second conviction carried a 15-day to one year jail sentence and fine of $500 to $1,500 and six months suspension of driver's license. A third conviction required a mandatory 120-day jail term, a fine of $1,000 to $5,000 and the loss of driver's license for two years.

The bill also passed creating the Department of Air Transportation.

Though the crime package was approved by both Houses of the Legislature and signed by the governor, it never became law. The reason is one of the most fascinating political tales in the history of Alabama politics.

# — 26 —

# James' Clashes with
# Siegelman and the Alabama
# Supreme Court

In the last year of his term, James clashed head-on with Secretary of State Don Siegelman and the Alabama Supreme Court in three separate but overlapping issues—budget isolation, his 20-bill crime package and the current use bill.

The clash over the current use bill grew out of James' efforts to prevent it from passing, which he knew would reduce the amount of local funding going to public education, K–12.

Newspaper articles referred to the current use bill as "a property tax sought by large landowners."

Sam Duvall wrote in the Montgomery *Advertiser* that passage of the current use bill would reduce the amount of local funding for education and for other local services.

James had spoken out for a need for just the opposite—a need for local funding to be increased. Alabama ranked among the top five states in the nation in the percentage of state funding provided to education, but among the bottom five in the percentage of local funding provided for the purpose.

James for some reason was not joined in his opposition to the current use bill by Paul Hubbert, a man who normally would have been in the thick of any fight to prevent a raid on education dollars. The two, united, would have provided formidable opposition.

The current use bill surfaced in the 1982 regular session as one of

two controversial non-administration bills—one pushed by McCorquodale, one pushed by Hubbert—which in an election year divided
the Legislature as never before. McCorquodale pushed the current
use bill. Hubbert pushed a bill to create a statewide health insurance
plan for teachers. First estimates indicated that such a plan would
need $22 million in addition to the money already being provided by
the state to local school systems for teacher insurance. Teachers are
not employees of the state. They work for local systems. Those systems
in 1982 provided insurance plans for them.

The House sponsor for the current use bill was McCorquodale's
right-hand man, Speaker-Pro-Tem Rick Manley.

The House passed the current use bill. The Senate passed a compromise version of the bill. In April, the House voted 62–32 to adopt
the Senate compromise.

There were only three days left in the session. James thought over
his options. If he vetoed the bill, McCorquodale and Manley had the
votes to override his veto. The only option he had, apparently, was to
stall and hope to generate enough public support to persuade a few
legislators to change their minds.

"We sat around at the mansion and tried to figure out some way
to stall," said Bob Geddie. Also present, in addition to Geddie and
James, were two legislators and Revenue Commissioner Ralph Eagerton. "Finally we came up with the idea of closing the governor's office
to avoid receiving the bill. We knew it wouldn't work in the long run.
We just needed a little time. If we got that, we could hopefully focus
the public on who would benefit from current use."

Thus it was when legislative officials tried to officially deliver the
current use bill to James April 8, they found he was not in his office.
No one was in the governor's office. He had taken the unprecedented
step of closing his office on a day in which the Legislature was in
session. He hung a "Gone Fishing" sign on his office door.

Reporters were informed by a spokesman with a straight face that
James had given his overworked employees a day off and was himself
in Gulf Shores.

Reporters noted in their columns that James was somewhat notor-
ious for the opposite action, working his employees even on state
holidays. They wrote that the closing of the office was "an apparent
move to slow final action on the current use bill."

Angry sponsors of the bill asked the Alabama Supreme Court for
an opinion on whether James could take such action. The request for

the opinion was made by State Sen. Albert McDonald of Huntsville, who also happened to chair the Senate Rules committee which reporters noted was at that moment "sitting on the pay raise" for the Supreme Court.

Emotions ran high. Another legislator asked the Alabama Supreme Court if James had "vacated" his office and therefore should be replaced by Lt. Gov. McMillan.

The Supreme Court supposedly bases its decisions on non-political grounds. The justices had to be aware, however, that one of the first stands James took as governor in 1979 was to oppose a 22 percent increase in their salaries. Except for that opposition, which induced legislators to cut the increase by nearly two-thirds, the salary increase would have automatically taken effect upon recommendation of the judicial commission.

The Supreme Court is "privileged but not required" to issue an advisory opinion when requested to do so by the governor or the Legislature, the court wrote in turning down one request by the Legislature.

On April 12, the Court had the "privilege" of complying with the Legislature's request to decide whether James legally could close his office. The Court wrote that all the Legislature had to do to officially deliver a bill to the governor was to make a "bona fide effort." Such an effort satisfied the constitutional requirement and started the clock ticking which limited the governor to six days in which to take action on the bill. If he did not amend the bill and send it back to the Legislature within those six days, it became law.

McDonald's committee approved the court's pay increase.

Reporters noted that the court in siding with the Legislature had chosen to stick to the "letter of the law."

On many occasions in the past, reporters wrote, the Supreme Court had refused to get involved in legislative brouhahas. An example commonly cited was the court's repeated refusal to inject itself into the dispute over whether legislators could legally set the clock back on the last night of the session to avoid adjourning at midnight.

James was vocal in letting the state know he was incensed that the same judges who refused to enforce the constitutional mandate to adjourn the Legislature at midnight would suddenly worry about the "letter of the law."

An April 27 editorial quoted James as saying "the high court should not and cannot be trusted to rule on conflicts between the governor and the Legislature because the justices get their salaries from the Legislature and right now there is a pay raise proposal pending."

James muttered that he should ask the judicial ethics commission if the Supreme Court had a conflict of interest in ruling on McDonald's request while their pay raises hinged upon approval of McDonald's committee.

The ensuing stand-off of James against the court drew the battle lines for a war which would continue for his remaining months in office.

The same political pundits who had scoffed at James' lack of political motivation four years earlier clucked their tongues at his challenge of the court. Everybody needs the court sooner or later. Everybody knows you don't make the court angry. And most certainly everybody knows that questioning the ethics of a judge is a 100 percent sure-fire way to make him angry.

The Birmingham *News* on April 16 addressed the ruckus in an editorial.

> It's a shame that posturing over the so-called "current use" bill—a blatant piece of special interest lawmaking—has precipitated a showdown between the governor and the highest court in the state.
>
> The high court ruled earlier this week, in an advisory opinion issued without benefit of testimony or cross-examination, that James had acted improperly in closing his office just as lawmakers were about to present the irresponsible "current use" measure for his signature...

Attention should be focused not on the governor and the court, the *News* argued, but on lawmakers who "moved heaven and earth to steamroll an election year plum" for large landowners.

The current use bill became law despite James' fierce opposition. He eventually vetoed it. The Legislature overrode his veto.

Hubbert, in a 1988 interview, blamed McCorquodale for passing the legislation.

"Fob was violently opposed to the current use bill but McCorquodale rammed it through the Legislature. If Fob had really built some bridges of his own with legislators he could have stopped it," Hubbert said.

On the heels of James' clear implication that the Supreme Court unethically traded an opinion for an increase in salary, legislators appealed to the court in an effort to remove James' budget isolation amendment from the September ballot and prevent people from being allowed to vote on it.

Amendments to the constitution, unlike general bills, do not become law when approved by the Legislature and signed by the governor. Amendments must be ratified by a majority of voters in an election.

This approval, however, was a mere formality where the budget isolation amendment was concerned. Voters had been as incensed as James when legislators in 1981 had been unable to agree on an education budget.

Legislators were aware of the intensity of public support for the amendment.

That support was not shared by key legislators in powerful positions, however, for a simple reason.

If put into effect, James' amendment would "isolate" far more than the budgets. After the budgets were approved, all other legislation would stand alone in the glaring spotlight of public scrutiny. Special interest legislation would no longer be enveloped and overlooked in the cloak of parliamentary footwork known to a few highly skilled players in the legislative game.

The bottom line was that James' amendment would put a damper on a lot of back-room antics.

The small but powerful clique who depended on legislative clout for their livelihood could not let it become law.

Nervous legislators looked for a solution which would allow them to kill the amendment without arousing the public's ire.

James had succeeded in focusing public attention on his budget isolation legislation, which accounted for the legislators' quandary. They were pressured on one hand to kill it by the lobbyists who financed their campaigns and on the other to pass it by James and their constituents.

How did they resolve the quandary?

Ostensibly, the Legislature approved the budget isolation amendment. It was set for a vote of the people in September, 1982.

What appears to be the case, when talking politics, is not necessarily the case and in fact is not usually the case. This was true of the bill substituted for James' budget isolation amendment in the House.

James' amendment was introduced in both the Senate and the House. When it was obvious the bill was moving quickly through Lt. Gov. McMillan's Senate, the House version was substituted with an almost identical bill which would allow temporary budget isolation to be imposed on the next year's legislature. Without this bill, budget isolation even if approved by the people in a vote at the earliest date possible would not take effect until after James left office.

Both the permanent budget isolation amendment and the temporary budget isolation statute were approved by legislators in 1981. The legislation invoking permanent budget isolation did so through an amendment to the constitution which had to be approved by voters. The legislation providing for temporary budget isolation, as substituted, accomplished the purpose through a statute. Unlike an amendment, a statute does not have to be approved by the people. Both the amendment and the statute required that none except "emergency" legislation be approved by the Legislature prior to passage of the budgets.

Reporter Ralph Holmes in 1982, prior to revelation of the obvious shenanigans which had taken place during passage of the trial-run bill, explained the situation thus: "James asked for an isolation bill. What he got was two. One, under which the Legislature is now operating, is a statute, a test act to see how things will work. The other is a proposed constitutional amendment that is supposed to go to the voters for statewide ratification in September unless the Legislature changes its mind..."

Some legislators did not have to "change" their minds. They had adroitly planned each step taken on the budget isolation amendment with the intent of preventing it from ever being imposed on the Alabama Legislature.

It took fancy footwork by a true master of parliamentary procedure and what appears to be a bit of blatant legislative blackmail to do so. The fancy footwork can be reconstructed from official records of the House Journal and of the Alabama Supreme Court.

The legislator whose name is on most of the documentation is Rep. Bob Gafford of Birmingham. Gafford may have been the sole legislator opposing budget isolation. Or he may have been the "up-front" man. After James told new legal advisor Mike Waters to work on a new constitution in 1979, he directed waters to seek advice from House Speaker McCorquodale.

"Fob told me to call Joe McCorquodale to get advice," Waters said. "I did. Mr. McCorquodale told me there were three people I needed to call, that I should rely on their advice."

Those three were Rep. Rick Manley, whom Waters came to know as "McCorquodale's right hand man," Rep. Jack Venable, who had worked on constitutional revision for a number of years, and Gafford, whom Waters came to know as "McCorquodale's point man. He did the dirty work."

Did Gafford do McCorquodale's "dirty work" in the budget isolation fight? We may never know. Gafford says the episode was so long ago, eight years, he doesn't remember all the details of the strategies and maneuvers.

Legislators, even before the special session ended in which the budget isolation bills were passed, began calling on the Alabama Supreme Court to help set them aside.

On Aug. 13, 1981, the same day the Senate approved the temporary budget isolation bill, a resolution was approved asking the Supreme Court whether substitution of a statutory bill for a constitutional amendment made any law resulting from such a substitution "null and void." The resolution cited a section of the state constitution which stated no bill could be changed so much as to alter its original meaning between the time it was introduced and the time it passed.

Such a substitution altered the original meaning, maintained Gafford, who sponsored the resolution. He called on James to ask the Supreme Court for a ruling as to the legality of the temporary budget isolation statute.

James ignored him.

The Supreme Court declined to issue an advisory opinion, explaining that the bill had become law. Once a bill becomes law, the court noted, the proper challenge is filed in circuit court.

Holmes later backgrounded the situation: "The Legislature, by the manner in which 'budget isolation' was approved, sealed [the bill's] fate by including the parliamentary quirk of first introducing a constitutional amendment and then substituting a general bill in its place."

The second special session of 1981 began Sept. 9.

On Sept. 30, the House in a resolution asked the same question of the Supreme Court about a bill which had nothing to do with budget isolation. Though the bills were seemingly unrelated, the subject matter of the request was identical. The bill had been introduced as a constitutional amendment, then substituted with a statutory bill. Was this legal? The Court was not fooled. Refusing to issue an opinion, the Court stated the request was the same as had been made concerning legislation which was now law. The same conclusion applied—only by filing a challenge in circuit court could the Legislature get a ruling.

On Oct. 20, Gafford filed suit in Montgomery Circuit Court asking that the "trial-basis" budget isolation bill be declared unconstitutional. Court documents reflect that in the suit Gafford "claims there was substituted for HB 38 an altered or amended bill..."

Legislative intent is obvious eight years later, reading the House Journal, newspaper clippings and Supreme Court opinions. Gafford never intended for budget isolation to become law.

They intended to request in a resolution that the Supreme Court declare the *temporary* budget isolation bill "null and void." If that failed, a lawsuit would be filed to achieve the same purpose. The *permanent* Budget Isolation Amendment? They would postpone putting it to a vote by the people until James was out of office and there would be a new governor. Gafford, a past floor leader for Gov. George C. Wallace, had to be aware that Wallace was thinking of running for governor again. Inner circles were aware that James had given his word that he would not run for re-election, though he would realize later what a mistake he made in not seeking a second term. All Gafford needed to do to get rid of permanent budget isolation, he thought, was to stall for time.

The Third Special Session of 1981 began Nov. 3. Legislators in a joint House resolution set the date for the budget isolation amendment to go before voters. The legislation had specifically set the date for the election: it would go before voters in the first election which was held more than three months after the 1981 Legislature adjourned. James wanted time to campaign for the amendment. Therefore he wanted it on the primary ballot in September of 1982 or on the November general election ballot.

Other constitutional amendments which had been approved during the first, second or third special sessions were to be voted upon March 2, 1982.

On Jan. 5, 1982, Montgomery Circuit Judge Perry O. Hooper ruled against Gafford. The temporary budget isolation act "does not violate the constitution of the State of Alabama," Hooper ruled.

The clock was running out. The Legislature would convene in a week and, unless a higher court ruled with Gafford, the session would be conducted under budget isolation.

Gafford appealed to the Alabama Supreme Court.

On Jan. 12, the Legislature convened in the 1982 regular session. Under budget isolation, the budgets had to be passed before anything else.

Immediately, there began a flurry of resolutions asking the Supreme Court for advisory opinions as to whether any aspects of budget isolation were unconstitutional.

There was also a flurry of bills to provide benefits for every segment of the court system, from adding new judges to some circuits to providing additional staff and attorneys with the money to pay for them.

On the second day of the session, Gafford introduced a bill to repeal the budget isolation amendment.

On the fourth day, Manley as chairman of the Judiciary Committee reported that it had been voted out of his committee. It was read a second time and placed on the calendar.

On Feb. 23, the court declined to comment on any of the questions asked by legislators in their requests for advisory opinions on budget isolation. However, the court noted, "...It is apparent to the Justices of this court that members of the Legislature are concerned about the operative effect of [budget isolation] on the business of the Legislature currently being conducted."

The resolutions raised questions about an issue which happened also to be the subject of a pending lawsuit, the Court noted.

Therefore the court agreed to "expedite" Gafford's lawsuit.

It was expedited so greatly, in fact, that a ruling was issued that same day. Signed by Chief Justice C. C. "Bo" Torbert and the other judges, the court declared James' trial-run budget isolation law "null and void" because it had been altered to the extent that the bill which passed did not reflect its original purpose.

If the man on the street had been asked the "original purpose" of James' budget isolation bill, he would probably have said, "to force the Legislature pass a budget in 1982."

The court explained otherwise.

"The substitute bill proposed a statute, the 'purpose' of which was to establish a paramount duty on the Legislature to (pass budgets before other bills)" the court explained.

The purpose of James' original bill, however, was to propose a constitutional amendment, the court ruled.

Thus, the court concluded, the original purpose had not been "manifested and effectuated."

The wording of the opinion made it clear the court had not been forced by legal precedent to rule as they did. It stated they ruled with "no precedents or authority from prior case law."

Bolstered by the court's decision, legislators in a joint resolution attacked the remaining budget isolation bill—the amendment scheduled to go before the people for a vote in September or November a few months hence.

Legislators approved a resolution on March 23 postponing the date of the referendum until 1984, when James would be out of office.

James quickly called a news conference and disputed the Legislature's legal right to recall a constitutional amendment with a simple resolution.

Isolation would remain on the ballot, he vowed.

This is the point at which then–Secretary of State Don Siegelman becomes involved.

Legislators decided they could with Siegelman's help remove the isolation amendment from the ballot. Reporters wrote that the duties of prior secretaries of state had consisted of little more than logging new laws on the books. Siegelman had expanded the duties of the office, however, giving himself far more power than previous occupants. He made no secret of aspiring to higher office.

On April 1, Gafford introduced a resolution which contained accusations which would chill the heart of any aspiring young politician. It stated:

> WHEREAS, it has become obvious to this legislature that Secretary of State Don Siegelman has for some time been attempting to use his current public office to further his future political ambitions; and
>
> WHEREAS, the official duties of the Secretary of State are very limited; so limited as to be almost nonexistent, and so limited that the legislature has, on occasion, considered abolishing the office; and
>
> WHEREAS, the legislature has noted with dismay that Secretary of State Siegelman has, without any authorization or statutory authority, caused to be printed and distributed at public expense a pamphlet that he has entitled "A Citizen's Guide to the 1982 Elections"; and
>
> WHEREAS, he is holding question and answer sessions across the state at dates in May and June in order to tell people 'how to get involved in politics'; and

WHEREAS, this legislature understands Secretary of State Siegelman plans to use public money and a public vehicle to attend
and conduct said meetings; and

WHEREAS, it is a fact that Secretary of State Siegelman, along
with the "Chicago Seven," attempted to disrupt the Democratic
Convention in Chicago, Illinois, in 1968; and

WHEREAS, he clerked for Allard Lowenstein, a known left-
winger; and

WHEREAS, the legislature does not feel that the citizens of
this state need any political advice from a man such as Mr. Siegelman whose political views are obviously far to the left of those
entertained by the average citizen of this state; and

WHEREAS, the topics that he proposes to discuss at his meetings are properly the function of the political parties of this state;
and

WHEREAS, the major political parties carry out these functions very well; and

WHEREAS, the legislature feels that Mr. Siegelman's actions
in this entire matter border very closely upon a misuse or possibly
an illegal expenditure of public funds; now therefore,

BE IT RESOLVED BY THE HOUSE OF REPRESENTA-
TIVES OF THE ALABAMA LEGISLATURE, That they do
admonish Secretary of State Don Siegelman that nowhere is he
authorized to use his state vehicle to travel to or claim per diem
while participating in the so called seminars or sessions he has
scheduled during May and June across this state and nowhere has
he been authorized to expend public money in preparing and distributing pamphlets of the type he is currently distributing.

BE IT FURTHER RESOLVED, That the Clerk of the House
serve a copy of this resolution personally upon Mr. Siegelman in
order that he might know of this legislature's displeasure with his
actions.

BE IT FURTHER RESOLVED, That the Examiners of Public
Accounts are instructed to investigate this matter and determine
if any public funds have been misused or misspent or if any state
laws have been violated.

Did Gafford seriously try to get the above resolution approved by
his cohorts? There is reason to believe he did not; that it was introduced solely as a bargaining tool. The House voted overwhelmingly
not to *kill* but to *postpone* the resolution. Did it hang over Siegelman's
head as a warning? Fall in line, or the resolution could be approved
at any time. Adding weight to the argument that it was introduced as

a ploy is the fact that Gafford didn't even vote on it.

Siegelman's official comment was a blistering condemnation of Gafford in which he referred to the solon as "sleazy." Reporters were assured that a resolution did not carry the weight of law. Thus even if it passed, the Department of Examiners of Public Accounts would not have to carry out the investigation requested by the resolution.

On April 4, the Senate "resolved" that Siegelman return the budget isolation amendment to the Legislature for "further consideration." Legislators stated in the resolution that the resolution was not to be given to the governor.

It is obvious that behind-the-scenes negotiations had to be going on to convince Siegelman to do as the Legislature asked. Gafford appeared to be the key mover and shaker behind the request. Why should Siegelman go out of his way to help Gafford? Also, the action would sabotage legislation James had campaigned for fiercely. Siegelman, unable to get money for his office from the Legislature, had come to James for bail-outs several times, Bob Geddie remembers. Legislators had to have known Siegelman would not do their bidding unless he had a reason to do so.

That is conjecture. What is not conjecture is the resolution Gafford introduced April 6, the 24th day of the session and two days after his scathing condemnation of Siegelman.

That resolution was approved, a seemingly complimentary resolution which actually contained scathing sarcasm.

The two resolutions and the manner and timing surrounding their introduction bring questions to mind which can only be answered by conjecture.

The first resolution appears in its entirety in the House Journal. The second resolution does not. There is only a synopsis which describes it erroneously as a resolution commending Siegelman for the manner in which he carried out his duties. The resolution actually repeats much of the language from the first one, thinly masking it as commendation at the beginning.

Why the deceptive description? Obviously because Gafford for some reason wanted it to appear as a resolution of commendation. He achieved his purpose through knowledge of House rules.

Gafford introduced his first Siegelman resolution as a House Joint Resolution (HJR). Under House rules, every word of an HJR is recorded in the House Journal, even though it is postponed and never voted upon. Gafford's second resolution was introduced simply as a

House Resolution (HR). Under House rules, only a short synopsis of HRs appear in the Journal. In order to discover that the synopsis is erroneous in describing it as praise, one must go to the Department of Archives and request that the resolution be brought from the basement to read it.

Was there a behind-the-scenes agreement that Gafford would atone for his past sins by introducing a resolution praising Siegelman and that Siegelman would return the budget isolation amendment to the House? If not, why did Siegelman comply with the House resolution which directed him to do so? The secretary of state was on record as declaring that House resolutions do not carry the weight of law and do not have to be obeyed. He adamantly made that clear earlier when Gafford's resolution requested an audit of Siegelman's office.

Siegelman said his decisions were made according to the law as he interpreted it.

One week after Gafford introduced his first resolution, on April 13, a bill increasing Siegelman's salary from $25,800 per year to $45,000 per year was sent to the House Ways and Means Committee after passing the Senate. It also provided for pay increases to take effect in the next term for the governor, the commissioner of agriculture and industries and the state auditor.

Meanwhile, James' argument against Siegelman returning the budget isolation amendment to the Legislature appeared to be on solid legal ground: the Legislature made the request to Siegelman in a resolution. The Alabama Constitution required that all resolutions passed by the Legislature be sent to the governor. Therefore James asked Siegelman to give him the resolution.

AP wrote on April 16 that it was a "rare and unusual move" for the resolution not to be sent to the governor.

"The amendment, for now, is scheduled to be on the ballot this fall. If the Legislature recalls the amendment, the lawmakers could kill it. But if Siegelman sends the recall resolution to James, the governor could kill the resolution."

Siegelman, who less than three weeks earlier had downplayed the weight of resolutions, apparently had a change of heart. He decided this particular resolution had more weight than the Constitution. Regarding the Constitutional requirement that resolutions must be sent to the governor, Siegelman explained that the Constitution also gives the Legislature the right to determine its own rules. The Legislature had determined that James should not get the resolution. Siegelman was therefore complying with the resolution and returning the budget isolation amendment to the Legislature.

If James and the Supreme Court had not been at such odds, it appears to a layman that Siegelman's reasoning could have been successfully challenged in court. Applying Siegelman's logic, what was to stop the Legislature from "determining its own rules" on all legislation? Why not routinely include in any bill which the governor might veto language directing that the bill be routed around the governor and directly to the Secretary of State?

In returning the budget isolation amendment to the Legislature, Siegelman commented, "The recall of a constitutional amendment proposed in a previous session of the Legislature, but yet to be voted on by the people, is an event which has not heretofore occurred in Alabama history."

Court records reflect that Siegelman, "custodian" of the amendment, returned it to the House April 19, six days after his pay raise bill was received from the Senate by House Ways and Means.

The pay raise bill was approved by Ways and Means the day after Siegelman returned the amendment to the House. It was placed on the calendar that day, the 29th day of the session, read a second time and placed on the calendar in position to be voted upon. It stalled on the next day of the session, however, failing to pass as repeated attempts were unsuccessful to get enough votes to take it up out of order.

What was James' reaction? He stated publicly on every occasion given the chance that the Legislature had approved the amendment and it would be placed on the ballot for a vote of the people in September.

It was at this point that Siegelman introduced a new issue: He said the amendment could not be voted on unless the Secretary of State "certified" it and placed it on the ballot.

James' legal adviser Jimmy Samford challenged Siegelman to show where in the constitution his duties included anything more than the clerical chores of officially recording legislation which had been enacted into law.

Siegelman announced he would not put the budget isolation on the ballot.

The *Post-Herald* quoted Siegelman as saying he could not certify the amendment to go on the ballot because he had given the paperwork back to the Legislature and had "no document to certify."

He "contends the 1982 Legislature legally recalled the measure with a joint resolution and it should not appear," Holmes wrote in the *News*. "He has refused to certify the ballots."

He quoted Siegelman as saying, "The governor is throwing the entire process into a state of chaos."

"Siegelman said he has sent the governor a letter urging him to ask the high court for a legal opinion," Holmes wrote, adding that Siegelman said he would certify the amendment only if the high court ordered him to.

James responded that he had no intention of asking anyone whether the budget isolation amendment should be on the ballot. It had been approved by both houses of the Legislature and the people were going to get a chance to vote on it.

Samford retorted that Siegelman "...is acting beyond the scope of his authority. He doesn't have to certify constitutional amendments."

Also pending was a bill to allow the Supreme Court Justices to hire six additional staff attorneys, with their pay to come from the General Fund.

The bill had been read for the second time, which meant it could be read for the final time and voted on if four-fifths of the House agreed to suspend the rules and take it up out of order.

Gafford made a motion to do so on the 29th day. It was defeated in a 25–16 vote.

He made the motion a second time later in the day. It was defeated by a 31–8 vote.

Rep. Mann Minus made the motion on the third try. It was defeated 46–19.

Rep. Jim Smith made the motion on the fourth try. It was defeated 43–13.

Gafford's only chance to get the Supreme Court's bill approved was for Speaker McCorquodale to put it on the Special Order Calendar for a vote on the last day.

The House Journal reflects the bill was third on the Special Order Calendar the last day of the session. It was approved 72–4.

As one of its final acts, the Legislature on April 26 approved a resolution returning the budget isolation amendment to Siegelman. The Secretary of State was directed to "keep such document which relates to amending the constitution and election date" within "exclusive possession of his official capacity" to ensure that the amendment did not appear on the ballot prior to 1984.

Legislators further resolved that the resolution "does not require the signature of the governor" and that it would not be sent to him.

James' response is best described in records of the Supreme Court, which noted that on July 16 "without prior certification by the Secretary of State, the Honorable Fob James, governor, proclaimed Tuesday the 7th of September, 1982" as election date for the amendment and ordered the required advertising to begin statewide.

When the Third Special Session of 1982 began Aug. 9, the House Journal reflects that legislators once again turned to the Supreme Court to back them up in their efforts to keep the budget isolation amendment from going before voters.

In one resolution the Legislature postponed the date for the amendment to be voted until the general election in 1984.

In another resolution, sponsored by Gafford, the Legislature asked if the Legislature could legally reset the date for an election through a resolution.

On Friday, Aug. 13, the Supreme Court in a 7–2 vote responded with an opinion that the Legislature could.

The court stated that the Legislature could change the date of an election by resolution. The Court also addressed the issue of whether James could put the amendment on the ballot Sept. 7 as stipulated in the legislation which was approved by the Legislature. No, the court said, James did not have that authority after the Legislature approved a resolution to postpone it.

The court went further. Did James' action constitute "an encroachment by the executive branch of the powers of the legislative branch and thereby render the results of such an election null and void?"

The question was not answered.

"But James threatened to ignore the court," the *Post-Herald* wrote. The opinion by the Supreme Court Justices was only an advisory ruling, Samford explained. "Unless we are challenged in court, I don't see us stopping it."

Said James, "I refuse to accept the proposition that the Alabama Supreme Court can, by advisory opinion, deny Alabama citizens their right to vote on this critical issue of state government."

At that point, probate judges were brought into the fracas. Answerable to the Supreme Court as part of the judicial system and answerable to Siegelman as part of the electoral process, probate judges in every section of the state began announcing they would not include budget isolation on the ballots in their counties.

If they did not, James threatened, he would sue each and every probate judge who refused to let the people vote on the issue.

AP writer Phillip Rawls, quoting Siegelman, said probate judges in several urban counties were either going to lock the levers on voting machines or not count the votes.

Siegelman, however, would not name those judges to Rawls.

Samford got on the phone and personally called as many probate judges as he could reach. He announced shortly thereafter that 40 probate judges had confirmed to the governor's office that they would put budget isolation on their ballots. Samford said no probate judges informed the governor's office they would not do so.

On September 1, Siegelman acknowledged that the amendment would be on ballots throughout the state. But he said that many major cities, like Montgomery and Huntsville, would block it out on the voting machines so that people could not vote on it. Siegelman said smaller counties were seemingly intending to let people vote on it because they did not want to get sued.

James had six days.

Rawls described the course James took four days before the election: "Gov. Fob James jetted across the state Friday waving the tattered flag of 'budget isolation'...

> James held airport news conferences in Mobile, Montgomery, Birmingham and Huntsville to ballyhoo his proposed constitutional amendment...
>
> James has singlehandedly tried to force a referendum on budget isolation on Tuesday's ballot. His actions have conflicted with the Legislature, which voted to delay the referendum for two years, and the Alabama Supreme Court, which issued an advisory opinion [backing up the Legislature]...
>
> James rejected the Legislature's two-year delay because, he said, the legislators overwhelmingly passed a law setting a referendum on budget isolation for Sept. 7 and then they delayed it two years by passing a resolution, which is not the same as a law.
>
> The governor told reporters that the taxpayers want budget isolation but opponents are using "chicanery" to confuse them and hide how tax dollars are being spent.
>
> James threatened to sue the state's probate judges if they did not put it on the ballot, and he said Friday that all 67 have agreed.
>
> But...Siegelman...said probate judges in several metropolitan counties are either going to lock the levers on voting machines or

not count the votes...

An aide to [Siegelman] said the probate judges who are defying the governor do not want their names revealed for fear they will be harassed by the governor.

Siegelman has opposed putting budget isolation on the ballot because of the Supreme Court's advisory opinion issued three weeks ago.

But James said he is ignoring it. "That was nothing more than an advisory opinion. It is not law," the governor said.

"Anybody standing against the isolation bill is standing against letting the people of Alabama vote on knowing how their tax dollars are being spent," James said.

The Supreme Court at the last moment ruled that the budget isolation amendment should not be on the September, 1982, ballot. The court in doing so agreed that the Legislature had been legally entitled to postpone with a resolution until 1984 the vote which had been set through legislation for 1982.

That gave opponents two years.

In the 1984 Regular Session of the Legislature, a resolution was passed directing Siegelman to keep the budget isolation amendment in his office and not to put it on the ballot.

Siegelman, who was serving his second term, had changed his mind again on the weight carried by a resolution. He refused to comply with the resolution. In 1984 he fought as fiercely for the amendment to be put on the ballot as he had fought two years before to keep it off. Why? A Siegelman supporter would surely argue that the legalities differed. A cynic would argue that he realized how popular the budget isolation amendment was with the voters and was looking ahead to the attorney general's race.

Regardless of motive, Siegelman announced the amendment would be put on the ballot in the March 13, 1984 election.

Assuming Siegelman's role of two years before, Gov. George Wallace instructed probate judges not to count the votes.

Siegelman sued Wallace and Attorney Gen. Charles Graddick in Montgomery Circuit Court, asking that probate judges be required to count the votes and "perform all other constitutional responsibilities with regard to" the election.

The amendment was overwhelmingly ratified by the March 13 vote.

On March 26, Montgomery Judge William R. Gordon ordered

probate judges to certify the election results.

Wallace dropped his opposition. A former legislator who was involved in fighting the budget isolation amendment said Wallace did so because of the obvious strong support of voters for budget isolation.

Legislators on April 2 sought an advisory opinion from the Supreme Court as to the "validity" of the proposed amendment.

The Court declined to issue an opinion, explaining that its "policy of allowing the questions to be answered in [an] adversarial proceeding stems from the preference for using a process that allows all interested parties to have their day in court..."

The amendment was added to the Alabama Constitution.

It has never been enforced as James intended, however. Legislators seized on the "out" provided by James in case emergency legislation needed to be considered. James defined "emergency" as something on the order of Hurricane Frederic. Legislators today routinely step up to the microphone, ask for a three-fifths vote to suspend the budget isolation requirements, and most times get that vote from fellow legislators as an unspoken "common courtesy."

"It could still be carried out as Fob intended," Geddie says. "All it would take would be for a strong speaker or a strong lieutenant governor or a strong governor to speak out for the adoption of rules to implement the constitutional amendment as intended by the people."

Meanwhile, the passage of state budgets is still of secondary importance to too many members of the Legislature.

In 1987, Gov. Guy Hunt's budget failed to pass in the regular session or in the first special session. It made it on the third try.

James has not wavered in his insistence that the majority of voters in the state want the budgets passed before any other business of the Legislature.

"They showed that by the vote," he said. "Legislators may not listen when the governor talks. But they listen when the voters talk. If voters in every district in the state let their legislators know that they won't put up with any more game playing with the budget isolation amendment, you would see it working the way it's supposed to."

## The Half-Million-Dollar Semi-Colon

A picture of James on Aug. 24, 1981, with pen in hand, surrounded by smiling legislators, shows a happy man.

He was posing for the traditional governor-signs-bills-into-law shot, which in this instance was of special significance.

The 20 bills were his "crime package," which had been mostly rejected in the regular session and almost totally approved in a special session.

His signature was all that was needed to turn the bills into law. That's what the caption under his picture stated. Some reporters noted the afterthought that one final step remained, that of routing the bills on to the Secretary of State for him to put them officially on the books.

James was effervescent. The new laws would strengthen a lot of weak ones, close gaps, toughen sentences. He praised the members of the commission on crime, headed by Montgomery Circuit Judge Joe Phelps, who had spent so many hours seeking input for the legislation in public hearings all over the state.

James maintained that the package in the long run would reduce the number of inmates in prison, though there might be some "short-term" increase because of the new laws.

"Every citizen of Alabama is living under a Criminal Code that gives them greater protection than when this special session started," James said. He praised State Sen. Reo Kirkland for pushing the package.

It included laws which:

- mandated jail sentences for second and third DUI offenses;
- made escape from work release a felony;
- made it a criminal offense to deal in illegal food stamps:
- prohibited bid rigging;
- raised the minimum sentence of Class C felonies from one to five years;
- tightened child pornography laws;
- allowed judges to try juveniles as adults in serious felony cases;
- provided for hearings for defendants convicted on insanity charges for commitment to mental hospitals.
- allowed two or more defendants to be tried at the same time;

- barred perpetrators of violent crimes from being enrolled in neighborhood work release centers.

The Legislature sent James not only his crime package but a host of other measures.

James pocket-vetoed three of the 27 House bills because of what he called technical errors.

Two constitutional amendments which did not require his signature were sent directly to the secretary of state.

It is difficult to ascertain from newspaper files when the rumblings started that powerful behind-the-scenes opposition was uniting to kill the crime package and with it most of the other legislation which had been approved in the session.

Birmingham political writer Frank Bruer obviously heard the gossip. He wrote a column about the casualness with which legislators and judges ignored breaches of constitutional mandates:

> Someday when someone gets tired of the winking and blinking that goes on about how laws are enacted in Alabama the roof will fall in.
>
> Example: all 60 of the bills passed by the Alabama Legislature during the recent special session may be, and probably are, unconstitutional.
>
> Example: Both the education and general fund budgets were passed illegally during the regular session.
>
> Why are the 111 resolutions and bills, including Gov. Fob James' own crime package, probably unconstitutional?
>
> It's because of Article V, Section 125 of the Alabama constitution. Section 125 says to become law all bills passed by the Legislature must be signed and presented to the Secretary of State within 10 days after final adjournment of a legislative session.
>
> In effect, James may have technically pocket-vetoed every measure passed during the session by not delivering them to Secretary of State Don Siegelman's office on last Monday...not the first bill was delivered by the governor's office to Siegelman's office until last Tuesday, 11 days after the Legislature adjourned on Aug 13...
>
> The bills in question include James' package of 25 crime-fighting measures and a bill to require mandatory jail terms for second and third convictions of driving under the influence.
>
> Then was everything passed in the session invalid and unconstitutional?

Probably no more so than the hundreds of bills the Legislature has passed over the years by stopping the clock on the final day of the session.

The Legislature passed both budget bills during the regular session after midnight of the last legal day for meeting.

By law, a general session is limited to 30 legislative days and 105 calendar days. Both budgets and both pay raise bills passed on the 31st legislative day and the 106th calendar day.

The courts, which also are funded in the general fund, have winked at the procedure for years. They have ruled consistently that the separation of powers doctrine prevents the courts from looking behind the journals of the Senate and the House of Representatives.

The journals will reflect such things as 15 bills passing in a chamber at 11:45 p.m., 30 at 11:52 and maybe 45 at 11:57, something that is technically and physically impossible to do. Also something that the members of the Alabama Supreme Court know is impossible to do.

James threatened this year to close his books at midnight on the final night of the regular session. He claimed the Legislature had been acting illegally for years and that he would have no part in passing illegal bills.

However, not only did he keep the office open after the witching hour but agreed about 2:20 a.m. on April 27 to a compromise executive amendment on both the 15 percent teacher and 11 percent state employee pay raise which go into effect Oct. 1

However, no Legislative act is unconstitutional until the courts have ruled it so...

Rumors increased that James' crime package would be subjected to standards not hitherto imposed on other legislation.

Reporters discovered James had signed the 109 bills and resolutions well within the 10-day time limit.

Siegelman, however, stamped the bills "late" and declared them pocket-vetoed.

Once again, Samford and Siegelman engaged in a running verbal battle.

A pocket veto is a method by which a governor kills a bill by refusing to sign it, Samford said. The fact that the bills were duly signed by James made it clear he had no intent to pocket veto them, that he meant them to become law.

The question was whether the crime bills had been delivered to Siegelman on time. If they *were* late, was their delivery to the Secretary of State a formality or was it a key, vital step in a bill becoming a law? What had been the custom with past governors and secretaries of state? The questions were not addressed.

After James signed the bills, they were given to Samford, Siegelman's verbal sparring partner during the months of angry confrontation over the budget isolation amendment.

Samford did not at first take Siegelman's challenge of the crime package seriously, news articles reflect. He said Siegelman's role in the law-making process as defined by the Constitution was a clerical one—the Secretary of State's job was to log new laws on the books after they were passed by the Legislature and signed into law by the governor.

When he realized the issue was perceived as a serious one, Samford dragged out the Constitution and showed reporters that whether the bills had been delivered to Siegelman a day *late* or a day *early* depended upon how the law was interpreted. One sentence in the constitution stipulates the methods by which bills are killed or become law after being approved by the Legislature. The sentence gives the governor six days to sign the bills and get them to the Secretary of State during a session and 10 days to do the same if the session had ended. Sundays were clearly excluded in the first part of the sentence when referring to bills passed during the session. Sundays were neither excluded or included in the second half of the sentence, referring to bills on the governor's desk after the session ended. It was common logic, Samford said, to assume if the framers of the Constitution had changed their mind about Sundays between the first part of the sentence and the last, they would have gone out of their way to make that point clear.

Therefore, Samford said, if you left out the two Sundays in the 10 days involved in the crime package, Siegelman got them a day early.

Newspaper files in the archives do not reflect that the issue was ever treated by the news media as a two-sided one. Siegelman's statement that the bills were "a day late" was accepted at face value. Reporters then sought to discover why the governor "forgot" to sign his crime package. Newspaper files do not reflect that any newspapers made an effort to discover the answers to tantalizing questions: Previous Secretaries of State had interpreted their constitutional duty to be one of recording the legislation passed by the Legislature and signed by the governor. Did the constitution give the Secretary of State the authority Siegelman assumed? How had previous secretaries of state and governors interpreted the 10-day period? What had been the custom in previous administrations and in the James administration on sending bills to the Secretary of State?

The issue became a judicial one after Montgomery County District Attorney Jimmy Evans relied on a new law in the crime package to appeal when a judge in a pre-trial ruling refused to allow Evans to try a defendant on an assault charge.

The charges stemmed from a New Year's Eve incident in which a Hope Hull woman was injured in an accident in which the other driver was an intoxicated State Senate security officer. Evans indicted the Senate official on first degree assault. He tried him first on the drunk driving charge and convicted him. The Senate official then asked the judge to dismiss the assault charge, pleading "former jeopardy." The judge agreed and dismissed the assault charge. Evans appealed the decision under a law in the new crime package which allowed prosecutors to appeal some procedural rulings.

The defendant's attorney argued that the law was unconstitutional because Siegelman had stamped it "late" when it was delivered to him.

James jumped in on behalf of his crime package.

James' argument to the Court of Criminal Appeals revolved around the one sentence in the Constitution which stated how many days the governor had to decide what action to take on a bill.

The fate of the entire crime package hung on a semi-colon: The phrase, "Sundays are excluded," is not repeated after the semi-colon in the second part of the sentence.

James' attorneys argued that the framers of the constitution made it clear they wanted to exclude Sundays from the days in which the governor had to deliberate over the fate of bills passed by the Legislature by stating so at the first of the sentence. What reason would there have been to repeat the same words in the same sentence?

The Court of Appeals found the subject weighty, however.

Yes, they admitted, Sundays were "specifically excluded" in the sentence.

However, "That provision is separated from the rest of the sentence by a semi-colon," the judges explained in a written opinion that James had pocket-vetoed the bill.

How could the court say James pocket-vetoed legislation he signed and sent to the Secretary of State?

Assistant Attorney General Joe Marston said that filing a bill with a Secretary of State is a bookkeeping procedure. He asked the court,

"Do we go with absurdity or do we go with common sense?"

The argument was apparently wasted. The judges couldn't get past the semi-colon.

They ruled "...the bill did not become law. Instead it became the object of pocket veto."

AP wrote on Oct. 22, 1982, that James would "make a last-ditch appeal to the Alabama Supreme Court to save his package of anti-crime bills hanging in legal limbo..."

But, said AP, "sources say not only the 20-bill anti-crime package but also 40 other bills and 49 joint resolutions are dead."

That is indeed what happened.

On Dec. 17, 1982, the Alabama *Journal* reported that the Supreme Court, upholding a lower court opinion, struck down all the bills, "including bills against the insanity defense and cracking down on drunk drivers and violent crimes by juveniles."

The Journal stated "The court action virtually wiped out all legislation taken during the session which cost taxpayers an estimated $500,000."

The majority ruling by the Supreme Court included no written opinion. In dissent, however, Judge James Faulkner said that by refusing to review the case, the courts are "running the ship of state too strictly and too narrowly."

Attorney Gen. Charles Graddick commented that it was "absurd" for legislation to be invalidated in such manner. Such a decision would "give the clerks the power to veto the people, the Legislature and the governor," Graddick said.

It was Judge Faulkner who leveled the harshest criticism at his fellow judges.

Arguing that the framers of the Constitution clearly meant Sundays to be excluded from the governor's time limits, Faulkner said the courts were not only misinterpreting the law.

"They also misunderstood the grammar," he commented.

The "misunderstanding" ranged far wider than the judicial bench, however.

The complex interplay of words and deeds and resolutions and advisory opinions when pieced together eight years later puts the picture sharply into focus.

It is obvious that awesome power was and is concentrated in the offices of those who control the Legislature, the Judicial and the Executive branches of government.

Seldom, perhaps never, has this power been concentrated as it was in 1982, intent upon using any and all means available to preserve the status quo, to prevent monumental changes in the heart of the system from which the power came.

In 1983 and in the years which followed, the good-old-boy politicians and hangers-on and the "political whores" decried by James moved back into Montgomery and fought among themselves to reclaim their territory.

They bristle at the very mention of the name Fob James, and, having learned early in politics that truth is whatever is said loud enough and long enough, dismiss James with a snicker.

"You mean the governor who was so dumb he forgot to sign his crime package?" they ask.

Many people—the casual observer or the newcomer or the man or woman who is too young to remember—perhaps accept the statement at face value, as too many other statements were accepted without challenge in 1982.

The James folks who were part of it all draw a deep breath and reply, "Well, there was a little more to it than that."

# — 27 —

# The War Against Illiteracy

"**S**outhern states were the first to respond to the clarion call of *A Nation At Risk,* the 1983 Report of the U.S. Commission on Excellence in Education. Indeed, some states anticipated its findings, and began improving their public schools well before the national outcry for better public education hit the press. Southern governors and legislators have remained in the forefront of the reforms throughout, setting the pace for the rest of the nation in terms of educational innovations and new investments.

> The South may have set the pace, but it also started farther back than the rest of the nation. We still spend 20 percent less per student than the national average, and only 68 percent of our ninth graders graduate from high school. Our seniors score lower on college board tests than those from most other states. We are still behind on per capita spending and teacher pay...
>
> One in four southern adults never went beyond the eighth grade; for black adults, the figure is three out of every eight.
>
> ...Not only does ignorance drain individual success, it also drains the public purse. Functional illiterates earn 44 percent less than those with a high school diploma, are more likely to resort to crime, and are highly dependent on welfare.
>
> ...in 1986, too many students entering southern colleges still need remedial work. It is unjust to keep recruiting students, particularly minority students who have been especially deprived of the basics, to enter college and then leave them to sink or swim. Many will sink. Many are sinking now.
>
> — from *Halfway Home and a Long Way to Go,* the report of the

Commission on the Future of the South, Southern Growth Policies
Board, 1986.

In 1978, five years before *A Nation At Risk* sounded the alert that
the deterioration of America's educational system jeopardizes our our
social and economic survival, Fob James rode into the Alabama governor's office on a yellow school bus sounding the advance alarm.

The school bus, dubbed the "Reading, 'Riting and 'Rithmetic Special," was a concrete object which brought home the point that the
top item on James' agenda was education.

No other subject occupied James' thoughts as did education, as he
tried to find a rational reason why so many Alabama youngsters were
functional illiterates. The California Achievement Test showed that
nearly 30 percent of Alabama students ranked a grade level or more
below where they should have ranked in basic skills. Why? What factors were to blame?

James was frustrated at the lack of answers. He was not alone.

Parents were as frustrated as he.

Businessmen were as frustrated.

Teachers, who had committed their lives to educating Alabama's
children, were the most frustrated of all.

For years, the public had searched for answers within the then-
127 separate school systems in the state and, overwhelmed by the
bureaucracy and diversity of funding, had been unable to determine
at whom to point the finger of blame.

Did education money go where it was supposed to go?

Every now and then, a prosecutor sent to jail someone who had
pocketed school money in kickback schemes or equipment purchases.
There was, however, no reason to believe that graft was widespread
enough or on a big enough scale to be blamed for the poor education
system.

In certain areas of the state, politicians began to blame teachers
they said were poorly educated, citing third-grade words which were
misspelled in notes sent home by teachers to parents.

Throughout the state, what began as a murmur of suspicion grew
to a groundswell of accusation: Perhaps teachers were at fault. Perhaps they should be tested, just as their pupils were in certain grades.

Teachers banded together for protection. They joined the Alabama Education Association, which would assume an adversarial role
against James.

James rejected the assessment that teachers were to blame, based on memories of the dedicated teachers who had molded his young life. There were certainly some unqualified people in the teaching profession, as in all other professions, he knew. But there had to be other, more basic reasons for the illiteracy which choked all of the South, including Alabama.

James in his campaign provided a voice for the frustration which had turned to divisive anger, pitting parent against teacher, the public against the education community. That voice on election day was decisively given the go-ahead to "do something" about education.

It was James' mandate. It was his move.

The public was anxious to support him.

James focused all attention, all efforts, on improving those schools at the bottom of the educational ladder.

Why were they there?

It was a question traditionally shrugged off with a one-word answer, money: If we spent more money, we'd have better schools.

Each school system in the state spent a different amount per pupil, a quirk not of the state but of local governments. The state ostensibly divided its money equally, giving each system the same amount of money per student but based on the number of days the student actually attended. The amount of money provided by local governments, however, was left by Alabama law to local governments in each of the 67 counties and in the cities which had separate school systems.

There was no requirement by the state that local funding be adequate.

Despite the inequality of funding, James believed that money was not the key ingredient. The gap between the amount spent on students in some systems and the amount spent on students in other systems was unconscionable. But James could point to the small town elementary school he had attended as proof that a system's ability to provide a solid basic education depended on the presence of other factors as well.

What were those factors which had combined to make the mill town school he attended a good one? How could you isolate those factors, put them on a check list and use that check list to figure out what was lacking in schools which were not providing students with good educations?

James' logical business mind, his analytical engineering mind, told him the cloudy education picture would become crystal clear with an honest assessment of key conditions in each school system—management, teacher-pupil ratio, parental support, teacher competency, discipline and so forth.

"I knew fundamentally what I wanted to do," he said. "There were three points to my program. The first thing we had to do was to test students on a regular basis, every year, to establish a benchmark. Take any school. If you started in 1979 giving an aptitude test that measured basic skills, if you gave that same test every year, then you could chart the results and determine whether or not that school was making progress.

"I wanted a test that would show whether that school was moving forward when compared year after year with itself, not necessarily relative to another school," James said.

The next step in his program was equally simple.

"With the test scores in hand, what could be simpler than saying to ourselves, here is a school that simply is not performing. Let's find out why," James said.

> The way to do that was to require each school to tell us on a simple form how it spent its money, a uniform disclosure which a trained eye could look at and tell what the priorities were. With that form in hand, it should be easy to compare how the schools which were doing good jobs spent their money with the schools which were not. After enough comparisons, there would be a standard by which to judge. You could look at a school with 300 kids, compare how much money went for instruction, for administration, for counseling, etc. If the school's priority has supposedly been to bring the teacher/pupil ratio down, you could tell by looking at the form if money was spent for that purpose or went instead to increase the overhead.

When he had the charts from the systems in hand, when it could be determined how schools should be spending money, the third step was obvious to James. He would send teams of the best teachers and administrators in the state into the schools where students tested at the bottom of the ladder. The master teachers would help and advise, and one by one institute good management and good teaching practices in all Alabama schools.

Obviously, he anticipated full support from each member of the State Board of Education and from the superintendent of education in implementing the plan.

Each year he would test and revise his master plan, taking schools off the priority list as they rose in excellence and putting others which needed help in their place.

No one should object to the testing program, James believed. If money was the only arbiter of success, the test results would reflect it. A list of schools ranked by achievement scores would be a mirror image of a list which ranked schools by the amount of money spent per pupil.

Baldwin County native Dr. Robert Lager was James' "point man" for day-to-day coordination of his education program.

Lager's resume included a lot of work for the Foreign Service Institute, the language school belonging to the State Department. Competent to varying degrees in nine languages, Lager was the man who set up the program to train overseas operators for the Washington-Moscow hot line.

Lager said he left his globe-trotting post to work for James because, "What Fob said was very Democratic, to an extent populist...what struck me was his real and honest concern for poor people, for unemployed people...his complete commitment for good public education for all students, not just Mountain Brook, but Hale and Lowndes counties as well."

Mountain Brook is known as the wealthiest city in Alabama. Hale and Lowndes are among the poorest counties.

"Our idea was that we wanted to emphasize K–12," Lager said. "It's important to understand that Fob was not attacking colleges. Nor were we trying to take anything away. We were trying to broaden the emphasis. We felt that in the annual budget scramble in Montgomery, all the colleges and universities have lobbyists. Theoretically, the lobbyist for K–12 is supposed to be Dr. Wayne Teague, the state superintendent. In reality, Teague does what people in power tell him to do."

Additionally, "in talking to many colleagues in two- and four-year schools, most of them would admit their main problem was that K–12 graduates were not sufficiently prepared to do college-level work in many cases," Lager said.

Because Lager's position was a new one in Alabama government, he had no counterpart in the Wallace administration to brief him on his duties. Therefore, he said, he wandered around the Department of Education gathering information to come up with a plan to carry out James' War on Illiteracy.

Because sound management was a necessity at every level of education, James told Lager to analyze the "in-service training programs" in the State Department of Education, which should have been the vehicle used to train top-notch administrators.

Lager said he discovered the Department of Education relied on training programs offered by the colleges and universities in the state to train principals and administrators. Dozens of programs were available, Lager said, though educators confided to him confidentially that "none of them was worth a flip."

James' initial War on Illiteracy plan was a 42-page, $80 million program to upgrade education.

It contained $750,000 for a "management improvement program," and $3 million (scaled to $2.5 million in the final plan) for a "model school program" which targeted the 13 worst-scoring schools in the state for help by the Special Skills Teams.

It called for spending $16 million to reduce the teacher-pupil ratio in classrooms; $43 million for teacher pay raises; $10 million in discretionary funds for the governor to use as emergencies were revealed; $5.4 million to add 300 of the 2,000 new kindergarten classes James wanted to add; $2.23 million for emergency construction; and $250,000 to provide liability insurance for teachers.

The insurance was a relatively small item, but James believed it was only right that teachers be supported and protected in their efforts to maintain discipline. He says not to do so would be "unthinkable in this age of lawsuits and today's overly litigious society."

James was the new kid on the block in the education world, trudging ahead often on the toes of the existing bureaucracy.

He announced his testing program to editors gathered at a meeting of the Alabama Associated Press Association.

After the weekend editors' meeting, the *Advertiser* followed up with a story: "By Tuesday the state Writing Committee for Minimum Competency [which was] meeting in Montgomery for two days was wondering if its project had been altered in favor of a new plan of the governor's."

The committee was part of a "basic competency education program" being developed by the State Department of Education. It had since 1977 been planning a pilot testing program of minimum competency tests for grades 3, 6 and 9.

James had told editors his testing would begin within 60 days.

Was the governor throwing out the window everything the committee members had worked on for more than a year?

Their anger was reflected in the news article.

Teague stepped in to soothe their ruffled feathers, meeting first with James, then announcing to news media that the governor's testing program would not affect the committee's work.

"He is the best education governor we've ever had," Teague said after that meeting, adding that it would "cost a lot" to do the sort of testing desired by the governor.

James later used the committee as a vehicle for funding his testing program. However, the incident serves as an example of how early in the administration he alienated the very groups who, if they understood his programs, would have been his most enthusiastic supporters.

In mid-March, just prior to the April legislative session, James revealed some of his education plans. He spoke to 2,000 teachers at a meeting of the Alabama Education Association.

James did not name a total figure for his War on Illiteracy, telling teachers he would ask that $60 to $70 million be diverted from "within the total education umbrella" to fund education reforms.

The money would come from holding down appropriation increases to colleges and universities as he began upgrading the educational ladder from kindergarten up, he said.

"...I believe if we don't put emphasis on primary and secondary education children won't learn the basics and they will have problems later in life," he said.

He would find additional money in other areas.

The $800,000 to $900,000 needed to test students statewide, the first step in his war, had been "scrounged up out of my office," he said at the time. It was taken from the governor's discretionary fund, normally used by governors for "special projects," in districts of the state in which they feel it will bring them support or to legislators for special projects in return for favorable votes on the administration's legislation. James continued to dip into his discretionary fund for testing when needed.

News coverage reflected that AEA reacted unenthusiastically to James' revelations of his War on Illiteracy. The teacher-members did not welcome his program with open arms for a simple reason—they relied on AEA lobbyist Dr. Paul Hubbert to tell them who was friend and who was foe. Hubbert made it clear from the start that James was foe.

James was "foe" during the campaign when Hubbert supported first Brewer then Baxley in the governor's race. He became more a foe than ever when he made it clear that he would work closely with Joe McCorquodale, Hubbert's major political enemy.

James stopped preaching and started meddling when he announced he would take over the State Board of Education with the authority given him by law as president of the board; Hubbert had formed a strong alliance with Board Vice President Dr. Harold Martin of Birmingham, who ran the board prior to James' involvement.

He alienated Hubbert seemingly beyond repair when he decided to provide teachers with free liability insurance. AEA provided liability insurance to teachers; it was the number one lure held out to prospective members to convince them to join. Hubbert saw James' plans as a political effort to cripple AEA's strength.

"I had no idea that anyone would object to the state providing liability insurance, certainly not the man whose job it was to obtain benefits for teachers," James said. "Paul printed some front page articles in his journal that were just outrageous untruths. I remember when I first saw them I said, 'nobody will believe this nonsense.' But they did."

"We all take wherever we go an attitude that was formed years ago," James said. "I was lucky. I had great teachers in Lanett Grammar School. I remember them as a boy. They were loving but tough, bright people, the most respected folks in town. I guess even as governor I didn't think anybody could fool them. But the world has changed. I had to realize the world of the forties and fifties was different from the seventies and eighties."

Prior to James, it was no secret that Hubbert and University of Alabama at Birmingham lobbyist Rudy Davidson had a great deal of input into the education budget.

James felt lobbyists' roles should be secondary to those of elected state officials.

"I felt a governor should be willing to listen to any citizen, any lobbyist," James said of his term in office. He included Hubbert. "But when it got down to decision-making, you worked with those who were elected by the public to make the decisions on education, the members of the State Board of Education. We were responsible for policy, expenditures, and performance of public schools."

This was a radically different attitude for a governor, as shown by Gov. Wallace's inclusion of lobbyists in his budget-planning before and after James' term: "As Wallace prepared for the 1983 session to begin...," Ira Harvey wrote, "he appointed a select committee as he had done in 1976 and 1977 to develop education budget recommenda-tions." Among the lobbyists included were Hubbert and Randy Quinn, lobbyist for the Alabama Association of School Boards.

After taking a leading role in writing the budgets in 1976 and 1977, Hubbert must have been resentful when James essentially locked him out of the process.

James in 1979 injected the State School Board into the budget-making process for perhaps the first time in the history of the state. He did this in response to a legislative resolution urging him to create a blue-ribbon committee to work up an education budget. Instead of lobbyists and university presidents, James named the state board mem-bers—and only the state board members—to the "Blue Ribbon" com-mittee.

"Hubbert often times has blinders on to other education needs because he is so totally directed toward getting salary increases for teachers," Don Bryan says. "Frankly, education has suffered because of this."

The outgoing AEA president, speaking to the group after James in the spring of 1979, questioned spending money on large-scale test-ing "when we are on proration."

What jumps out at a researcher reading the news coverage of James' speech was that for some incredible reason he did not mention to teachers that day that $43 million of the money he requested for his War on Illiteracy was for raises for them.

James has no explanation for not doing so, except that he was trying to get teacher-support for those of his programs which needed their support. He knew he would have their support on the pay in-creases.

House legislative aide Bryan blames himself and other members of the James' administration for not fully informing teacher and other lobby-groups of the administration's intentions before paid lobbyists got to them first.

"Most of the time, if Fob's critics had been informed of what he was trying to do, they would have been in there trying to help him. If Fob had paid as little attention to public relations in building Diver-sified Products as he did to public relations as governor, he wouldn't have been the success he was," Bryan said.

"You can't get anything done standing out on the capitol steps telling folks what a great education program old Fob came up with or what great legislation old Fob's got," James said. "You have to pick up that list of schools every day and say to yourself every morning, 'Greene County,' then you have to live with Greene County and the other counties you're trying to improve day in and day out."

While James wallowed among stacks of figures, Hubbert busied himself "working the Legislature," confident among a group in which about half owed him at least a thank you for donating money and volunteer workers to their campaigns.

After being told by every veteran on Goat Hill there was no conceivable possibility legislators would appropriate $80 million for the War on Illiteracy, Lager said, "We went back to the drawing board and worked with legislators and came away with a request we thought we could get."

In his first State of the State address, James announced his intention to serve actively as chairman of the State Board of Education.

He also asked that $20 million of a projected $30 million surplus be used to fund his War on Illiteracy, but said, "...dollars won't win the war without mass commitment from parents who will support their children, teachers and principals."

James said he wanted to ensure quality in the state's junior colleges and universities. "But it all starts in grammar school, and all too often for too many children in reality it ends there."

A comparison of James' scaled-down request with his original "war" plan reveals that it was essentially the same minus two big chunks. One of these was the $43 million for teacher pay raises, which James said was not in the War on Illiteracy request because its proper place in the budget was as a line item. The second item not in his revised request was $16 million for reducing the pupil/teacher ratio. Aware that the anticipated surplus was only $30 million, James temporarily postponed his plan to reduce the pupil/teacher ratio.

Other figures were scaled down: The request for funds for emergency construction was lowered from $2.25 million to $1 million; the amount requested for teachers' liability insurance was firmed up at $135,000 instead of the initial estimate of $250,000.

James' $20 million War on Illiteracy retained the heart of his program, however—$13 million for the 96 teacher-specialists who would be divided in teams and spread across the state to help the lowest-scoring school systems improve students' basic skills. It also included funding for 20 more kindergarten classes than he originally thought could be provided—$5.8 million for 320 kindergarten classes.

James emerged from the first legislative session with only half of the $20 million he had requested—the other half was to be held as a reserve. It wasn't what he wanted. But he would make it do.

Meanwhile, he was learning the political realities of having to depend on a man to carry out his orders who did not regard him as boss.

James thought it a simple matter when he issued an executive order to Superintendent of Education Teague to begin the student testing which was needed and to develop a standard disclosure form for each system in the state. Data provided on the form would enable James to compare how money was spent by systems with high-scoring students to systems which had low-scoring students.

Once those two tasks were accomplished, James told Teague, he wanted him to get out of Montgomery, to spend his time in the lowest-scoring 20 percent of school systems in the state.

James told Teague to sit down with the local board members and the superintendents in the districts of those low-scoring schools, to have heart-to-heart talks with them. Teague would have to be firm, James told him. He would have to say, "Okay, you have some problems which must be worked out. Here are the changes you need to make. We'll test each year for the next three years to see if you've turned things around. If you can't turn it around, we're going to have to make some changes at the top."

However, "Getting Teague to do anything was like pulling hen teeth," James said. "He would sit there for hours, agreeing with what I wanted done. Then he'd leave and I wouldn't hear anything else about it. When I'd call him in to ask why there was no progress, he'd hem and haw and it took me three years to figure out he never was going to do anything."

"Fob entered into the project thinking Teague was the kind of guy you could work with," Bryan said. "What can I say? Wayne Teague is a politician. He has done what it takes to get himself appointed again and again."

James' problem in getting Teague to carry out his instructions was a fundamental one, inherent in the system, a fault not so much of Teague as the structure of the bureaucracy.

James felt it was his duty, and his right, as governor to put into effect the changes he had promised the electorate.

Teague simply did not recognize his power as governor to do so.

A survivor of political wars of past administrations, Teague explains that he does not work for the governor. He works for the State

Board of Education of which the governor by law is president. The governor wields more power as president of the board than the other members, each of whom are elected from a congressional district, only because of the vast resources he commands as governor. Under the provisions of state law, the governor posses no greater power than any other board member. He has, as do other board members, only one vote.

"I work with the governor," Teague said, "but when the governor and the board go different ways, you'll find me with the board. The day I'm not, I'll hand in my resignation."

Teague admits he is in a "precarious" position, constantly thrust between the governor and the board.

"I work behind the scenes trying to get the governor and the board together many times," he said.

"I don't remember any problem we had with testing, once Fob got the funding through the Legislature," Teague said. "He wanted every student tested every year. We pointed out to him it was not necessary to test every year because we were testing the same grades every year."

An educator who knew Teague long before the James administration explained why James found it difficult to work with the superintendent:

> Teague's biggest weakness is that he wants to please, to be liked. He surrounds himself with people who constantly assure him that he is making the right decisions, people who know better than to tell him the governor is angry with him or the legislators are upset with him. Teague should never go into a meeting one-on-one, the way he did with James. When he does, he will agree to something quickly, without thinking of the personal or political ramifications. Then, when he has time to reflect, from time to time he will change his previous position without going back to the person he told he would do otherwise, without telling him, "I made a mistake. I can't do it."

A friend of Teague describes him as "an enormously private person whose family are his only true confidants. His wife is a fabulous lady who is tremendously supportive of Wayne. Wayne is not one for small talk or gossip. Any gossip you hear which quotes Wayne on a sensitive political issue is, I assure you, speculation. Wayne doesn't engage in idle talk."

If the word "Fob" was substituted for the word "Wayne" in the above paragraph, the description would remain an accurate one. It is possible to visualize the two men meeting, talking, each thinking the other understood his position, both being wrong. Teague sought a private meeting with James when it was known a new president would have to be named for Auburn University. He asked James if he had decided on a candidate to push for the position. James told Teague, truthfully, that he did not.

Later, when some reporters wrote that James supported Highway Director Rex Rainer for the job, Teague during the long, drawn-out process of choosing a president decided that James had double-crossed him.

James did not support Rainer for the presidency, but he did not dispute such written reports. As he did in so many incidents in which his position was erroneously reported by "sources close to the governor," James ignored the controversy. He says he did not, as reported, secretly arm-twist any of the Auburn Board of Trustees for a particular candidate. He made his pronouncements public, cast his lone vote, and left the news media to scurry around looking for secondary sources to quote on what he had or had not done behind the scenes.

The episode was one in a series of miscommunications which eventually erected a firm barrier between James and Teague, who were poles apart philosophically anyway.

Teague, a one-time Auburn city superintendent of schools, was appointed state superintendent by Wallace at the united behest of the superintendents of local systems all over the state. At that time president of the superintendents' state association, Teague had gained prominence when he debated Hubbert statewide on the issue of collective bargaining.

"Teague owed his job to the superintendents and he never forgot it," a longtime observer said. "He was always sensitive to what the superintendents wanted, and their desires rated higher than those of the governor."

The observer occupies a top spot in education. He was not a James supporter and had no contact with James during his administration. The observer does not want to be named because his fellow educators will resent the assessment he makes of his chosen field:

> For years, the solution for education problems in this state was to throw money at them. Higher education was overbuilt. The junior college system was a joke. Education was routine-ized, to its great, great detriment. That means there was a routine for

everything and the education community said, 'Don't change anything.' They never realized, or they didn't care, that the operation of too much of education was based not on students' needs, but on the convenience of the administrators. Then Fob James came along, an accident. He was a revolutionary. "Change things," he said. And it scared the hell out of every educator in the state.

When the rumors became rampant that James wanted to fire Teague, it created anxiety, Teague's friend said. "As a result of that threat, he rallied to the board. He had to find security somewhere, and he found it in the board."

Or—to be more specific—in Board Vice President Martin, who listened attentively when Hubbert spoke.

The echelon of bureaucracy just beneath Teague, dependent upon him for their jobs, reacted to the rumors by rallying to Teague's defense and fighting James' programs, according to one of them. "The word among the top group was, 'We've got to save Wayne's job,' " he said.

Did these undercurrents affect James' education program?

"Certainly, there was not a popular willingness to cooperate on the part of the people who made up the hierarchy of the Education Department," the educator said.

In 1979, Teague wrote in the report, "Instructional services were further reduced due to further cuts in appropriations."

He stated, "Personnel cuts in the Division of Instruction caused major changes in...implementation; among services cut were workshops and test analysis. Staff was reduced; specialists in other sections had to be utilized on a very limited basis; essential tasks had to be delayed or eliminated."

Hubbert says James used the wrong approach to getting his objectives carried out, that he could should have courted state board members so that they would instruct Teague to carry out his wishes. This was the way George Wallace did it, Hubbert says.

John Tyson Jr., as vice president of the State Board of Education, has presided over most meetings of the board since James left office. Tyson strongly differs with Hubbert's assessment: "As a new board member in 1981, I found that Gov. James went to extraordinary lengths to communicate with the board. He even had us picked up in the state plane on the days before the meetings and put us up at the Governor's Mansion the night before."

Not only did James put board members up at the mansion—he

invited their families. One of Tyson's most cherished mementoes is a picture of daughter Elizabeth on the stairs at the mansion. James also thought of board members when making appointments to education posts; he named Tyson to the State Tenure Commission.

Tyson said late night brain-storming at the mansion, when board members chatted casually, head to head, later culminated in board action.

"That's the way it came about that the board decided to take the results of the teacher certification tests and go back to the colleges of education with the ones showing poor performance and make the changes that were needed," Tyson said. "It was the logical follow-up to Gov. James' program isolating the high schools with low-scoring students.

"Jim Allen Jr. was also new on the board and our fathers had been good friends. We had a lot to talk about. Fob was in and out of the room. At some point in time, we started talking about what could be done to improve the scores of the new teachers."

Tyson said the board made changes in the programs of every college of education in the state despite a lengthy (and unsuccessful) court challenge of their right to do so by Hubbert's assistant, Dr. Joe Reed.

Reed had also challenged the certification tests which the board approved on Tyson's resolution. Graduates of colleges of education were required to pass the tests before being certified to teach in the state.

"Dr. Martin, who was vice president of the board, settled that case with Reed in a Birmingham motel room without knowledge of the board," Tyson said. Anger toward Martin by board members because of the action paved the way for Tyson to unseat Martin as board vice president.

If James did not fail to communicate with the Board, why did Hubbert say he did?

"Before Fob took office, Martin ran the State Board of Education," Tyson said.

What was the relationship between Martin and Hubbert?

"He jumped everytime Paul said 'boo,'" Tyson said.

Thus when James asserted his leadership of the State Board of Education as its president, he not only robbed Martin of clout—he antagonized Hubbert. James did not jump when Hubbert said boo. He fought for his programs. He got what he wanted bit by bit, taking two steps forward and one step back, learning each time how to avoid the mistakes he had made during the process, getting a little more the next time he tried.

Each step of the way, frustration was intermingled with success.

"I even got down and brawled about what classes should be taught," James said. "I laugh about it now, but I seriously thought about drafting a piece of legislation requiring schools to teach phonics."

Tyson said he presided the majority of the time during Gov. Guy Hunt's first three years because Hunt missed more meetings of the board than he attended.

Tyson says there is no similarity between the manner in which James worked with the board and the manner in which Hunt has worked with the board.

To illustrate, he tells a story:

In 1987, the Birmingham *News* revealed that Charles Payne, the man serving in the position created by James as chancellor of the state's two-year colleges, had faked key elements of the resume he had submitted to the board when interviewing for the job. The fabrications included listing himself as holding a doctorate when he did not, and describing himself as a Vietnam veteran when he never set foot in Vietnam.

Of the nine members of the board, only Tyson and Isabel Thomasson of Montgomery called for Payne to resign after his deception was revealed.

"The first thing I did was to go to Gov. Hunt's office and talk to him about it," Tyson said. "Here you had in Payne a man who was the role-model for students in 42 schools and colleges. They know they would get kicked out of school if it was learned they got in by faking a transcript. What were they supposed to think if we turned our heads the other way when we learned the chancellor cheated? Gov. Hunt and I agreed in that meeting that the single most important thing we could do to maintain credibility was to get rid of Charles Payne."

Tyson thought he had the five votes needed to fire Payne when the board met behind closed doors to discuss the issue.

"I soon found out that there were two cases of amnesia and one double-cross," Tyson said. Hunt was the double-cross.

"He waffled," Tyson said. "Far from calling for Payne to be fired, he said nice things about the man."

Tyson said Hunt was "telling me he would do one thing in private and doing another and leaving me out front to take the heat."

Tyson did not know why Hunt waffled. He learned that pro-Payne sentiment was being orchestrated from the offices of the Alabama Education Association, where Payne's responses to news media were said to be originating.

After weeks of stalls from Hunt and opposition from AEA forces, Tyson resorted to chartering a small plane for a one-day marathon of press conferences which smacked of the tactics of former Gov. James. He called on citizens to let their school board members know how they felt about allowing this "doctor who isn't a doctor, this Vietnam veteran who isn't a Vietnam veteran" continue to serve as role-model for their children.

The public brought such pressure to bear on Hunt and the board that Payne was forced to resign. He did not leave Montgomery empty-handed, however. A cushy $40,000-a-year-plus job was created for Payne as head of the Alabama Fire College in Tuscaloosa and guests who turned out to wish him well at his going-away party included Gov. Hunt.

"Gov. Hunt did chime in publicly to help me before the fight was over," Tyson said. "But only after another board member leaned over to him at a meeting and whispered, 'This is all going to be over with in a matter of days. He's going to resign.'

> I compare this to how Gov. James handled the situation when one of the two-year presidents was indicted in connection with discrepancies in the college bookwork. We had the books. We knew how bad it was, but there was a push coming from somewhere to keep him on the job. I was new and I didn't know where it was coming from. Gov. James called a meeting of the State Board to fire him. I'll never forget him telling the board, "Now, I've got all night and it's okay with me if we stay all night. But we're not leaving until we do the right thing."

It took quite a few hours to convince board members he meant what he said, Tyson said, but before they adjourned they fired the president.

> That's the difference between Gov. James and Gov. Hunt in working with the board. Gov. James circled the wagons. He didn't give up. Gov. Hunt came to the meetings a lot when he was first elected, but after the first six months he either gave up or lost interest. We don't see much of him on the board. Gov. James, now, he was there every time you turned around. Board members didn't

do everything he asked, but they respected him as a genuine, real person.

Hunt, on the other hand, has only asked the State Board of Education for one thing during his entire term of office, Tyson said in September of 1989.

"The only thing he has asked us to do is to ban hazardous chemicals in chemistry classes," Tyson said.

James has been criticized by his opponents at one time or another as being arrogant, headstrong, a stubborn man who does not listen enough to the opinions of others. All of these are subjective criticisms, true or false in the eyes of the beholder.

Yet even James' most severe critics concede that education was more than a campaign issue to him, that it was the guiding light which he followed steadily, never losing sight of, never wavering in commitment. Those who disagreed with him vocally, adamantly, violently, sometimes victoriously, on his approach to solving Alabama's education problems in retrospect voice no doubt as to his sincerity.

Referring to James' inaugural address, in which he said, "Our children cannot seek their own destinies without literacy. We must have literacy and by the Grace of God, we shall have literacy," Harvey wrote, "This theme was to dominate his four years as governor and came as no surprise to anyone."

James said the answer to solving the problem of illiteracy should be a simple one for a governor:

> Assume the responsibility and use the authority currently given you by law. It's there. You don't need to wait on reports of blue ribbon committees or wait for legislation to be passed. You have the authority if you will seize it.
>
> Isolate the problem schools. We very easily can determine the status of a school, we have the data available to do that. At that point, get with the superintendent of education and tell him to go meet with those folks and fix it.
>
> What do you mean, fix it? I mean, look at management, priorities of the local board, teacher-pupil ratios, discipline, and other elements that determine academic performance. If you have a 300-student grammar school, we've been in the business long enough to know you need a principal, an assistant and a certain number of teachers. There ought to be a standard on how many teachers we need. If there isn't, something is awfully wrong.
>
> If you find such a school with a large number of non-instruc-

tional employees and a 40-to-1 teacher ratio in the first grade when you should have a 20-to-1 ratio, you don't have a money problem. You have a bureaucratic problem, a political problem, a mismanagement problem in many cases.

James compiled the results from the first statewide student testing in chart form.

That chart became his "Bible."

Regardless of his other duties as governor, James' thoughts constantly returned to the schools in Alabama which were not giving their students the basic education needed to survive economically in the 21st century.

Alabama's illiteracy was pinpointed on that chart, a blatant reproof that money alone was not the answer. The chart proved that in many cases there was no correlation between the amount of money spent and how well a school system educated its students.

There was, however, an obvious correlation between pupil performance and the demographic make-up of the county. There was a further correlation between pupil performance and the ability of the system's management.

Students in mainly rural counties with a high poverty level scored far worse on pupil performance than students in urban areas comprised mainly of middle-income families.

Why? Because many of the schools in those counties traditionally were black schools which were always funded at a lower level than white schools. The inequities of a dual system of education cannot be erased overnight.

James studied the figures:

In expenditure per student, Arab city schools spent less per student than 119 of the 129 systems, $1,147.52 per student. But in performance, the Arab system ranked 5th highest in the state.

Enterprise city schools spent less per student than 104 systems in the state—$1,118.52—yet scored 17th highest in pupil performance.

Two school systems which were outspent by nearly every system in the state—Carbon Hill city schools, 125th in expenditure, and Roanoke city schools, 126th—placed almost exactly in the middle of the chart on pupil performance. In 1979–80, Carbon Hill students placed 64th on performance, Roanoke students placed 54th.

The Greene County school system, spending $1,819.52 per student, was outranked in spending by only one other system in the state. Yet Greene County students placed 120th in terms of performance in

1979–80.

Perry County schools, number three in expenditure per student, placed 117th in pupil performance.

Anniston city schools, outspent by only five school systems in the state, ranked 98th on pupil performance.

Nine of the 20 school systems which spent the most were among the 27 worst systems in the state in terms of pupil scores.

James was frankly puzzled. "I sat there and said to myself, 'what's going on?' "

> Don't ever let anybody tell you the social and economic background of a child doesn't have a direct bearing on how he does in school unless his teacher compensates for the difference. If you put a kid in kindergarten or first grade and there hasn't been a book in that kid's house, and he sits next to a kid who has grown up with parents who read books and who read to him, you don't have an even situation to start with.
>
> Look at all the school systems in the state. That's what I spent most of my time doing. I would sit with that chart in front of me, thinking. Now, here is a school that simply is not performing. Most of our illiteracy is in 20 to 25 percent of our school systems. There is not much illiteracy in Mountain Brook or Enterprise. The Mobile school system is about halfway down. But you go to Greene County, that's where it swells up, at the bottom, I thought that bottom was like an anchor on this state. You're putting our kids literally out in the world ignorant...some of them can't count money. It's that basic. They go into a store and pay for their purchase with a ten-dollar bill and they don't know if they're getting the right change back.
>
> I'd come in to my office in the morning and play with the numbers on that chart. I'd say, "Homewood city. Their expenditure per student enrolled was $1,851.52. They are number one in the state on dollars spent per student. How did their students do in the testing?"

And so on, with every system in the state.

The course to follow was clear to James.

"Once we established which schools were the problem schools, it should have been a simple matter for Teague to go to those systems, meet with those boards and say 'Okay, we have a problem and we have to work it out. We'll continue testing for three years and if you can't turn it around in that time, I'll make the necessary changes in management," James said.

"It's that simple," he said. "I came to the conclusion that where you had a good principal you had a good school."

In his 1980 State of the State address, James had the statistics he needed to move ahead with his War on Illiteracy.

"The results of the California Achievement Test given to all Alabama school children in the spring of 1979 show that approximately 205,000 of the nearly 725,000 children in our public schools rank one year or more below grade level in the basic skills," he said.

"The reasons for this are two-fold, poor management and lack of parental involvement and support—financial and otherwise," James said. "Other deficiencies, such as discipline, teacher-pupil ratio, teacher performance, etc. result from a failure in these two areas."

He asked the Legislature for $3 million to fund a "principal program" to provide incentives to induce administrators to meet high standards, and requested a scaled-down $2 million for his War on Illiteracy.

He also called for a major reduction in money for the Department of Education. With proration again a distinct possibility as the economy continued its downward plunge into recession, James singled out two areas in which costs could be cut. He asked legislators to make driver's education optional and to eliminate funding to some lunch room programs in which parents were able to pay for the lunches and therefore could be self-supporting.

To hedge against proration, his budget left a $23.5 million reserve in the Special Education Trust Fund.

In 1980, Teague's report noted that James' Basic Skills Teams, cut to four from the 13 James originally envisioned, went to work helping teachers and administrators in the lowest-scoring schools. In many cases, Teague wrote, the first step in some of the schools had to be basic renovation.

Also in 1980, remedial workshops were conducted and training was provided to those who administered James' testing program, Teague wrote.

"In both cases," Teague stated, "improved morale and dedication to teaching and learning were observed."

In 1981, the state and the nation slumped into what economists predicted was the deepest curve of the economic recession.

James slashed funding requests for state government across the board. He cut his request for War on Illiteracy funding from $8.6 million to $2 million.

"Three Basic Skills Teams were eliminated due to cuts in appropriations," Teague wrote. "The one which remained concentrated its work in West Alabama."

The team went to work in the district of state board member Victor Poole of Moundville.

"Fob used my district to try out his ideas for several reasons," Poole said. "It contained counties which had scored the lowest on the statewide tests. And I was quite willing to go along because I thought it was good politics."

Grinning, Poole quips, "Also, I was the only one on the board who had too little sense to realize it could be a political liability."

Why a liability? "Because the word got out that we would have to publicize low scores and board members thought people in the districts with low scores would be incensed," said Poole, elected by the people of that district. "But they weren't. It had the opposite effect."

There was resentment, Poole said. But it came from school boards and superintendents, not from parents.

"When we went into the low-scoring schools, we [Poole and the special team] approached with the angle of always finding something to brag about. We tried to keep the negative publicity from getting out."

Poole said superintendents were resentful of James because, "nobody had ever paid any attention to their schools before, nobody before had really called on them, interfered, told them how they had to run things, especially in the Black Belt.

"One of the biggest problems was the lack of attendance by students and the lack of concern shown by educators toward improving that attendance," Poole said.

In Alabama, schools receive state money only for the days students attend. Poole said many school systems for that reason have encouraged teachers not to report absences.

"For years the saying was, 'Don't take that pencil and mark yourself out of a job,' or 'Don't call the roll till everyone gets there,' " Poole said. "Suddenly there was this guy from Montgomery looking over their shoulder. They had to keep accurate records.

"Sure, there was resentment at first," he said. "Once they found out the team wasn't trying to get their jobs, or run anybody off, the resentment faded somewhat."

Parents, though not resentful, were at first suspicious. They had no faith that the skills teams would be able to better their children's education.

"One time we were in Perry County, another low-scoring school system. We had made the first presentation [to parents] and I had got on them good about poor attendance for not making their children go to school," said Poole, a crusty-talking banker known for his mince-no-words style.

"The superintendent got up to speak, but before he could, a parent in the back, a big, big man, started getting up to speak. He was so big it seemed like he got up and got up and got up. He finally said, 'All y'all doing in Perry County is greetin' and eatin'.'"

Sumter County had the worst scores in the state.

Poole said he called meetings of teachers and principals and parents in Sumter County and told them, "not in a very nice way, that I wasn't going to have any system in my district on the bottom of the scale."

That, and similar, meetings accomplished the purpose of "putting people on notice, the principals, the teachers, the parents...," Poole said.

When students were tested after a year of help from the skills teams, educators were jubilant. Poole was excited. James was ecstatic. Teague was enthusiastic. The test results, compared with the test results from the year before, proved that James' special skills teams concept worked.

"An analysis of test scores indicated statistically significant gains in achievement in ten of the twelve schools," Teague wrote in his four-year-end report to James. "The remaining two showed gains but they were not statistically significant."

It was a start. But it was important. No one could scoff or doubt. James and Poole had the statistics to prove it.

Continuing the program as James envisioned it, concentrating on the lowest-scoring schools in the state and yearly updating the list, would ultimately create an Alabama school system second to none in the nation.

Poole is frankly perplexed as to why so little was written on what he calls the "fantastic results" of James' model schools program.

"There wasn't anything written except in the Tuscaloosa *News* about what we were trying to do or what we did. And the Selma *Times-Journal* had a few articles," he said.

The Anniston *Star* was another paper which wrote on the subject.

In an article on education in December of 1981, the *Star* wrote:

"While James did push achievement tests, he did not initiate teacher competency tests, administered for the first time this year.

"But James was 'instrumental,' Teague says, in extending the testing to teachers who move up in rank (from a bachelor's to master's degree, for example) or change area of specialization."

The *Star* talked about the pilot schools with Bill Berryman, director of the Education Department's Division of Instrumental Services.

The *Star* reported that test scores in 10 of the 12 "so-called" pilot schools improved "significantly." In the other two schools, the scores "went up slightly."

The *Star* wrote:

> James also secured federal funds for 10 other low-scoring schools, including Constantine Elementary in Anniston and Jonesview Elementary in Talladega. Test scores improved significantly at all 10 schools, Berryman says.
>
> Constantine received $100,000 in the first two years, says Anniston School Superintendent J. V. Sailors. The money has been used to hire two teachers to work with individual students and small groups and a parent-community coordinator to work with parents in reducing unexcused absences.
>
> The War's most ambitious initiative was sending "basic skills teams" to work with teachers. Four teams were assigned to separate areas of the state. The six-to-eight member teams consisted of elementary school teachers with "particular strengths" in math, reading, language arts or administration, Berryman says.

The *Star* also interviewed Annette Cox, Title I coordinator of Anniston city schools, who said after funds were cut for the program only one team was left. That team worked with the seven systems in the Tuscaloosa area.

Ms. Cox described the work of the North Alabama team while it was in existence. She said they "visited 55 school systems and advised teachers how to use those scores to 'build on the students' strengths.'"

Poole calls it "one of the great mysteries of politics" that Alabama teachers are not only unaware of the things James did for education and for teachers' salaries, but actually have animosity toward him.

"Teachers never had a better friend than Fob James," Poole said. "They made more progress in salary raises than under any other governor.

"He has always been his own worst enemy," Poole said. "He should have been talking about what he was doing for teachers and education while he was doing it."

James has done a lot of thinking about the events which occurred from 1979–1983.

He has modified his thinking on some stances, refined it on others, remaining adamant on the thrust of his education beliefs.

James took office believing education needed strong direction from the state level on policy. "I came away thinking that only in school districts which are academically bankrupt should changes be made from the top, and those changes should be administrative ones," he said. "If you don't, you leave thousands of youngsters to the fate of becoming functional illiterates. Fundamentally, though, education is not a federal issue and not a state issue; it is a local issue, although we fund 80 per cent of it from state."

He remains insistent that the efforts of the State Department of Education, the State Board, the governor and the superintendent of education should be totally directed toward problem schools.

"When there is a proven lack of performance, you need a tough state superintendent who will step in—it is that simple," James said.

> You look at some of the schools, the good ones, they should never hear from the state department of education operationally. There are dozens of school systems that the state superintendent and the governor shouldn't even pick up the phone to call, except to say thank-you for a job well done. Those are the ones with strong local school boards, strong citizens on the school board, a good capable superintendent, they're doing their job. Our efforts should be directed toward those systems which haven't made progress in a long time, which are drowning in illiteracy, ignorance, and squalor.
>
> It's not easy. It's not a lot of fun teaching some of those classes. When I was governor, I went to Birmingham and taught for four days in the third grade in a poor section of town. Sarah Swindle, a Birmingham teacher who was president of AEA that year, invited me. I went because I wanted people to talk about education. They had a good teacher who explained the lesson plans to me and I took them and went over them and we had some kids who were two or three years older than they should have been. Some were very poor. Some came from homes not in the best of circumstances. Some didn't have breakfast and were hungry. Some were dirty. I had two or three little boys who were mischievous as hell. I cuffed them once or twice and hugged them. There was one girl three or four years older than the others, overweight, must have weighed 200 pounds, and one little boy went up behind her

and pinched her or something. I remember that child, she swung at that boy, and I couldn't believe the language that came out of her mouth (and I've heard it all) but this was a 10-minute fight right in the middle of class that you had to jump in and grab one and grab the other.

I'll never forget a tiny little girl. I talked to her once or twice. The next day I complimented her on her home work. The third day, I said something about her good homework and she ran put her arms around my neck and her legs around my waist. If you've ever seen a child starved for affection, she was. It broke your heart.

The teacher had three groups, three round tables, three different lesson plans. I had to figure out how I could teach three different lesson plans at the same time. Some were far behind. Some of those kids just couldn't read. They'd sit there in third grade and know no more what you were talking about than a jaybird. Some were 12 years old. They were children...they loved recess, they loved to play.

The invitation from Mrs. Swindle to James to walk a mile in teachers' shoes was printed in the *AEA Journal* on July 15, 1980.

"Governor, You're Invited," the headline read. It invited James to leave the governor's office for a few days to become a "real" classroom teacher, to "do lessons, plans, grade papers, bus duty, hall duty," etc.

"We know you care about schools and children. You campaigned in a school bus and you talked about schools," the invitation read.

It suggested that James take the lead and hoped that other officials, from members of the State Board of Education to legislators to newspaper editors and publishers, would follow his lead.

"The issue of education seemed to have slipped from the minds of the public," James said, explaining his motives for accepting the invitation. "I was looking for a vehicle to get it back in the forefront, to get people talking about schools and school students and I thought this would be the way to do it."

Mrs. Swindle said she chose the school knowing it was one which would give James a good taste of what teachers go through each day. It was old. It was being renovated, so the sound of construction interfered with classes. Its students came from a variety of backgrounds.

"They sized him up right away as someone who loved to play," she said. "When they went out to play, the children told him they were hungry and he took them to lunch early. The principal had to reprimand him."

Several months later, Mrs. Swindle said, James invited the class to his office for a reunion, gave them a tour and fed them "Happy Meals" from McDonald's. They would be seniors in 1990.

James said he spent a lot of time after his experience as a teacher thinking about what role the governor should play, what role the state should play.

> How deep a responsibility does the state have in educating your child, I wondered, what responsibility rests on the shoulders of the governor, the state school board, the state superintendent, the principal, and finally, the one on the firing line, the teacher, to educate your child, to a large extent today raise your child? Where does the state get their responsibility? We have chipped away at parental responsibility by kindergarten, which is necessary and good. But how much can you ask of a teacher?

The job of principal is the key link in the education chain, James said. He or she is the one "to make the daily on-line decisions that impact every aspect of a school."

"There are thousands of men and women who do good jobs as principals, as teachers, evidenced by the record, and you can't attack the system as a whole because the majority of the whole is good," James says.

"To be harsh about it, we've put hundreds of millions of dollars more into education and there is no one who will say, show me in tangible terms where we stand in each school system," James says. "I'm not attacking individuals, I'm pointing out the need to have someone in authority who will assume the responsibility to change situations which need changing."

Poole, when he was interviewed, had on the dashboard in his car the latest testing results from the 144 schools in his district.

"I've just been to the PTAs in the two schools that scored highest and presented them with $100 awards," Poole said. "Next I'm going to visit the school with the most improved score and do the same thing."

He planned a fourth visit which would not be so pleasant, to a school which had dropped incredibly in the rating.

"I'm going to check first and make sure there's not a mistake in the tallying," Poole said. "If there's no mistake, I'm going to give them hell."

The monetary awards are an offshoot of a plan James came up with just prior to leaving office, Poole said. He wanted to offer mon-

etary incentives to schools on a statewide basis to improve their test
scores above and beyond the score shown as "possible" by the aptitude
test.

James figured out how it could be done with a one-time $5 million
investment, Poole said.

A resolution to do so was passed by the board, but time ran out
and James left office, Poole said.

When James ran for governor in 1986, Poole presented him with
a framed chart comparing the test scores of students in three counties
of his district before James' model schools program was initiated and
after James' term in office.

The scores reflected the improvement brought about because of
James, he said.

"Fob will have my everlasting gratitude not only because he backed his plan with funds, but because he encouraged me and Teague to
get started," Poole said. "As I say, the politics were unknown, so it
took political courage to do it. We made excellent progress.

> Today, we are not only able to look at and compare all the
> systems, but schools within those systems, classrooms within those
> schools and kids in the classroom.
>
> When we first started out, we were lumping all 127 systems
> together in comparing test scores. Mountain Brook always came
> out on top. We are now giving them an aptitude test so we can
> look in one column and see what they did and look in the other
> column and compare it with what they're capable of doing. We can
> correlate the test to within five percent of the ability or achieve-
> ment of the student.

"We've come a long way, but Fob James was the trailblazer," Poole
said.

Hubbert was the undisputed chief major foe of James from 1979–
1983. Yet he said in a 1988 interview:

> Fob was ahead of his time in that he stressed the need for
> literacy before national reports, before at-risk studies were done
> on drop-outs, before major attention was focused on adult illit-
> eracy.
>
> Fob had an issue in which he strongly believed, an issue he
> articulated strongly, from the standpoint of seizing on the fun-
> damental need for literacy.

James and Hubbert found there were a number of issues they

could work together on.

Pay raises, of course, was number one.

Bryan said, "We found a number of issues we could go with Hubbert. The beauty of Fob was that he waded into those situations without hidden agendas."

As the administration settled in, Bryan said he believes Hubbert formed a "healthy respect" for James.

"I don't think he ever viewed Fob as an enemy. There was never any hostility between them. I think Paul got to respect Fob for his honesty and how he tried to act in government," Bryan said. "I think there grew a great appreciation for Fob in that when Paul wanted to come sit down and talk about what he thought was good, and make a proposal, the door was always open, he had access.

"Fob didn't always agree but there were moments when he did," Bryan said. "Fob knew only too well the problems faced by teachers. His mother had been a teacher and his father had been a teacher and a football coach. My mother had been a teacher."

It was a two-way street of appreciation. James said he was unaware as governor that teachers are often the victims of education politics.

"I've discussed this with Paul, and he says on many occasions teachers are treated unfairly due to nepotism and weak management. I investigated this enough to find there is a substantial amount of truth to it."

Poole, first appointed by then-Gov. George Wallace to the State School Board then elected to four consecutive terms, was in 1990 the veteran board member.

"Fob was as effective as any of the other five governors I've worked under," said Poole. "He has hidden his light under a bushel as far as I'm concerned. He was a much better education governor than given credit for. The things he pushed us to do ten years ago are what the education world is pushing now.

"It was Fob's idea that the board should assess the local system as to the instruction students were getting. Before that, emphasis had always been on teacher certification and finances. About the time he came along the use of the computer became prevalent, a sign of the times. It was Fob's idea to use the computer to assess scholastic scores."

James had to take on the entire education establishment to do so, Poole said. "Educators say you can't measure scholastic achievement with test scores, because you need to assess more than test scores. I kind of agree but scores are the only way lay people can assess. We can look at them and make up our own mind."

Today, James zeroes in on the need for strong principals and superintendents as the key to having an education system second to none.

"The key to those schools that do well is the principal and the superintendent. That became very obvious while I was governor," he said. "I realized that, where you had an individual who knew his or her business, they wouldn't tolerate a bad teacher, or the misuse of funds to hire Tom, Dick and Harry instead of the good teacher they needed for the second grade. When you went to those schools and walked through the halls, you could see it, feel it, you knew whether or not there was a good administrator. Getting rid of non-performing principals and superintendents and replacing them with winners is the key."

Teague said James was the best governor education ever had.

What were James' strong points? "He believed in the involvement of all of the education community," Teague said. "I met with the governor for many hours, at his office in the capitol and at his office in the mansion. He believed in a good, solid, basic education and in good discipline; that says a lot."

What were James' weaknesses? "He had blinders on concerning how long it takes to get things done, which is not uncommon for people who don't know what the education world is all about. He thought changes could be made overnight," Teague said. "If you make major changes, you should start in the early grades, or in the 9th grade in high school. Then you have to wait to see the effects."

Teague said James was "headstrong," following the comment with "Make sure you understand that I consider him a personal friend. We had our differences, which is not unusual in this situation, but I have respect for him. He was impatient to the point that it influenced his politics. Politics is by definition the art of compromise and Fob refused to compromise."

James, in Teague's estimation, was "a little disenchanted with politics because he couldn't change things overnight. I think if he had won in 1986 you would have seen an effective governor, someone who has learned you have to work with people to get things done, not run over them as though you're carrying a football."

"Fob's view of government was that he was the Chief Executive Officer, that he would issue an order and it would get carried out,"

Hubbert said. "He spent a lot of time running at a structure he wanted to change rather than using his office as a pulpit to strengthen education."

Hubbert said James should have worked more with board members, informing them about what he wanted to accomplish in a program prior to the time he brought it up at a board meeting.

When James brought something up "out of the blue," Hubbert said board members many times felt threatened, feeling that his actions were directed toward them. Hubbert said if James had explained what he wanted done prior to the board meetings, he would have had board members with him.

Teague has nothing but praise for the model schools concept.

"We strongly supported the model school concept, in which we sent teams in to help at the local level," Teague said. "We used test results to pinpoint weaknesses. Then we sent experts in to help correct the weaknesses. We helped design the program and we are proud of it. We can show you great things the program accomplished. In every school in which we had a team working we can show you test results which rose."

The program was not continued as James intended it to be run after he left office because no funding was provided for it in future budgets, Teague said.

"If we had instructional teams in 25 schools now," Teague begins, then stops and smiles, "you wouldn't believe the improvements we could make."

Some of James' programs are still being carried out, but not in the manner in which James originated them, Poole said.

The testing James initiated is still being done, but not as he did it. When Gov. Hunt cut the money for testing from the Education Budget in 1989, the State Board of Education united against him to keep the money intact. The board voted to hold hostage (until they got testing funds) the nearly $8 million in "pork barrel" money which had been given to the board with instructions to spend it on the pet projects of various legislators.

"We knew we didn't have a legal ground to stand on," said Tyson, an attorney, "but we raised enough of a ruckus before we let the pork go that we got our testing money."

"The model school program, now, we're doing that now," Poole said. "There are some differences, however.

"Fob gave me a team of people stationed in my district, in Tuscaloosa. The special skills team concept is still there in the Department of Education, but Teague has centralized it in Montgomery," Poole said. "We still assess schools and still send teams. But nobody's concentrating on it."

Nobody.

The test results are calculated on a chart, but there is no anxious middle-aged man with shirt sleeves rolled up taking surreptitious puffs on a cigar waiting impatiently to grab that chart, put it on his desk and make it his "Bible."

Nobody requires school systems in Alabama to fill out disclosure forms revealing how they spend their money. But it really does not matter.

Nobody sits in Montgomery night after night, poring over those figures in the lamplight until the wee morning hours, waking aides excitedly at 2 a.m. to announce he has isolated a key factor between good schools and bad schools.

There is nobody to take that chart to the people, to fly from city to city, laughing at critics, daring politicians and hangers-on to challenge his figures, a rabble-rouser hawking education as effectively as a New Orleans pitchman extols the delights of a Bourbon Street stripper.

There is nobody to throw open the board rooms of the bureaucracy and the back rooms of the Legislature so that the howls of the people can pervade and prevail, and in doing so guide one school at a time, starting at the bottom with the worst, from the darkened corridors of ignorance into the bright light of literacy.

# Assessment

What kind of a governor was Fob James?

As I write this, I know it is a simple question with a simple answer. Two years ago, there appeared to be nothing simple about either.

What is a governor supposed to do? There are few requirements, really. No definitive list of duties and responsibilities for the job exists; each person who takes the office of governor writes the definition for his term. The majority of voters obviously felt that a governor who did what Fob James said he would do in his campaign would be a good governor. If not, they would not have elected him. All I had to do to answer the question, therefore, was to learn what James promised he would do and compare that with what he actually did.

I collected his speeches and borrowed thick volumes of the 1979–1982 House and Senate Legislative Journals from the bookshelves of friends. I also spent months making notes from the newspaper coverage of his four years in office. Gradually, the stacks of research material piled up in my living room, records from various state departments, budgets, a terrific reference book on education finance written by Ira Harvey and various other documents and scrapbooks.

As I studied them, the blank sheet of paper which was the administration of Fob James within my mind began to fill in with form and substance. He was a busy governor. The notes I stored on computer grew by several hundred pages each time I printed them out.

Even before making a list of people to interview, I started asking in casual conversations, "What did you think of the Fob James administration?" The answers echoed with a sameness.

"I think he tried hard. But he didn't get anything done."

"We supported Fob, but we were disappointed. We thought he would do more."

"I didn't have any use for Fob in the first place and he didn't do anything in office to change my mind."

"He was honest. But he didn't do anything much, did he?"

*He didn't do anything.*

Whether they gave the answer right off or only after I pushed them to say more, the bottom line was mostly the same, "He tried *but...*"

People liked James; they trusted him. But for the life of them, they could not list any accomplishments he achieved in office.

I had no such trouble. My problem even in the early stages of writing was deciding what to cut. A department-by-department synopsis of computerization, reorganization, consolidation, cost-cutting and legislation was over 400 pages long.

Why the discrepancy between the solid facts of accomplishment which stared me in the face and the attitudes of people who thought James did nothing?

Frustrated former aides had wrestled with the question for nearly eight years.

"Fob got 80 percent of his legislation passed," Bob Geddie told me early-on. "Because he tackled so many major reforms in every session, his successes were overlooked."

I did not take Geddie's word for it, of course. Neither did I take the word of Bobby Davis, who insisted that James' frugal penny-pinching and concentration on efficiency had saved the state tens of millions of dollars. Neither did I accept on face value the contention of Jim Foy that James daily rode herd on ethics and honesty, requiring cabinet members and department heads to think only of the taxpayer when making decisions. Or...the list could go on.

I did listen to them, however. Their insistence that proof was there, if I just looked hard enough, countered somewhat the authoritarian black headlines which asserted through their bulk that James suffered loss after loss. If I had relied solely on headlines to form my opinion of his legislative sessions, I would have thought he wasted the first one on a constitution and failed on an equally important gas tax increase to fund his highway program.

With his State of the State address in front of me, and spending hours every Monday morning prying into his thoughts and philosophy, I knew Fob James did not consider a new constitution his major order of business. It was not even a campaign promise. I looked instead for what happened to his War on Illiteracy.

It was top on his legislative and all other agendas.

For that "War" in 1979, he asked legislators for $20 million to send teams of skilled teachers into schools which scored low on the tests he financed in part from his discretionary fund. Other governors have used the fund for political rewards, I knew. James used it to put heat in cold classrooms, to patch roofs which otherwise allowed rain to seep through attics and rot wood and drip on students. James' rationale was as simple as his goal: How could first-graders learn to read and write if they were cold and wet? James got half of what he asked that first year, $10 million. Remembering how James had pushed campaign fund-raiser Jud Salter to *raise* $100,000 for his kickoff, and how ecstatic Salter remembers James was to learn $86,000 had been pledged, I had a feeling James was equally ecstatic about that $10 million. His War funds had to be scaled down each year in his administration. But so did all other costs as recession deepened. What James could not get from the Legislature, he found in other areas. The four-year-end report by Lynda Hart, director of CETA, reveals that James repeatedly took advantage of the agency's federal funding to bend it to fulfill his as well as CETA's goals.

In 1979, James took over what the layman would call a bankrupt state. The Legislature had met for the first time ever in an election year in 1978 and spent some $70 million in surplus which had been generated by double-digit inflation. Anticipating another such surplus in 1979, the Legislature spent the predicted surplus in addition to the actual surplus. This would not have caused a problem if tax revenue had continued each year to increase. Between the end of that session and the day James took office, however, the recession which had been ever-present on the horizon enveloped Alabama and the nation. Less tax revenue was collected in the first quarter of the fiscal year, which runs October 1 through September 30, than had been appropriated. There would be no surplus. There would instead be a deficit, which is forbidden by law. The state would not have enough money coming in to pay its bills.

Worse, unemployment was growing, with 443,167 out-of-work people registering for unemployment checks in 1979. They were joined in 1980 by another 50,000, a figure which continued to increase until the recession bottomed out after James left office. Unemployed people don't buy washing machines and automobiles and don't pay income tax; less tax money is available to pay unemployment checks. Such is the vicious reality of recession.

Looking back, it was clear that Alabama had not been in such a crisis since the 1930s. The Unemployment Compensation Fund from which unemployment checks were written was broke at the beginning of 1979. The federal government had advanced the fund $27 million prior to James' taking office. Medicaid was $34 million in the red when James took office and had been operating at a deficit for four years. Cities and counties had not since 1976 been paid by the state for housing the overflow of inmates from state prisons which were under court order not to admit more prisoners.

James in 1979 without fanfare repaid the $27 million loan to the unemployment fund; it is touted as an achievement only in one line in a four-year-end report. Keeping state government afloat had to be a staggering task, yet James turned Medicaid around his first year in office and by the time he left office had reimbursed cities and counties for housing state prisoners. In 1980, "extremely high" unemployment triggered extended benefits to those who would otherwise been cut off because they had exceeded the maximum number of days for unemployment compensation. Extended benefits were triggered twice in 1981 for the same reason.

James completely restructured Medicaid through legislation which brought costs down. Permission first had to be obtained from federal officials to make changes in the rules and regulations which were in effect in all states. James flew to Washington, D.C., and convinced the Reagan administration to allow him to make the needed changes.

It was not the only time James intervened personally with federal officials to convince them to go along with changes he wanted to make. The Military Department is another example.

James was particularly interested in taking whatever steps were necessary to provide the best training possible for members of the Alabama National Guard.

James was too young to be involved in the Korean Conflict. But three of his friends were called to active duty. One, a member of a National Guard unit, did not return. Believing strongly in the historical concept of a "people's army," James set out to develop a system of "rapid deployment" whereby troops could be mobilized in 60 to 90 days. Ever mindful that the quality of training directly affects the number of casualties, James was disturbed that Alabama guardsmen could not be trained properly in the "maneuver and fire" tactics of tank warfare. Tanks shoot for miles, so a tank firing range must be huge. Camp Shelby, Mississippi, where Alabama guardsmen trained, had no such range. Bobby Davis remembers the months-long battle James had with military officials in Washington, D.C., before he got what he was after—approval for construction of a tank firing range at Eglin Air Force Base in Florida. It is today described by a Guard spokesman as continuing to provide "the best possible training" for armored units—not just from Alabama but also from other states.

When viewed through department-by-department tunnel vision, the changes James set in motion may not appear to have resulted in a great overall effect. However, as surely as a bricklayer through the repeated stacking of brick upon brick builds a solid wall, James through his relentless daily efforts to redirect the focus of state departments shifted the direction of the whole of state government. He awoke the sleeping giant of sluggish bureaucracy, replaced lethargy with purpose and direction, and left behind a map on which the route to service and productivity was clearly delineated.

With dozens of different reforms pending in the Legislature at various times, James was attacked often for trying to do too much. The criticism was accurate for James' first two years, if the critic meant that reform legislation is easier to pass in small doses. It is not accurate if the critic is insinuating that James haphazardly grabbed at every reform which caught his attention.

It is clear from James' speeches, however, that he ran for governor with very basic goals in mind. He pledged to figure out how to make literacy a reality, not a dream; to do whatever was necessary to ensure that taxpayers' dollars were spent efficiently and to see that those dollars delivered the services government is charged by law with providing; and to do whatever it took to bring order to the chaos that existed as Alabama's criminal justice system. Most of all, he promised voters that by electing him they would have a governor who lived every day with their welfare and concerns foremost on his mind.

Every piece of legislation James pushed, every decision he made, every speech he gave, can be traced directly to these campaign promises.

James was perhaps the most stubborn man who has held the office of governor in Alabama. Anything he wanted, he went for again and again, as he did the legislation to provide highway and bridge construction funding with an increase in the gas tax. It passed the second session it was introduced and James has since been proven right in his rationale for supporting it: the price of gasoline did increase nation-wide as he predicted and the gas tax increase was swallowed in that increase as he predicted.

The record proves that James eventually passed the majority of the legislation which engendered headlines of defeat when it failed the first session it was introduced, from a bill to consolidate environmental agencies to that which reformed the state merit system. The only legislation which he repeatedly failed to pass was that such as retirement reform which was falsely portrayed to state teachers and employees as an attempt to take away their benefits. The lobbyists who did so early-on in the James administration used the legislation as a battle cry to distort the true intent of James' legislation. They created a state of fear among the rank and file which sent them running for protection to join the Alabama Education Association and the State Employees Association. These lobbyists beat James in a game he would have excelled at if he had chosen to play—salesmanship.

The legislation speaks for itself: James' proposals would have strengthened retirement systems, ensuring that retirees would receive every penny of their retirement. There is, however, no need to wade through legislative Journals to prove the validity of this statement. Former State Sen. John Teague was quoted in 1982 saying that "everyone agrees" steps had to be taken to save the retirement system and predicting that James' legislation would pass because it did not take away benefits from those covered by the retirement plans. Teague was so staunchly supportive of state employees that they later hired him as their lobbyist. Teague has been equally supportive of teachers. In 1989, he was hired by Hubbert's gubernatorial campaign.

Retirement is no longer an issue today. The state today does not have to bail out the retirement systems annually as it did in 1982; the same double-digit interest rates which smothered the average citizen in 1982 allowed the retirement systems to gain stability.

With the advantage of hindsight, one tantalizing aspect of James' behavior is explained. When he was in office, James was sometimes perceived by news media as unpredictable. He launched new projects when least expected to. He took off seemingly at the drop of a hat on barnstorming jaunts to elicit support for projects. Looking back, it is clear that James' unpredictability has been one of his greatest assets. Shug Jordan called James "the greatest broken field runner" he ever coached. When James realized he was getting nowhere in the direction in which he ran on the football field, he searched for daylight and in the blink of an eye switched directions. The crowd which rose to their feet in cheers could clearly see the goal for which he ran. The problem James encountered as governor was that when he switched directions he most times left behind him politicians and "observers" who were unaware of his intent and more interested in discussing the apparent defeat he left behind. The crowd, or the public in this case, did not have the advantage of watching the overall situation from an upper deck. For interpretation of James' moves and motives, they had to depend upon people who not only shared their lack of vantage point but often had placed their bets on the opposing team.

In every session, James passed dozens of bills. In three of his four years, James' bills rewrote insurance laws for consumers, protecting policyholders if companies go out of business, regulating insurance plans for legal services and dental services.

James' legislation provided teachers with liability insurance from his first year in office. Hubbert fought unsuccessfully to do away with the insurance, which competed with that offered as a membership incentive by AEA. The Legislature did away with state-provided liability insurance for teachers a few months after James left office.

James also supported successful bills requiring companies which mined coal to replant the area with trees or take other steps to leave the land better than they found it.

In three of James' four years, the budgets he sent to the Legislature were the basis for the final budgets which were approved. There were changes and additions, but he got what he asked for to run the departments under him and to administer his programs. It is difficult for one who knows of James' attention to minute budgetary detail to sit still without squirming when reading of department heads under Gov. Guy Hunt submitting budgets to the Legislature which Hunt knows little of.

In 1981, when the Legislature did not approve either James' version or any other version of the Education Budget, he reacted typically. He called legislators back into a special session in which they not only approved his Education Budget, they passed his amendment to the constitution mandating that in the future state budgets had to be approved prior to any but emergency legislation. What was typical was that James acted quickly, not content to solve the problem at hand, determined to get to the root of the problem and "fix it." The two words had to be James' favorites. If it was broke, he set out to fix it.

In that session, James discovered the power of the "special" session to fix what needed fixing. In a special session, a governor forces legislators to concentrate on the subjects he names. Approval of any other legislation requires a greater vote. Using special sessions, James fought banking interests and the most powerful lobbyists in the state to get approval of a $657 million Public Works project. It was made possible by approving James' plan to invest a $449 million "windfall" from the sale of leases of petroleum-rich bottomlands.

Today, state and federal elected officials throughout the nation are parroting the warnings James gave in 1981 when urging legislators to use the bond money to "rebuild the state's infrastructure"—roads, schools, buildings, etc. Our physical plant is wearing out, we hear today. James said it in 1981, in convincing legislators to vote for his plan for using the windfall. If James had not been there, bankers would have convinced legislators to put the $449 million windfall in the bank and each year build whatever the interest would pay for. Politicians would have squabbled each year over the projects and there is little doubt that architects and attorneys would have captured their share of the money and then some. Under James' plan, some $657 million was spent on school construction, roads, bridges, prisons, mental health, etc. Moreover, the projects were agreed upon at the time, leaving nothing for future politicians to haggle over. Because James was there, the original windfall will remain intact when the bond issue is paid off.

James harped so much on cutting the cost of bureaucracy that only the "insiders" realized how he pumped the money saved into needed social services, stressing youth and the elderly. Legislative records are filled with special appropriations pushed by James which popped up with regularity giving money to the Department of Youth Services and the Alabama School for the Deaf and the Blind.

James increased the annual appropriation to Youth Services from $8.8 million in 1979 to $11.2 million during his term and gave the department $500,000 conditional funding in 1980. He included $6 million in his giant public works bond issue for improving Youth Services' student housing and other needs, the first capital outlay money given the department in its history.

Perhaps the most significant and lasting thing James did for youth services was to push successful legislation which recognized the educational system of the Youth Services Department as a separate school district. The department now gets its share of the education money in the state when that money is divided according to law among all school systems in the state.

Despite the drop in tax revenues, James increased the funding to the Women, Infants and Children Nutrition program by $400,000 which State Health Officer Dr. Ira Myers believed directly contributed to the decline in Alabama's infant mortality rate in 1979, 1981 and 1982.

James through 1981 legislation increased the amount paid by the state to those who took foster children into their homes. The Department of Pensions and Security cracked down on errant fathers, increasing the amount of child support collected from $5.8 million in 1980 to $6.4 million in 1981 to $7.5 million in 1982.

For senior citizens, James pushed legislation in 1981 which regulated Medicare supplement contracts and required companies providing such policies to provide buyer's guides. Though he tightened the belts of other agencies, James increased the annual budget of the Commission on Aging from $8.9 million in 1979 to $13 million in 1982. In an effort to make tax dollars go further, the office of the commission was relocated in 1980 to quarters which contained less but more usable space at reduced costs. When the contract ran out with the vendor who provided 13,000 meals statewide for the elderly, a statewide competition was announced to select a new vendor. It resulted in a five percent annual reduction in costs. An ombudsman program was set up to provide a means by which nursing home patients and their families could file complaints.

James pushed dozens of bills which changed procedures and reorganized the more than three-dozen departments under his control.

Where are the pictures which should have filled newspaper columns when violence flared during the truckers' strike and James defiantly joined a convoy and rode shotgun with truckers who wanted to take their goods to market? Where are the headlines when James flew into Birmingham after dark settling a strike with black coffee and a threat to prolong the all-night session for as long as it took for both sides to come to an agreement? Where are the editorials praising James for making good his threat to keep the State School Board "all night if need be" to fire a college president who needed firing?

The blame for not publicizing James' accomplishments must lie primarily with James. Journalists are not supposed to act as public relations conduits for office holders. However, journalists must shoulder the responsibility for making sure not only that what they write is correct but that it is complete, that it provides readers and listeners with an accurate understanding of the total picture. When James left a void by not informing people of what he was doing, the "political observers" and "reliable sources" stepped into that void. They were desperately anxious to restore the status quo which prior to James had been so politically rewarding. Their perception and observations reflected such.

There is no doubt that an old-fashioned press agent would have been in a publicists' heaven to have been handed the task of promoting Fob James as governor.

If James had packaged his revamp of state government with the same gusto he displayed in pushing his barbells, the public would today think of him as the man who proved a tax dollar can be spent efficiently.

If James had allowed his staffers to ballyhoo the escapades he instead refused them permission to discuss, Alabama citizens would have been realized how intent he was upon crushing drug traffic. The biggest topic of conversation for weeks would have been his sneaking off to join undercover officers for the biggest drug bust of the decade.

If James had realized that the accomplishments of a governor, much like the proverbial tree falling in the forest, must be seen or heard to affect the attitudes of the populace, the $600 million in housing mortgage money created in his administration would have monopolized newspapers and television sets from Maine to California. Tens of thousands of low and middle income families who have been able to buy homes only because of that bond issue would today be unable to hear the name of Fob James without feeling a warm glow.

The Legislature today daily violates James' Budget Isolation Amendment, endorsed overwhelmingly by voters in a referendum vote. Other departments of state government violate other reforms James put in place. An example is the sale of wine by the ABC Board. That is prohibited in legislation James sponsored which was intended to make the board more responsible. How can laws be violated? Because no strong voice challenges the violation.

James was a strong governor. He was not afraid to challenge, to trudge ahead where meeker or less-motivated men or more politically-influenced officeholders would not go. The image of James as governor sharpens as the men and women who worked with him talk of those years. He is energetic, questioning, pushy, relentless, certain that an answer can be found if the right people work long and hard enough. He does not know the meaning of the word quit. He was a great enough contrast to his predecessor for Ralph Holmes to write a mood piece describing how the former silence of the governor's office was alive with sounds of typewriters clicking, heels clacking and telephones ringing.

James must have spent so much time at his desk that he wore out the upholstery.

He closeted himself with a stack of No. 4 pencils, revenue projections and a list of essentials requested by department heads, sat down at his desk and wrote the budget for the State of Alabama. He ordered a ten percent cutback in spending and his department heads complied.

He sat at his desk, going over the weekly expense statements from three dozen departments, picking up the phone when an expense increased, calling the department head to demand why.

He sat at his desk late at night poring over test scores from every school district in the state, comparing, charting, hell bent to isolate those factors which determine whether a child gets a good education, and make the good ones work for all schools.

James set in motion a contagious enthusiasm for getting the most out of a dollar. Four-year-end reports written by department heads brag of seemingly inconsequential savings—until added up. There runs throughout the reports a recurring theme of massive re-organization, of contagious cost-consciousness, of efforts to increase efficiency, and of an overall turn to computerization as the means by which to do it. Offices were relocated to save money and to bring employees together under one roof who though they worked for the same department had been scattered in different offices. There are innumerable listings of small savings which added up as bank accounts were consolidated, forms were cut in size and paperwork reduced.

Today, state employees who are in positions to see the overall figures—those in the State Personnel Office and the Auditor's Office—say Fob James was the best thing that ever happened to them. His reclassification plan, the first reform of the Merit System in 30 years, removed the favoritism built into it in three decades of politics. State employees make higher salaries because of this reclassification plan.

Today, his push for literacy is recognized as being a decade ahead of the rest of the nation's realization that Americans must be literate to compete economically with the rest of the world in the 21st century.

A law was passed allowing Alabamians to pray in schools while James was in office.

Roads and bridges were built in every county of the state.

Black employment rose from 19 to 24 percent.

James was truly color and gender-blind.

When he called Jack Miller to describe the man he was appointing to the Alabama Supreme Court, James described Oscar Adams' accomplishments as an attorney.

When Miller got a call later in the day asking if he knew James had appointed the first black to the Supreme Court, he had to answer "no." It was a detail James had not mentioned.

When James announced he would not run for re-election, he was surrounded by cabinet members, the majority of whom were women and veteran state employees promoted on merit.

In his speech that night, James quoted the same lofty beliefs and ideals he voiced the day he was inaugurated.

He could say that he cut Medicaid costs, but increased benefits, that he provided the first capital outlay money in history for troubled and handicapped youths.

He could say he seized opportunity when it arose—to settle strikes, to restructure the system, to provide for the future—with the common thread of public interest weaving through his actions.

Most importantly, he could honestly say that he had followed through with every commitment he made to Alabama citizens.

Yes, he had his negatives. He had his failures. But they grew out of failure to communicate and failure to accept the fact that all battles can't be won simply by trudging ahead. He did not fail in motive or in effort or in results.

That is why the question, "What kind of a governor was Fob James?" is a simple one, with a simple answer.

He was a very good one.

# About the Author

**S**andra Baxley Taylor is a veteran journalist who has covered general news and the political scene in Alabama for 18 years. She worked as a reporter for the Tuscaloosa *News,* the Charleston, S. C. *News and Courier*, the Birmingham *News* and Mobile *Press Register,* as state editor and director of weekly newspapers for the *Press Register,* and as campaign coordinator for former U.S. Sen. Jeremiah Denton.

Mrs. Taylor is the author of *Faulkner (Jimmy, That Is),* the biography of politician/businessman/journalist James H. Faulkner, and *Me 'n' George, A Story of George Corley Wallace and his Number One Crony Oscar Harper.* She also writes a weekly syndicated column for Associated Features.

She has served as president of the Mobile chapter of the Society of Professional Journalists, and in 1976 was a founder of Alabamians for Open Government, which was dedicated to strengthening the open meetings law in the state.

She won Troy State University's prestigious Hector Award for career journalism in 1986.

She won first-place honors and community service awards from both the Alabama Press Association and the Alabama Associated Press Association as leader of a team of Birmingham News reporters which exposed illegal loan practices by State Treasurer Melba Till Allen—a series which led to Mrs. Allen's conviction and removal from office.

That same series was named by the Associated Press Managing Editors' Association as one of the top 10 stories in the nation in 1978.

She also was honored by APA and AAPA for 1973 Mobile *Press Register* stories on a prison riot and conditions in Alabama prisons.

Married to *Press Register* Executive Editor Tom Taylor, the author has three children, Steven R. Baxley, Samantha Lee Baxley and Thomas A. (Tommy) Taylor IV; and three stepchildren, Sean Taylor, Julia Taylor Lolley and Stephen A. Taylor. The Taylors have three granddaughters, Randi Lolley, Stephanie Taylor and Ashley Taylor.

# INDEX

Adams, Charles, 314
Allen, Charles Robertson, 85
Allen, Jim, Jr., 395
Allen, Melba Till, 3
Arnold, Norman, 150

Bailes, George Lewis Jr., 70
Banks, "Sarge", 77
Barrow, Willie, 142
Baxley, Bill, 3, 51, 55, 72, 74
Beasley, Becky, 81
Beasley, Jere, 53, 55, 73
Beasley, Rebecca, 260, 306
Bedell, Willie, 21
Bekurs, Don, 4
Bell, John, 145
Bell, Stephanie Wolfe, 246
Bennett, Jim, 229
Berkeley, Bill, 174
Berryman, William, 132, 404
Beto, George, 188
Biddle, Jack, 220
Black, Charles, 90
Black, Hugo, 346-347
Blanchard, Frank, 196, 223
Bledsoe, Jimmy, 66
Blount, Winton "Red", 59
Blue, John, 163
Boles, Hugh, 246
Bolling, Bill, 246
Bouler, Jean Lufkin, 217
Brewer, Albert, 12, 53, 55, 73
Britnell, Charlie, 226, 247, 252
Britton, Robert, 190, 191, 192, 193, 194, 196, 189, 236
Broadwater, Joe, 78, 160, 161, 162, 163, 164, 165, 166, 167, 170

Bronner, Dr. David, 76, 101, 143, 282, 283
Bruer, Frank, 204, 216, 222, 224, 229, 247, 375
Bryan, Don, 25, 31, 66, 75, 113, 115, 121, 122, 124, 220, 221, 226, 286, 389, 409
Bryant, Paul "Bear", 73
Bryant, Ted, 72, 111, 116, 117, 118, 121, 126, 149, 205, 228, 251, 252, 255
Byrne, Bradley, 63

Callahan, H.L. "Sonny", 265, 268, 318
Campbell, Larry, 67
Cannon, Vivian, 321, 322
Cardwell, Beth, 66
Cardwell, John, 66
Carroll, John, 194
Carter, Jimmy, 138
Cates, Eric, 229, 239, 259
Childress, Joe, 30
Childress, Mark, 85
Clark, George, 258, 270
Clemon, U.W., 156
Cobb, Henry H. Jr., 79, 139, 148, 150
Cobb, Wayne, 247
Cobun, Pete, 348
Cockrell, Eldridge, 40
Cockrell, Liz, 66
Coggin, Mrs. Freida, 163
Collier, Ben C., 79
Cook, Douglas, 116
Cooper, Gary, 79, 84, 138, 142, 333
Cooper, Melvin, 178, 332
Counts, Braxton II, 59, 289
Counts, Braxton Comer III, 66, 85
Counts, John, 59

Cox, Annette, 404

Dahlen, Debra Jane, 75
Davis, Bobby, 94, 100, 101 171, 179,
    187, 277, 280, 306, 321
Davis, T. K., 55, 56
Deep, Toofie, Jr., 144, 145
Dees, Morris, 63
deGraffenried, Ryan, Jr., 318, 329
Denton, Bobby, 226
Denton, Jeremiah, 7
Dirksen, Everett, 347
Dixon, Ed, 81
Dixon, Larry, 232
Dooley, Vince, 27, 30, 31, 38
Douglas, William O., 346
Drain, George, 156
Dunson, Ron, 77
Duvall, Sam, 225, 226, 270, 322, 323

Eagerton, Ralph P. Jr., 79, 123, 130,
    356
Edwards, Jack, 5, 280
Egger, Roscoe L., Jr., 280
Ellington, Calvin, 22, 23
Ellington, Rebecca, 22
Elliott, Lou, 130, 132, 204
Ervin, Sam, 339, 340, 346, 347
Evans, Jimmy, 4, 144, 179, 180, 378
Evans, John Louis, III, 181

Faulkner, Jimmy, 8
Faulkner, James, 379
Finney, Reuben, 80
Fleming, Eliza, 27
Floyd, Holmes, 39
Folsom, James Elisha "Big Jim", 8, 13,
    74
Ford, Joe, 246

Ford, Johnny, 283
Forster, Dick, 5, 6, 66
Fox, Al, 127, 255
Foy, James E., 31, 32, 80, 82, 78, 94,
    95, 149,
Freeman, Bobby, 30
Friend, Jack, 53, 54
Funk, Tim, 257

Gafford, Bob, 268, 314, 360, 361, 362,
    363, 364, 365, 366, 367, 369, 370
Gaston, Warren, 182, 196
Gaut, Bill, 147
Geddie, Bob, 75, 78, 81 101, 106, 108,
    115, 120, 122, 128, 129, 205, 220,
    221, 226, 230, 269, 270, 271, 303,
    320, 344, 353, 356, 373,
Genatoski, Lane, 269
Goodson, Peter, 269
Goodwin, Earl, 104
Gordon, William R., 373
Graddick, Charles, 4, 5, 110, 178, 179,
    180, 188, 195, 198, 199, 208, 372,
    379
Graves, Bibb, 159
Gresham, Janet, 349
Grimsley, George Harold, 246
Grizzard, Lewis, 8
Gulledge, Bob, 226
Gunter, Annie Laurie, 268, 282

Hale, John, 193
Hall, Bob, 246
Ham, Jon, 61, 180
Ham, Kay, 61, 73, 75, 78
Hammett, Seth, 246
Hammonds, Dave, 149
Hand, Brevard, 186, 345, 349, 350, 351
Harbert, John M., III, 163, 237
Harper, Oscar, 8

Harper, Taylor, 94

Harris, Nancy, 26

Harrison, Don, 215

Hart, Lynda, 81, 301

Harvey, Ira 99, 103, 211, 228, 229, 232, 240, 248, 249, 258, 312, 317, 388

Hawkins, Dr. Jack, 301, 302

Helms, Jesse, 349, 350

Hendrix, Johnny, 180

Higginbotham, G.J. "Dutch", 247, 252, 336

Hill, Thomas F., 138

Hilliard, Earl, 252

Hitchcock, Billy, 39

Hitt, Dr. James E., 26

Hobbs, Homer, 26

Holley, Jimmy, 220, 314

Holloway, Willis, 4

Holmes, Alvin, 205

Holmes, Donald, 116

Holmes, Ralph, 1, 121, 133, 134, 135, 180, 198, 222, 225, 230, 232, 233, 259, 265, 270, 313, 354, 360, 369

Hooks, David, 67, 79

Hooper, Perry O., 362

Hope, Robert M., 140

Hudson, Leonard, 69

Hunt, Guy, 3, 74, 75, 94, 109, 373, 396, 397, 398

Hylands, James R., 141


Ingram, Bob, 251, 305

Ireland, Glenn, 235


Jackson, James, 175

Jaffree, Ishmael, 345, 349

James, "Mama", 21

James, Aunt "Sis", 65

James, Bob, 15, 65

James, Calvin, 20 30, 41, 44, 45, 60, 65

James, Cynnie, 42

James, David, 42, 55, 64, 84

James, Dora, 65

James, Dottie, 65

James, Edward, 22, 65

James, Fob III, 33, 42, 66, 85, 96, 343

James, Fob Sr., 19, 20, 21, 22, 24, 27, 39

James, Gregory Fleming, 34, 36, 37, 39, 42, 43, 84

James, James Edward, 21

James, Linda Lee, 29, 59

James, Louie, 21, 22, 65

James, Michael, 84

James, Miriam, 65

James, Patrick, 43, 84, 96

James, Rebecca, 36, 65

James, Robert Edward (Bob), 20

James, Timothy Ellington, 42, 84, 96

James, William Everett "Ebb", 20, 21, 22

Jaworski, Leon, 346

Jennings, "Mr. Rube", 20

Johnson, Imogene, 66

Johnson, Frank M., Jr. 130, 186, 187, 188, 235

Johnson, Roy, 255, 344, 345, 125, 220, 226, 314, 319

Jones, Ebbie, 67

Jordan, "Shug", 21, 26, 27, 63, 85


Keener, Larry, 226, 227

Kelley, Claude D., 107

Kelley, Phil, 231, 265

Kemp, Bobby Joe, 235, 236, 287, 288, 289, 290,

Kennedy, Anthony, 337, 338

Kennedy, Judge Cain, 174

Kennedy, Mark, 72

Kennedy, Yvonne, 246

Kerns, W.H. (Hoke), 79, 239, 260

Killough, Lee, 144
King, Dr. Martin Luther, Jr., 12
Kirkland, Reo, 374
Krebs, Tom, 180

Lager, Dr. Robert, 60, 68, 73, 77, 80,
   123, 132, 217, 219, 386, 385
Lamb, "Sis", 66
Lambert, Ealon M., 297
Lea, Charlie, 269
Leavell, Windy, 197
Lemaster, James, 246
Lewis, Duane, 354
Little, Tandy, 109
Little, Ted, 336
Littleton, James A., 80
Long, James W. "Jimmy", 25, 26, 30,
   31, 37, 38
Lord, Wayne, 65
Lowenstein, Allard, 365
Lufkin, Jack C., 297

Manley, Richard, 223, 227, 205, 220,
   251, 264, 319, 328, 363, 356, 361
Mann, Floyd, 163, 168, 169, 170, 171,
   181
Marston, Joe, 378
Martin, Dr. Harold, 388. 394, 395
Mason, Dr. David Pierce, 8
McCartha, Kenneth, 80, 109
McCorquodale, Joe, 93, 94, 104, 105,
   109, 110, 112, 113, 114, 118, 122,
   124, 124, 128, 142, 188, 203, 204,
   208, 215, 216, 220, 248, 251, 257,
   265, 303, 305, 313, 314, 315, 317,
   320, 321, 335, 336, 344, 356, 358,
   361, 369,
McDonald, Albert, 357, 358
McDonald, Sid, 53, 233
McElmore, Marie, 66
McMillan, Lt. Gov., 104, 105, 109, 110,
   112, 115, 125, 134, 188, 203, 204,
   208, 251, 256, 270, 271, 310, 313,
   319, 320, 335, 336, 357, 360
Meyer, Hermine Herta, 345, 346, 347
Middleton, Dave
Miller, Charles, 106
Miller, Gov. Benjamin M., 103
Miller, John C. H. (Jack), 58, 59, 60,
   61, 63, 64, 65, 66, 68, 70, 71, 79,
   115, 294
Miller, Susan, 60
Millican, Dot, 40
Milstead, Clint, 66
Minus, Mann, 369
Mitchell, Gene, 77, 100, 148, 178, 179,
   182, 280
Mitchell, Pat, 177
Mitchem, Hinton, 231
Mooney, R. F., 27
Mooney, Roy, 66
Mooney, Thomas Coy, 27
Moore, Jack, 39
Morgan, Sam, 38
Moseley, Max 30
Moynihan, Sen. Daniel Patrick, 350
Murray, Manson, 174

Nachman, Rod, 181, 188, 191, 199, 200
Nassar, Edward, 181
Nevett, C. Howard, 344
Noonan, Ruby, 54
North, Jim, 269, 278, 279, 281

O'Neal, Emmett, 103
Odom, Ed, 4
Owens, Walter, 222, 227, 248, 319

Parks, Rosa, 12
Patterson, Joe, 193
Payne, Charles, 396, 397

Pearson, J. Richmond, 125, 246, 247, 258, 353
Pegues, Leigh, 222
Persons, Gordon, 80
Persons, Maida, 80
Phelps, Joe, 173, 311, 374
Phyfer, George, 268, 298, 299, 300
Poole, Victor, 402, 403, 405, 407, 408, 409, 410, 412
Powell, Lewis F., 195
Prat, Marie, 329
Pruett, Linda, 150

Quinn, Randy, 389

Raiford, Jimmy, 234
Rainer, Rex, 79, 286, 287, 324, 393
Ravan, Jack E., 151, 152
Rawls, Phillip, 125, 130, 249, 314, 371
Ray, Jerry C., 79, 147, 154
Reagan, Ronald, 340, 341, 350
Reed, Dr. Joe, 395
Reeves, Frank, 31
Rehnquist, William, 182, 337
Reynolds, William Bradford, 327
Rhodes, Guy, 150
Ritter, Wayne, 181
Rivers, Phil, 323
Robertson, Sue Reece, 22

Salter, Jud, 39, 40, 41, 55, 56, 57, 58, 61, 61, 64, 102
Samford, Bill, 39
Samford, Jimmy, 197, 198, 368, 369, 370, 376, 377
Samford, Yetta, 39, 104
Sandusky, Tommy, 120, 329
Sasser, James, 220, 247
Scalia, Antonin, 337

Scott, Jud Jr., 39
Sellers, Bill, 111
Sellers, John, 32
Sewell, Roy, 31
Shoemaker, Col. Jerry, 79, 107, 139, 140, 145, 148, 150, 174, 176, 177, 178, 183, 234
Siegelman, Don, 355, 364, 366, 367, 368, 369, 371, 372, 376, 377, 378
Slaughter, Bill, 269, 278, 279
Sloat, Bill, 69
Slone, Sam B., III, 143, 144
Smith, Cynthia, 270, 323
Smith, Jim, 369
Smith, Maury, 349
Smith, Sen. Bill, 354
Smith, Starr, 53, 54
Smith, William French, 350
Sorrells, Tom, 174
Sparkman, John, 58, 59, 74, 78
St. John, Finis, 112
Stack, Moss, 6
Stallworth, Clarke, 139
Starkey, Nelson R., Jr., 222
Starr, Bart, 42
Stewart, Helen, 66
Stewart, Potter, 341, 342
Stewart, William H., 103
Still, Ed, 70
Stout, J. David, 246
Summerford, Roy, 127
Sumrall, Hal, 61, 65, 78, 82, 133, 141
Swindle, Sarah, 405, 406

Tate, Robert, 150
Taylor, Cordy, 252
Teague, John, 270
Teague, Dr. Wayne, 99, 131, 133, 207, 255, 305, 309, 391, 392, 393, 394, 400, 401, 410, 411

Thigpen, Morris, 201

Thomas, James D., 103

Thomasson, Isabel, 396

Tobert, C.C. "Bo", 75, 104, 322, 363

Tonsmeire, Arthur, 66

Tuten, Lucendy Wallace, 27

Tuten, Newtia Gladys, 27

Tyson, John, Jr., 394, 395, 396, 397, 412


Vacca, Pat, 298, 299

Valeska, Don, 4

Vann, David, 148

Varner, Robert, 188, 194, 197

Venable, Jack, 361

Ventress, Tom, 81


Walker, Deloss, 54, 55, 58, 60, 63

Walker, Jacob, 39, 156

Wallace, Cornelia, 72

Wallace, George C., 8, 9, 12, 14, 15, 16,
  69, 72, 84, 165, 362, 372

Wallace, Gerald, 8

Wallace, Jack, 72

Wallace, Lurleen, 12

Ward, Shelby Dean, 343, 344

Waters, Michael D. "Mike", 6, 73, 104,
  105, 110, 113, 114, 128, 182, 189,
  361

Weaver, Kendal, 203, 204, 303, 309,
  320, 322, 328

Whatley, John Lewis, 39

White, Dewey, 315, 316, 320

Williams, Bob, 66

Williams, David H., 296, 297

Williams, Ron, 349

Wolfe, Dr. Fred H., 343

Woodard, Jeff, 204, 224

Woods, John, 271

Wyatt, Cecil, 125

Wynette, Tammy, 84